VIETNAM

A Comprehensive Bibliography

by

JOHN H. M. CHEN

The Scarecrow Press, Inc.
Metuchen, N. J.   1973

016.9597
C 518

Library of Congress Cataloging in Publication Data

Chen, John Hsüeh-ming, 1921-
  Vietnam: a comprehensive bibliography.

  1. Vietnam--Bibliography. I. Title.
Z3228.V5C47   016.91597   72-10549
ISBN 0-8108-0562-6

To:

  Cassandra, Alicia, Paul, Dean and Susan;

  Children in Vietnam;

  All children in the world.

          With love,

          John H. M. Chen

CONTENTS

Page

PREFACE

Even children five years old know about the Vietnam War.
They may not know where Vietnam is, but they do know that there
is a war there. They know about it through their parents, who talk
about the war and watch the war action on the television screen.
The Vietnam War is the longest war in modern history, and no one
knows when it will end. I sympathize with the Vietnamese people
who are living under the most miserable conditions, created by the
tragedy of war, and I sincerely hope that the nations involved in the
Vietnam War will soon forego their selfishness and reach a peace
settlement.

Because of the tragedy of the Vietnam War, I was stimulated
to compile this comprehensive bibliography. I started to collect materials for this work nearly five years ago, although I never thought
it would be published because I expected that before this bibliography
was completed, the war would already be over. I continued to collect materials and the war is continuing. Finally, toward the end
of February, 1972, I decided to complete the bibliography and have
it published, because there is still no indication when the war will
end.

This is a comprehensive bibliography covering all written
languages and publications in book form. There is no bias in the
selection, either pro-war or anti-war. I tried my best to find all
publications related to Vietnam; however, some items may not be
included, especially publications written in other than Western
languages. Because the Vietnam War directly involves the neighbor
countries in the Southeast Asia, selected publications related to those
countries are also included.

Due to various technical problems involved in compiling a
comprehensive bibliography including material in other than Western
languages, the titles of those languages have been translated into

English and the native spellings have been romanized. It is sometimes a problem to identify such publications, but the bibliographical data for each publication include the Library of Congress classification and the Dewey Decimal Classification numbers, and it is hoped that these will aid the user in finding the original publications in libraries, especially the Library of Congress and the British Museum. The Library of Congress has all publications listed in this bibliography and the British Museum has most of them.

Main entries in the bibliography are arranged alphabetically by author. The entry for each publication lists the author, the title, the place of publication, the publisher, and the date of the publication. Following the main entry is the Library of Congress classification, the Dewey Decimal Classification, and the L.C. card number, if any. At the beginning of each entry is an item number which is used as a guide number for indexes.

The Subject Index consists of three parts and it is based on the Library of Congress subject headings. Part I covers publications related to Vietnam and to countries in Southeastern Asia. The coverage of Vietnam is as complete as possible; coverage of other countries in Southeastern Asia is selective. The publications in Part II are related solely to North Vietnam from 1946 to the present. In Part III publications dealing with the Vietnamese conflict after 1961 are included.

The Title Index is alphabetically arranged by title with an item number as a guide to the main entry in the comprehensive bibliography.

This work seeks to bring together all the significant publications in all written languages related to Vietnam from its beginning to February, 1972. It is hoped that this bibliography will be of value to research scholars by presenting new items, preventing further duplication, and suggesting topics for further study. Corrections and additions to this work will be very gratefully received.

In compiling this work I was not personally able to examine each publication and I ask the user's indulgence if I have made any erroneous assumptions in categorizing the entries or have omitted any materials which rightfully belong within the scope of this bibliography.

This bibliography, like any bibliography, cannot make claims to completeness; it is and will remain a "work-in-progress" for years to come. However, for the period covered, every effort has been made to make it as inclusive as possible.

One thing I should mention here is that the impetus for compiling this bibliography was solely my personal interest. No government financial assistance of any kind was received from any nations involved with the Vietnam War, nor from any private foundations or individuals; so this publication has no political ties. It is a product only of sincere personal concern about the Vietnam War, and of hope that this War will soon end.

John H. M. Chen

April 20, 1972

Written in the
General Reading Room
Library of Congress
Washington, D.C.

A GENERAL DESCRIPTION OF VIETNAM

Vietnam is located on the eastern coast of Southeast Asia in the area known as Indochina. It is bordered on the North by mainland China. Laos and Cambodia are located to the west. The South China Sea and the Gulf of Tonkin provide boundaries to the south and east. It has a total area of 129,000 square miles.

Vietnam may be divided geographically into three regions: Tonkin, Annam, and Cochin China. Tonkin is the northern part of Vietnam and is bordered by China to the north and Laos to the west. The Red River Delta is located in this section. The area surrounding this delta is heavily populated. The borderline areas between Tonkin and Laos and Cambodia are mountainous.

Annam is the central area connecting Tonkin and Cochin China. This area is characterized by a narrow plain on the east along the coast of the South China Sea, rising to plateaus and finally to mountains along the boundaries between it and Laos.

The southern area of Vietnam is known as Cochin China. Here is found the Mekong Delta. As in Tonkin, a large share of the population is found in this area. The Mekong Delta is the most productive agricultural region in Vietnam. The soil here is extremely fertile.

The climate is regulated by the monsoons. In Tonkin, the monsoons begin in May and end in October. This period is characterized by heavy rains and typhoons. From November to April, the climate is generally damp and cool. In Annam, the climate is drier and cooler than in either Tonkin or Cochin China. Also, it is not affected as drastically by the monsoons as are the other two regions. Cochin China experiences the monsoons from April to October. Almost all of the rain comes during this summer period. From November through May, the weather is dry and cool.

With the war in progress and the division of Vietnam, it is

1

impossible to get an accurate population count. However, the population is estimated at 39,625,000, with South Vietnam having
18,130,000 and North Vietnam 21,495,000. Vietnam has a density
of 311 people per square mile. The density is higher in North
Vietnam (351 square mile) than in South Vietnam (275 per square
mile). The population centers in Vietnam, both North and South,
are the delta regions.

Most of the people in Vietnam are of a race traced to a
Mongolian-Indonesian background. These Vietnamese, who make up
about ninety percent of the population, prefer to live in the delta
areas in villages. Most of them are rice farmers. The second
largest race of people in Vietnam are the Montagnards, who number
approximately one million. These are the mountain dwellers. They
live by fishing, hunting, and farming. The Vietnamese consider
these mountain dwellers to be savages. Some are descendent from
aborigines. A third large group in Vietnam are the Chinese, num-
bering about 850,000, and generally found in the southern urban
areas. Most of them are commercial businessmen. Other minor
groups found in this country are: Indians, Khmers (Cambodians),
Malays, Pakistanis, French, and Chams (remnants from the Champa
Empire which was overrun by the Vietnamese). Together, the
Indians and Pakistanis number 4,000. Many of these people in
Vietnam hold French citizenship, a factor stemming from the former
colonial affiliation with France.

Vietnam has its own language, Vietnamese. It is like
Chinese in that it is tonal and monosyllabic, with strict word order.
Slight changes in the pronunciation or tone can lead to a change in
meaning. However, the language is not believed to be related to
Chinese, although it has borrowed some vocabulary from the
Chinese. Vietnamese was written in codified Chinese characters
until the seventeenth century. Then, it was adapted to the Roman
alphabet with many diacritical marks and tonal signs. This means
of writing Vietnamese is called quoc-ngu. It was developed by a
Jesuit working in the area.

The economy of Vietnam is highly dependent on agriculture.
In South Vietnam, the main crop is rice. This used to be a leading

export. However, due to war conditions, the South has had to begin
to import it. Rubber forms the main export for the South. There
are numerous secondary crops grown in South Vietnam such as sugar
cane, peanuts, fiber crops, cocoa, tea and corn. The government
has developed programs aimed at diversification and increased production in farming. These programs have been severely hampered
by the war. Saigon is the industrial center of South Vietnam. The
main type of industry found in this area centers on food processing
of sugar and rice and production of such light items as textiles,
pharmaceuticals, matches, and bikes. The South is not as industri-
alized as North Vietnam. This factor dates back to the period of
colonial rule under the French. Under the French, the North was
the area where most of the industrialization was carried out. Even
there, industrialization was held to a minimum as in most colonial
territories of the time. The minerals found in South Vietnam are
not exploited as much as they are in the North, though in recent
years there has been more coal mining in the South. Another recent development is the building of hydroelectric plants to harness
water power. In addition, U.S. intervention in the war has stimulated the construction business. However, most of this construction
is in military buildings.

The economies of the North and South differ. In North Vietnam, farming is done on collectivized farms. Rice is the main
crop, although there are numerous secondary crops, such as corn,
tea, vegetables, and fiber crops. Flooding in this area causes much
crop damage. The North has to import some foodstuffs as a result;
most of this trade is being done with Communist China. One industrial advantage the North has over the South is that it has larger
coal deposits within its borders. Tin and iron ore are also located
in this area, and are exploited more than deposits found in the
South. The industries in North Vietnam may be generally classified
as light, but there has been some expansion in building larger industries under Communist rule. This has been largely aided by
other Communist countries. The North Vietnamese did have steel
mills, small shipworks, and a large tool factory, but these have
been greatly damaged by the war. Recent industrial growth has

also led to the building of factories producing tile, rubber, plastics, fertilizers, and electrical machinery.

One of the greatest natural resources of Vietnam as a whole is its fertile delta areas surrounding the Mekong River in the South and the Red River in the North. It is in these areas that most of the cities are located. These are the most densely settled regions, too. Most of the people in Vietnam are rice farmers. Both the North and South Vietnam governments are working towards greater diversification in agriculture. The forests of Vietnam are another great natural resource. The types of wood found here range from bamboo, which is used locally in a variety of ways, to luxury woods such as teak, mahogany, and ebony. However, like the mineral resources, these forests remain little touched. This may be due in part to the Vietnamese fear of the woods. It is their belief that the forests are inhabited by beasts and savages. This is one of the reasons they prefer to live in the crowded delta regions rather than spread out into the forests and mountains.

A variety of game was found in the forests of Vietnam, including stags, boars, pheasants, and rhinoceros. In the past Vietnam was an ideal spot for big game hunts. This has been reversed by the war. The animals have generally migrated westward into Laos, Cambodia and Thailand.

There are a variety of small deposits of minerals in Vietnam. The largest, perhaps, is that of coal. Others found in North Vietnam are iron ore, manganese, phosphate, tin, and zinc. In the South one finds lead, limestone, molybdenum, peat, and zinc. The resources in the South are not as well exploited as in the North and little is being done to remedy this situation.

There is no national religion in Vietnam. The main religion is Buddhism, mixed with such other beliefs as Taoism and Confucianism. The Vietnamese believe in nature spirits and ancestor worship. Local sects found in South Vietnam are Cao Dai, which is a combination of Buddhism, Confucianism, and Christianity with a belief in reincarnation and hero worship; and Hoa Hao, which is a form of extreme Buddhism. There are some Catholics in Vietnam as a result of French colonization and the resulting missionary

work done by the Catholics. In fact, French acquisition of Vietnam
as a colony came as a result of mistreatment of Catholic mission-
aries by the natives. There has been religious strife in South Vietnam in recent years under the rule of Diem. Diem was Catholic.
The Buddhists charged that he persecuted members of their religion,
and many Buddhist monks and nuns publicly burned themselves as a
means of protest. Since the end of Diem's rule, this strife has les-
sened.

The majority of the Vietnamese live in the delta areas where
they farm rice. They live in villages. The houses consist of walls
of wood with dirt floors, no water, and no electricity. Planks
serve as beds. The diet consists of spiced rice, seafoods, poultry,
some pork, and vegetables such as sweet potatoes or okra. They
eat very little beef. Little livestock is raised in these areas. The
people prefer this type of existence rather than moving to the less
settled forests and mountain areas. Nevertheless, government programs to persuade the people to move to such areas are underway
and are meeting with some success.

Theoretically, the government of North Vietnam is a democratic republic. The constitution of 1959 provides for a President,
Council of Ministers, Premier, and National Assembly. The National
Assembly is the central legislative body. It has 450 members who
are elected for four-year terms by universal suffrage of those over
eighteen years of age. The National Assembly elects the President
and Vice-President, may amend the constitution, appoints the Premier at the President's recommendation and appoints the Ministers at
the Premier's recommendation. The National Assembly meets twice
yearly. When it is not in session, the Standing Committee carries
out its legislative functions. The President serves a four-year
term. The Premier heads the Council of Ministers which is sup-
posed to be the highest executive organ. It is held accountable to
the National Assembly. In reality, the picture is quite different.
Ho Chi Minh, who had been President since 1945, was in fact a dic-
tator. The government follows the Russian and Chinese pattern of
democracy--on paper but not practiced. The Lao Dong (Worker's
Party), a communist organization, controls the government at the

national and local levels.   Opposition to the communist party or its
ideologies, if expressed, is quickly suppressed.

South Vietnam's most recent constitution, written in 1967,
calls for a constitutional system with presidential leadership.   The
President is elected by the public.   He appoints the Prime Minister
who is responsible to the President rather than to the legislature as
in North Vietnam.   The Cabinet is headed by the Prime Minister.
The legislature, too, is popularly elected.   It is divided into two
houses: the Senate and the Assembly.   By a two-thirds vote, the
legislature can remove the Prime Minister from office, but only
after he has been in office for one year.   The constitution also calls
for a judicial system separate from the other two bodies.

The history of Vietnam dates back to prehistoric times.   During the Neolithic Age, a people of Negrito origin lived in the area
now known as Vietnam.   They generally lived in caves.   In the
Bronze Age, a division of the Mongoloids, referred to as the Dongsonians, moved into this area.   These Dongsonians moved in from
the north, and as they did, they pushed the existing population into
the hills.   This latter group was of an anthropological group similar
to the Indonesians or Polynesians.   Iron found in this area is dated
back to the first centuries A.D.   The group that introduced this iron
is classified as Han Mongoloid.   It is believed that this group was
based on a clan type organization that is still found in many areas
of Southeast Asia today.   These people populated the Red River
Delta in North Vietnam, formerly designated as Tonkin.   Eventually,
the rice economy grew out of this region.   It was only natural for
this crop, which grows well in this area, to become the basic food
of the people.   Not only that but the development of a rice oriented
economy led to the establishment of power centers.   Such an economy made it possible to support the armies needed to maintain control.   The result was the evolution of a kingdom centered in Tongking.   The Vietnamese people of this Pre-Chinese period developed
during the era from the second century B.C. to the tenth century
A.D.   Indonesians in the area intermarried with a Thai people who
immigrated to the area in the sixth century B.C., and with the
Mongols from the southern Yangtze River area who came between

the fifth and third centuries B.C.   Thus, the intermingling of these
three groups led to the development of a new ethnic group, the
Vietnamese.   The Annamese of central Vietnam trace their particular ancestry to the tribe known as Giao-chi.   This tribe emigrated
southward from southern China to Tongking, and finally to Annam.

For a variety of reasons, the rulers of Imperial China became very interested in this area to the south and desired to control it.   For one reason, they did not wish to have a powerful
southern neighbor.   The Chinese were also anxious to monopolize
the trade in this area which was an important step toward trade with
India to the west.   And trade with India led toward trade in the Medi-
terranean region.   Finally, the Chinese were interested in establishing a buffer zone between themselves and what they considered the
savages of Southeast Asia.   For these reasons, the Chinese moved
south to take over the area to the Mekong River Delta, in the region referred to as Cochin China where the Hindus were located.
This Chinese rule lasted from the third century B.C. until the tenth
century A.D.   At first, the Vietnamese were merely subject to the
military and naval power of their strong neighbor to the north.
Later, they were put under the Chinese administrative system.
Finally, they were forced to accept the civil service and character
language of the Chinese empire.   About 207 B.C. a Chinese general
who had been appointed the imperial delegate to the Red River Delta
proclaimed himself king of Nam-Viet (the southern land).

This was the first of many such states which were established, taken by China, and re-established during the next 2,000
years of Chinese rule.   This state was taken by the Chinese army
during the Han dynasty.   From 111 B.C., this region was re-established as a part of the Chinese empire.   It was labelled as the
province of Giaochi.   The small rice-growing bays along the more
southern coastlines maintained their separation from the Chinese
empire.   This area was referred to as Annam during the late Han
period.   The regions of Tongking and Annam were more closely
associated with China during this period and much of their influence
still remains.   Under the rule of the Chinese, the nation of Vietnam, which had only begun to emerge, was led by governors

appointed by the Chinese imperial court. During times of internal strife, Vietnam was ruled by the dynasty controlling the southern part of China. Under the Han and T'ang dynasties in particular, the civilization of Vietnam was greatly affected by the Chinese. This included introduction to Chinese religions, philosophies, methods of cultivation and administration, and their literature. The Vietnamese also used the Chinese system of ideographic writing. During the dynasties mentioned, scholars of Vietnam were equally acceptable for posts in the Chinese courts.

Although the Vietnamese adopted the ideas, customs, and skills of the Chinese, they never actually became a part of the Chinese people. The peasants in particular only superficially accepted the Chinese rule. One example of the lack of true identification with the Chinese is the fact that the Vietnamese frequently attempted to throw out the Chinese and regain their independence. One revolt was led by the sisters Trung Trac and Trung Nhi in 40 A.D. This succeeded in establishing a separate kingdom after pushing the Chinese back. However, their success was only temporary. Three years later, the Chinese were again in control. Rather than actual revolt, it was more common for an imperial viceroy to declare himself the local king. This was generally immediately followed by military reprisals from the Chinese dynasty to return the straying area to its control. Thus, the adoption of the Chinese written language and administration did not lead to true unification. The Vietnamese succeeded in winning relatively permanent freedom in the tenth century. During the early part of the fifteenth century, the Ming dynasty of China did regain control of Vietnam but the Chinese had been removed by 1428, and the Vietnamese remained independent until they were colonized by the French. Kublai Khan attempted to invade the Red River Delta with his powerful Mongol army in 1284 but was repelled by the Vietnamese under the leadership of General Trang Hung Dao.

The coastline of Cochin China was under the influence of the civilization of the Hindu. It also served as the center of the kingdom of Champa, the economy of which was based on the sea. These people were very active in the trading of tropical spices, ivory, and

aloes. Their trade took them to Java and as far west as India and
the Middle East. Champa was made up of several city-states. The
Cham Kingdom lasted for a thousand years. However, it was con-
stantly made aware of its more powerful northern neighbors of Nam-
Viet and China, and because of this pressure the capital of the Cham
kingdom was gradually moved further south. This area was eventually taken over by the Annamites during the late fifteenth century.
Champa was taken by Le Thanh-Ton. During his forceful rule, the
Annamites established themselves in the inland areas neglected by
the seagoing Cham people, who were primarily interested in developing the coastal areas. Later leaders of the Le dynasty were weak
and actual power came into the hands of the Trinh family in the
north and the Nhuyen family in the south. By the early seventeenth
century, rivalry between these two sections was so intense that a
wall was built by the people of the south. This division was the result of a rebellion led by the Tayson brothers. Thereafter, the
area north of the wall was referred to as Tongking and the kingdom
south of the wall was called Cochin China. The Cham people were
lost as the Annamites and Tongkingese invaded the area. However,
the area of the Mekong River Delta was under the control of the
Hindu-oriented kingdoms of Fu-nan and Chen-la and was not overtaken by the Annamites and Tongkingese. It remained under the
control of the aforementioned kingdoms until they gave way to the
Cambodian kingdom. The Mekong Delta was not overtaken by the
Vietnamese until the late seventeenth and early eighteenth centuries.

A prince who had been exiled as a result of the division of
Vietnam, Nguyen Anh, was aided by the French explorers in the
1790's. A bishop of Adran, Pigneau de Behaine persuaded the
French to aid Nguyen, realizing that helping the prince would be a
means of establishing French influence in Indo-China to equalize the
English presence in India. Prior to this, Gia-long (formerly called
Nhuyen Anh) had agreed to give France Tourane and Pulo-Condore
in exchange for French assistance in regaining his throne. This
treaty between Louis XVI and Gia-long was the beginning of French
political influence in the general area of Indo-China. Nguyen
eventually proclaimed himself emperor in 1802. The Nguyen dynasty

was the source of Vietnamese emperors until Bao Dai abdicated
in 1945.

The rulers who followed Gia-long opposed the presence
of the French in their country. As a result, Christian mis-
sionaries and converted natives were persecuted, and things became even worse during the reign of Tu-duc in the mid-nine-
teenth century. The French insisted that the freedom of religion
be recognized. When the Vietnamese rulers refused to comply,
a French and Spanish fleet entered the area. They began by
capturing Tourane and moved on to take Saigon, which became
the center of operations. However, for over a year these
French and Spanish had to suffer a blockade. When reinforce-
ments arrived, the Annamites were defeated. A revolt against
the ruler and the suspension of rice supplies from Cochin China
forced Tu-duc to sign a treaty essentially giving Cochin China
to France. Ratification of the treaty required further military
action on the part of the French. Admiral de la Grandière was
appointed the first governor of Cochin China. Much was accomplished during his time in this office. In 1863, Cambodia came
under French control. La Grandière arranged for the exploration of the Mekong River. He made possible the addition of
three provinces of Cochin China that were left to Annam. Approximately two decades later, after an involved war, France
gained control of Annam and Tongking.

The French were initially interested in Cochin China because they felt that this area along the Mekong River would be
a good trading center. When they discovered that the area
lacked people and trade potential, the French turned their at-
tention to the more developed areas of Annam and Tongking.
Although the French had gained control of most of Vietnam during the 1880's, Vietnamese resistance continued for twenty years.
The Vietnamese called in the Black Flag Society, a Chinese
mercenary group, to aid them in their fight against the French.

The French attempted to unify this whole area into one
colony in spite of the fact that it had been comprised of three
relatively distinct countries. A governor-general was appointed

to administer this area in 1887. Emphasis was placed on unification via one budget and a single administration of public
works, the latter aimed at building a communication network
to act as a physical and economic link. The French administration took the power for the intellectual-office class of Vietnam. As well as developing a railway network, the French
established rubber as a cash crop in Cochin China and began
exporting rice. They also developed the coal deposits found in
Tongking. However, the French did not do much to develop
the local industries, particularly those that might have become
a source of competition to the French factories.

The rural population of Vietnam bore most of the bur-
dens of French colonialism. The financial demands of the
French rule, added to the high rural birth rate, led to increasing poverty in the countryside. The peasants also suffered
from the disappearance of local administration which led to the
closing of the local schools. As a result, when a program for
better education was begun in the 1920's, much of the rural
population was completely illiterate. However, a Vietnamese
middle class was developed as a result of French actions. During the initial period of French rule, some communities had
been deserted. This land was taken over by the French and
sold to those Vietnamese who had aided the French. These
people also bought land in newly opened territories to expand
their rice production, and they loaned their money to the poor
at high interest rates. They were able to educate their children, but they failed to develop banking, industry, and commerce. The rise of this middle class that was yet unable to
achieve economic and political stations gave impetus to the rising feeling of nationalism in this country.

At first, rebellions had been led by the replaced scholar-
officials. After World War I, the desire for freedom was expressed by the middle class and by some soldiers, as well.
Uprisings resulted in harsh reprisals by the French. One nationalistic group was the Indochinese Communist Party under the
leadership of Ho Chi Minh. This organization eventually became

the main nationalistic party as the others were suppressed. This
party based its campaign on the unhappiness of the farmers.
Due in part to French repression, there was a great increase in
the spread of Cao Dai, a faith combining Catholic, Buddhist,
Taoist, and Confucian religious beliefs with a structure like a
political party. It was particularly strong in the south where it
had its own pope and clergy. Another group that was political
and religious in nature was the Hoa Hao, which attracted the
simple peasants of the Mekong Delta region. As a result, wide-
ly differing nationalist movements early marked a separatism
between North and South Vietnam, the north being dominantly
Communist-nationalist, the south often semi-religiously nationalist.

     In the 1930's, Ho Chi Minh's party entered into a united
front with the Trotskyist party based on the Saigon working
class. After World War II began, the French police destroyed
the Trotskyist group but the Communists survived by going under-
ground. Between 1941 and 1945, Indochina was occupied by the
Japanese. Early in this period, Ho Chi Minh established the
League for the Independence of Vietnam which was called Viet-
minh. This was a front movement, dominated by the Communists, but it included several Vietnamese nationalist parties. During the war its guerrillas were armed by the Allies, and it
was active in North Vietnam and supplied information to the
Allies. However, its guerrillas did little against the Japanese,
rather saving their arms for later use against other nationalists
or the French. The Japanese imprisoned the French authorities
in Vietnam in the spring of 1945 and gave pseudo-independence
to Emperor Bao Dai, who set up an ineffective government.
Following the Japanese surrender, the Vietminh declared Vietnam
an independent republic and formed a government, with Bao Dai
abdicating. Chinese troops occupied North Vietnam and British
troops the south. In the meantime, the French began to suppress
the nationalists in Cochin China by force.

     In 1946, the French signed an agreement with the Vietminh,
recognizing Vietnam as a free state but still under the French
Union. When later negotiations ended unsuccessfully, the Vietminh

attacked the French in Hanoi. The French held all the main towns
in Vietnam. The Vietminh controlled the countryside. After some
months of light military action the French government, embarrassed
with the situation, proposed that the three divisions of Vietnam
might combine to form a single state. Bao Dai was agreeable to
this arrangement. A government, led by Bao Dai, was formed to
control all of Vietnam. Many organizations, including the Cao Dai,
accepted the leadership of Bao Dai. He became the chief of state
in 1949 when the Territorial Assembly of Cochin China voted to remain a part of Vietnam. However, the Vietminh opposed French
control.

The 1949 revolution in China afforded Ho Chi Minh an oppor-
tunity to gain powerful and experienced military aid from Communist
China. His forces captured French outposts on the Chinese border
and opened the way for free movement of weapons into Vietnam.
The resulting pressure reduced the French holdings in North Vietnam to the Red River Delta area, even though the French had received increased supplies and support from the United States. By
1952, the U.S. government, feeling that the developments in Indo-
china were linked with the Korean War, was giving full support.
By creating in 1951 a common front with opposition groups in Cambodia and Laos, the Vietminh became clearly revolutionary, not
only in Vietnam but in all of Indochina. Guerrilla activity was ex-
panded. During the war, the French continued to broaden the defi-
nition of what it would accept as independence in Vietnam. All
powers and functions of government were transferred to Bao Dai's
ministers. Yet the war continued and in 1954 the French lost a
vital position.

During the summer of 1954, an armistice was signed as a
result of the Geneva Conference. The agreements were not signed
by the United States or the Bao Dai government. According to
these agreements, Vietnam was to be divided at the seventeenth
parallel with the Vietminh getting the northern zone and the Bao
Dai government receiving the southern part. It was agreed that all
Vietnamese would be allowed to choose their own zones to live in
and that the armed forces of the two sides would be regrouped.

India, Canada, and Poland were grouped into an international commission to supervise the implementation of the agreements. National elections in preparation for reunification were planned for 1956, but were not held.

The North Vietnamese government was able to consolidate its political power even though many anti-Communists moved out of the area and the peasants tried to revolt. It planned vast agricultural reforms and instituted economic planning with an eye toward industrializing the country. In its efforts to modernize the economy, it was aided by other Communist countries. As the war continued, the internal political situation in South Vietnam was also disturbed. The Diem regime became more and more unpopular. Persecution of the members of the Buddhist religion led to the sacrificial suicides by burning of a number of Buddhist monks and nuns. The government was finally overthrown on November 1, 1963 by a military coup d'état in which Ngo Dinh Diem and Ngo Dinh Nhu were killed. After several military coups, a military group of three, headed by Major General Nguyen Van Thieu, gained control of the government. Nguyen Cao Ky, commander of the Air Force, became premier. The Ky regime was violently opposed by the militant Buddhists. Buddhist unrest reached a peak in the late spring of 1966 when Hue and Da Nang were in a state bordering on rebellion. However, Ky regained control. In 1967, a new constitution was written and a new election was held. Premier Ky, originally the leading candidate for the presidency, was forced by differences with President Thieu to run as vice-president on a ticket with him.

After the Geneva Conference, the United States attempted to establish a separate anti-Communist state south of the seventeenth parallel. In addition to substantial economic support, the U.S. provided weapons and military training to the South Vietnamese. However, by 1960 the Viet Cong had approximately 20,000 men. Although outnumbered ten to one by the South Vietnamese Army, they were strong enough to attack South Vietnamese forts and army units. Their strength lay in the guerrilla tactics they used in striking unexpectedly at various places. Under these conditions, the army of South Vietnam was unable to protect the entire country.

The National Liberation Front (NFL) was organized in Hanoi to help the Viet Cong. The Front set up local councils to govern areas of South Vietnam controlled by the Viet Cong, built factories to produce weapons, and supplied ammunition, medical supplies, and money to the Viet Cong. Many of these supplies were transported from North Vietnam over a system of roads and trails called the Ho Chi Minh Trail. By 1961, the Viet Cong had become so successful in South Vietnam that the U.S. was forced to choose between allowing the collapse of the South Vietnamese government and increasing its support.

It was at this point that the United States decided to exceed the number of military advisers permitted by the Geneva Agreements. The United States also sent helicopter pilots into the area. In 1965 combat units of the United States Army, Navy, Marines, Air Force, and Coast Guard began to take part. Smaller units were sent from South Korea, Australia, and a few other nations. On the Communist side, the Viet Cong were aided by regular units of the North Vietnam People's Army and supplies from Russia and China. The fighting in South Vietnam started on a small scale when the guerrillas began to attack government officials in South Vietnam. It eventually evolved into a savage, full-scale war that threatened world peace. The war became a test of strength between the Communist and the non-Communist nations.

The United States believed that a non-Communist South Vietnam was necessary for the defense of Southeast Asia. The Communists called the struggle in Vietnam a war of national liberation. They accused the South Vietnamese government of being a puppet of the United States. They pledged to overthrow the government. They wanted to unite Vietnam under one rule, as stated in the Geneva Accords of 1954, which had ended the Indochina War and resulted in the division of Vietnam.

In the early 1960's, the guerrillas began to gain ground. Their methods varied from propaganda and persuasion to military force and terror. They conquered many villages and sometimes defeated South Vietnamese army units in battle. They tried to turn the villagers against the Saigon government through speeches, radio

broadcasts, pamphlets, posters, and meetings. The Communists
hoped to cause the collapse of the government by a revolution. By
1964 about four million of the fifteen million South Vietnamese were
under Viet Cong control. After the United States attack on North
Vietnamese bases in the Gulf of Tongking, in retaliation for attacks
reported on United States destroyers in 1964, the military struggle
began to pass from a guerrilla state, though the main strength of
the Viet Cong still lay in surprise attacks and terrorism in South
Vietnamese territory.

In 1965 U.S. military participation became direct with the
sending of 3,500 Marines to the Da Nang air base. Sustained aerial
bombardments of North Vietnam began. Military operations at times
approached the conventional rather than guerrilla warfare. United
States operations were mainly sweep and clear actions. In 1967,
the heaviest fighting was in the northernmost provinces of South
Vietnam just below the demilitarized zone. In early 1968, the
Marine base at Khe Sanh came under heavy attack and Viet Cong
raids on Saigon and Hue, among other cities, were repulsed after
initial success.

War was never officially declared. Nevertheless, in 1968
approximately 1,355,000 soldiers from South Vietnam, the United
States and other non-Communist countries were fighting against an
estimated 300,000 Communists. There was no fixed battle line.
Instead, the Communists used guerrilla war tactics which consisted
of ambushes, hit-and-run raids, and hand-laid bombs and mines.
Non-Communist forces used air raids and "search and destroy"
operations in which troops were transported by helicopter. Ground
and air forces were supported by the U.S. Navy.

The Vietnam war prompted a national debate in the U.S. on
the necessity, objectives, and strategy of U.S. involvement. The
war also became an issue in many other non-Communist countries.
Persons holding the most extreme views on the war were called
"hawks" or "doves." The "hawks" wanted to increase the attacks on
North Vietnam, while the "doves" opposed U.S. participation in the
war. Many Americans believed U.S. participation was necessary to
stop Communist aggression and to maintain U.S. prestige. A

Communist victory in South Vietnam, they argued, would lead to Communist takeovers elsewhere. This argument was based on the "containment policy." Others argued that U.S. involvement tended to unite the Communists and was hampering friendly relations between the U.S. and Russia at a time when the Cold War seemed to be easing. Others argued that the conflict was a civil war in which the U.S. should not have become involved. They cited the fact that the United Nations remained neutral, whereas in the Korean War it recommended that United Nation members send troops to aid South Korea. Another group feared U.S. bombings would bring Communist China into the war. Some military experts urged that the United States increase military pressure. They argued that the Communists would give in only if the war were carried to North Vietnam by bombing or other means. Others disagreed, and wanted more emphasis placed on counter-guerrilla methods in South Vietnam. They also stressed programs of political, social, and economic reform to win the allegiance of the South Vietnamese people.

This is the story of a relatively small country which has somehow come to be of major importance in today's world which lies under the threat of annihilation as a result of nuclear war. It appears that Vietnam has become the testing ground to see if the major world powers can disagree without resorting to the use of nuclear weapons.

BIBLIOGRAPHY

1. Abad, Angel. Vietnam: independencia, guerra civil, con-
    flicto internacional. [1. ed.] Barcelona, Editorial Nova Terra,
    [1966].
    DS557.A5A56   959.7   67-45659

2. Abaya, Hernando J. Betrayal in the Philippines. New York,
    Wyn, 1946.
    DS686.4.A7   991.4   46-8075

3. Abu, comp. Verdicts on Vietnam: a world collection of car-
    toons; edited by Abu and introduced by James Cameron.
    London, Pemberton in association with Barrie & Rockliff,
    1968.
    DS557.A61A65   959.7'04   72-374391

4. Accords franco-vietnamiens du 8 mars 1949. The Franco-
    Vietnamese agreement of March 8th, 1949. [Saigon, Impr.
    francaise d'outre-mer, 1949]
    DS557.V5A6   959.7   50-33817

5. Adair, Dick. Dick Adair's Saigon: A Vietnam Sketchbook.
    Weatherhill, John, Inc. 1971.

6. Adler, Bill, ed. Letters from Vietnam. [1st ed.] New York,
    Dutton, 1967.
    DS557.A69A3   959.7'04   66-27396

7. Agcaoili, T. D., ed. Philippine writing; an anthology.
    Manila, Archipelago Pub. House, 1953.
    PS9992.P4A7   54-2784

8. Akademiia nauk SSSR. Institut gosudarstva i prava. U.S.
    aggression in Vietnam; crime against peace and humanity.
    [Ed. compiled by Institute of State and Law, USSR Academy
    of Sciences. Moscow] Novosti Press Agency [1965 or 6]
    DS557.A6A64   66-8304 rev.

9. Akademiia nauk SSSR. Institut narodov Azii. Demokraticheskaia
    Respublica V'etnam, 1945-1960, (Democratic Republic of
    Vietnam). (In Russian). Moscow, 1960.
    DS557.A7A6

10. Akademiia nauk SSSR. Institut narodov Azii. Noveishaia
    istoriia V'etnama; sbornik statei, (The Recent Vietnamese

History; collected Papers). (In Russian). Moscow, 1963.
DS557.A5A58

11. Akademiia nauk SSSR. Institut narodov Azii. Plechom k ple-
chu; vospominaniia sovetskikh spetsialistov, (Shoulder to
Shoulder; Recollections of Soviet Specialists). (In Russian).
Moscow, 1965.
DK68.7.V5A75

12. Albinski, Henry Stephen. Australian policies and attitudes
toward China, by Henry S. Albinski. Princeton, N. J.,
Princeton University Press, 1965.
DU113.5.C5A6   327.51094   66-10548

13. _____. Politics and foreign policy in Australia; the
impact of Vietnam and conscription [by] Henry S.
Albinski. Durham, N. C., Duke University Press, 1970.
DU117.A7   327.94   76-101128

14. Alisjahbana, Sutan Takdir, 1908-   Indonesia: social and cul-
tural revolution, by S. Takdir Alisjahbana. Kuala Lumpur,
Oxford University Press, 1966.
DS615.A68 1966   919.1033   S A 66-7740

15. All Viet-Nam Congress of the National United Front, Hanoi,
1955. Viet-Nam Fatherland Front; resolutions, manifesto,
programme, and statutes. Rev. ed. Hanoi, Foreign
Language Pub. House, 1956.
JQ898.F33A5 1955g   58-21409

16. Allen, George Cyril and Donnithorne, Audrey Gladys. Western
enterprise in Indonesia and Malaya; a study in economic development. London, Allen & Unwin, 1957.
HC447.A8   338   58-492

17. Allen, James de V. The Malayan Union [by] James de V.
Allen. [New Haven] Southeast Asia Studies, Yale University;
[distributed by Cellar Book Shop, Detroit, 1967]
DS597.A65   959.5'03   67-21150

18. Allen, Luther A. A Vietnamese district chief in action [by]
Luther A. Allen [and] Pham Ngoc An. [Saigon] Michigan
State University, Vietnam Advisory Group [1961?]
JS7225.V5A65   64-64285

19. Allen, Sir Richard Hugh Sedley, 1903-   Malaysia: prospect
and retrospect: the impact and aftermath of colonial rule
[by] Richard Allen. London, New York, Oxford University
Press, 1968.
DS597.A67   959.5'04   68-31964

20. Alley, Rewi. Buffalo Boys of Viet-Nam. Hanoi, Foreign
Language Publishing House, 1956.
DS557.A5A6   57-38127

21. Alley, Rewi, 1897-   The mistake; poems. [Christchurch, N.
     Z., Printed at the Caxton Press, 1965]
     PR6001.L6725M5   821'.9'12   67-121254

22. Allocutions prononcées à l'occasion de l'investiture du gouverne-
     ment Buu-Loc à Saigon, le 16 janvier 1954. [Saigon, 1954]
     DS557.A5A62   62-31696

23. Alsheimer, Georg W. Vietnamesische Lehrjahre, sechs Jahre
     als deutscher Arzt in Vietnam 1961-1967. [Von] Georg W.
     Alsheimer. [Frankfurt a. M.] Suhrkamp [1968].
     R512.A45A3   959.7'04   68-68979

24. al-Takriti, Salim Taha. Vietnam. Bagdad, Matba'at al-Ma'
     arif, 1950.
     DS557.A5T295

25. Alvarez Rios, René. Vietnam: historia y politica; por qué
     pierden los Estados Unidos la guerra? [La Habana, Instituto
     de Politica Internacional, Ministerio de Relaciones Exteriores,
     1965]
     DS557.A5A67   67-45650

26. Alvear, Carlos Torcuato de. Viet-Nam, ahora. Buenos
     Aires, Emecé Editores [1965]
     DS557.A6A66   66-9691

27. Ambekar, C. G. Viet-Nam; a reading list. [n. p.] 1958.
     Z3228.V5A7   016.9597   59-27908

28. American aircraft systematically attack dams and dikes in the
     D.R.V.N. Hanoi, Foreign Languages Publishing House; [dis-
     tributor: Xunhasaba, Hanoi] 1968.
     DS557.A65A64   959.7'04   77-230470

29. American Civil Liberties Union. Southern California Branch.
     Day of protest, night of violence, the Century City peace
     march; a report. [Los Angeles] Sawyer Press, 1967.
     F869.L8A5   979.4'94'05   68-7809

30. The American crime of genocide in South Viet Nam. [Saigon?]
     Giai Phong Publishing House, 1968.
     DS557.A67A67   959.7'04   74-9621

31. American Failure & Dry Season Offensives. China Books and
     Periodicals, 1969.

32. American Friends of Vietnam. A symposium on America's
     stake in Vietnam. New York, [1956]
     DS557.A5A15   959.7   56-58707

33. American Friends Service Committee. Peace in Vietnam: A
     New Approach in Southeast Asia. Rev. ed. Hill & Wang, 1967.
     DS557.A692F7 1967   327.73'0597   67-20981

22   Vietnam

34. American heroes of Asian wars, by the editors of the Army
     Times. New York, Dodd, Mead [1968]
     E747.A679   951.9'042'0922   68-21902

35. American Institute of Pacific Relations. Books on Southeast
     Asia; a select bibliography. Rev. ed., with supplements cov-
     ering the period June 1956 to March 1959. New York, 1959.
     Z3221.A5   016.9159   59-2680

36. American Management Association. International Management
     Division. Doing business in and with Australia. [New York,
     1966]
     HG5892.A76   338'.0994   67-1850

37. American University, Washington, D. C. Foreign Areas
     Studies Division. Area handbook for North Vietnam. Co-
     authors: Harvey H. Smith [and others] Washington, For Sale
     by the Supt. of Docs., U.S. Govt. Print. Off., 1967.
     DS557.A7A63   915.97   68-60367

38. _____. Foreign Areas Studies Division. Area handbook
     for South Vietnam. Co-authors: Harvey H. Smith [and
     others] Washington, For Sale by the Supt. of Docs., U.S.
     Govt. Print. Off., 1967.
     DS557.A5A717   915.97'03'4   67-62089

39. _____. Foreign Areas Studies Division. Area handbook
     for Vietnam. Washington, 1962.
     DS557.A5A72 1962   67-115018

40. American use of war gases and world public opinion. Hanoi,
     Foreign Languages Publishing House, 1966.
     DS557.A68A4   959.7'04   67-2227

41. Amerikanerne i junglen. Udg. af Arhus-konferencens Køben-
     havns-udvalg. [København, Svend Jensen, Tomsgardsvej 68/2,
     1966]
     DS557.A6A67   67-75791

42. An, Ching, ed. Yueh-nan moin chu kung ho kuo mei shu tso
     pis hefisn chi, (Selected Art Collections of Dem. Rep. of
     Vietnam), (In Chinese). Peking, 1957.
     N7314.A5

43. Anders, Gunther, 1902- Nurnberg und Vietnam. Synoptisches
     Mosaik. (2. Aufl. Frankfurt/M., Edition Voltaire, 1968.)
     AC30.V58 Nr.6   72-472866

44. _____. Visit beautiful Vietnam; ABC der Aggressionen
     heute. Köln, Pahl-Rugenstein [1968]
     DS557.A6A675   68-124027

45. Andersen (Arthur) and Company. Tax and trade guide:

Australia. [Chicago?] 1962.
HJ3106.A53   62-21347

46. Andrus, James Russell. Burmese economic life. Stanford,
     Calif., Stanford University, 1948.
     HC437.B8A65   330.9591   48-5422

47. Anh-Van. Mouvements nationaux et lutte de classes au Viet-
     Nam [par] Anh-Van et Jacqueline Roussel. [Paris] Publica-
     tions de la Vie Internationale [1947]
     DS557.A7A64   65-55690

48. Annam. . . . Bulletin administratif . . . Hue
                   J8.F31   44-11620

49. L'Annam en 1906. Marseille, Govt., 1906.

50. Annam. Laws, statutes, etc. . . . Code annamite. Lois et
     reglements du royaume d'Annam; traduits du texte chinois
     original par G. Aubaret . . . Pub. par ordre de Chasseloup-
     Laubat, ministre de la marine et des colonies . . . Paris,
     Imprimerie imperiale, 1865.
                                              F-3351 Revised

51. _____. Laws, statutes, etc. . . . Le code annamite,
     nouvelle traduction complete, comprenant: Les commentaires
     officiels du code, traduits pour la premiere fois: de nom-
     breuses annotations extraites des commentaires du code
     chinois: des renseignements relatifs a l'histoire du droit,
     tires de plusieurs ouvrages chinois; des explications et des
     renvois. Par P.-L.-F. Philastre . . . Imprime par ordre
     du gouvernement de la Cochinchine francaise . . . Paris, E.
     Leroux, 1876.
                                                        34-11711

52. _____. Laws, statutes, etc. . . . Le code annamite,
     nouvelle traduction complete, comprenant: Les commentaires
     officiels du code, tr. pour la premiere fois; de nombreuses
     annotations extraites des commentaires du code chinois; des
     renseignements relatifs a l'histoire du droit, tires de plusieurs
     ouvrages chinois; des explications et des renvois, par P.-L.-F.
     Philastre . . . Imprime par ordre du gouvernement de la
     Cochin-chine francaise. 2. ed. . . . Paris, E. Leroux, 1909.
                                                        12-29643

53. _____. Laws, statutes, etc. Code civil de l'Annam . . .
     [livre II] Hoang-viet ho-luat (quyen II) Hue, Imprimerie Phuc
     Long, 1938.
                                                        41-40678

54. _____. Laws, statutes, etc. La justice dans l'ancien An-
     nam; code de procedure, traduction et commentaire, par
     Raymond Deloustal. Hanoi, Imprimerie d'Extreme-Orient, 1919.

55. _____. Laws, statutes, etc. Recueil de la legislation en
vigueur en Annam et au Tonkin, depuis l'origine du protec-
torat jusqu'au I mai, 1895. 2. ed., publiee d'apres les
textes officiels et classee dans l'ordre alphabetique et chrono-
logique par D. Ganter . . . Hanoi, F. H. Schneider, 1895.
F-3365 Revised

56. _____. Laws, statutes, etc. Recueil des principales
ordonnances royales edictees depuis la promulgation du Code
annamite et en vigueur au Tonkin. Traduction de R.
Deloustal. Revue, annotee et completee d'une table alphabetique et analytique de ce recueil et du Code annamite (traduction Philastre) par Gabriel Michel. Hanoi, Impr. type-
lithographique F. H. Schneider, 1903.
KA61+1903

57. _____. Laws, statutes, etc. Regime de la propriete
fonciere dans les concessions francaises en Annam et au
Tonkin; (decreta des 21 juillet 1925 et 6 septembre 1927)
Hanoi, 1927.

58. _____. Ministere de l'economie rurale. . . . Rapport
. . . 1936- . Hue, 1937-
HC443.A6A3   330.9598   40-21273

59. Annuaire general du Vietnam. Tong nien giam Viet-Nam.
General directory of Vietnam. 1952/53-Saigon, A. V. T.,
Bureaux d'etudes techniques et economiques.
DS557.A5A18   54-27693

60. Ap Bac; les grandes batailles, 1963-1964, au Sud Vietnam.
Hanoi, Editions en langues etrangeres, 1965.
DS557.A6A684   68-47883

61. Aptheker, Herbert, 1915- Mission to Hanoi. With prefaces
by Tom Hayden and Staughton Lynd. [1st ed.] New York,
International Publishers [1966]
DS557.A7A67   327.730597   66-21952

62. Arguilla, Manuel Estabillo. How my brother Leon brought
home a wife, and other stories. Manila, Philippine Book
Guild, 1949.
PZ3.A688HO2   41-9238 rev.

63. Armbruster, Frank E. et al. Can We Win in Vietnam?
Hudson Institute Series on national security and international
order. New York, Praeger, 1968.
DS557.A6C3   959.7'04   68-21355

64. Armstrong, John P. Sihanouk speaks. New York, Walker
[1964]
DS557.C26A76   959.6   64-16118

65. Army Times Editors. American Heroes of the Asian Wars.
    Dodd, 1968.
    E747.A679   951.9'042'0922   68-21902

66. Arora, Gloria. Vietnam under the shadows; a chronological
    and factual book that records the tragedy of Vietnam. Fore-
    word by R. K. Karanjia. Bombay, Jaico Publishing House
    [1965]
    DS557.A6A7   S A 66-2489

67. Arts musulmans. Extreme-Orient: Inde, Indochine, Insulinde,
    Chine, Japon, Asie centrale, Tibet. Paris, Colin, 1939.
    N5300.H47   709.5   40-5491

68. Ashmore, Harry S. Mission to hanoi; a chronicle of double-
    dealing in high places, a special report from the Center for
    the Study of Democratic Institutions, by Harry S. Ashmore
    and William C. Baggs. With a chronology of American in-
    volvement in Vietnam by Elaine H. Burnell. New York,
    Putnam [1968]
    DS557.A692A7 1968b   959.7'04   68-54160

69. Asian Culture. Saigon. Vietnamese Association for Asian
    Cultural Relations.
    DS1.A4735   S A 65-8868

70. Asian Peoples' Anti-communist League. Vietnam. The Quynh
    Luu uprisings. [n. p., 1957?]
    DS557.A7A8   959.7   58-31448

71. Asiatic mythology; a detailed description and explanation of
    the mythologies of all the great nations of Asia, by J. Hack-
    ing and others. New York, Crowell, 1963.
    BL1031.M83   291.13   63-20021

72. Die Asiatischen Lander der Volksdemokratie. Lehrheft der
    Erdkunde fur das 8. Schuljahr. [Bearb. von der Verlags-
    redaktion Erdkunde unter Mitwirkung von Karl Troeger] 4.,
    durchgesehene Aful. Berlin, Bolk und Wissen, 1953.
    DS518.1.A78 1953   61-23540

73. Association of British Orientalists. A select list of books on
    the civilizations of the Orient. Ed. by W.A.C.H. Dobson.
    Oxford, Clarendon, 1955.
    Z3001.A85   55-14732

74. Association of the United States Army. Vietnam in perspec-
    tive; a time for testing. Washington [1968]
    DS557.A63A8   959.7'04   68-1359

75. Ausenev, M. M. Democratic Republic of Vietnam: Economy
    & Foreign Trade. New York, Crowell Collier &
    Macmillan, 1960.

.

76. Austin, Albert Gordon. Australian education, 1788-1900;
     church, state, and public education in Colonial Australia. Mel-
     bourne, Pitman, 1961.
     LA2101.A8   370.994   61-2964

77. Australia. Army. Royal Australian Regiment. 3d Battalion.
     3 RAR in South Vietnam, 1967-1968; a record of the opera-
     tional service of the Third Battalion, the Royal Australian
     Regiment in South Vietnam, 12th December 1967, 20th No-
     vember 1968, edited by R. F. Stuart. [Brookvale, N. S. W.,
     Printcraft Press, 1968]
     DS557.A64A8   959.7'04   70-449738

78. Australia. Committee of Economic Enquiry. Australian eco-
     nomic background, from the Report of the Committee of Eco-
     nomic Enquiry. [Melbourne] Economics Standing Committee.
     Victorian Universities and Schools Examinations Board [1966]
     HC605.A624   330.994   67-79567

79. Australia. Department of External Affairs. Select documents
     on international affairs. 1963- . no. 1- Canberra [Govern-
     ment Press]
     DU113.A88

80. _____. Viet Nam, February 1966 to October 1966. Can-
     berra [Government Press] 1966.
     DS557.A6A8 1966,   959.7'04   67-78481
     no. 9

81. _____. Viet Nam, first half of 1965. Canberra, 1965.
     DS557.A6A8 1965, no. 2   66-54953

82. _____. Viet Nam, June 1965 to February 1966. Canberra
     [Government Press] 1966.
     DS557.A6A8 1966,   959.704   66-73050
     no. 7

83. _____. Viet-Nam, November 1966 to June 1967. [Canberra,
     Government Press] 1967.
     DS557.A6A8 1967,   959.7'04   68-116596
     no. 11

84. _____. Viet Nam; questions & answers. [Canberra, Govern-
     ment Press, 1966]
     DS557.A6A84   959.704   66-69215

85. _____. Viet Nam since the 1954 Geneva agreements.
     Canberra [1964]
     DS557.A6A8 1964, no. 1   66-42074

86. Australia; official handbook. Melbourne.
     DU95.A8   52-26270 rev.

87. Australian Council for Educational Research. Research series.
     no. 1- Melbourne.
     LB5.A85

88. Australian Institute of International Affairs. Australia and the
     Pacific, by members of the Australian Institute of International
     Affairs. Issued under the auspices of the International secre-
     tariat, Institute of Pacific relations, and the Australian institute
     of international affairs. Princeton, Princeton University
     Press, 1944.
     DU113.A885   327.94   A 44-2151

89. Australian Institute of Political Science. Communism in Asia:
     a threat to Australia? proceedings of 33rd Summer School.
     [Edited by John Wilkes. Sydney, Angus and Robertson [1967]
     DU113.A88   335.43'095   67-114203

90. _____. Victorian Group. Winter Forum. 1st, Melbourne,
     1953. The Australian political party system, by S. R. Davis
     and others. Sydney, Angus & Robertson, 1954.
     JQ4098.A1A8   54-39484 rev.

91. Australian national bibliography. January, 1961. Canberra,
     National Library of Australia.
     Z4015.A96   63-33739

92. Australian poetry. Sydney, Angus & Robertson, 1941-
     PR9551.A1A85   821.91082   ·   A42-2468

93. Australian short stories. 1st- series. Selected by Walter
     Murdoch et al. London, Oxford University, 1951-

94. Australiana facsimile editions. no. 1- Adelaide, South
     Australia Public Library, 1962-
     DU80.A88

95. Auvade, Robert. Bibliographic critique des oeuvres parues
     sur l'Indochine francaise, un siecle d'histoire et d'enseigne-
     ment. Paris, G.-P. Maisonneuve & Larose [1965]
     Z3226.A85   68-38733

96. Avelane, Gerard, 1910- Indochine cruelle; roman. Paris,
     Nouvelles Editions Debresse [1964]
     PQ2601.V42 I 5   67-55799

97. Avsenev, Mikhail Mikhailovich. Demokraticheskaia Respublika
     v'etnam; ekonomika i vneshnaia torgovlia, (Democratic Repub-
     lic of Vietnam; its economy and foreign trade). (In Russian).
     Moscow, 1960.
     HC443.V5A85

98. Azeau, Henri. Ho Chi Minh, derniere chance, la conference
     franco-vietnamienne de Fontainebleau, juillet 1946 . . .

Paris, Flammarion, 1968.
DS550.A95   320.9'597   68-99353

B

99.   Ba, Lanh. She Made Love Not War: The Secret Diary of
      Ho Chi Minh's Daughter. Lancer Books, 1971

100. Bain, Chester Arthur, 1912-   The history of Viet-Nam from
      the French penetration to 1939. Ann Arbor, University Mi-
      crofilms [1957]
      Microfilm AC-1 no. 17,524   Mic 57-971

101. _____. Vietnam: the roots of conflict [by] Chester A.
      Bain. Englewood Cliffs, N. J. , Prentice-Hall [1967]
      DS557.A5B23   959.7   67-18701

102. Baker, Richard Terrill, 1913-   Darkness of the sun; the
      story of Christianity in the Japanese Empire. Nashville,
      Abingdon-Cokesbury Press [1947]
      BR1305.B3   275.2   47-6831

103. Ball, George W. The issue in Viet-Nam [by] George W.
      Ball. [Washington] Department of State; [for sale by the
      Superintendent of Documents, U.S. Government Print. Office,
      1966]
      DS557.A6B29   327.730597   66-60784

104. _____. Viet-Nam, free-world challenge in Southeast Asia.
      [Washington, Office of Public Services, Bureau of Public Af-
      fairs, Department of State, 1962]
      DS557.A6B3   62-61621

105. Balraves, John. Australian libraries. Hamden, Conn.,
      Archon Books, 1966.
      Z870.A1B3   021.00994   66-7060

106. Balsiger, Peter. Vietnam. [Kriegsreportage. Zurich, AG
      fur Presse-Erzeugnisse, 1968.)
      DS557.A6B32   75-359981

107. Ba Maw, U, 1892-   Breakthrough in Burma; memoirs of a
      revolution, 1939-1946 [by] Ba Maw. New Haven, Yale Uni-
      versity Press, 1968.
      DS485.B89B28   959.1'04'0924   67-24504

108. Barber, Noel. A sinister twilight; the fall of Singapore,
      1942. Boston, Houghton Mifflin, 1968.
      D767.55.B3   940.542'5   68-16479

109. Barinova, Antonina Nikolaevna. Uchebnik v'etnamskogo
      iazyka dlia pervogo goda obuchenia, (Textbook of Vietnamese
      Language for the First Year of Teaching.) (In Russian).

Moscow, 1965.
PL4373.B3

110. Barnett, A. Doak, ed. Communist strategies in Asia; a comparative analysis of governments and parties. New York, Praeger, 1963.
DS35.B3   950   63-10823

111. Baruch, Jacques. Bibliographie des traductions francaises des litteratures du Viet-Nam et du Cambodge. Bruxelles, Editions Thanh-Long, 1968.
Z3229.L5B3   68-121923

112. Bassett, Marnie (Masson) 1889-   Behind the picture; H. M. S. Rattlesnake's Australia-New Guinea cruise, 1846 to 1850 [by] Marnie Bassett. Melbourne, New York [etc.] Oxford University Press, 1966.
QH11.B3   919.4   67-72001

113. Bastin, John Sturgus, 1927-   ed. Malayan and Indonesian studies; essays presented to Sir Richard Winstedt on his eighty-fifth birthday. Ed. by John Bastin, R. Roolvink. [New York] Oxford University Press, 1964.
DS503.4.B3   915.95   64-56618

114. _____. comp. Malaysia; selected historical readings, compiled by John Bastin and Robin W. Winks. Kuala Lumpur, Oxford University Press, 1966.
DS596.B33   959.5   S A 67-771

115. _____. The native policies of Sir Stamford Raffles in Java and Sumatra; an economic interpretation. Oxford, Clarendon, 1957.
                                            57-59585

116. Bator, Victor, 1891-   Vietnam, a diplomatic tragedy: the origins of the United States involvement, by Viktor Bator. Dobbs Ferry, N. Y. , Oceana Publications, 1965.
E183.8.V5B3   327.73   65-17939

117. Baturin, Andrei Alekseevich. Skhvatka v dzhungliakh, (Pursuit in Jungles). Moscow, 1963. (In Russian).
DS557.A6B35

118. Baudesson, Henry. Indo-China and its Primitive People. London, Hutchinson & Co. , 1919.
GN635.I6B3   20-1224

119. Baume, Michael. The Sydney Opera House affair. Epilogue by Peter Hall. [Melbourne] Nelson [1967]
NA6840.A79S9   725'.822   67-112485

120. Bauza, Obdulio. Cartas de Vietnam; poemas de guerra. Ilus.

de Rafael Muzzio Diaz. San Juan, P. R. [Orsini-Bristto]
1966 [i. e. 1967]
PQ7439.B34C29   68-50520

121. Baxter, Gordon, 1923-   Vietnam; search and destroy,
      Cleveland, World [1967]
      DS557.A61B3   959.7'04'0222   67-13129

122. Beaglehole, John Cawte. The discovery of New Zealand. 2d
      ed. London, Oxford University, 1961.
      DU410. B4   993.101   61-1997

123. Beatty, William Alfred. A treasury of Australian folk tales
      and traditions. London, Ward, 1960.
      GR365. B37   398.0994   60-51936

124. Beechy, Atlee. Vietnam: who cares? By Atlee and
      Winifred Beechy. Scottdale, Pennsylvania, Herald Press
      [1968]
      DS557.A68B4   959.7'04   68-20543

125. Der Befreiungskampf der Volker von Vietnam, Khmer und
      Pathet Lao. [1 Aufl.] Berlin, Dietz, 1954.
      DS557.A5B414   56-57030

126. Begbie, Peter James, d. 1864. The Malayan Peninsula.
      Introduction by Diptendra M. Banerjee. Kuala Lumpur, New
      York, Oxford University Press, 1967.
      DS592.B3 1967   915.9   67-9446

127. Behavioral science research in New Guinea; a report of a
      conference, Honolulu, Hawaii, August 18-25, 1965. Washing-
      ton, National Research Council, 1967.
      DU740. B44   390   67-60099

128. Belshaw, Cyril S. In search of wealth; a study of the
      emergence of commercial operations in the Melanesian society
      of southeastern Papua. Menasha, Wisconsin, American
      Anthropological Association, 1955.
      GN2.A22   572.995   55-2724

129. Belshaw, Cyril S. Island administration in the South West
      Pacific; government and reconstruction in New Caledonia,
      the New Hebrides, and the British Solomon Islands. New
      York, Royal Institute of International Affairs, 1950.
      JQ5995. B4   354.93   50-6437

130. Belshaw, Horace, ed. New Zealand. Berkeley, University
      of California, 1947.
      DU405. B4   919.31   47-31349

131. Benda, Harry Jindrich. The crescent and the rising sun;
      Indonesian Islam under the Japanese occupation, 1942-1945.

New York, The Institute of Pacific Relations, 1958.
DS643.5.B4   991   A58-5772

132. Benda, Harry Jindrich, ed. Japanese military administration
      in Indonesia: selected documents [by] Harry J. Benda,
      James K. Irikura [and] Koichi Kishi. [Translated by James
      K. Irikura, Margaret W. Broekhuysen, and Iman J. Pamoedjo.
      New Haven] Yale University Southeast Studies [1965]
      JX5003.B365   341.320991   65-26388

133. Benedict, Ruth (Fulton). That culture and behavior; an un-
      published war-time study dated September, 1943. Ithaca,
      N.Y., Cornell University, 1962.
                                                      55-37033

134. Benjafield, David Gilbert. Principles of Australian adminis-
      trative law, by D. G. Benjafield and H. Whitmore. 3rd ed.
      Sydney, Melbourne [etc.] Law Book Company, 1966
      TB467p   340   67-70795

135. Bensberger Kreis. Die Christen und der Krieg in Vietnam.
      Ein Memorandum deutscher Katholiken. Hrsg. vom Bens-
      berger Kreis. Mainz, Matthias-Grunewald-Verlag (1969).
      DS557.A68B45   77-448827

136. Benthem van den Bergh, G. van. Vietnam en de ideologie
      van het Westen. Amsterdam, De Bezige Bij, J. M. Muelen-
      hoff, 1967 [1968]
      DS557.A6B4   68-80977

137. Berlitz, V. A. Vietnamese phrase book, and English-Viet-
      namese dictionary, prepared by V. A. Berlitz. New York,
      New American Library [1968]
      PL4375.B4   495'.922'83   68-7956

138. Bernad, Miguel Anselmo. Bamboo and the greenwood tree;
      essays on Filipino literature in English. Manila, Bookmark,
      1961.
      PR9797.P6B4   820.9   61-11905

139. Du Berrier, Hilaire, 1906   Background to betrayal; the
      tragedy of Vietnam. Boston, Western Islands [1966, c.
      1965]
      DS557.A6D8   959.704   65-24091

140. Berrigan, Daniel. Night flight to Hanoi; war diary with 11
      poems. New York, Macmillan [1968]
      DS558.H3B47   959.7'04   68-56045

141. Bershadskii Rudol'f IUl'evich. V dvukh shagakh ot ekvatora,
      (Two steps from the Equator). (In Russian). Moscow, 1962.
      DS557.A7B4

32	Vietnam

142. Bertolino, Jean. Vietnam sanglant, 1967-1968. Paris, Stock, 1968.
DS557.A6B4   959.7'04   68-122206

143. Binh, Duong T.   Tagmemic Comparison of the Structure of
English & Vietnamese Sentences. Humanities Press, Inc. 1971.

144. Binyon, Laurence. The spirit of man in Asian art, being the
Charles Eliot Norton lectures delivered in Harvard university,
1933-34. Cambridge, Harvard University, 1935.
N7260.B53   709.5   35-3032

145. Bird, James, 1923- Seaport gateways of Australia. London,
New York [etc.] Oxford University Press, 1968.
HE559.A8B5   387.1'0994   68-141404

146. Bishop, Isabella Lucy (Bird). The Golden Chersonese and the
way thither [by] Isabella L. Bird. Introduction by Wang Gungwu
[1st ed. reprinted. Kuala Lumpur, London, New York, Oxford
University Press, 1967]
DS592.B62 1968   915.95'03'3   68-111938

147. Bisignano, Flavio. Vietnam--why? An American citizen looks
at the war. Torrance, California, Frank Publications [1968]
DS557.A69B5   959.7'04   68-27773

148. Bitsch, Jorgen. Why Buddha smiles. Tr. [from Danish] by
Gwynne Vevers. New York, Taplinger [1966, c. 1964]
DS485.B84B53 1966   915.9   66-12946

149. Bixler, Norma. Burmese journey. [Yellow Springs, Ohio]
Antioch Press, 1967.
DS485.B84B59   915.91'03'50922   67-11440

150. Blainey, Geoffrey. The tyranny of distance; how distance
shaped Australia's history. Melbourne, Macmillan; New York,
St. Martin's Press, 1968, [c. 1966]
DU110.B54   994   67-89825

151. Blanchet, Marie Therese. La naissance de l'Etat associe du
Viet-Nam. Paris, M. T. Genin [1954]
                                        A 55-3723

152. Bloomfield, Lincoln Palmer, 1920-   The U. N. and Vietnam
[by] Lincoln P. Bloomfield, New York, Carnegie Endowment
for International Peace, 1968.
JX1977.2.V5B6   341.13'9'597   68-2907

153. Blume, Isabelle, 1892-   De la frontiere du Laos a la riviere
Ben Hai. Hanoi, Editions en langues etrangeres [pref. 1961]
DS557.A7B6   65-57520

154. Bly, Robert, ed. A poetry reading against the Vietnam War;
collection gathered by Robert Bly and David Ray. [Madison,

Minnesota] American Writers Against the Vietnam War; distributed by the Sixties Press, 1966.
DS557.A6B55   808.803   66-4861

155. Boba, Antonio. Saigon Diary. Vintage Press, Inc., 1970.

156. Bodard, Lucien. La Guerre d'Indochine. Paris, Gallimard,
1963.
DS550.B62   63-58532

157. _____. The quicksand war; prelude to Vietnam. Translated
and with an introduction by Patrick O'Brian. [1st ed.] Boston,
Little, Brown [1967]
DS550.B6213   959.7'03   67-11226

158. Boeke, Julius Herman. Economics and economic policy of dual
societies, as exemplified by Indonesia. New York, International
Secretariat, Institute of Pacific Relations, 1953.
HC447.B663   330.991   53-13196

159. _____. The evolution of the Netherlands Indies
economy. New York, Institute of Pacific Relations,
1946.
HC447.B664   330.991   47-17557

160. Boettiger, John R. comp. Vietnam and American foreign
policy, edited with an introduction by John R. Boettiger.
Boston, Heath [1968]
DS557.A63B6   959.7'04   68-25862

161. Bøgholm, Karl, 1898- Vietnam kalder. [Af] K. Bøgholm.
København, Nyt Nordisk Forlag, 1967.
DS557.A6B557   67-88927

162. Bogo, Generoso. Imagens e paisagens do Vietnam. [Porto
Alegre, Composto e impresso nas oficinas da Editora Escola
Grafica Dom Bosco, 1969 or 70]
DS557.A5B58   70-493449

163. Bommarito, John E. The truth about Viet Nam, by John E.
Bommarito. St. Louis, Alert Publications, 1966.
DS557.A6B56   335.432   66-26618

164. Bone, Robert C. The dynamics of the Western New Guinea
(Irian Barat) problem. Ithaca, N. Y., Modern Indonesia
Project, Southeast Asia Program, Department of Far Eastern
Studies, Cornell University, 1958.
DU744.5B6

165. Bone, Robert C., Jr. Contemporary Southeast Asia. New
York, Random [c. 1962]
DS518.1.B6   959   62-10675

166. Bonnet, Gabriel Georges Marcel. La guerre revolutionnaire
      du Vietnam, histoire, techniques et enseignements de la
      guerre americano-vietnamienne . . . Paris, Payot, 1969.
      DS557.A6B57   76-396747

167. Bonosky, Phillip. Beyond the borders of myth, from Vilnius
      to Hanoi. New York, Praxis Press, 1967.
      DK511.L2B6   915.97'04'4   68-188

168. Bornemann, Paul, 1935-   Die Teilnahme politisch geteilter
      Staaten an der Arbeit internationaler Organisationen. [Köln,
      1964]
      JX1995.B6   65-66379

169. Bortniak, Iakym Mykolaiovych. Demokratichna Respublika
      V'etnam, (Democratic Republic of Vietnam). (In Ukrainian.)
      Kiev, 1960.
      AS262.T563

170. Bourne, Peter G.   1939-   Men, stress, and Vietnam [by]
      Peter G. Bourne. [1st ed.] Boston, Little, Brown [1970]
      DS557.A68B67   959.7'04   72-101754

171. Bouscaren, Anthony Trawick. The last of the mandarins:
      Diem of Vietnam. Pittsburgh, Duquesne University Press,
      1965.
      DS557.A6B6   923.1597   65-16136

172. Bowditch, Nathaniel, 1733-1838. Early American-Philippine
      trade: the journal of Nathaniel Bowditch in Manila, 1796.
      Edited and with an introduction by Thomas R. McHale and
      Mary C. McHale. New Haven, Yale University, Southeast
      Asia Studies; distributed by the Cellar Book Shop, Detroit,
      1962.
      HF3126.B6   63-25180

173. Bozek, David A. Artillery Medic in Vietnam. Vantage Press,
      Inc. 1971.

174. Brackman, Arnold C. Indonesian communism, a history.
      New York, Praeger [1963]
      HX402.B7   335.430991   63-9391

175. Brake, Brian. New Zealand, gift of the sea. Brian Brake:
      photos. Maurice Shadbolt: text. [1st ed. Christchurch]
      Whitcombe and Tombs [1963]
      DU412.B7   919.31   64-1692

176. Brandon, Henry, 1916-   Anatomy of error; the inside story
      of the Asian war on the Potomac, 1954-1969. Boston, Gambit,
      1969.
      DS557.A63B7   959.7'04   75-95232

177.   _____. Anatomy of error: the secret history of the
        Vietnam war. London, Deutsch, 1970.
        DS557.A63B7 1970   959.7'04   75-492575

178.   Brass, Alister John Douglas. Bleeding earth; a doctor looks
        at Vietnam [by] Alister Brass. Foreword by Harrison E.
        Salisbury. Melbourne, Heinemann [1968]
        DS557.A677B72   959.7'04   68-108559

179.   _____. Bleeding Earth: A Doctor Looks at Vietnam.
        Melbourne, Tri-Ocean, 1968.
        DS557.A677B72   959.7'04   68-108559

180.   Braun, Volker, 1939-   Kriegserklarung. Halle (Saale) Mit-
        teldeutscher Verlag, 1967.
        DS557.A61B7   68-96524

181.   Brebion, Antoine. Bibliographie des Voyages dans l'Indo-
        chine Francaise, 800-1800. B. Franklin, 1971.
        Z3221.B72 1970   78-132542

182.   _____. Livre d'or du Cambodge, de la Cochinchine et
        de l'Annam, 1615-1910. B. Franklin (Franklin, Burt, Pub.)
        1969.

183.   _____. Livre d'or du Cambodge, de la Cochinchine et
        de l'Annam, 1625-1910. B. Franklin. (Franklin, Burt, Pub.)
        1971.

184.   Brecher, Michael. The new states of Asia, a political analy-
        sis. New York, Oxford University Press, 1963.
        JQ96.B7   320   64-549

185.   Brelis, Dean. The face of South Vietnam. Text by Dean
        Brelis.   Photos by Jill Krementz. Boston, Houghton Mifflin,
        1968 [1967]
        DS557.A6B62   959.7'04   67-24416

186.   Brett, Peter, ed. Cases and materials in criminal law, by
        Peter Brett and Peter L. Waller. Melbourne, Butterworths,
        1965.
        CB845 c1965   63-5798

187.   Briand, Rena. No tears to flow; woman at war. Melbourne,
        Heinemann [1969]
        DS557.A69B7   959.7'04'0924   70-465498

188.   Briley, John. Traitors. Putnam, 1969.
        PZ4.B856Tr   813'.5'4   78-81568

189.   Brinch, Esther. Vietnam. [Af] Esther Brinch-Nogle grund-
        traek af Vietnam-problemet. [Af] Gotfred Appel. København,
        Vietnam-Komiteen, 1966.
        DS557.A6B63   67-93917

190.   Briscoe, Edward.   Diary of a Shortimer in Vietnam.   Vantage
       Press, Inc.   1970.

191.   Brissenden, Paul Frederick, 1885-   The settlement of labor
       disputes on rights in Australia, by Paul F. Brissenden.   Los
       Angeles, Institute of Industrial Relations, University of Cali-
       fornia [1966]
                                331. 890994   67-63059

192.   Broekmeijer, M. W. J. M.   1894-   South-Vietnam, victim
       of misunderstanding.   [By] M. W. J. M. Broekmeijer.
       Bilthoven, H. Nelissen [1967]
       DS557. A6B64   915. 97'03'4   68-71016

193.   Bromley, Dorothy (Dunbar).   Washington and Vietnam; an
       examination of the moral and political issues.   Dobbs Ferry,
       N. Y. , Oceana Publications, 1966.
       DS557. A6B65   959. 704   66-28741

194.   Brookings Institution, Washington, D.C.   Vietnam after the
       war; peacekeeping and rehabilitation [by] H. Field Haviland,
       Jr. [and others] Washington, Brookings Institution, 1968.
       DS557. A692B7   959. 7'04   69-18821

195.   Broughton, Jack 1925- Thud Ridge.   With an introduction by
       Hanson W. Baldwin.   [1st ed.]   Philadelphia, Lippincott [1969]
       DS557. A65B7   959. 7'04   69-16959

196.   Brown, David Alexander.   The geological evolution of Australia
       & New Zealand, by D. A. Brown, K. S. W. Campbell [and]
       K. A. W. Crook.   [1st ed.] Oxford, New York, Pergamon
       Press [1968]
       QE340. B7 1968   551. 7'00994   66-29583

197.   Brown, James Patrick.   Era of challenge [by] James Patrick
       Brown [and] James A. Kearns III.   Ed. by Herald M. Doxsee
       with a foreword by William C. Addison.   St. Louis, B.
       Herder Book Company [1970]
       DS557. A63B76 1970   959. 7'04   77-109441

198.   Brown, Robert McAfee, 1920- Vietnam: crisis of conscience
       [by] Robert McAfee Brown, Abraham J. Heschel [and] Michael
       Novak.   New York, Association Press [1967]
       DS557. A68B7   959. 7'04   67-21994

199.   _____ .   Vietnam: Crisis of Conscience.   Herder &
       Herder, 1971.

200.   Brown, Sam & Ackland, Len, eds.   Why Are We Still in
       Vietnam.   Random, 1970.
       DS557. A63W48   959. 7'04   73-127532

201.   Browne, Malcolm W.   The new face of war [by] Malcom W.

Browne. Indianapolis, Bobbs-Merrill [1965]
DS557.A6B7   959. 7   65-17701

202. _____. The new face of war [by] Malcolm
W. Browne. Rev. ed. Indianapolis, Bobbs-Merrill [1968]
DS557.A6B7   959. 7'04   68-15805

203. _____. Vietnam, Il nuovo volto della guerra. [Di] Malcolm
Browne. Con una prefazione di Henry Cabot Lodge. Tra-
duzione di Enrico Mattioli. Roma, G. Casini, 1967.
DS557.A6B716   70-383287

204   Brune, Jean. Viet-Nam, bataille pour l'Asie. Paris, Com-
pagnie francaise de librairie, 1967.
DS557.A6B73   959. 7'04   68-112577

205. Buchanan, Keith M. The Southeast Asian world; an introductory essay [by] Keith Buchanan. New York, Taplinger [1967]
DS511.B8   309. 1'59   67-20243

206. Buck, Peter Henry. Anthropology and religion. New Haven,
Yale University, 1939.
BL2600.B8   299. 9   40-488

207. _____. The coming of the Maori. 2d ed.
Wellington, Whitcombe & Tombs, 1950.
DU423.B83   993. 1   51-25987

208. Buckley, Charles Burton, 1844-1912. An anecdotal history
of old times in Singapore, from the foundation of the settlement under the Honorable the East India Company on February
6th, 1819, to the transfer to the Colonial Office as part of the
colonial possessions of the Crown on April 1st, 1867. Kuala
Lumpur, University of Malaya Press [New York, Oxford, c.]
1965.
DS598.S7B9   959. 52   SA66-1471

209. Buckley, Vincent. Essays in poetry, mainly Australian.
Carlton, Melbourne University, 1957.
PR9471.B8   821. 09   A58-207

210. Budanov, Anatolii Gavrilovich. Gosudarstvennyi stroi Demo-
kraticheskoi Respubliki V'etnam, (State Organization of the
Republic of Vietnam). (In Russian). Moscow, 1958.
JQ815.B8

211. Buell, Harold G. Viet Nam: land of many dragons, by Hal
Buell. New York, Dodd, [1968]
DS557.A5.B76   915. 97'03   68-24027

212. Buhler, Alfred et al. The art of the South Sea Islands, including Australia and New Zealand. New York, Crown, 1962.
                                                         62-11806

213.   Bui-kong-Chyng, 1905-   Severnyi V'etnam na puti postroeniia
        sotsializma, (North Vietnam on the Road to Building Socialism).
        (In Russian).   Moscow, 1959.
        HC443.V5B8

214.   Bui-quang-Tung.   Contribution à l'étude des colonies viet-
        namiennes en Thailand.   Saigon, France-Asie [1958?]
        DS570.V5B8   S A 65-5288

215.   Bundy, McGeorge, 1919-   The fourth Cosmos Club award:
        McGeorge Bundy.   Washington, Cosmos Club, 1967.
        DS557.A6B75   959.7'04   67-9462

216.   Bundy, William P. , 1917-   South Viet-Nam: reality and
        myth.   [Washington] Bureau of Public Affairs, Department
        of State [for sale by the Superintendent of Documents, U.S.
        Government Print. Office, 1965]
        DS557.A6B8   65-62425

217.   Burchett, Wilfred G.   1911-   The furtive war; the United
        States in Vietnam and Laos.   New York, International Pub-
        lishers [1963]
        DS557.A6B8   327.73059   63-18721

218.   _____. My visit to the liberated zones of South
        Vietnam [by] Wilfred Burchett.   Hanoi, Foreign Lan-
        guages Publishing House, 1964.
        DS557.A6B82   65-89518

219.   _____. My visit to the liberated zones of South Vietnam
        [by] Wilfred Burchett.   Hanoi, Foreign Languages Publish-
        ing House, 1966.
        DS557.A6B82 1966   959.7'04   68-5185

220.   _____. North of the seventeenth parallel.   Delhi, People's
        Publishing House, 1956.
        DS557.A7B8   959.7   59-30440

221.   _____. Partisanen contra Generale.   Sudvietnam 1964
        [von] Wilfred G. Burchett.   (Aus dem Englischen übers. von
        Gerhard Bottcher [u. a.] Mit 43 Fotos des Autors. 2., vom
        Autor erg. Aufl.) Düsseldorf, Brucken-Verlag, 1966.
        DS557.A6B825 1966   959.704   66-68593

222.   _____. Pourquoi le Vietcong gagne [par] Wilfred Burchett.
        Traduit de l'anglais par J.-P. [Jean-Pierre] Rospars. Paris,
        F. Maspero, 1968.
        DS557.A6B8384   76-449698

223.   _____. Vietná Norte [por] Wilfred G. Burchett.   Trad.
        de Affonso Blacheyre. [Rio de Janeiro] Civilização Bra-
        sileira [1967]
        DS557.A7B837   68-123722

224.   . Vietnam--a guerrilha vista por dentro [por] Wil-
fred G. Burchett. [Trad. Daniel Campos] Rio de Janeiro,
Graf. Record, 1967.
DS557.A6B837   959'.7'04   68-115138

225.   . Vietnam: inside story of the guerilla war, by
Wilfred G. Burchett. New York, International Publishers
[1965]
DS557.A6B83   959.7   65-18719

226.   . Vietnam: Inside Story of the Guerrilla War. International Publishers Company, Inc. 1968.

227.   . Vietnam North, by Wilfred G. Burchett. [1st ed.]
New York, International Publishers [1966]
DS557.A7B83   959.7'04   66-28970

228.   . Vietnam North, by Wilfred G. Burchett. With a
preface by Bertrand Russell. [2d ed.] New York, International Publishers [1967, c1966]
DS557.A7B83 1967   959.7'04   67-7619

229.   . Vietnam will win! Why the people of South Vietnam have already defeated U. S. imperialism--and how they
have done it--by the internationally famous Western corres-
pondent whose first-hand dispatches from Vietnam have become
a part of the history of our times, Wilfred G. Burchett. New
York, Distributed by Monthly Review Press, 1968 [i.e. 1969,
c1968]
DS557.A6B838   959.7'04   68-59046

230. Burdon, Randal Mathews. King Dick, a biography of Richard
John Seddon. Christchurch, N. Z., Whitcombe & Tombs,
1955.
DU422.S4B8   923.2931   56-30649

231.   . New Zealand notables. Christchurch, N. Z., Cax-
ton, 1941-
DU402.B8   920.0931   A42-2699rev2

232. Burkhill, Isaac Henry. A dictionary of the economic products
of the Malay peninsula. London, Crown Agents for the
Colonies, 1935.
HC497.P2B8   330.9595   Agr36-171

233. Burley, Kevin. British shipping and Australia 1920-1939.
London, Cambridge University Press, 1968.
HE916.B95   387'.0994   68-10328

234. Burroughs, Peter. Britain and Australia 1831-1855: a study
in imperial relations and crown lands administration. Oxford,
Clarendon P., 1967.
HD1035.B87   354.94'0082   67-100191

235.   Bushner, Rolland H., ed. American dilemma in Viet-Nam; a
        report on the views of leading citizens in thirty-three cities.
        Edited by Rolland H. Bushner. New York, Council on Foreign
        Relations [1965]
        DS557.A6B85   65-29668

236.   Business International Corporation, New York. Doing
        business in the new Indonesia. [New York, c1968]
        HF3806.5.B87   330.991   68-59252

237.   Buttinger, Joseph. Der kampfbereite Drache. Vietnam nach
        Dien Bien Phu. [Aus dem Engl. v. Walter Hacker.] Wien,
        Europa-Verlag [1968]
        DS557.A5B79   71-487470

238.   _____. The smaller dragon; a political history of Vietnam.
        New York, Praeger [1958]
        DS557.A5B8   959.7   58-7748

239.   _____. Smaller Dragon. Praeger Publishers, 1970.

240.   _____. Vietnam: a dragon embattled. London, Pall
        Mall P., 1967.
        DS557.A5B83 1967b   959.7   68-70118

241.   _____. Vietnam: a dragon embattled. New York,
        Praeger [1967]
        DS557.A5B83   959.7   66-13682

242.   _____. Vietnam; a political history. New York, Praeger
        [1988]   [1968
        DS557.A5B84   959.7   68-23351

243.   Butts, Robert Freeman. Assumptions underlying Australian
        education. New York, Columbia University, 1955.
        LA2101.B8   370.994   55-14854rev

244.   Buxton, Gordon Leslie. The Riverina, 1861-1891: an
        Australian regional study [by] G. L. Buxton. [Melbourne]
        Melbourne U.P.; London, New York, Cambridge University
        Press, 1967 [i.e. 1968]
        S471.A82R56   994'.4   67-30092

245.   Buxton, Leonard Halford Dudley. The peoples of Asia. New
        York, Knopf, 1925.
        GN625.B8   25-21999

C

246.   Cadiere, Leopold Michel, 1869-1955. Syntaxe de la langue
        vietnamienne. Paris, Ecole francaise d'Extreme-Orient, 1958.
        PL4373.C33   59-53048

247.   Cady, John Frank, 1901-   A history of modern Burma.
        Ithaca, N. Y., Cornell University Press, 1958.
        DS485.B86C2   959.1   58-1545

248.   _____. Thailand, Burma, Laos & Cambodia [by] John F.
        Cady. Englewood Cliffs, N. J., Prentice-Hall [1966]
        DS509.3.C3   915.9   66-28105

249.   Les Cahiers franco-vietnamiens. année 1- [Saigon, 1948-]
        DS557.A5A24   54-17872

250.   Caiden, Gerald E. The Commonwealth bureaucracy [by]
        Gerald E. Caiden. [Melbourne] Melbourne University Press;
        London, New York, Cambridge University Press [1967]
        JQ4047.C33   354.94'006   67-12145

251.   Cairns, James Ford. The eagle and the lotus; western inter-
        vention in Vietnam 1847-1968 [by] J. F. Cairns. [Melbourne]
        Lansdowne Press [1969]
        DS557.A5C28   959'.704   75-480525

252.   _____. Lotus and the Eagle: European Inter-
        vention in Vietnam 1847-1968. Verry, Lawrence, Inc., 1969.

253.   Caldwell, John Cope, 1913-   Let's visit Malaysia [by] John
        C. Caldwell. New York, John Day [1968]
        DS592.C33   915.95   68-26341/AC

254.   _____. Let's visit Vietnam [by] John C. Caldwell. [rev.]
        New York, John Day Company [1969]
        DS557.A5C3 1969   915.9'7'03   78-12338

255.   _____. Let's visit Vietnam. New York, John Day [c.1966]
        DS557.A5C3   915.97   66-15092

256.   Callado, Antonio. Vietnã do Norte: advertencia áos agressores.
        Rio de Janeiro, Civiliazçao Brasileira, 1969.
        DS557.A7C24   76-466305

257.   Calley, William & Sack, John. Lt. Calley: An American
        Tragedy with a Complete Account of My Lai Four & Exclusive
        Coverage of the Trial. Viking Press, Inc., 1971.

258.   Calley, William Laws, 1943-   Lieutenant Calley: his own
        story as told to John Sack. Viking, 1971.
        DS557.A67C33 1971   959.7'0434   73-153127

259.   Cambodia. Letter dated 16 April 1964 from the Permanent
        Representatives of Cambodia addressed to the President of the
        Security Council, and attached documents. [New York, United
        Nations, 1964]
        JX1977.A2 S/5666   65-1323

260.   Cameron, Allan W., comp. Viet Nam crisis, a documentary
        history. Cornell University Press, 1971.
        DS557.A5C32   959.7'03   72-127600

261.   Cameron, James, 1911-   Here is your enemy; complete re-
        port from North Vietnam. [1st ed] New York, Holt, Rinehart
        and Winston [1966]
        DS557.A7C25   915.97044   66-20860

262.   _____. Witness. London, Gollancz, 1966.
        DS557.A7C3   915.97044   66-70127

263.   _____. Our tropical possessions in Malayan India. Intro-
        duction by Wang Gungwu [New York] Oxford [c.] 1965.
        DS592.C18   915.95033   66-610

264.   Cammack, Floyd M. and Saito, Shiro. Pacific island bibli-
        ography. New York, Scarecrow, 1962.
        Z4001.C3   016.99   62-10126

265.   Campbell, Alex. Unbind Your Sons: The Captivity of Amer-
        ica in Asia. Liveright, 1970.
        DS35.C33   327.5'073   79-114382

266.   Campbell, Enid Mona, 1932-   Legal research: materials
        and methods by Enid Campbell and Donald MacDougall. Syd-
        ney, Melbourne, [etc.] Law Book Co., 1967.
                                                               68-96652

267.   Can we win in Vietnam? [by] Frank E. Armbruster [and
        others] With the assistance of Thomas F. Bartman and
        Carolyn Kelley. New York, Praeger [1968]
        DS557.A6C3   959.7'04   68-21355

268.   Can we win in Vietnam? The American dilemma [by] Frank
        E. Armbruster [and others] With the assistance of Thomas F.
        Bartman and Carolyn Kelley. London, Pall Mall Press, 1968.
        DS557.A6C3 1968b   959.7'04   68-117678

269.   Canberra, Australia. National Library. Annual catalogue of
        Australian publications. no. 1-25; 1936-60. Canberra.
        Z4011.C22   38-9570 rev

270.   Cannon, Terry. Vietnam, a thousand years of struggle. [San
        Francisco, Peoples Press, 1969]
        DS557.A5C33   959.7   75-14831

271.   Carey, Alex E. Australian atrocities in Vietnam, by Alex
        Carey. [Sydney, Gould, Convenor, Vietnam Action Campaign,
        1968]
        DS557.A67C37   959.7'04   77-492396

272.   Casey, Richard Gardiner, 1890-   Friends and Neighbors.

East Lansing, Michigan State College Press [1955]
DU113. C37 1955   327. 94   55-7676

273.   Castles, Lance. Religion, politics, and economic behavior
        in Java: the Kudus cigarette industry. [New Haven]
        Southeast Asia Studies, Yale University [distributor: Cellar
        Book Shop, Detroit, 1967]
        HD9149. C42J33   309. 191   67-18731

274.   Cave, Sydney. An introduction to the study of some living
        religions of the East. London, Duckworth, 1959.
                                                                A22-386

275.   Center for the Study of Democratic Institutions. War and
        Revolution Today. Santa Barbara, (California) 1965.
        DS557. A6C4   66-1605

276.   Center for War/Peace Studies. Experimental Education Pro-
        gram. Understanding Vietnam; a citizen's primer. Cam-
        bridge, Massachusetts [1967]
        DS557. A63C4   959. 7'04   68-446

277.   Chaffard, Georges. Les deux guerres du Vietnam; de Valluy
        a Westmoreland. [Paris. La Table ronde, 1969]
        DS557. A5C43   73-465011

278.   _____. Indochine; dix ans d'independance. Paris, Cal-
        mann-Levy [1964]
        DS500. C47   65-81212

279.   Chai, Hon-chan. The development of British Malaya, 1896-
        1909. Kuala Lumpur, New York, Oxford University Press,
        1964.
        DS596. C43   S A 66-5980

280.   Chaliand, Gerard, 1934- Peasants of North Vietnam. Wiles,
        Peter, tr. Penguin Books, Inc., 1970.

281.   _____. The peasants of North Vietnam.
        With a pref. by Philippe Devillers. Translated by Peter Wiles.
        Baltimore, Penguin Books [1969]
        HN700. V5C5313   301. 3'5'09597   78-11515
        1969b

282.   _____. The peasants of North Vietnam; with a preface by
        Philippe Devillers; translated [from the French] by Peter
        Wiles. Harmondsworth, Penguin, 1969.
        HN700. V5C5313   301. 3'5'09597   73-473125

283.   Champassak, Sisouk Na, 1928- Storm over Laos, a con-
        temporary history. New York, Praeger [c.1961]
        DS557. L28C5   959. 4   61-11107

284.   Ch'ang-cheng, pseud. Lun Yueh-nan pa yueh ko ming, (Viet-
       namese August Revolution, (In Chinese).   1948.
       DS557.A7C485

285.   La Chanson des deux rives, poemes. [Traductions de G.
       Boudarel, Le van Chat et P. Gamarra. Illustrations de Diep
       Minh Chau] Hanoi, Editions en langues etrangeres, 1963.
       PL4283.F3C48   67-122920

286.   Chants pour le Vietnam, 80 poemes, 75 poetes de 28 pays.
       Paris les Editeurs francais reunis, 1967.
       DS557.A61C45   68-96052

287.   Chapman, Robert McDonald and Bennett, Jonathan Francis,
       comps. An anthology of New Zealand verse. London, Oxford
       University, 1956.
       PR9657.C5   821.082   56-3148

288.   Chau, Phan Thien Long. Transitional nationalism in Viet-
       Nam 1903-1931.   Denver, 1965.
       LB2378.U6 1965   Microfilm T 46.423

289.   Chaumont, Charles Marie. Analyse critique de l'intervention
       americaine au Vietnam [par] Charles Chaumont . . . Bruxelles,
       Commission permanente d'enquete pour le Vietnam, (1968).
       DS557.A6C515   77-374021

290.   _____. A critical study of American intervention in Viet-
       nam [by] Charles Chaumont.   Brussels, Permanent Committee
       of Enquiry for Vietnam [n. d.]
       JX1573.C5   327.73   74-38414

291.   Chaunu, Pierre. Les Philippines et le Pacifique, des
       Iberiques (XVI, XVII, XVIII siecles).   Paris, S.E.V.P.E.N.,
       1960.
                                                             63-52669

292.   Cheeseman, Harold Ambrose Robinson. Bibliography of
       Malaya. . . New York, Longmans, Green, 1959.
       Z3246.C5   016.9191   60-27688

293.   Le Chemin du bonheur et de la prosperite. Hanoi, Editions en
       langues etrangeres, 1963.
       HC443.V5C45   66-95204

294.   Ch'en, Hsiu-ho. Chung Yueh liang kuo jen min ti yu hao kuan
       hsi ho wen hua chiao liu, (Sino-Vietnamese Friendship &
       Cultural Exchange), (In Chinese).   Peking, 1957.
       DS740.5.V5C48

295.   Ch'en, Huai-nan. Yueh-nan jen min ti chieh fang tou Cheng,
       (Vietnamese People Struggle for Freedom), (In Chinese) 1954.
       DS557.A765

296.   Ch'en, I-ling, 1913-   Yuen-nan hsien shih (Present situation
       in Vietnam) (In Chinese), Taipei, Taiwan, 1957.
       DS557.A5C48

297.   Chen, King C., 1926-   Vietnam and China, 1938-1954, by
       King C. Chen. Princeton, N. J., Princeton University Press,
       1969.
       DS740.5.V5C484   327.51'0597   78-83684

298.   Chen, Mong Hock. The early Chinese newspapers of Singa-
       pore, 1881-1912. Singapore, University of Malaya Press;
       [sole distributors: Oxford University Press, London] 1967.
       PN5449.S55C5   079.595'2   68-2061

299.   Chen, Tse-ming. The Chinese Communists' role in the war
       in Vietnam. [Taipei] Asian Peoples' Anti-communist League,
       Republic of China, 1965.
       DS557.A635C5   327.51'0597   67-37113

300.   Chesneaux, Jean. Contribution à l'histoire de la nation viet-
       namienne. Paris, Editions sociales [1955]
                                                        A 56-914

301.   _____. Le Vietnam (etudes de politique et d'histoire).
       Paris, F. Maspero, 1968.
       DS557.A5C534   959.7   68-110210

302.   _____. Vietnam; Geschichte und Ideologie des Wider-
       standes. [Aus dem Franzosischen ubertragen von Gisela
       Mandel. Frankfurt am Main] Europaische Verlagsanstalt
       [1968]
       DS557.A5C5345   957.7   70-376323

303.   Chiang, Chun-chang, 1906-   Yueh-nan lun ts'ung, (Collected
       Essays of Vietnam), (In Chinese). 1960.

304.   Chicago. University. Philippine Studies Program. Selected
       bibliography of the Philippines, topically arranged and anno-
       tated. Fred Eggan, director. Preliminary ed. New Haven,
       Human Relations Area Files, 1956.
       Z3291.C45   016.9914   57-4424

305.   Chien si nhan dan; tap truyen ngan ky su phuc vu le ky niem
       15 nam ngay thanh lap quan doi nhan dan Viet-Nam 22-12-59
       [cua] Nguyen-minh-Chau [et al.] [Hanoi] Thanh Nien, 1959.
       DS557.A7C54   S A 68-1044

306   Child, Frank C. Essays on economic growth, capital forma-
       tion, and public policy in Viet-Nam. Saigon, Michigan State
       University Viet-Nam Advisory Group, 1961.
       HC443.V5C5   62-62535

307.   _____. Toward a policy for economic growth in Vietnam

[by] Frank C. Child. [Saigon] Michigan State University,
Vietnam Advisory Group [1962?]
HC443.V5C53   338.9597   64-64286

308. China. Ching chi fang wen t'uan. Report on Vietnam's agri-
      culture and industry, by Economic Good Will Mission of the
      Republic of China to Vietnam. [Taipei?] 1958.
      HD2080.V5C513   66-92640

309. La Chine et le Vietnam, un probleme pour la conscience
      chretienne [par] Lily Abeg, Carl-J. Keller-Senn, Ernst Kux,
      Alois Riklin . . . [et al.] Traduit par [l'abbe] Marcel
      Grandelaudon. Mulhouse, Editions Salvator; Paris, Tournai,
      Casterman, 1968.
      BT736.2.C5414   76-448280

310. Chinnock, Frank W. Kim--a Gift from Vietnam. Paperback
      Library, 1971.

311. Chomsky, Noam. American power and the new mandarins. New
      York, Pantheon Books [1969]
      E744.C514   327.73   69-11864

312. _____. At War with Asia. Pantheon, 1970.
      DS557.A63C47 1970   959.7'04   78-129983

313. _____. At War with Asia. Random House, Inc., 1971.

314. Chuang, Wei. Ya-chou ti jen min min chu kuo chia, (Demo-
      cratic Countries of Asian Peoples), (In Chinese), 1955.
      DS932.C55

315. Chung, Ly Q., ed. Between Two Fires: The Unheard Voices
      of Vietnam. Praeger Publishers, 1970.

316. Chung Yueh yu hao jen min kung she. Wo men ho Yueh-nan
      jen min ti chan tou yu i, (Chinese-Vietnamese Friendship
      during Wartime), (In Chinese). Peking, 1965.
      DS740.5.V5C5

317. Chung-kuo ch'ing nien ch'u pan she, Peking. Shin jih Yueh-
      nan, (Vietnam Today), (In Chinese). Peking, 1956.

318. Ciuffi, Sergio. Vietnam 1858-1967: un secolo di lotte.
      Firenze, Cultura, 1967.
      DS557.A5C55   68-98132

319. Civic Education Service, Washington, D.C. Two Viet Nams
      in war and peace, by the eds. of Civic Educ. Serv. Washing-
      ton [1967]
      DS557.A5A46   959.7'04   67-3780

320. Clark, Alan, 1928-   The lion heart; a tale of the war in

Vietnam. New York, Morrow, 1969.
PZ4.C5898Li 3   823'.9'14   69-11569

321.   Clark, Andrew Hill.   The invasion of New Zealand by people,
        plants and animals: the South Island. New Brunswick,
        Rutgers University, 1949.
        DU410.C5   993.1   49-50393

322.   Clark, Charles Manning Hope. A history of Australia. New
        York, Cambridge University Press, 1962-
        DU110.C48   994   63-5969

323.   Clark, Joseph S. China and the Vietnam war--will history
        repeat? Report to the Committee on Foreign Relations, United
        States Senate, by Joseph S. Clark. Washington, U.S. Govern-
        ment Print. Office, 1968.
        DS557.A64C43   68-61937

324.   _____. Stalemate in Vietnam. Report to the Committee on
        Foreign Relations, United States Senate, by Joseph S. Clark on
        a study mission to South Vietnam. Washington, U. S. Govern-
        ment Print. Office, 1968.
        DS557.A6C58   959.7'04   68-61039

325.   Clarkson, James D.   The cultural ecology of a Chinese village;
        Cameron Highlands, Malaysa [sic] by James D. Clarkson.
        [Chicago, Department of Geography, University of Chicago]
        1968.
        H31.C514 no. 114   301.3'5'09595   67-28490

326.   Clifford, Mary Louise. The land and the people of Malaysia.
        [1st ed.] Philadelphia, Lippincott [1968]
        DS592.C64   915.95   68-24412

327.   Clodd, Harold Parker.   Malaya's first British pioneer; the
        life of Francis Light. London, Luzac, 1948.
        DS596.C58   959.5   49-2107

328.   Clutterbuck, Richard L. The long, long war; counterinsur-
        gency in Malaya and Vietnam. Foreword by Harold K. John-
        son. New York, Praeger [c.1966]
        DS596.C59   959.504   66-13678

329.   Coates, Austin. Rizal. Philippine nationalist and martyr.
        Hong Kong, New York, Oxford University Press, 1968.
        DS675.8.R5C57   991.4'02'0924 (B)   78-304

330.   Coe, Charles. Young man in Vietnam. New York, Four
        Winds Press [1968]
        DS557.A69C6   959.7'04   68-27270

331.   Coedes, George. Angkor: an introduction; translated [from
        French] edited by Emily Floyd Gardiner, photogs., by George

Bliss unless otherwise credited.   Hong Kong, New York [etc.]
Oxford University Press, 1966 [i.e. 1967]
DS558.A6C583 1967   915.96   68-108294

332.   Cole, Allan Burnett, ed.   Conflict in IndoChina and interna-
       tional repercussions; a documentary history, 1945-1955.
       Ithaca, N. Y., Cornell University, 1956.
       DS550.C6   959   56-14338

333.   Cole, David Chamberlain 1928-   Financing provincial and
       local government in the Republic of Vietnam. Ann Arbor,
       Michigan, University Microfilms [1959]
                                                    Mic 59-4898

334.   Cole, Fay Cooper.   The peoples of Malaysia. New York, Van
       Nostrand, 1945.
       DS601.C63   919.1   45-5386

335.   Collins, Sir Charles Henry.   Public administration in Hong
       Kong. New York, Royal Institute of International Affairs,
       1952.
       JQ675.C6   354.5125   52-11532

336.   Collotti Pischel, Enrica, comp.   Il Vietnam vincera. Po-
       litica, strategia, organizzazione. Scritti di Ho Chi Minh,
       Vo Nguyen Giap, Pham Van Dong, Nguyen Kach Vien, Pham
       Ngoc Thach, Truong Son, Enrica Collotti Pischel. Torino,
       G. Einaudi, 1968.
       DS557.A5C63   78-383833

337.   Colquhoun, Archibald R.   Amongst the Shans. New York,
       Scribner & Welford, 1885.
       DS560.C72   5-7349

338.   Columbia Broadcasting System, Inc.   CBS News. Vietnam
       perspective; CBS News special report. Analysis by Walter
       Cronkite. New York, Pocket Books [c.] 1965.
       DS557.A6C65   959.704   65-29653

339.   Combe, Gordon D.   Responsible government in South Australia.
       Adelaide? South Australia, 1957.
       JQ4911.C6   57-39512

340.   Committee for Economic Development. The national economy
       and the Vietnam war; a statement of national policy by the
       Research and Policy Committee of the Committee for Eco-
       nomic Development. [New York] 1968.
       HC106.6.C6   338.973   68-26845

341.   Committee of Concerned Asian Scholars. Indochina Story:
       A Critical Appraisal of American Involvement in Southeast
       Asia. Pantheon Books, 1971.

342.   _____. The Indochina story: a fully documented account.
        Bantam, 1970.
        DS557.A63C64 1970b   959.7'043373   71-22211

343.   Committee on Vietnam. Research Sub-Committee. A source
        book on Vietnam; background to our war. [Wellington? N. Z.]
        Printed at Standard Press, 1965.
        DS557.A6A54   67-56990

344.   Condliffe, John Bell and Airey, Willis Thomas Goodwin. A
        short history of New Zealand. 9th ed. Christchurch, Whit-
        combe & Tombs, 1960.
        DU420.C6   62-47882

345.   Conference de juristes d'Europe occidentale sur le Vietnam,
        Brussels, 1966. Vietnam. Reunion des representants des
        associations nationales de juristes democrates d'Europe occi-
        dentale, Bruxelles, 10-11 decembre 1966. [Travaux] Bruxelles,
        Association internationale des juristes democrates [1967?]
        JX4481.C6 1966   959.7'04   68-90617

346.   Conference on Investment Conditions in Vietnam, New York,
        1958. Investment conditions in the Republic of Vietnam: a
        symposium. Based on a conference sponsored by the American
        Friends of Vietnam. Edited by Gilbert Jonas. [New York,
        American Friends of Vietnam, 1958]
        HG5750.V5C6 1958   332.6709597   58-13451

347.   Conference on Social Development and Welfare in Vietnam,
        New York, 1959. [Addresses, papers, etc. n. p., 1959]
        HN700.V5C6 1959   60-25213

348.   Conference on the Strengthening and Integration of South Asian
        Language and Area Studies, New York, 1961. Resources for
        South Asian area studies in the United States; report. Ed. by
        Richard D. Lambert. Philadelphia, University of Pennsylvania,
        1962.
        DS510.7.C65   915.9   62-11263

349.   _____. Resources for South Asian area studies in the
        United States; report of a conference convened by the Commit-
        tee on South Asia of the Association for Asian Studies for the
        United States Office of Education. Ed. by Richard D. Lambert.
        [Philadelphia] University of Pennsylvania Press [c. 1962]
        DS335.C65   915.9   62-11263

350.   Connell, Gordon. Stories of Australia. [Melbourne] Melbourne
        University Press; London, New York, Cambridge University
        Press [1967]
        DU115.C63   Aus 67-768

351.   Connell, Robert. Firewinds; poems [on the Vietnam War]
        Sketches by David Ogg and Chris Amitzboll. Sydney, Wentworth

Press, 1968.
PR6053.048F5   821   68-141365

352.   Cooke, David Coxe, 1917-   Vietnam: the country, the peo-
        ple [by] David C. Cooke. [1st ed.] New York, W. W.
        Norton [1968]
        DS557.A5C65   915.97'03'4   68-16572

353.   Cooke, Joseph R.   Pronominal reference in Thai, Burmese
        and Vietnamese, by Joseph R. Cooke. Berkeley, University
        of California Press, 1968.
        P25.C25 vol. 52   495   79-626769

354.   Cooper, Chester L.   Lost Crusade: America in Vietnam.
        Dodd, 1970.
        DS557.A63C66   959.7'04   79-135539

355.   Coquia, Jorge Rioflorido, 1918-   The Philippine presidential
        election of 1953. Manila, Distributed by University Publishing
        Company [1955]
        DS686.5.C6   324.914   56-37162

356.   Corson, William R.   Betrayal.   Ace Books (Ace Publishing
        Corporation) 1968.

357.   _____. The betrayal [by] William R. Corson. [1st ed.]
        New York, W. W. Norton [1968]
        DS557.A6C6 1968   959.7'04   68-15753

358.   Costa, Horacio de la. The background of nationalism and
        other essays [by] H. de la Costa. Manila, New York,
        Solidaridad Publishing House [c1965]
        HC453.C6   320.9914   66-31328

359.   Cosyns-Verhaegen, Roger. Arriere-plan revolutionnaire de
        la guerre du Vietnam. Bruxelles, Les Ours, 1968.
        DS557.A6C68   72-406689

360.   Coupland, Sir Reginald.   Raffles of Singapore. 3d ed. Lon-
        don, Collins, 1946.
        DS646.26.R3C65   923.5595   46-4989

361.   Cowan, Charles Donald.   Nineteenth-century Malaya; the
        origins of British political control. London, New York, Ox-
        ford University Press, 1961.
        DS596.C6   959.5   61-1559

362.   Cowan, James. The New Zealand wars. A history of the
        Maori campaigns and the pioneering period. Wellington,
        W. A. G. Skinner, government printer, 1922-23.
        DU420.C65   45-40073

363.   Crawford, Ann (Caddell). Customs and culture of Vietnam.

Illus. by Hau Dinh Cam. Rutland, Vermont, Tuttle [1966]
DS557.A5C7   915.97   66-16721

364. Crawford, Sir John Grenfell. Australian trade policy 1942-
      1966; a documentary history, by J. G. Crawford assisted by
      Nancy Anderson and Margery G. N. Morris. Canberra,
      Australian National University Press, Toronto, University of
      Toronto Press, 1968.
      HF1625.C7   382'.0994   68-12555

365. Crawford, John Grenfell et al. Wartime agriculture in
      Australia and New Zealand, 1939-50. Stanford, Stanford
      University, 1954.
      HD2152.C7   338.1   54-7161

366. Crawfurd, John, 1783-1868. Journal of an embassy to the
      courts of Siam and Cochin China. [1st ed. reprinted]; intro-
      duction by David K. Wyatt. Kuala Lumpur, London, New
      York, Oxford University Press 1967 [i.e. 1968]
      DS565.C885 1828a   915.93'03'3   78-351303

367. Cressey, George Babcock. Asia's lands and peoples; a
      geography of one-third the earth and two-thirds its people
      2d ed. New York, McGraw-Hill, 1951.
      DS5.C7   915   51-11381

368. Critchfield, Richard. The long charade; political subversion
      in the Vietnam war. [1st ed.] New York, Harcourt, Brace &
      World [1968]
      DS557.A6C7   320.9'597   68-28815

369. Csapó, Gyorgy. Az arany teknosbeka foldjen; vietnami utirajz.
      Budapest, Gondolat, 1961.
      DS557.A7C75   62-65306

370. Cumberland, Kenneth Brailey and Fox, James W. New Zea-
      land, a regional view. Christchurch, N. Z., Whitcombe &
      Tombs, 1959.
      DU412.C8   919.31   60-39597

371. Cumming, Ian. Glorious enterprise; the history of the Auck-
      land Education Board, 1857-1957. Christchurch, N. Z.,
      Whitcombe & Tombs, 1959.
      LA2129.A8C8   379.153   60-39938

372. Cung-giu-Nguyen. Le domaine maudit; roman. Paris,
      Fayard [1961]
                                                            A 62-909

373. Curnow, Allen. The Penguin book of New Zealand verse.
      Harmondsworth, Penguin, 1960.
      PR9657.C8   61-66264

D

374.   Dam, Nguyen C. & Linh, Tran C.   Vietnam, Our Beloved
        Land.   C. E. Tuttle (Tuttle, Charles E., Company, Inc.),
        1968.

375.   Dan-chu dang, Vietnam.   American blood for freedom or tyran-
        ny? [Foreward [sic] by General Thai-son. Edited by Nguyen-
        thai-Binh] [Paris] 1963.
        DS557. A6D36

376.   Dane, Barbara, comp.   The Vietnam songbook.   Comp., ed.
        by Barbara Dane, Irwin Silber.   [New York, The Guardian]
        Dist. by Monthly Review [1969]
        M1650. D   784. 7'1   72-76819

377.   Dang, Nghiem.   Viet-Nam: Politics & Public Administration.
        Eastwest Center Press, 1966.
        JQ831. N46   354. 597   65-27935

378.   Danois, Jacques.   Envoye special au Vietnam. Bruxelles, P. De
        Meyere, (1967).
        DS557. A6D3   959. 7'04   67-106162

379.   . . . .   Les moineaux de Saigon.   Photos: Philippe Fran-
        chini. (Bruxelles), J. Verbeeck, (1968).
        DS557. A68D3   78-364902

380.   _____. Speciale opdracht in Vietnam. Naar het Frans
        bewerkt door M. Stevens. Nukerke, Uitg. De Riemaecker,
        [1967]
        DS557. A6D335   959. 7'04   68-71240

381.   Dansk fredskonference.   Krigen i Vietnam i økonomisk og
        folkeretslig belysning. [Af Ellen Brun m. fl. [København]
        Knabrostraede 3, 1967.
        DS557. A6D34   68-102457

382.   Dao-duy-Anh.   Viet-nam van-hoa su-cuong.   Esquisse d'his-
        toire de la civilisation annamite. Hué, Quan-Hai-Tung-Thu,
        1938.
        DS557. A5D26   S A 68-1045

383.   Dao-duy-Phuc.   Realization of the production plan for the first
        six months of 1958 (North Vietnam) New York, U.S. Joint
        Publications Research Service, 1959.
        AS36. U57 no. 1280   338. 9597   59-60983

384.   Dareff, Hal.   From Vietnam to Cambodia: a background book
        about the struggle in Southeast Asia.   Parents' Magazine
        Press, 1971.
        DS557. A6D37   959. 7'043   78-143177

385.   . The story of Vietnam; a background book for young people. New York, Parents' Magazine Press [1966]
DS557.A5D3   959.7   66-31807

386. Davies, Alan Fraser, ed. Australian society; a sociological introduction. Edited by A. F. Davies and S. Encel. New York, Atherton Press [1965]
HN843.5.D35   309.194   65-21217

387. Davies, S. Gethyn, ed. Central banking in South and East Asia. Hong Kong, Hong Kong University, 1960.
HG3266.D3   332.11095   60-51219

388. Davin, Daniel Marcus, comp. New Zealand short stories. London, Oxford University, 1953.
A54-474

389. Davis, Solomon R. The government of the Australian States. London, Longmans, 1960.
JQ4099.A1D3   342.9409   60-41542

390. Day and Zimmermann, Inc. General industrial survey of seventeen industries for Viet Nam. Washington, Technical Aids Branch, Office of Industrial Resources, International Co-operation Administration [1959]
HC443.V5D3   338.09597   61-60139

391. Deakin, Alfred. The federal story; the inner history of the federal cause, 1880-1900. 2d ed. Parkville, Victoria, Melbourne University, 1963.
JQ4011.D4   342.9409   64-3607

392. Deane, Hugh. The war in Vietnam. New York, Monthly Review Press, 1963.
DS557.A6D4   63-19862

393. Dedra, Don. Anybody here from Arizona? A look at the Vietnam war. [Phoenix] The Arizona republic [1966]
DS557.A69D4   959.7'04   67-1662

394. The Democratic Republic of Viet Nam. Hanoi, Foreign Languages Publishing House, 1960.
DS557.A7D4   959.7   S A 62-629

395. Democratic Republic of Viet-Nam; 15th anniversary, 2-9, 1945-1960. [Rangoon, News Service of the Democratic Republic of Vietnam, 1960?]
DS557.A7D415   S A 67-7821

396. Democratic Republic of Vietnam, 1945-1960; impressions of foreigners. Hanoi, Foreign Languages Publishing House, 1960.
DS557.A7D42   S A 62-1234

397. Democratic Republic of Vietnam Is Twenty-Five Years Old.
      China Books and Periodicals, 1970.

398. Demokraticheskaia Respublika V'etnam, (Democratic Republic
      of Vietnam). (In Russian). Moscow, 1963.
      DS557.A7D44

399. Denison Vietnam Colloquium. Denison University. 1966.
      Vietnam. [Morton L. Shagrin, others, eds. Contributors:
      Barbara Adee, others] Granville, Ohio, 1966.
      DS557.A6D43   959.7   66-9025

400. Development of the Economy of the Chinese, Vietnamese,
      Korean, & Mongolian Peoples Republic in 1961.
      CCMIC. (Subs of Crowell Collier & Macmillan Inc.) 1961.

401. Devillers, Philippe, 1920- End of a war; Indochina, 1954 [by]
      Philippe Devillers and Jean Lacouture. [Translated by Alex-
      ander Lieven and Adam Roberts] New York, Praeger [1969]
      DS550.D463   959.7'04   69-12705

402. _____. Histoire du Viet-Nam de 1940 a 1952. Paris,
      Editions du Seuil, 1952.
      DS557.A5D45   52-43585

403. _____. Vietnam and France. Paris, Comite d'etudes des
      problemes du Pacifique; distributed by International Secretari-
      at, Institute of Pacific Relations, New York, 1950.
      DS557.V5D413   959.7   54-31120

404. Dewey, Alice G. Peasant marketing in Java. [New York]
      Free Press of Glencoe [1962]
      HF3809.J4D4   658.809922   62-10585

405. De Young, John E. Village life in modern Thailand. Berke-
      ley, University of California, 1958.
                                                               55-9879

406. Le Differend khmero-vietnamien devant le Conseil de securite
      des Nations-Unies, mai, juin, juillet, 1964; document. Saigon,
      Ministere des affaires etrangeres, 1964.
      DS557.A6D5   S A 67-3031

407. Doan-trong-Truyen. Building an independent national economy
      in Vietnam [by] Doan trong Truyen [and] Pham thanh Vinh.
      Hanoi, Foreign Languages Publishing House, 1964.
      HC443.V5D65   S A 65-4251

408. _____. L'edification d'une economie nationale independante
      au Vietnam (1945-1965) [por] Doan Trong Truyen [et] Pham
      Thanh Vinh. 2. ed. revue et augm. Hanoi, Editions en
      Langues Etrangeres, 1966.
      HC443.V5D62

409. Dobby, Ernest Henry George. Monsoon Asia. Chicago,
      Quadrangle, 1961.
      DS10.D59   915   61-13967

410. Dodds, Gordon Barlow. The Salmon King of Oregon; R. D.
      Hume and the Pacific fisheries. Chapel Hill, University of
      North Carolina, 1959.
      HD9469.S23072   926.6   63-3158

411. Doeker, Gunther, 1933-   The treaty-making power in the
      Commonwealth of Australia. The Hague, M. Nijhoff, 1966.
      JX4165.D63   341.2'94   67-8401

412. Dollerup, Preben, 1927-   Vietnam krigen i perspektiv [af]
      Preben Dollerup og Ebbe Reich. [København] Rhodos [1965]
      DS557.A6D62   67-59708

413. Dommen, Arthur J. Conflict in Laos; the politics of neutrali-
      zation [by] Arthur J. Dommen. New York, Praeger [1964]
      DS557.L28D6 1964   959.4   64-21661

414. Donlon, Roger H. C. Outpost of freedom [by] Roger H. C.
      Donlon, as told to Warren Rogers. Foreword by Robert F.
      Kennedy. New York, McGraw [c.1965]
      DS557.A6D64   959.7040924   65-25516

415. Donoghue, John D. My Thuan: the study of a delta village
      in South Vietnam [by] John D. Donoghue and Vohong-Phuc.
      Saigon, Michigan State University Advisory Group, 1961.
                                                 NUC64-35323

416. Dooley, Thomas A., M.D., 1927-1961. Deliver us from evil;
      the story of Viet Nam's flight to freedom [New York] New
      American Library [1961, c.1956]
      DS550.D6   959.7

417. _____. Dr. Tom Dooley's three great books: Deliver us
      from evil, The edge of tomorrow [and] The night they burned
      the mountain. New York, Farrar, Straus & Cudahy [1960]
      RA390.U5D583   926.1   60-51236 rev

418. Dorsey, John T. Report and recommendations on the re-
      organization of the Presidency of Vietnam. Submitted to the
      President of the Republic, November 15, 1955, by John T.
      Dorsey, Michigan State University, Vietnam Advisory Team.
      [Saigon?] 1955.
      JQ841.D6   354.59703   59-63320

419. Dourness, Jacques. En suivant la piste des hommes sur les
      hauts-plateaux du Vietnam. Paris, R. Julliard, 1955.
      DS539.M6D6   56-57019

420. Do-vang-Ly. The stork and the shrimp; The claw of the

golden turtle and other Vietnamese tales. New Delhi [Siddhartha Publications] 1959.
GR310.D6   308.2   60-39741

421.   Do-Van-Minh. Viet nam; where East & West meet. [2d, rev. and enl. ed.] New York, Paragon Book Reprint Corp. [1968]
DS557.A5D6 1968   915.97'04'4   72-3117

422.   Doyon, Jacques, 1938-   Les Viet Cong . . . Paris, Denoel, 1968.
DS557.A6D68   959.7'04   68-113051

423.   Drachman, Edward R. 1940-   United States policy toward Vietnam, 1940-1945, by Edward R. Drachman. Rutherford, Fairleigh Dickinson University Press [1970]
E183.8.V5D7   940.532'2'73   71-86293

424.   Le Drapeau-repere; recits de la resistance vietnamienne [par] Huu Mai [et al.] Hanoi, Editions en langues etrangeres, 1964.
DS557.A6D7   65-85620

425.   Draper, Theodore, 1912-   Abuse of power. New York, Viking Press [1967]
DS557.A63D7   959.7'04   66-18668

426.   _____. Abuse of Power. Viking Press, Inc. (orig.), 1971.

427.   _____. Les Pieges de la puissance, les Americains au Vietnam et ailleurs. Traduction de Raymond Albeck. Paris, Fayard, 1968.
DS557.A63D714   959.7'04   78-369724

4 !8.   Drendel, Lou. Air War in Viet Nam. Arco Publishing Company, Inc., 1969.

4. 9.   _____. The air war in Vietnam. Text and illus. by Lou Drendel. New York, Arco Publishing Company [1968]
DS557.A65D7   959.7'04   68-56217

430.   Drinan, Robert F. Vietnam and Armageddon; peace, war and the Christian conscience, by Robert F. Drinan. New York, Sheed and Ward [1970]
BT736.2.D7   261.8'73   71-101550

431   DRV in the Face of U.S. Aggression. China Books and Periodicals, 1966.

432.   Du Berrier, Hilaire. Background to Betrayal: Tragedy in Vietnam. Western Isl., 1965.
DS557.A6D8   959.704   65-24091

433.   Dudman, Richard. Forty days with the enemy. Liveright, 1971.
DS557.A675D8   959.7'04'37   70-157097

434. Duffett, John, ed. Against the Crime of Silence. S&S, 1970.
JX6731.W3I46 1967b   341.3'1   70-119018

435. Duhacek, Antun. Vijetnam, savest covecanstva. Beograd,
"Narodna armija, " 1968.
DS557.A6D82   68-120577

436. Dumont D'urville, Jules Sebastien Cesar. The voyage of the
Astrolabe, 1840; an English rendering of the journals of
Dumont d'Urvill and his officers . . . by Olive Wright.
Wellington, Reed, 1955.
DU410.D815   919.31   55-4069

437. Duncan, David Douglas. I protest! [New York] New American Library [1968]
DS557.A62K55   959.7'04   68-4828

438. Duncan, Donald, 1930-   The new legions. London, Gollancz,
1967.
DS557.A69D8 1967b   959.7'04   71-351714

439. _____. The new legions. New York, Random House [1967]
DS557.A69D8   973.923'0924   67-14471

440. Duncan, Ross. The Northern Territory pastoral industry,
1863-1910. [Melbourne] Melbourne University Press [and]
Monash University [1967]
HD9433.A83N63   330.994'29   67-102653

441. Duncanson, Dennis J. Government and revolution in Vietnam
[by] Dennis J. Duncanson. London, New York, [etc.] issued
under the auspices of the Royal Institute of International Affairs [by] Oxford University Press, 1968.
DS557.A5D75   320.9'597   68-19954

442. Dunn, Mary Lois. The man in the box; a story from Vietnam.
New York, McGraw-Hill [1968]
PZ7.D9217Man   68-19488

443. Dunn, William Brothers. American Policy and Vietnamese
Nationalism 1950-1954. Chicago, University of Chicago Press,
1960. (Microfilm).
                                          Mic 61-7264

444. Dunsdorfs, Edgar. The Australian wheat-growing industry,
1788-1948. Melbourne, University Press, 1956.
HD9049,W5A86   338.17311   56-14588

445. Du'o'ng-Chau. The seventeenth parallel. Translated from the
original Vietnamese by Viet-nam Translation Service. Saigon,
Cong Dan, 1958.
DS557.A7D83   59-37494

58   Vietnam

446.   Durand, Maurice M.   Introduction a la litterature viet-
       namienne, par Maurice M. Durand . . . Nguyen Tran-Huan
       . . . Paris, G. P. Maisonneuve et Larose, 1969.
       P14378.D8   74-494455

447.   Durdin, Tillman.   Southeast Asia, New York, Atheneum, 1966
       [c.1965]
       DS513.D8   915.90342   65-27529

448.   Dykes, Hugh, 1939-   Vietnam: threat and involvement, by
       Hugh Dykes & Reginald Watts.   London, Bow Publications
       [1966]
       DS557.A6D9   959.7'04   67-76087

                                 E

449.   East, William Gordon and Spate, Oskar Hermann Khristian,
       eds.   The changing map of Asia, a political geography.   3d ed.
       rev.   New York, Dutton, 1958.
       DS35.E3   915   59-1411

450.   Eby, Omar, 1935-   Edgar County, Illinois, Knox County,
       Missouri.   [n. p.] 1968.
       DS557.A62H85   959.7'04   74-4101

451.   Echols, John M.   Preliminary checklist of Indonesian imprints
       during the Japanese period (March 1942-August 1945) with
       annotations.   Ithaca, N. Y., Modern Indonesia Project, South-
       east Asia Program, Department of Asian Studies, Cornell
       University, 1963.
       Z3278.A5E3   64-1794

452.   Echols, John M. and Shadily, Hassan.   An Indonesian-English
       dictionary.   Ithaca, Cornell University Press, 1961.
       PL5076.E25   499.2   61-1250

453.   Eckardt, Andre, 1884-   Vietnam; Geschichte und Kultur
       [von] Andre Eckardt [und] Nguyen Tien Huu.   Freudenstadt/
       Wurtt., Eurobuch-Verlag [1968]
       DS557.A5E25   75-382740

454.   Economic impact of the Vietnam war.   [New York] Renaissance
       Editions, 1967.
       HC106.6.E25   330.973   67-26130

455.   Economic Survey Mission to the Republic of Vietnam.   Toward
       the economic development of the Republic of Vietnam; report.
       New York, 1959.
       JX1977.A2 ST/TAO/K 338.9597   60-1205

456.   Economical evolution in Vietnam in 1952. (In Vietnamese).
       Saigon, 1953.

457.   Economist Intelligence Unit, Ltd., London. The economic ef-
        fects of the Vietnamese war in East and South East Asia.
        London, [1968]
        HC412.E25   330.95   71-5545

458.   Eden, Sir Anthony.   Toward Peace in Indochina.   Boston,
        Houghton Mifflin, 1966.
        DS550.E3   320.9597   66-23562

459.   Edinger, George Adolphus.   The twain shall meet.   New York,
        T. Yoseloff [1960]
        DS596.E3   915.95   59-12188

460.   Edogawa, Shikei.   Betonamu, Kashimiru senso to sono hai-
        kel: (Vietnam and Kashmir wars and their background) (In
        Japanese), Tokyo, 1965.
        DS518.1.E36

461.   Effros, William G., ed.   Quotations Vietnam: Nineteen
        Fifty to Nineteen Seventy.   Random House, Inc., 1970.

462.   _____., comp.   Quotations Vietnam: 1945-1970, compiled
        by William G. Effros.   New York, Random House [1970]
        DS557.A61E33   959.7'04   74-127535

463.   Eggleston, Sir Frederic William, 1875-1954. Reflections on
        Australian foreign policy.   Edited by Norman Harper. With
        a biographical sketch by Tristan Buesst. Melbourne, Pub-
        lished for the Australian Institute of International Affairs [by]
        F. W. Cheshire [1957; label: New York, Distributed by the In-
        stitute of Pacific Relations]
        DU113.E34   327.94   57-4394

464.   Eide, Asbjørn.   Intra-statlige konflikter og intervensjon uten-
        fra: Folkerett og politikk i var tid.   En analyse med Viet-
        nam som utgangspunkt.   Oslo, Universitetsforlaget, 1968.
                                                        68-140396

465.   Einbinder, Harvey.   Mah name is Lyndon; a play.   Illustrated
        by Florence Safadi.   New York, Lady Bird Press [1968]
        PS3555.I47M3   812'.5'4   68-20361

466.   Eliot, Sir Charles Norton Edgecumbe.   Hinduism and Bud-
        dhism; an historical sketch.   New York, Barnes & Noble,
        1957.
        BL1031.E6   294   54-14201

467.   Elkin, Adolphus Peter.   Art in Arnhem Land.   Melbourne,
        Cheshire, 1950.
        N7402.A7E4   709.94   51-5133

468.   Elliott, Charles Burke.   The Philippines to the end of the
        Commission government; a study in tropical democracy.

Indianapolis, Bobbs-Merrill, 1917.
DS685.E4   17-23950

469.   Embree, John Fee.   Southeast Asia, a selected bibliography.
       New York, American Institute of Pacific Relations, 1955.
       Z3001.E52   016.9159   56-3544

470.   Embree, John Fee and Dotson, Lillian Ota.   Bibliography of
       the peoples and cultures of mainland Southeast Asia.   New
       Haven, Yale University, 1950.
       Z3001.E5   016.9159   50-14198

471.   Emerson, Rupert.   Malaysia; a study in direct and indirect
       rule.   New York, Macmillan, 1937.
       DS592.E5   959.5   37-22906

472.   Encel, S.   Cabinet government in Australia.   Parkville,
       Melbourne University, 1962.
       JQ4042.E5   342.94   62-6443

473.   Ennis, Thomas Edson.   Vietnam: land without laughter.
       [Morgantown, W. Va.] Cooperative Extension Service,
       West Virginia University [1966]
                                                       A 68-7076

474.   Eriksson, Erik, 1937-   Dagbok fran Nordvietnam.   Stockholm,
       Prisma, [Solna, Seelig].   1969.
       DS557.A72E7   75-493059

475.   _____ .   Vietnam--USA: s krig.   Diskussionskurs.   [Av
       Erik Eriksson och Bengt Liljenroth.   Utg. pa uppdrag av och
       i samarbete med ABF.   Studiehandlednig till Sven Oste: Viet-
       nam--hokens ar och John Takman: Napalm]   Stockholm, ABF;
       Brevskolan, 1967.
       DS557.A6E7   68-133575

476.   Eskelund, Karl, 1918-   Den gale krig.   En rejse i Vietnam.
       Fotografier af forfatteren.   København, Gyldendal, 1966.
       DS557.A6E8   67-80797

477.   Evans, Barbara.   Caduceus in Saigon: a medical mission to
       South Viet-Nam.   London, Hutchinson, 1968.
       DS557.A677E9   959.7'04   68-140016

478.   The Evolution of Vietnamese literature: from "nom" to
       romanized characters.   Special ed.   Saigon, Horizons [1957?]
       PL4378.05.E9   S A 64-3867

479.   Ewers, John Keith, 1904-   Creative writing in Australia;
       a selective survey by John K Ewers.   [5th i. e. 4th ed.]
       Melbourne, Georgian House [1966]
       PR9412.E9 1966   820   68-78644

F

480.   Faber, Franz. Rot leuchtet der Song Cai. Berlin, Kongress-
        Verlag, 1955.
        DS557.A5F3   56-23956

481.   Facts and dates on the problem of the reunification of Viet-
        Nam. Hanoi, Foreign Languages Publishing House, 1956.
        DS557.A6F3   959.7   60-29962

482.   Falk, Richard A. The six legal dimensions of the Vietnam
        war, by Richard A. Falk. [Princeton, N. J., Center of In-
        ternational Studies, Princeton University] 1968.
        JX1573.F29   341.6'5   73-1785

483.   _____. A Vietnam settlement: the view from Hanoi, by
        Richard A. Falk. [Princeton, N. J.] Center of International
        Studies, Princeton University,1968.
        DS557.A692F3   959.7'04   74-965

484.   _____., comp. The Vietnam war and international law,
        edited by Richard A. Falk. Princeton, N. J., Princeton Uni-
        versity Press, 1968.
        JX1573.F3   341.3   67-31295

485.   _____., ed. Vietnam War & International Law, Vol. 1.
        Princeton University Press. 1967.

486.   Fall, Bernard B., 1926-1967. Hell in a very small place: the
        siege of Dien Bien Phu [by] Bernard B. Fall. Philadelphia,
        Lippincott, 1967 [c1966]
        DS550.F28   959.704   66-23242

487.   _____. Last Reflections on the War. Garden City, N.Y.,
        Doubleday, 1967.
        DS557.A5F32   956.7   67-28638

488.   _____. Military developments in Viet Nam, by Bernard B.
        Fall. [Washington?] 1962.
        DS557.A6F33   67-1911

489.   _____. Political Development of Vietnam. Ann Arbor,
        University Microfilm, 1955.
                                                  Mic 56-4369

490.   _____. Street without joy. [4th ed.] Harrisburg, Pennsyl-
        vania, Stackpole Company [1967]
        DS550.F3 1967

491.   _____. Street without joy; insurgency in Indochina, 1946-
        63. 3d rev. ed. Harrisburg, Pennsylvania, Stackpole
        [c1961,63]
        DS550.F3   959.7   63-9160

492.   _____. The two Vietnams; a political and military analysis [by] Bernard B. Fall. 2d rev. ed. New York, Praeger
[1967]
DS557.A5F34 1967   959.7   66-14505

493.   _____. The two Viet-Nams; a political and military analysis. New York, Praeger [1963]
DS557.A5F34   959.7   63-10719

494.   _____. Le Viet-Minh, la Republique democratique du Viet-
Nam, 1945-1960. Pref. de Paul Mus. Paris, A. Colin, 1960.
H31.F6 no. 106   61-27178

495.   _____. The Viet-Minh regime; government and administra-
tion in the Democratic Republic of Vietnam. Ithaca, N. Y.,
Department of Far Eastern Studies, Cornell University, 1954.
JQ815. F3   959.7   54-11255 rev.

496.   _____. The Viet-Minh regime; government and administration in the Democratic Republic of Vietnam. Rev. and enl.
ed. Issued jointly with the Southeast Asia Program, Cornell
University. New York, Institute of Pacific Relations, 1956.
JQ815.F3 1956   959.7   56-9452

497.   _____. Viet-Nam, dernieres reflexions sur une guerre
[par] Bernard Fall. Traduit de l'americain par Daniel Martin.
[Preface de Dorothy Fall] Paris, R. Laffont, 1968.
DS557.A5F3214   72-379083

498.   _____. Viet-Nam witness, 1953-66 [by] Bernard D. Fall.
New York, Praeger [1966]
DS557.A5F35   959.704   66-18898

499.   Fall, Bernard B. & Raskin, Marcus G. , eds. Vietnam Reader. Random, 1965.
DS557.A6R3   959.704   65-26331

500.   Fallaci, Oriana. Niente e cosi sia. [2. ed.] Milano, Rizzoli,
1969.
DS557.A69F3 1969   79-464569

501.   Faltis, Joseph. Quickie lessons in Vietnamese, using the absorbomatic method. Illustrated by Christian Jan Faltis.
Woodland, California. [Foto Features]; J. Winston Company,
distributors, Palo Alto, California [1967]
PL4375. F3   495'.922'8342   67-20511

502.   Fam Tkhan'Vin'. Ekonomika Iuzhnogo V'etnama, (The Economy of South Vietnam). (In Russian). Moscow, 1959.
HC443.V5F35

503.   Farmer, James. Counterinsurgency: principles and practices
in Viet-Nam. [Santa Monica, California, Rand Corporation]

1964.
AS36.R28 no. 3039   65-5762

504. Favre, Claude Pierre. Les os du tigre. Paris, Editions
France-Empire [1965?]
PQ2666.A97308   66-75469

505. Fawzi, Muhyi al-Din. Vitnam Al-chenobia Towachih Al-
asiffah. (Vietnam in the storms of war). (In Arabic). Cairo,
1964.
DS557.A6F37

506. Feinberg, Abraham L. Rabbi Feinberg's Hanoi diary. [Don
Mills, Ont.] Longmans [c1968]
DS558.H3F4   959.7'04   77-374920

507. Feith, Herbert. The decline of constitutional democracy in
Indonesia. Published under the auspices of the Modern Indo-
nesia Project, Southeast Asia Program, Cornell University.
Ithaca, N. Y., Cornell University Press [1962]
DS644.F4   991.03   62-19171 rev

508. _____. The Indonesian elections of 1955. Ithaca,
N. Y., Cornell University, 1957.
JQ778.F4   324.91   57-44892

509. Feng, Chien-wei. Hung-ho ch'en ko, (Singing Morning Songs
Along the Red River), (In Chinese). Peking, 1963.
DS740.5.V5H8

510. Ferdinand-Lop, Samuel, 1891- La France et le Viet-Nam,
la Paix qui s'impose [par] Ferdinand Lop. Paris, l'auteur,
1967.
DS557.A6F44   959.7'04   68-86701

511. Ferguson, John Alexander. Bibliography of Australia. Sydney, Angus & Robertson, 1941-
                                            A42-1362rev

512. Fernandez, Benedict J. In opposition; images of American
dissent in the sixties, by Benedict J. Fernandez. Pref. by
Aryeh Neier. New York, Da Capo Press, 1968.
E839.F4   322'.4   68-55520

513. _____. In Opposition: Images of American Dissent in the
Sixties. Plenum Publishing Corporation, 1971.

514. Ferrari, Leon, 1920- Palabras ajenas; conversaciones de
Dios con algunos hombres y de algunos hombres con algunos
hombres y con Dios. [Traducciones del frances y del ingles
en colaboracion con Alcica Ferrari y Lidia Gomez respec-
tivamente. Traducciones del italiano del autor. Buenos Aires]
Falbo [1967]
PQ7798.16.E728P3   68-80609

515.   Ferreira, Jose Ribamar, 1930-   Por voce, por mim [por]
        Ferreira Gullar. [Rio de Janeiro] Ediçao Sped [1967]
        PQ9697. F3743P65   68-76754

516.   Fiedler, Arkady, 1894-   Dzikie banany; u bujnych Tajow i
        meznych Meo. [Wyd. 2.] Warszawa, Iskry, 1967.
        DS557. A7F48 1967   68-43089

517.   _____. Im lande der wilden Bananen; Begegnungen mit
        den Thai und Meo. [Aus dem Polnischen ubertragen von
        Julius Schultz] Leipzig, F. A. Brockhaus, 1959.
        DS557. A7F485   60-22328

518.   Field, Michael. The Prevailing Wind. London, Methuen,
        1965.
        DS550. F5   959   65-5728

519.   Field, Thomas Parry. Postwar land settlement in Western
        Australia. Lexington, University of Kentucky, 1963.
        HD1116. F5   63-12387

520.   XVth anniversary of the Democratic Republic of Viet Nam.
        1945-1960.   Hanoi, Foreign Languages Publishing House [1960?]
        DS557. A7F53

521.   Fifth Avenue Vietnam Peace Parade Committee. In the teeth
        of war; photographic documentary of the March 26th, 1966,
        New York City demonstration against the war in Vietnam.
        Photos by Martin Berman and others. Introduction by Dave
        Dellinger. Additional text from speeches at the demonstration
        by Juan Mari Bras [and others] New York City; [Sole selling
        agent: OAK Publications, New York] 1966 [i. e. 1967]
        DS557. A68F5   974. 7'04   67-17651

522.   Figueres, Leo. Je reviens du Viet-Nam libre (notes de
        voyage) Pref. de Marcel Cachin. Paris, 1950 [i. e. 1951]
        DS557. A7F5   58-47518

523.   _____. V svobodnom V'et-Name. Perevod s frantsuzskogo
        E. Dubashinskoi i dr. (In the Free Vietnam). (In Russian).
        Moscow, 1951.
        DS557. V5F517

524.   Finan, John Joseph, 1905-   Guns and blood for butter, by
        John J. Finan. [1st ed.] New York, Vantage Press [1969]
        DS557. A63F5   959. 7'04   70-15528

525.   Findlay, P. T. Protest politics and psychological warfare;
        the communist role in the Anti-Vietnam War and anti-con-
        scription movement in Australia by P. T. Findlay. Mel-
        bourne, Hawthorn Press [1968]
        DS557. A68F53   322'. 4   70-362886

526.   Finkle, Jason Leonard, 1926-   Provincial government in Viet
        Nam; a study of Vinh Long province [by] Jason L. Finkle
        and Tran-van-Dinh.   Saigon, Michigan State University, Viet
        Nam Advisory Group and National Institute of Administration,
        1961.
                                                              NUC64-29879

527.   Firth, Raymond William.   Malay fishermen: their peasant
        economy.   London, Paul, Trench, Trubner, 1946.
        HD9466.M32F5   338.372   46-5465

528.   Fischer, Louis.   The story of Indonesia.   New York, Harper,
        1959.
        DS634.F5   991   59-12442

529.   Fishel, Wesley R.   The United States and Viet Nam; two views,
        by Wesley R. Fishel and T. A. Bisson.   [1st ed.   New York,
        Public Affairs Committee, 1966]
        E183.8V5F5   66-6488

530.   _____-., comp. Vietnam: anatomy of a conflict.
        Edited by Wesley R. Fishel.   Contributors: Hanson Baldwin
        [and others] Itasca, Ill., F. E. Peacock [1968]
        DS557.A6F48   959.7'04   68-21870

531.   _____. Vietnam: is victory possible? [New York] Foreign
        Policy Association [1964]
        E744.H34   959.7   64-15201

532.   Fisk, Ernest Kelvin, ed.   New Guinea on the threshold; as-
        pects of social, political, and economic development, edited
        by E. K. Fisk.   With a foreword by Sir John Crawford.   Can-
        berra, Australian National University Press [1966]
        DU740.F55   919.503   66-72231

533.   Fitch, Florence Mary.   Their search for God; ways of wor-
        shpi in the Orient.   New York, Lothrop, Lee & Shepard, 1947.
        BL1055.F5   294   47-11705

534.   Flood, Charles B.   War of the Innocents.   McGraw, 1970.
        DS557.A69F54 1970   959.7'04   71-132342

535.   For a political solution of the Vietnam issue.   [Cairo, The
        Permanent Secretariat of the Afro-Asian Peoples Solidarity
        Organization, 1969]
        DS557.A6F57   959.7'04   78-961018

536.   Forbes, William Cameron.   The Philippine Islands.   Boston,
        Houghton Mifflin, 1928.
        DS685.F6   29-229rev

537.   Ford, Daniel.   Incident at Muc Wa.   [1st ed.] Garden City,
        N. Y., Doubleday, 1967.
        PZ4.F6929In   67-12876

538.   Ford, Herbert.   No guns on their shoulders.   Nashville,
        Southern Publishing Association [1968]
        DS557.A677F6   959.7'04   68-21277

539.   Foreign Policy Association.   Vietnam: issues for decision
        [by] the eds. of the Foreign Policy Association [New York,
        1968, c1967]
        DS557.A6F59   959.7'04   68-27299

540.   _____.   Vietnam; vital issues in the great debate.   [New
        York, c1966]
        DS557.A6F6   959.7'04   66-29508

541.   Forney, Inor.   Nhan, a boy of Viet-Nam.   Told & illustrated
        by Inor Forney.   Story edited by Joanne Robinson.   Rutland,
        Vermont, Tuttle [1969]
        PZ9.F6223Nh   915.97'03'4   75-77116

542.   _____.   Our friends in Viet-Nam; coloring book.   Drawings
        by Inor Forney.   Stories by E. H. Forney.   Rutland, Ver-
        mont, C. E. Tuttle Company, 1967.
        DS557.A6F65   j915.97   67-22361

543.   Fortune, Reo Franklin.   Manus religion; an ethnological study
        of the Manus natives of the Admiralty Islands.   Philadelphia,
        American Philosophical Society, 1935.
        BL2620.A4F6   299.912   36-2179

544.   Foucar, Emile Charles Victor, 1894-   I lived in Burma.
        London, D. Dobson [Chester Springs, Pennsylvania, Dufour,
        1965]
        DS485.B89F6   959.1   57-1125

545.   Fourniau, Charles.   Le Vietnam de la guerre a la victoire
        . . . Paris, Editions du Pavillon, 1969.
        DS557.A6F67   79-396587

546.   _____.   Le Vietnam face a la guerre.   Paris, Editions
        sociales, 1966.
        DS557.A6F6   959.704   66-77357

547.   _____.   Le Vietnam face a la guerre.   2 edition, revue et
        mise a jour.   Paris, Editions sociales, 1967.
        DS557.A6F66 1967   959.7   68-99747

548.   Fox, Len.   Druzhestvennyi V'etnam, (Friendly Vietnam).   (In
        Russian. Translated from English).   Moscow, 1959.
        DS557.A7F67

549.   _____.   Friendly Vietnam.   Hanoi, Foreign Languages
        Publishing House, 1958.
        DS557.A5F6   915.97   60-35936

550. France. Commissariat de la Republique française dans le
      Nord Viet-Nam Bulletin officiel. 1. -4. annee; 15 jan.
      1948-15 dec. 1951. Hanoi.
      J641. T7N152   56-29398

551. France, Treaties, etc., 1947-1954 (Auriol). Accords franco-
      vietnamiens du 8 mars 1949. Conventions d'application. La
      presente publication est faite d'accord parties entre le gou-
      vernement du Vietnam et le Haut Commissariat de France en
      Indochine. [Saigon, Ideo, 1950?]
      JX945. V5A513   54-23208

552. Frankenstein, Alfred Victor. Angels over the altar; Christian
      folk art in Hawaii and the South Seas. Honolulu, University
      of Hawaii, 1961.
      N7410. F7   704. 9482   61-8433

553. Frederic-Dupont, Edouard, 1902-   Mission de la France en
      Asie. Paris, Editions France-Empire [1956]
      DS550. F75   58-26756

554. Freeman, Roger A. Socialism and private enterprise in
      equatorial Asia, the case of Malaysia and Indonesia, by Roger
      A. Freeman. Stanford, California, Hoover Institution on War,
      Revolution, and Peace, Stanford University, 1968.
      HC59. F735   330. 991   67-31386

555. Frei, Bruno. Vruhling in Vietnam; Vericht einer Reise.
      Berlin, Aufbau-Verlag, 1959.
      DS557. A5F67   60-33869

556. French, W. Pattern for victory [by] W. French. [1st ed.]
      New York, Exposition Press [1970]
      DS557. A6F667   959. 7'04   70-114057

557. Fresnoza, Florencio. Essentials of the Philippine educational
      system. Rev. ed. Manila, Abiva, 1957.
      LA1292. F75   379. 914   57-48968

558. Fridland, V. M. Physical Nature of North Vietnam. CCMIC
      (Subs of Crowell Collier & Macmillan Inc.), 1961.

559. Fried, Erich. Und Vietnam und. Einundvierzig Gedichte.
      (Mit einer Chronik) Berlin, Wagenbach (1966)
      PT2611. R596U5   66-68620

560. Friend, Theodore. Between two empires; the ordeal of the
      Philippines, 1929-1946. New Haven, Yale University Press,
      1965.
      DS685. F7   991. 403   65-12541

561. Friends, Society of. American Friends Service Committee.
      Peace in Vietnam; a new approach in Southeast Asia; a report

prepared for the American Friends Service Committee. New
enl. ed. New York, Hill and Wang [1967]
DS557.A692F7 1967   327.73'0597   67-20981

562. _____. La Tragedie vietnamienne vue par des Quakers
americains (American Friends Service Committee). Proposi-
tions nouvelles pour la paix. Preface du P. Alfred Kastler
. . . Paris, les Editions du Pavillon, 1967.
DS557.A692F714   327.73'0597   78-356239

563. Friends, Society of. London Yearly Meeting. Friends Peace
and International Relations Committee. Vietnam: facts and
figures. London, Friends Peace and International Relations
Committee [1967]
DS557.A6F72   959.7'04   68-97475

564. Froehlich, Walter, ed. Land tenure, industrialization, and
social stability: experience and prospects in Asia. Milwaukee,
Marquette University, 1961.
                                                 61-10914

565. Front unifie des forces nationalistes du Viet-Nam. Le
probleme meconnu du Sud Viet-Nam pese dangereusement sur
les efforts tentes pour un equilibre mondial; memoire presente
par la Mission permanente du Front unifie des forces nationalistes du Viet-Nam. [Paris, Impr. central du Croissant, 1955]
DS557.A5F7   56-44457

566. Fuchs, Lawrence H. "Those peculiar Americans": the
Peace Corps and American national character [by] Lawrence
H. Fuchs. [1st ed.] New York, Meredith Press [1967]
HC455.F78   309.2'235'7309914   67-18494

567. Fulbright, J. William. Vietnam Hearings. Random House,
Inc., 1966.

568. _____., introduced by. Vietnam Hearings. Random
House, Inc., 1971.

569. Fundamental Problems. China Books and Periodicals, 1966.

570. Furer-Haimendorf, Elizabeth Von. An anthropological bibliography of South Asia, together with a directory of recent
anthropological field work. Paris, Mouton, 1958-
                                                 A59-1034

571. Furnivall, John Sydenham. Netherlands India; a study of
plural economy. New York, Macmillan, 1944.
DS634.F   991   A45-4116

G

572. Gabelic, Andro. Vijetnamski rat. Naslovna strana: Pavle
      Ristie. Beograd, "Sedma sila, " 1967.
      D839. 3. S4 br. 169   959. 7'04   67-112713

573. Gage, William W.   Verb constructions in Vietnamese [by]
      William W. Gage [and] H. Merrill Jackson. [Ithaca, N. Y. ,
      1953]
      PL4379. G3   54-44684

574. Galbraith, John Kenneth, 1908-   Come uscire dal Viet Nam.
      Una soluzione realistica del piu grave problema del nostro
      tempo. Torino, G. Einaudi, 1968.
      DS557. A63G36   959. 7'04   72-377874

575. _____. How to get out of Vietnam; a workable solution to
      the worst problem of our time. [New York] New American
      Library [1967]
      DS557. A63G3   959. 7'04   68-1111

576. Gamba, Charles. The origins of trade unionism in Malaya;
      a study in colonial labour unrest. With a foreword by Victor
      Purcell. Singapore, Publi⸱ ⸱y D. Moore for Eastern Uni-
      versities Press, 1962.
      HD6815. M3G33   65-36507

577. Gaucheron, Jacques H. , 1920-   Onze poemes pour le Vietnam.
      [Poemes de Jacques Gaucheron et Armand Monjo. Dessins de
      Mireille G. Miailhe.] [n. p.] 1967.
      PQ2613. A68606   68-80097

578. Gazette de Saigon. Preuves sanglantes; recueil des histoires
      vecues, publiees par "La Gazette de Saigon, " septembre-
      decembre 1955. [Saigon, 1955]
      DS550. G35   56-38069

579. Geertz, Clifford. Agricultural involution; the process of
      ecological change in Indonesia. Berkeley, Published for the
      Association of Asian Studies by University of California Press,
      1963.
      HC447. G4   338. 10991   63-20356 rev.

580. _____. Peddlers and princes; social change and economic
      modernization in two Indonesian towns. Chicago, University
      of Chicago, 1963.
      HC448. M58G4   338. 0991   63-18844

581. _____. The religion of Java. Glencoe, Illinois, Free
      Press, 1960.
      BL2120. J3G42   299. 9222   59-13863

582. Geertz, Clifford James. The development of the Javanese

economy: a socio-cultural approach. Cambridge, Mass.,
Center for International Studies, Massachusetts Institute of
Technology, 1956.
HC447.G44

583.   Gelber, Harry Gregor. Australia, Britain and the EEC, 1961
        to 1963 [by] H. G. Gelber. Melbourne, New York [etc.]
        Oxford University Press, 1966.
        HC241.25.A85G4   67-93167

584.   Gellhorn, Martha, 1908-   A new kind of war. Manchester,
        Manchester Guardian & Evening News [1966]
        DS557.A68G4   915.97'03'4   67-83199

585.   Geneva Conference, 1954. The 1954 Geneva Conference:
        Indo-China and Korea. New introduction written especially
        for the Greenwood reprint by Kenneth T. Young. New York,
        Greenwood Press [1968]
        DS921.7.G4 1954ab   915.9'042   68-57791

586.   Georg, Anders. Opgør i Vietnam. København, Berlingske
        forlag, 1966.
        DS557.A6G4   959.704   67-70509

587.   Gerasimov, Gennadii. The key to peace in Vietnam [by] Gen-
        nady Gerasimov. [Moscow] Novosti Press Agency Publishing
        House [1968?]
        DS557.A63G45   77-491313

588.   Gerassi, John. North Vietnam: a documentary; with a fore-
        word by Conor Cruise O'Brien. London, Allen & Unwin,
        1968.
        DS557.A7G53 1968b   959.7'04   68-107893

589.   _____. North Vietnam: a documentary. With an introduc-
        tion by Conor Cruise O'Brien. Indianapolis, Bobbs-Merrill
        [1968]
        DS557.A7G53 1968   959.7'04   68-11154

590.   Germany (Federal Republic, 1959-). Statistisches Bundesamt.
        Landerberichte: Nord-Korea, Nord-Vietnam. 1963-
        HA1857.A2G4   67-46434

591.   Gershen, Martin. Destroy or die: the true story of Mylai.
        Arlington House, 1971.
        DS557.A67G47   959.7'04'342   76-139887

592.   Getnam, Aleksandur. Vietnamsko surtse, (Heart of Vietnam).
        (In Bulgarian). Sofia, 1960.
        DS557.A5G45

593.   Gettleman, Marvin, et al., eds. Conflict in Indochina: A
        Reader on the Widening War in Laos & Cambodia. Random.
        DS557.C28C6   959.7'04   72-139571

594.   Gettleman, Marvin E., ed.   Viet Nam, history, documents,
       and opinions on a major world crisis.   Ed., introduction by
       Marvin E. Gettleman.   Greenwich, Connecticut, Fawcett
       [c. 1965]
       DS557.A5G47   959.704

595.   _____.   Vietnam.   NAL (New American Library) 1970.

596.   Gheddo, Piero.   Cattolici e buddisti nel Vietnam.   Il ruolo
       delle comunita religiose nella costruzione della pace.   Firenze,
       Vallecchi, 1968.
       DS557.A6G45   70-397055

597.   _____.   The cross and the Bo-tree; Catholics and Bud-
       dhists in Vietnam.   Translated by Charles Underhill Quinn.
       New York, Sheed and Ward [c1970]
       DS557.A6G4513   959.7'04   70-101547

598.   Giap, Vo Nguyen.   Banner of Peoples' War: The Party's
       Military Line.   Praeger, 1970.
       UA853.V5V62   959.7'04   72-120153

599.   _____.   Big Victory Great Task: North Vietnam's Minister
       of Defense Assesses the Course of the War.   Praeger, 1968.
       DS557.A6V58   959.7'04   67-31381

600.   _____.   Military Art of People's War.   Selected Writings.
       Stetler, Russell, ed.   Monthly Review Press, 1970.

601.   _____.   People's War, People's Army.   New York,
       Praeger, 1962.

602.   Gigon, Fernand, 1908-   Les Americains face au Vietcong.
       Paris, Flammarion, 1965.
       DS557.A6G5   959.704   66-71106

603.   Ginsburg, Norton Sydney.   Malaya, by Norton Ginsburg and
       Chester F. Roberts, Jr., with the collaboration of Leonard
       Comber [and others]   Seattle, University of Washington Press,
       1958.
       DS592.G55   959.5   58-6372

604.   _____., ed.   The pattern of Asia.   Englewood Cliffs,
       N. J., Prentice-Hall, 1958.
       DS5.G5   915   58-8513

605.   Giuglaris, Marcel, 1922-   Vietnam: le jour de l'escalade,
       reportage.   [Paris] Gallimard, 1966.
       DS557.A6G55   959.704   66-78823

606.   Glaser, Horst.   Palmen, Soldner, Partisanen.   Berlin,
       Deutscher Militarverlag, 1962.
       DS557.A7G55   67-119407 rev.

607.   Glebova, Iveta Ivanovna.   Nachal'nyi kurs V'etnamskogo
       iazyka, (The Beginner's Course of the Vietnamese Language).
       (In Russian).   Moscow, 1963.
       PL4373.G55

608.   Glimpses of Viet-Nam.   [Published on the occasion of the 3d
       World Youth and Student Festival.   n. p.] 1951
       DS557.A5G54   959.7   53-22981

609.   Glorvigen, Bjørn.   Ved fronten i Vietnam.   Oslo, Elingaard,
       1967.
       DS557.A6G57   67-85988

610.   Glyn, Alan, 1919-   Witness to Viet Nam: the containment of
       communism in South East Asia.   London, Johnson, 1968.
       DS557.A6G59   959.7'04   68-98872

611.   Gobron, Gabriel, 1895-1941.   Histoire et philosophie du
       caodaisme; bouddhisme renove, spiritisme vietnamien, religion
       nouvelle en Eurasie.   Paris, Dervy, 1949.
       BL2055.G6   299.592   52-21242

612.   _____.   History and philosophy of Caodaism; reformed Bud-
       dhism, Vietnamese spiritism, new religion in Eurasia.
       Translated from the original French by Pham-xuan-Thai.
       [Saigon, Vietnam, Tu-hai, 1950]
       BL2055.G613   299.592   52-20667

613.   Golay, Frank H.   The Philippines: public policy and national
       economic development.   Ithaca, N. Y., Cornell University
       Press [1961]
       HC455.G6   338.9914   61-7869

614.   Gollwitzer, Helmut.   Vietnam, Israel und die Christenheit.
       München, Kaiser, 1967.
       BT736.2.G63   68-83260

615.   Gonzalez, Mario.   Neustros heroes en Viet Nam.   [New York?
       1967-   ]
       DS557.A64P83   959.7'04'0922   67-66304

616.   Goodwin, Richard N.   Triumph or tragedy; reflections on
       Vietnam [by] Richard N. Goodwin.   New York, Random
       House [1966]
       DS557.A6G6   959.704   66-23612

617.   Goralski, Wladyslaw.   Walka o Wietnam.   [Wyd. 1. Warszawa]
       Ksiazka i Wiedza, 1961.
       DS557.A5G56   62-47378

618.   _____.   Wietnamska lekcja.   [Wyd. 1. Warszawa]
       Ksiazka i Wiedza, 1965.
       DS557.A6G65   66-98038

619.   Gordon, Bernard K.   New Zealand becomes a Pacific power.
        Chicago, University of Chicago, 1960.
        DU421.G65   327.931   60-15106

620.   Gordon, Ernest.   Through the valley of the Kwai. [1st ed.]
        New York, Harper [1962]
        D805.J3G65   940.547252   62-11127

621.   Gore, Albert.   Eye of the Storm: A People's Politics for the
        Seventies.   Herder & Herder, 1970.
        E839.5.G67   959.7'04   78-110076

622.   Gouin, Eugene.   Dictionnaire vietnamien, chinois, francais.
        Saigon, Impr. d'Extreme-Orient [1957]
        PL4376.G56   59-42165

623.   Gourou, Pierre.   The peasants of the Tonk Delta, a study of
        human geography.   New Haven, Human Relations Area Files,
        1955.
        DS557.T7G62   915.99

624.   _____. L'utilisation du sol en Indochine francaise. Paris,
        Hartmann, 1940.
                                                          A44-1503

625.   Le Grand vent.   Hanoi, Editions en langues etrangeres, 1962.
        DS557.A7G7   S A 65-5192

626.   La Grande vague.   Hanoi, Editions en langues etrangeres, 1962.
        DS557.A7G73   S A 65-5193

627.   Grant, Bruce.   Indonesia. [Melbourne] Melbourne University
        Press; New York, Cambridge University Press [1964]
        DS634.G75 1964   919.1   64-6760

628.   Grant, Jonathan S., comp.   Cambodia: the widening war in
        Indochina.   Washington Square Press, 1971.
        DS557.C28G7 1971   959.7'04'34   77-20962

629.   Grauwin, Paul.   Doctor at Dienbienphu. New York, J. Day
        Company, 1955.
        DS550.G75   959   55-9933

630.   _____. 1915-   Seulement medecin.   Paris, Editions France
        Empire [c1956]
        DS557.A5G63   60-44169

631.   Green, Frank C., ed.   A century of responsible government,
        1856-1956.   Hobart, Tasmania, L. G. Shea, 1956?
        JQ5111.G7   354.946   57-28886

632.   Green, Henry Mackenzie. A history of Australian literature,
        pure and applied; Sydney, Angus & Robertson, 1962.
        PR9411.G7   820.9   62-38897

633.   _____., ed.   Modern Australian poetry.   2d ed.   rev.
        Carlton, Victoria, Melbourne University, 1952.
        PR9551.G7   821.91082   52-11526

634.   Greene, Felix.   Vietnam! Vietnam!   In photographs and text,
        by Felix Greene.   Palo Alto, California, Fulton Publishing
        Company [1966]
        DS557.A5G72   959.7040222   66-28359

635.   Greene, Graham, 1904-   The quiet American.   New York,
        Viking Press [c1955]
        PZ3.G8319Qui 2   56-6281

636.   Greenhaw, Wayne, 1940-   The making of a hero: the story
        of Lieutenant William Calley Jr.   Touchstone Publishing Com-
        pany, 1971.
        DS557.A67G74   959.7'04'32   79-166284

637.   Gregory, Gene.   A glimpse of Vietnam, by Gene Gregory,
        Nguyen-Lau and Phan-thi-Ngoc-Quoi. [Saigon?] 1957.
        DS557.A6G7   915.97   59-40262

638.   Grey, Sir George.   Polynesian mythology, and ancient tra-
        ditional history of the Maori as told by their priests and
        chiefs.   Christchurch, Whitcombe & Tombs, 1961.
        BL2615.G7   299.9   57-41672

639.   Griffiths, Philip Jones.   Vietnam Inc.   New York, Macmillan,
        1971.
        DS557.A61G7 1971   959.7'0431   73-167932

640.   Grimes, Annie E.   An annotated bibliography of climatic
        maps of North Vietnam, by Annie E. Grimes.   Silver Spring,
        Md., U.S. Environmental Data Service, 1968.
        Z6683.C5G7   016.9121'551609597   76-603928

641.   Groslier, Bernard P.   The Art of Indochina.   New York,
        Crown Publishers, 1962.
        N7311.G713   709.597   62-11805

642.   _____.   Indochina.   Cleveland, World Publishing Company,
        1966.
        DS525.5.G713   915.9'03   66-29161

643.   Groslier, Bernard Philippe.   Angkor et Cambodge au XVI
        siecle d'apres les sources portugaises et espagnoles.   1 ed.
        Paris, Pr. Universitaires de France, 1958.
        DS1.P35

644.   _____.   Indochina.   Translated from French by James
        Hogarth.   Cleveland, World [1967] c.1966.
        DS525.5.G713   915.9'03   66-29161

645.   . Indochina; translated from the French by James
Hogart. London, Muller, [1967]
DS525.5.G713 1967   915.9'03   67-1008

646.   Grousset, Rene. A history of Asia. New York, Walker, 1963.
DS33.G823   950   63-17553

647.   Gruening, Ernest Henry, 1887-   Vietnam folly, by Ernest
Gruening and Herbert Wilton Beaser. Washington, National
Press [1968]
DS557.A6G73   959.7'04   67-29093

648.   Grunder, Garel A. and Livezey, William Edmund. The
Philippines and the United States. Norman, University of
Oklahoma, 1951.
DS685.G75   991.4   51-6997

649.   Gruning, Gerhard. Bruderkrieg in Vietnam. [Frankfurt, Ver-
band der Kriegsdienstverweigerer Gruppe Frankfurt (Main)
1965]
DS557.A6G75   67-35013

650.   Gt. Brit. Central Office of Information. Reference Division.
Vietnam: background to an international problem. London,
H. M. S. O., 1970.
DS557.A6G67   959.7'0431   73-586282

651.   Gt. Brit. Foreign Office. Recent exchanges concerning attempts
to promote a negotiated settlement of the conflict in Viet-Nam.
London, H. M. Stationery Office, 1965.
DS557.A6G68   66-99418

652.   . Vietnam and the Geneva agreements; documents
concerning the discussions between representatives of Her
Majesty's Government and the Government of the Union of
Soviet Socialist Republics held in London in April and May
1956. Mar. 20-May 8, 1956. London, H. M. Stationery
Office [1956]
DS557.A5G7   56-4457

653.   Guevara, Ernesto, 1920-1967. On Vietnam & World Revolution. New York, Pathfinder Press, 1971.

654.   . Guerrilla warfare; a method [by]
Che Guevara. "Special war"; an outgrowth of neo-colonialism,
by Nguyen van Hieu. Introduction by William R. Nelson.
Edited by Donald B. McLean. [Forest Grove, Or., Normount
Armament Company] 1966.
U240.G833 1966   355.425   66-22697

655.   . On Vietnam and world revolution [by] Che Guevara.
[New York, Merit Publishers, 1967]
D844.G78   959.7'04   67-7287 rev.

656.   _____. Open new fronts to aid Vietnam! [by] Che Guevara;
introduction by Ken Coates. London, The Week, [1967]
DS44. G77   909. 82   67-98802

657.   _____. Guerrilla Warfare. Monthly Review Press, 1961.

658.   Guillain, Robert, 1908-   Vietnam: the dirty war; translated
[from the French] by April Carter and others. London,
Housmans [1966]
DS557. A6G8   66-67115

659.   Gullick, J. M. Indigenous political systems of western
Malaya. London, Athlone, 1958.
JQ692. G8   354. 595   58-3735

660.   _____. Malaya. New York, Praeger [1963]
DS596. G8   959. 5   63-16984

661.   _____. Malaysia and its neighbours [by] J. M. Gullick.
New York, Barnes & Noble [1967]
DS597. 2. G8 1967   959. 5'05   67-5340

662.   Gupta, Bhupesh, 1914-   India and American aggression on
Vietnam. [New Delhi] Communist Party Publication [1966]
DS557. A6G86   S A 67-1773

663.   Gurtov, Melvin. First Vietnam Crisis: Chinese Communist
Strategy & United States Involvement, 1953-1954. Columbia
L. A., 1968.

664.   _____. The first Vietnam crisis; Chinese Communist
strategy and United States involvement, 1953-1954. New
York, Columbia University Press, 1967.
DS557. A5G8   327. 510597   67-12207

665.   Guzman, Raul P. de, ed. Patterns in decision-making;
case studies in Philippine public administration. Manila,
Graduate School of Public Administration, University of the
Philippines; distributed by the East-West Center Press,
Honolulu, 1933.
JQ1331. G8   63-23671

H

666.   Hadgraft, Cecil. Australian literature; a critical account to
1955. London, Heinemann, 1962.
PR9411. H3   820. 9   62-51808

667.   Hai Thu. North Vietnam Against the U. S. Airforce.
China Books and Periodicals,   1967.

668.   _____. Saigon a l'heure des coups d'etat [par] Hai Thu
[et] Binh Thanh. Hanoi, Editions en langues etrangeres, 1964.
DS557. A6H284   68-47476

669.   Halberstam, David.   The making of a quagmire.   New York,
       Random [c.1964, 1965]
       DS557.A6H3   959.7   65-11258

670.   _____ .   One very hot day; a novel.   Boston, Houghton
       Mifflin, 1968 [c.1967]
       PZ4.H1590n   67-27510

671.   Hall, Daniel George Edward, 1891-   Burma.   London, New
       York, Hutchinson's University Library, 1950.
       DS485.B86H24   959.2   A 51-8971

672.   Hall, Rodney, 1935-   comp.   New impulses in Australian
       poetry, edited by Rodney Hall and Thomas W. Shapcott.   [St.
       Lucia, Queensland] University of Queensland Press [1968]
       PR9558.H3   821   68-138837

673.   Halme, Pentti.   Vietnamin palavat tuulet [kirj.] Pentti Halme
       [ja] Mikko Valtasaari.   Helsinki, Kustannusosakeyhtio Tammi
       [1967]
       DS557.A5H24   68-131597

674.   Halpern, Joel M.   Government, politics, and social structure
       in Laos; a study of tradition and innovation.   Yale University
       Southeast Asia Studies [distributor Detroit, Cellar Book Shop,
       1964]
       HN700.L3H33   959.4   64-16987

675.   Halpern, Joel Martin.   Economy and Society of Laos; a brief
       survey [by] Joel M. Halpern.   [New Haven] Southeast Asia
       Studies, Yale University [distributor: Cellar Book Shop,
       Detroit, c1964]
       HC443.L3H3   309.1594   64-8763

676.   Halstead, Fred.   GIs speak out against the war; the case of
       the Ft. Jackson 8; interviews of participants.   New York,
       Pathfinder Press, 1970.
       DS557.A68H3   959.7'04   70-108714

677.   Hamilton, Michael P. (ed.)   The Vietnam War: Christian
       Perspectives.   Grand Rapids, Eerdmans, 1967.
       DS557.A68V5   959.7'04   67-28380

678.   Hammer, Ellen J.   The Struggle for Indochina Continues.
       Stanford, Stanford University Press, 1955.
       DS550.H352   959   55-10469

689.   Hammer, Ellen Joy, 1921-   The emergence of Viet Nam;
       study of recent political developments in Indochina prepared
       as part of a larger series of reports on nationalism and de-
       pendencies in the Far East.   Distributed by the Secretariat
       as a supplementary document for the information of interested
       research workers and organizations and for members of the

Tenth IPR Conference in Sept. 1947. New York, International
Secretariat, Institute of Pacific Relations, 1947.
DS550.H3   959.7   48-27497 rev.

680.   _____. The struggle for Indochina, 1940-1955 [by] Ellen
        J. Hammer. Stanford, California, Stanford University
        Press [1966, c1955]
        DS550.H353   959.703   66-24065

681.   _____. The struggle for Indochina. Stanford, Stanford
        University Press, 1954.
        DS550.H35   959.7   54-6815 rev.

682.   _____. Vietnam yesterday and today. New York, Holt
        [c.1966]
        DS557.A5H25   915.97   65-26445

683.   Hammer, Richard. The Court-Martial of Lieutenant Calley.
        Coward, 1971.
        KF7642.C3H3   343'.73'0143   72-169820

684.   _____. One morning in the war; the tragedy at Son My.
        New York, Coward-McCann [1970]
        DS557.A67H34 1970   959.7'04   78-121323

685.   Hammerbacher, Gerhart. Die volkerrechtliche Stellung Viet-
        nams; ein Beitrag zur Problematik der volkerrechtlichen
        Situation geteilter Staaten. Mit einem Geleitwort von F. J.
        Berber. Augsburg, Hofman-Druck Verlag, 1960.
        JX4084.V5H3   65-89192

686.   Handache, Gilbert. L'Œil de Cao Dai, roman. Paris,
        Julliard, [1968]
        PQ2668.A503   68-119974

687.   Hanh, Thich N. Cry of Vietnam. Unicorn Press, 1968.

688.   _____. Vietnam: Lotus in a Sea of Fire. Hill & Wang,
        Inc., 1967.

689.   Hanna, Willard Anderson, 1911- Bung Karno's Indonesia;
        a collection of 25 reports written for the American Universi-
        ties Field Staff. New York, American Universities Field
        Staff, 1960.
        DS644.H16   991.03   60-10485

690.   _____. The formation of Malaysia; new factor in world
        politics; an analytical history and assessment of the prospects
        of the newest state in Southeast Asia, based on a series of
        reports written for the American Universities Field Staff, by
        Willard A. Hanna. New York, American Universities Field
        Staff [1964]
        DS597.2.H3   915.95   64-19390

691.   _____. Sequel to colonialism; the 1957-1960 foundations
            for Malaysia; an on-the-spot examination of the geographic,
            economic, and political seedbed where the idea of a Federa-
            tion of Malaysia was germinated, by Willard A. Hanna. New
            York, American Universities Field Staff [1965]
            DS597.H3 1965   959.5   65-12895

692.   Hanoi. Chambre de commerce. Bulletin economique. [Hanoi]
            HC443.V5H3   57-41776 rev.

693.   Hanrahan, Gene Z. The Communist struggle in Malaya. New
            York, Institute of Pacific Relations, 1954.
            DS596.H33   54-4251

694.   Harahap, Parada. Vietnam merdeka! Djakarta, Tintamas,
            1948.
            DS557.A5H3   55-39862

695.   Hardy, Osgood and Dumke, Glenn S. A history of the Pacific
            area in modern times. Boston, Houghton Mifflin, 1949.
            DS511.H25   950   49-6930

696.   Harrigan, Anthony. A guide to the war in Viet Nam. Boulder,
            Color., Panther Publications, 1966.
            DS557.A6H34   959.7'04   67-1846

697.   Harriman, W. Averell. America & Russia in a Changing
            World: A Half Century of Personal Observation. Doubleday,
            1971.
            E183.8R9H19   327.47'073   71-138930

698.   Hart, Donn Vorhis, 1918-   The Philippine plaza complex: a
            focal point in culture change. [New Haven] Yale University,
            Southeast Asia Studies, 1955.
            HN161.S69Y35 no. 3

699.   Hartke, Vance. The American crisis in Vietnam. Indianapo-
            lis, Bobbs-Merrill Company [1968]
            DS557.A63H3   959.7'04   67-18650

700.   Harvey, Frank. Air war--Vietnam. [New York] Bantam
            Books [1967]
            DS557.A65H35   959.7'04   67-25661

701.   Harvey, Godfrey Eric, 1889-   History of Burma from the
            earliest times to 10 March 1824, the beginning of the English
            conquest [by] G. E. Harvey. New York, Octagon, 1967.
            DS485.B86   959.1'02   67-15860/CD

702.   Haskins & Sells. Taxation in Australia. The Sydney office of
            Haskins & Sells collaborated in the preparation. [New York,
            1965-]
            FR35.li   340   66-5903

703.   Haskins, James. War & the Protest: Vietnam. Doubleday,
        1971.
        DS557.A63H34   959.7'04'3373   73-131079

704.   Hassler, R. Alfred. Saigon, U.S.A. [by] Alfred Hassler.
        With an introduction by George McGovern. New York, R. W.
        Baron, 1970.
        DS557.A6H35   959.7'04   70-108966

705.   Hatta, Mohammad, 1902-   The co-operative movement in
        Indonesia. With an introduction by Roesli Rahim. Edited by
        George McT. Kahin. Published under the auspices of the
        Modern Indonesia Project, Southeast Asia Program, Cornell
        University. Ithaca, N. Y., Cornell University Press [1957]
        HD3544.A5H32   58-194

706.   _____. Past and future, an address delivered upon re-
        ceiving the degree of doctor honoris causa from Gadjah Mada
        University at Jogjakarta on November 27th, 1956. Ithaca,
        N. Y., Modern Indonesia Project, Southeast Asia Program,
        Department of Far Eastern Studies, Cornell University, 1960.
        DS675.H3

707.   Haviland, H. Field Jr., et al. Vietnam after the War:
        Peace Keeping & Rehabilitation. Brookings Institution, 1968.

708.   Hawley, Earle, ed. The face of war: Vietnam, the full
        photographic report! [North Hollywood, California, Milton
        Luros, 17600 Gledhill North, 1965]
        DS557.A6H36   959.7   65-3639

709.   Hay, Stephen N. and Case, Margaret H.   Southeast Asian
        history; a bibliographic guide. New York, Praeger, 1962.
        Z3221.H36   016.959   62-20439

710.   Hayden, Joseph Ralston. The Philippines, a study in national
        development. New York, Macmillan, 1942.
        DS686.H3   991.4   42-2760

711.   Heaton, Leonard D.   Military surgical practices of the United
        States Army in Viet Nam [by] Leonard D. Heaton [and others]
        Chicago, Year Book Medical Publishers [1966]
        RD1.C9 Nov. 1966   617'.02   67-4957

712.   Heisterkamp, Charles, 1933- Activities of the U.S. Army
        Surgical Team WRAIR--Vietnam; a technical report, for the
        period of 17 June 1967 to 20 January 1968. Compiled and
        edited by Charles Heisterkamp, III. Prepared for US Army
        Medical Research and Development Command. [Washington,
        1970]
        RC971.H42   617'.99'0072   79-606045

713.   Hendry, James Bausch. The study of a Vietnamese rural

community: economic activity by James B. Hendry assisted
by Nguyen van Thuan. [Saigon?] Michigan State University
Viet-Nam Advisory Group, 1959.
HC443.V5H4   330.9597   60-64217

714. Herbert, Jean, 1897-   An introduction to Asia. Translated
      by Manu Banerii. New York, Oxford University Press [1968,
      c.1965]
      DS5.H453   915.03   65-4782

715. Herman, Edward S. America's Vietnam policy; the strategy
      of deception, by Edward S. Herman and Richard D. Du Boff.
      Washington, Public Affairs Press [1966]
      E183.8.V5H4   327.597073   66-29854

716. _____. Atrocities in Vietnam: Myths & Realities. United
      Church, 1970.
      DS557.A67H45   959.7'04   79-130839

717. A Heroic people: memoirs from the revolution. 2d ed.
      Hanoi, Foreign Languages Publishing House, 1965.
      DS557.A7H4 1965

718. Heros et heroines des forces armees de liberation du Sud
      Vietnam. [Saigon? Editions Liberation, 1965]
      DS557.A6H44   66-89487

719. Herrera, Barbara Hand. Medics in action. Photos by John
      Steel. Mountain View, California, Pacific Press Publishing
      Association [c1968]
      DS557.A677H4   959.7'04   68-54400

720. Hersh, Seymour M. My Lai 4; a report on the massacre and
      its aftermath [by] Seymour M. Hersh. [1st ed.] New York,
      Random House [1970]
      DS557.A67H47   959.7'04   77-119900

721. Herz, Martin Florian. A short history of Cambodia from the
      days of Angkor to the present. New York, Praeger, 1958.
      DS557.C2H52   959.6   58-8537

722. Hetherington, John Aikman. Forty-two faces. London, Angus
      & Robertson, 1963.
      PR9453.H4   64-39183

723. Heymard, Jean. Verite sur l'Indochine. Paris, Nouvelles
      Editions Debresse, 1962.
      DS550.H48   63-50431

724. Heynowski, Walter. Piloten im Pyjama. Von Heynowski &
      Scheumann. (Ubersetzung aus dem Amerikanischen: Gunter
      Walch [und] Ernst Adler.) Fotos: Thomas Billhardt. (Ber-
      lin) Verlag der Nation (1968)
      DS557.A69H4   68-131500

725.   Hickey, Gerald Cannon, 1925-   Research report, the De-
        partment of Education [by] Gerald C. Hickey [and] Vo Hong-
        Phuc. [Saigon?] Michigan State University, Vietnam Ad-
        visory Group, Field Administration Division, 1957.
        LA1181.H5   379.597   59-63304

726.   _____. The study of a Vietnamese rural community:
        sociology [by] Gerald C. Hickey assisted by Bui Quang Da.
        [Saigon?] Michigan State University, Viet Nam Advisory
        Group, 1960.
        HN700.V5H5   301.3509597   60-64220

727.   _____. Village in Vietnam. New Haven, Yale University
        Press, 1964.
        DS557.A5H5   309.1597   64-20923

728.   Higgins, Benjamin Howard. Indonesia's economic stabilization
        and development. New York, Institute of Pacific Relations,
        1957.
        HC447.H52   338.991   57-14155

729.   Higgins, Marguerite. Our Vietnam Nightmare. New York,
        Harper & Row, 1965.
        DS557.A6H5   327.597073   65-26104

730.   Hinton, Harold C. China's Relations with Burma and Viet-
        nam. New York, Institute of Pacific Relations, 1958.
        DS740.5.B8H5   327.5109059   58-2644

731.   Hirsch, Phil, ed. Vietnam combat. New York, Pyramid
        (1967)
                                    959.7'04   X1654

732.   Historical interaction of China and Vietnam: institutional and
        cultural themes. Edgar Wickberg, compiler. [Lawrence]
        Center for East Asian Studies, University of Kansas: [sole
        distributors in the U.S.A. & Canada: Paragon Book Gallery,
        New York, c1969]
        DS740.5.V5H5   301.29'51'0597   78-627562

733.   Historical studies: selected articles, second series. Com-
        piled by Margot Beever and F. B. Smith. [Melbourne]
        Melbourne University Press [1967]
        DU110.H5   994'.008   67-29755

734.   Ho, ch'eng. Yueh Han tz'u tien, (Vietnamese-Chinese Dic-
        tionary). Peking, 1960.
        PL4377.Y8

735.   Hoang-quoc-Viet. A short history of the Vietnamese workers'
        and trade union movement. Hanoi, General Confederation of
        Labour of Vietnam, 1960.
        HX400.V5H6   S A 64-651

736.   Hoang-van-Chi. Du colonialisme au communisme, l'experi-
       ence du Nord-Vietnam . . . [Traduction de Pierre Nicolas]
       [Tours] Mame, 1965.
       DS557. A7H594   67-86657

737.   _____. From colonialism to communism; a case history
       of North Vietnam. With an introduction by P. J. Honey.
       New York, Praeger [1964]
       DS557. A7H59 1964   959. 7   63-10721

738.   _____. From colonialism to communism. New Delhi,
       Allied Pub. [dist. New York, Paragon, 1965]
       DS557. A7H59   959. 7   S A 65-2584

739.   _____., ed. and tr. The new class in North Vietnam.
       Saigon, Cong Dan, 1958.
       DS557. A7H6   959. 7   59-34272

740.   Hoang-van-Thai. Some aspects of guerilla warfare in Viet-
       nam. Hanoi, Foreign Languages Publishing House, 1965.
       DC557. A5H6   S A 66-6840

741.   Hobbs, Cecil Carlton, 1907-   Writings on southern Asia,
       1942-1968, by Cecil Hobbs. [Washington, 1968]
       Z3221. H56   016. 954   74-8143

742.   Ho-Chi-Minh. Against U. S. Aggression, for National Salva-
       tion. China Books and Periodicals, 1967.

743.   _____. Izbrannye stal'i i rechi, (Selected Articles and
       Speeches). (In Russian). Moscow, 1959.
       DS557. A7H58

744.   Ho-Chi-Minh, Pres. Democratic Republic of Vietnam, 1894?-
       Against U. S. aggression for national salvation. Hanoi, For-
       eign Languages Publishing House, 1967.
       DS557. A635H6   959. 7'04   68-522

745.   _____. Oeuvres choisies. Paris, F. Maspero, 1967.
       DS557. A76H64   68-109509

746.   _____. Journal de prison; poemes. [Traduction de Dang
       the Binh et al.] Hanoi, Editions en langues etrangeres [1960]
       PL4378. 9. H6   S A 65-6814

747.   _____. Oktiabr'skaia revoliutsiia i osvobozhdenie narodov,
       (The October Revolution and the Liberation of the East Asian
       people). (In Russian). Moscow, 1957.
       DS33. 2. H6

748.   _____. On revolution; selected writings, 1920-66. Edited
       and with an introduction by Bernard B. Fall. New York, Prae-
       ger [1967]
       DS557. A7H533   959. 7008   67-20481

749. _____. President Ho chi Minh answers President L. B.
Johnson. Hanoi, Foreign Languages Publishing House, 1967.
DS557.A692H6   959.7'04   68-355

750. _____. Prison diary. Translated by Aileen Palmer.
Hanoi, Foreign Languages Publishing House, 1962.
PL4378.9.H613   S A 65-6537

751. _____. Selected works. Hanoi, Foreign Languages Publishing House, 1960-62.
DS557.A7H53   S A 66-5336

752. _____. Tuyen tap. Hanoi, Su That, 1960.
DS557.A7H586   S A 68-1043

753. _____. Yu chung jih chi, (Diary in Prison), (In Chinese).
Hanoi, 1960.
DS557.A7H5833

754. Hodder, B. W. Man in Malaya. London, University of
London, 1959.
HN690.M38H6   309.1595   60-20843

755. Hoffman, Margret, comp. Vietnam viewpoints; a handbook
for concerned citizens. [Austin, Texas, 1968]
DS557.A6H56   959.7'04   68-5767

756. Holden, Willis Sprague. Australia goes to press. Detroit,
Wayne State University, 1961.
                                                    61-15295

757. Holland, William Lancelot, ed. Asian nationalism and the
West; a symposium based on documents and reports of the
eleventh conference, Institute of Pacific Relations. New York,
Macmillan, 1953.
DS518.1.H6   991   53-1116

758. Holt, Claire. Art in Indonesia; continuities and change.
Ithaca, N. Y., Cornell University Press [1967]
N7325.H6   709.91   66-19222

759. Holzer, Werner. Vietnam; oder, die Freiheit zu sterben.
München, R. Piper [1968]
DS557.A6H58   68-95613

760. Honey, P. J. Communism in North Vietnam, its role in the
Sino-Soviet dispute. Cambridge, Massachusetts, M. I. T.
Press [c.1963]
DS557.A7H64   959.7   63-22436

761. _____. Genesis of a tragedy: the historical background
to the Vietnam War [by] P. J. Honey. London, Benn, 1968.
DS557.A5H64   959.7   68-105261

762.   _____. Genesis of a Tragedy: The Historical Background of the Vietnam War. International Publications Service, 1968.

763.   _____ ed. North Vietnam today; profile of a communist satellite. New York, Praeger [1962]
DS557.A7H65   959.9   62-21093

764.   Hoopes, Townsend. Limits of Intervention. New York, David McKay, 1970.

765.   Hope, Bob, 1903-   Five women I love; Bob Hope's Vietnam story. Garden City, N. Y., Doubleday, 1966.
DS557.A6H6   959.704   66-28863

766.   Horlemann, Jurgen, 1941-   Vietnam. Achtergronden van een conflict. [Door] Jurgen Horlemann en Peter Gang. [Vertaling: B. Groen] Amsterdam, De Bezige Bij, 1967.
DS557.A5H652   959.7   68-70935

767.   _____. Vietnam. Genesis eines Konfliktes [von] Jurgen Horlemann [und] Peter Gang. (3. Aufl) (Frankfurt a.M.) Suhrkamp (1967)
DS557.A5H65 1967   959.7'04   67-102307

768.   Hoskins, Marilyn W. Life in a Vietnamese Urban Quarter. Carbondaie, (Ill.) Office of Research and Projects. (Master's Thesis), 1965.
                                               NUC 67-96984

769.   Hsiao, Yang. Chieh fang chung ti Yueh-nan, (Vietnam in Freedom), (In Chinese), Shanghai, 1954.
DS557.A7H8

770.   Htin Aung, U. Burmese drama, a study. New York, Oxford University, 1937.
PL3971.H7   895.8209   38-10511 rev.

771.   _____, ed. and tr. Burmese monk's tales, collected, translated and introduced by Maung Htin Aung. New York, Columbia University Press, 1966.
GR309.H7   398.2   66-10871

772.   _____. A history of Burma, by Maung Htin Aung. New York, Columbia University Press, 1967.
DS485.B86H77   959.1   67-25964

773.   Huard, Pierre Alphonse and Durand, Maurice. Connaissance du Viet-nam. Hanoi, Ecole francaise d'Extreme-Orient, 1954.
DS557.A5H8   A55-10639

774.   Huber, Bert. Vietnam. [1. Aufl.] Berlin, Verlag der Nation [1968]
DS557.A7H84   70-382728

775.   Huberman, Leo, et al. Vietnam: The Endless War. Monthly
        Review Press, 1971.

776.   Hughes, John, 1930-   Indonesian upheaval. New York, D.
        McKay Company [1967]
        DS644.4.H8   991'.03   67-26500

777.   Hughes, Larry, 1944-   You can see a lot standing under a
        flare in the Republic of Vietnam; my year at war. New
        York, Morrow, 1969 [c.1970]
        DS557.A69H77   959.7'04   76-100636

778.   Huke, Robert E. Shadows on the land; an economic geography
        of the Philippines. Detroit, Cellar Book Shop, 1963.
        HC455.H8   330.9914   64-4080

779.   Hull, Roger H.   Law and Vietnam [by] Roger H. Hull & John
        C. Novogrod.   Foreword by Myres S. McDougal.   Dobbs
        Ferry, N. Y., Oceana Publications, 1968.
        JX1573.H8   341.3   68-12440

780.   Human Relations Area Files, Inc. Laos; its people, its society,
        its culture, by the staff and associates of the Human Relations
        Area Files. Editors: Frank M. LeBar [and] Adrienne Sud-
        dard. New Haven, HRAF Press [1960]
        DS557.L2H8   959.4   60-7381

781.   _____. North Borneo, Brunei, Sarawak (British Borneo).
        New Haven, 1956.
        DS646.3.H8   919.11   57-1553

782.   Hunt, Chester L.   Sociology in the Philippine setting, by
        Chester L. Hunt [and others] Manila, Alemar's [1954]
        HN713.H8   54-42041

783.   Hurhal', Volodmyr Iosypovych. Neskorene sertse V'etnamu,
        (Undefeated Heart of Vietnam). (In Ukrainian). Kiev, 1966.
        DS557.A69H8

784.   Hutchens, James M. Beyond combat [by] James M. Hutchens.
        Foreword by Ellis W. Williamson. Chicago, Moody Press
        [1968]
        DS557.A69H83   959.7'04   68-31200

785.   _____. Beyond Combat, Moody Press, 1969.

786.   Huu-Mai.   La derniere hauteur, roman sur Dien Bien Phu
        [par] Huu Mai. Hanoi, Editions en langues etrangeres, 1964.
        PQ3979.2.H8D4   66-95508

787.   Huxley, Elspeth Joseclin (Grant) 1907-   Their shining El-
        dorado; a journey through Australia, by Elspeth Huxley. New
        York, Morrow, 1967.
        DU105.H88   919.4'04'5   67-46372

788. Huyen, N. Khac. Vision accomplished? The enigma of Ho
Chi Minh by N. Khac Huyen. Collier Books, 1971.
DS557.76H679 1971   959.7'04'0924   78-147929

789. Hymoff, Edward. The First Air Cavalry Division, Vietnam.
[1st ed.] New York, M. W. Lads [1967]
DS557.A6H88   959.7'04   67-24872

790. _____. First Marine Division, Vietnam. [1st ed.] New
York, M. W. Lads Pub. [1967]
DS557.A6H9   959.7'04   67-21378

I

791. Iljas, Bachtiar. Perang Vietnam & netralisasi Asia Tenggara.
[Tjet. 1] Djakarta, Delegasi [1964]
DS557.A6 I 4   S A 66-6505

792. Images du Viet-Nam. [Hanoi]
DS557.A7A25   71-212670

793. In Face of American Aggression: 1965-1967. China Books and
Periodicals, 1971.

794. In South Vietnam. U. S. biggest operation foiled (February-
March [i.e. April] 1967) Hanoi, Foreign Languages Publishing
House, 1967.
DS557.A6 I 54   959.7'04   68-980

795. In the name of America; the conduct of the war in Vietnam by
the armed forces of the United States as shown by published
reports, compared with the laws of war binding on the United
States Government and on its citizens. Director of research,
Seymour Melman. Research associates: Melvyn Baron [and]
Dodge Ely. [New York] Clergy and Laymen Concerned About
Vietnam, 1968.
JX6731.W3 I 45   341.3   68-21064

796. Independent Information Centre, London. Vietnam Legion? A
new Communist defamation campaign: a document; introduced
by John Hynd; [translated from the German by Robert Moore
and Henry Jessup] London, Independent Information Centre
[1966]
DS557.A6 I 53   959.704   66-71570

797. India (Republic). Consulate General. Vietnam. Report on
economic and commercial conditions in the Republic of Vietnam.
New Delhi, Director, Commercial Publicity, Ministry of
Commerce and Industry, Government of India.
HC443.V5 I 5   S A 62-1054

798. Indonesia, no. 1- , April, 1966- Ithaca, N. Y., Cornell
University, Modern Indonesia Project.
DS611.I5

799.   Indonesia. Departemen Penerangan. Basic information on
        Indonesia. [Djakarta] Ministry of Information [1953]
        DS615. A515   919. 1   S A 62-994

800.   _____. Ho Chi Minh dan negaranja. [Djakarta] Kemen-
        terian Penerangan [cover 1959]
        DS557. A7 I 5   S A 64-6120

801.   The Indonesian town; studies in urban sociology. Hague, W.
        van Hoeve [1958]
        HN703. I 53

802.   International Bank for Reconstruction and Development.   The
        economic development of Ceylon; report of a mission.   Bal-
        timore, Johns Hopkins, 1953.
        HC437. C4I6   330. 954   53-1066

803.   _____. The economic development of Malaya; report.
        Baltimore, Johns Hopkins, 1955.
        HC442. I5   330. 9595   55-12042

804.   International Commission for Supervision and Control in
        Vietnam. Interim report. 1st/2d- August 11, 1954--Febru-
        ary 10, 1955. London, H. M. Stationery Office.
        DS557. A5 I 55   56-19617

805.   _____. Special report to the co-chairmen of the Geneva
        Conference on Indo-China, Saigon, 13 Feb. 1965. London,
        H. M. Stationery Office, 1965.
        DS557. A5 I 56   65-84489

806.   _____. Special report to the co-chairmen of the Geneva
        Conference on Indo-China, Saigon, 27 February, 1965.
        London, H. M. Stationery Office, 1965.
        DS557. A6 I 55   959. 7'04   67-115025

807.   International Conference for Solidarity with the People of
        Vietnam Against U. S. Imperialist Aggression and for the
        Defence of Peace, Hanoi, 1964. International Conference
        for Solidarity with the People of Vietnam Against U. S.
        Imperialist Aggression and for the Defence of Peace, Hanoi,
        25-29 November 1964. [Hanoi, 1965?]
        DS557. A5A27 1964   320. 9597   S A 66-3936

808.   International War Crimes Tribunal, Stockholm and Copen-
        hagen, 1967. Against the crime of silence; proceedings of
        the Russell International War Crimes Tribunal, Stockholm,
        Copenhagen. Edited by John Duffett. Introduction by Ber-
        trand Russell. Foreword by Ralph Schoenman. [1st ed.]
        New York, Bertrand Russell Peace Foundation, 1968.
        JX6731.W3 I 46 1967 341. 3'1   68-55747

809. International War Crimes Tribunal, Stockholm and Roskilde,
      Denmark, 1967. Le Jugement final. Directeur de publica-
      tion: Jean Paul Sartre. Redactrice: Arlette El Kaim . . .
      [Paris] Gallimard, 1968.
      JX6731.W3 I 55 1967   75-484358

810. _____. Russelltribunalen. Fran sessionerna i Stockholm
      och Roskilde. Urval och redigering: Peter Limqueco och
      Peter Weiss. Oversattning av Teddy Arnberg m. fl. Stock-
      holm, PAN/Norstedt, 1968.
      DS557.A6 I 558 1967   70-438910

811. Intervention in Vietnam; [articles] Editorial Committee:
      R. Boshier [and others] Wellington, C. I., Committee on
      Vietnam, 1965.
      DS557.A6 I 56   67-6074

812. Irikura, James K. Southeast Asia: selected annotated bib-
      liography of Japanese publications. New Haven, Southeast
      Asia Studies, Yale University, in association with Human Re-
      lations Area Files, 1956.
      Z3221.I7

813. Irwin, Graham. Nineteenth-century Borneo; a study in dip-
      lomatic rivalry. 's-Gravenhage, Nijhoff, 1955.
      DS646.3.I7   991.1   56-3877

814. Isaac, Julius E. Wages and productivity [by] J. E. Isaac.
      Melbourne, Canberra, [etc.] F. W. Cheshire [1967]
      HD5100.I8   338'.012   67-22847

815. Isard, Walter, ed. Vietnam: Some Basic Issues & Alterna-
      tives. Schenkman Publishing Company, Inc., 1969.

816. Iscaro, Rubens. Un argentino en Vietnam. Buenos Aires,
      1965. Editorial Anteo, 1965.
      DS557.A6I8   67-84357

817. Iosart, Paul. Le phenomene national vietnamien, de l'inde-
      pendance unitaire a l'independance fractionnee. Pref. de
      Michel-Henry Fabre. Paris, Librairie generale de droit et
      de jurisprudence, 1961.
      DS557.A5.I75   62-33917

818. Ivanoff, Pierre. Headhunters of Borneo. London, Jarrolds,
      1958.
      DS646.3.I853   919.11   59-17237

819. Izobrazitel'noe iskusstvo V'etnama, (Paintings of Vietnam).
      (In Russian). Moscow, 1959.
      N7314.I9

J

820.   Jackson, James C. Planters and speculators: Chinese and
        European agricultural enterprise in Malaya, 1786-1921, by
        James C. Jackson. Kuala Lumpur, University of Malaya
        Press; [sole distributors: Oxford University Press, Lon-
        don, New York] 1968.
        HD1471. M34J3   338. 1'09595   68-7767

821.   Jaeggi, Urs Josef Viktor. Der Veitnamkrieg und die Presse
        [von] Urs Jaeggi, Rudolf Steiner [und] Willy Wyniger. Zurich,
        EVZ-Verlag [1966]
        DS557. A68J3   67-102265

822.   James, Brian, ed. Australian short stories: second series.
        London, Oxford University, 1963.
        PZ1. J226Au   63-25172

823.   Janse, Olov Robert T. . . . The People of French IndoChina.
        Washington, The Smithsonian Institute, 1944.
        GN4. S6   44-41029

824.   Jay, Robert R. Religion and politics in rural central Java.
        [New Haven?] Yale University, Southeast Asia Studies;
        [distributed by the Cellar Book Shop, Detroit, Michigan,
        1963]
        DS646. 27. J3   919. 22   63-20750

825.   Jen min ch'u pan she, Peking. Chan tou chung ti Yueh-nan,
        (Vietnam in Struggle), (In Chinese). Peking, 1951.
        DS557. A7J4

826.   _____. Chung Yueh yu i, (Long Life for Chinese-Viet-
        namese Friendship), (In Chinese). Peking, 1962.

827.   Jennings, Joseph Newell. Landform studies from Australia
        and New Guinea; edited by J. N. Jennings and J. A. Mab-
        butt, with a foreword by Professor E. S. Hills. Cambridge,
        London, Cambridge University Press, 1967.
        GB381. J4 1967b   551. 4'0994   67-13805

828.   Jensen, Fritz. Erlebtes Vietnam. Mit einem Nachwort von
        Erwin Zucker-Schilling. [1. Aufl] Berlin, Dietz, 1955.
        DS550. J4   56-23959

829.   Johnson, Lyndon Baines, Pres. U. S., 1908- The Nation's
        commitment in Vietnam. Statement by the President of the
        United States, July 28, 1965. Washington, U. S. Govern-
        ment Printing Office, 1965.
        DS557. A6J57   65-62549

830.   _____. U. S. halts bombing of North Viet-Nam [by]
        Lyndon B. Johnson. [Washington] Department of State [for
        sale by the Superintendent of Documents, U. S. Government

Printing Office, 1968]
DS557. A65J6   959.7'04   68-67391

831.   ____. Viet-Nam; the struggle to be free [by] Lyndon B.
Johnson. [Washington] Department of State [for sale by the
Superintendent of Documents, U. S. Government Printing
Office, 1966]
DS557. A6J59   959.704   66-61230

832.   ____. Viet-Nam: the third face of the war [by] President Lyndon B. Johnson. [Washington] Department of State
[for sale by the Superintendent of Documents, U. S. Government Printing Office, 1965]
DS557. A6J6   65-61755

833.   ____. We will stand in Viet-Nam [by] Lyndon B. John-
son. [Washington] Department of State [for sale by the
Superintendent of Documents, U. S. Government Printing
Office, 1965]
DS557. A6J65   65-62422

834. Johnson, Raymond W. Postmark: Mekong Delta [by] Raymond
W. Johnson. Westwood, N. J., Revell [1968]
DS557. A69J6   959.7'04   68-20181

835. Johnson, Rossall James, 1917- Business environment in an
emerging nation; profiles of Indonesian economy [by] Rossall
J. Johnson, Dale L. McKeen [and] Leon A. Mears. Evans-
ton, Northwestern University Press, 1966.
HF3806. J6   330.991   65-14422

836. Johnson, Ural Alexis, 1908- Viet-Nam today [by] U.
Alexis Johnson. [Washington] Department of State [for sale
by the Superintendent of Documents, U. S. Government
Printing Office, 1966]
DS557. A6J68   309.1597   66-60959

837. Johnstone, William Crane, 1901- Burma's foreign policy; a
study in neutralism. Cambridge, Harvard University Press,
1963.
DS485. B893J6   327.591   63-9550

838. Joint Development Group. The postwar development of the
Republic of Vietnam; policies and programs. Foreword by
David E. Lilienthal. New York, Praeger Publishers [1970]
HC443. V5J63 1970   338.9597   79-114437

839.   ____. The postwar development of the Republic of
Vietnam: policies and programs. Saigon, New York, 1969.
HC443. V5J63   338.9597   76-607087

840.   ____. Postwar development of Viet Nam; a summary
report. [Saigon] Vietnam Council on Foreign Relations [1969]
HC443. V5J64   338.9597   72-14336

841.   Joka, Milan.   Vijetnam demokratska republika u Istocnoj
        Aziji, (The Democratic Republic of Vietnam in East Asia).
        (In Yugoslav).   Beograd, 1948.
        DS557. V5J6

842.   Jones, Rennie C.   Vietnam; a select reading list, compiled
        by Rennie C. Jones, Melbourne, State Library of Victoria,
        1966.
        Z3228. V5J6   016. 91597   66-74044

843.   _____.   Vietnam; historical background, the 1954 Geneva
        Conference, the International Commission for Control, com-
        piled by Rennie C. Jones.   Melbourne, State Library of Vic-
        toria, 1966.
        Z3228. V5J62   016. 9597   67-79559

844.   Jones, Robert B.   1920-   Introduction to spoken Vietnamese
        [by] Robert B. Jones, Jr., and Huynh sanh Thong.   Rev.
        ed.   Washington, American Council of Learned Societies,
        1960.
        PL4375. J6 1960   495. 928242   60-53558

845.   Jones, Stanley Wilson.   Public administration in Malaya.
        New York, Royal Institute of International Affairs, 1953.
        JQ715. J6   354. 595   53-8786

846.   Jones-Griffiths, Philip.   Vietnam, Inc.   Sandum, Howard,
        ed.   Macmillan Company (Subs of Crowell Collier & Mac-
        millan, Inc.) 1971.

847.   Jumper, Roy.   Bibliography on the political and administra-
        tive history of Vietnam, 1802-1962, selected and annotated
        [by] Roy Jumper.   [Saigon] Michigan State University, Viet-
        nam Advisory Group [1964]
        Z3228. V5J8 1964   S A 64-6829

848.   _____.   Notes on the political and administrative history
        of Viet Nam,   1802-1962, by Roy Jumper and Nguyen Thi
        Hue.   [Saigon?]   Michigan State University, Viet Nam Ad-
        visory Group, 1962.
        DS557. A5J8   959. 7   S A 62-1217

849.   Jury, Mark.   The Vietnam photo book.   Grossman Pubs.,
        1971.
        DS557. A61J87   959. 7043'0222   76-161038

850.   Just, Ward S.   To what end; report from Vietnam [by]
        Ward S. Just.   Boston, Houghton Mifflin, 1968.
        DS557. A69J8   959. 7'04   68-17299

K

851. Kahin, George M. & Lewis, John W. United States in Viet-
      nam. Dell Publishing Company, Inc., 1967.

852. Kahin, George McTurnan. The Asian-African Conference,
      Bandung, Indonesia, April, 1955. Ithaca, N. Y., Cornell
      University, 1956.
      DS35. A8   950   56-897

853. _____, ed. Major governments of Asia, by Harold C.
      Hinton [and others] 2d ed. Ithaca, N. Y., Cornell Univer-
      sity, 1958.
      JQ5. K3   320. 95   58-3682

854. _____, ed. Major governments of Asia, by Harold C.
      Hinton [and others] 2d ed. Ithaca, N. Y., Cornell Univer-
      sity Press [1963]
      JQ5. K3 1963   342   63-15940

855. _____. Nationalism and revolution in Indonesia. Ithaca,
      Cornell University, 1952.
      DS644. K32   991   52-4383

856. _____. The United States in Vietnam, by George Mc-
      Turnan Kahin and John W. Lewis. New York, Dial Press,
      1967.
      DS557. A6K28   959. 7'04   66-21593

857. _____. The United States in Vietnam, by George Mc-
      Turnan Kahin and John W. Lewis. Rev. ed. New York,
      Dial Press, 1967   [i. e. 1969]
      DS557. A63K3 1969   959. 7'04   79-78461

858. Kaiko, Takeshi, 1930-   Betonamu senki (War report on
      Vietnam) (In Japanese), Tokyo, 1965.
      DS557. A6K3

859. Kalb, Marvin L. Roots of involvement: the U. S. in Asia,
      1784-1971 by Marvin Kalb & Elie Abel. Norton, 1971.
      DS557. A63K315 1971   959. 7'04'31   73-139381

860. Kang, Pilwon. The road to victory in Vietnam. [1st ed.]
      New York, Exposition Press [1970]
      DS557. A63K32   959. 7'04   72-12646

861. Karikhanis, Sarala Laxman, 1920-   Vhietanama (Vietnam).
      (In Marathi). 1965.
      DS557. A6K35

862. Karlsson, Per Olof, 1927-   Kriget i Vietnam. Av Per-
      Olof Karlsson. 2. Utokade uppl. Stockholm, Raben &
      Sjogren, 1966.
      DS557. A6K37 1966   67-81623

863.   _____. Kriget i Vietnam.   Stockholm [Raben & Sjogren]
       1965.
       DS557. A6K37   66-67944

864.   Karmen, Roman Lazarevich.   Po Stranam Trekh Kontinentov,
       (Through the Countries of Three Continents).   (In Russian).
       Moscow, 1962.
       DP269. 17. K3

865.   _____. Svet v dzhungliaky; zametki kinooperatora, (Light
       in Jungles; observations of a movie operator).   (In Russian).
       Moscow, 1957.
       DS557. A7K3

866.   _____. V'etnam srazhaestsia; zapiski sovetskogo kino-
       operatora, (Vietnam is fighting; Soviet movie operator's
       notes).   (In Russian).   Moscow, 1958.
       DS557. A7K32

867.   Karnow, Stanley.   Southeast Asia, by Stanley Karnow and
       the eds. of Life.   New York, Time, Inc. [c. 1962]
       DS508. 2. K35   915. 9   62-20816

868.   _____. Southeast Asia, by Stanley Karnow and the eds.
       of Life.   New York, Time-Life Books [1967]
       DS508. 2. K35 1967   915. 9'03   68-851

869.   Kaye, Barrington.   Upper Nankin Street, Singapore; a
       sociological study of Chinese households living in a densely
       populated area.   Singapore, University of Malaya, 1960.
       HN690. S47K3   309. 15952   60-51064

870.   Keesing, Felix Maxwell.   The ethnohistory of northern Lu-
       zon.   Stanford, California, Stanford University, 1962.
       DS688. L9K38   919. 141   62-9563

871.   Keesing's Publications Ltd.   South Vietnam: A Political
       History 1954-1970.   New York, Scribner, 1970.

872.   _____. South Vietnam: A Political History 1954-1970.
       New York, Scribner, 1971.

873.   Keith, Agnes (Newton).   Bare feet in the palace.   Boston,
       Little, Brown, 1955.
       DS686. 5. K4   919. 14   56-1543

874.   Kelly, George A.   Lost Soldiers.   Cambridge, Massachu-
       setts, M. I. T. Press, 1965.
       DC367. K4   355. 0330944   65-24922

875.   Kelly, Leslie G.   Marion Dufresne at the Bay of Islands.
       Wellington, N. Z., 1951.
       DU430. B2K4   923. 944   52-43600

876. Kemp, Ian, 1940-   British G. I. in Vietnam [by] Ian Kemp
      [in collaboration with Peter Kemp] London, Hale, 1969.
      DS557. A69K4   959. 7'04   75-479778

877. Kennedy, Joseph, 1919-   A history of Malaya, A. D. 1400-
      1959. [New York] St. Martin's Press [1962]
      DS596. K4 1962a   959. 5   62-4276

878. Kennedy, Raymond.   The ageless Indies.   New York, Day,
      1942.
      DS615. K4   919. 1   42-17780

879. _____. Bibliography of Indonesian peoples and
      cultures. Rev. and edited by Thomas W. Maret-
      zki and H. Th. Fischer. 2d rev. ed. [New Haven] South-
      east Asia Studies, Yale University, by arrangement with
      Human Relations Area Files, 1962.
      Z5115. K4 1962   016. 572991   62-20539

880. The Kennedys & Vietnam. (Interim History Ser: The Bridge
      Between Today's News & Tomorrow's History).   Facts on
      File, Inc. , 1971.

881. Kerry, John, 1943-   The new soldier, by John Kerry &
      Vietnam Veterans Against the War.   Macmillan, 1971.
      DS557. A69K44   959. 704'38   76-171990

882. Kessel, Joseph, 1898-   The valley of rubies.   Translated
      from French by Stella Rodway.   New York, D. McKay Com-
      pany [1961, c. 1960]
      PQ2621. E77V33   TR 915. 92   61-7987

883. Keyes, Jane Godfrey.   A bibliography of [North] Vietnamese
      publications in the Cornell University Library.   Ithaca,
      N. Y. , Southeast Asia Program, Department of Asian
      Studies, Cornell University, 1962.
      Z3228. V5K4   016. 91597   63-4361 rev 2

884. Khaing, Mi Mi, Daw.   Burmese family.   Illus. by E. G. N.
      Kinch. [Introduction by Santha Rama Rau] Bloomington,
      Indiana University [c. 1962]
      DS485. B84M5   915. 91   62-8981

885. Khrushchev, Anatolii Timofeevich.   Demokraticheskaia Res-
      publika V'etnam; lektsii, prochitannye v Vysshei partiinoi
      shkole pri TSK KPSS, (Democratic Republic of Vietnam;
      Lectures Delivered to the higher party school at the Central
      Committee of the Communist Party of the Soviet Union).
      (In Russian).   Moscow, 1956.
      DS557. A5K54

886. Kiki, Albert Maori, 1931-   Kiki: ten thousand years in a
      lifetime, a New Guinea autobiography.   New York, F. A.

Praeger [1968]
DU746. K5A3   995 (B)   68-30943

887.   Kim, Sung Yong, 1918-   United States-Philippine relations,
       1946-1956. Washington, Public Affairs Press [1968]
       E183. 8. P5K5   327. 73'0914   68-22601

888.   Kirban, Salem.   Goodbye Mister President.   Kirban, Salem,
       Pub. , 1968.

889.   _____.   Goodbye Mr. President; the story of one man's
       search for peace.   Huntingdon Valley, Pennsylvania, 1967.
       DS557. A69K5   915. 97'04'4   67-31531

890.   Kirk, Donald.   Wider War: The Struggle for Cambodia,
       Thailand, & Laos.   Praeger, 1971.
       DS518. 8. K56   959. 7'043   70-76790

891.   Kirk, Grayson Louis.   Philippine independence; motives,
       problems, and prospects.   New York, Farrar & Rinehart,
       1936.
       DS685. K57   991. 4   36-12281

892.   Kirsch, Richard, 1915-   Moskitos, Bambus und Bananen.
       Als Arzt in Vietnam.   [Ausgewahlt und zusammengestellt aus
       dem Tagebuch Prof. Dr. Kirschs von Edeltraud Scholz. 1.
       Aufl.] Berlin, Kinderbuchverlag [1960]
       DS557. A7K5   62-68441

893.   Klaveren, Jacob van.   The Dutch colonial system in the
       East Indies. ['s Gravenhage, M. Nijhoff] 1953.
       JQ762. K45   54-4658 rev.

894.   Klemm, Edwin O.   You, Viet-Nam and Red China [by Edwin
       O. Klemm. 1st ed. Saginaw, Michigan, Multicopy Printing
       Services, 1968]
       DS557. A63K55   959. 7'04   68-2242

895.   Klemm, Heinz, 1915-   Der Tiger kommt nicht mehr; viet-
       namesische Reisen. Leipzig, Brockhaus, 1960.
       DS557. A5K55   67-118127 rev.

896.   Klopotov, Kirill Konstantinovich.   Ocherki narodnogo
       Khoziaistva Demokraticheskoi Respubliki V'etnam, [A general
       description of the National Economy of the Democratic Re-
       public of Vietnam).   (In Russian).   Moscow, 1956.
       HC443. V5K6

897.   _____.   V strane Iura; zapiski o V'etname, (From the
       South; notes about Vietnam).   (In Russian).   Moscow, 1957.
       DS557. A7K54

898.   Knobl, Kuno, 1936-   Victor Charlie: the face of war in
       Viet-Nam.   Introduction by Bernard B. Fall.   Translated

by Abe Farbstein.   New York, Praeger, [1967]
DS557. A6K553   959. 7'04   67-18835

899.   .   Victor Charlie: Viet Cong, der unheimliche
Feind.   Ein Erlebnisbericht mit dokumentarischem Anhang.
(2. Aufl) München, Heyne (1968)
DS557. A6K55 1968   68-120680

900.   .   Victor Charlie, Vietcong.   Traduit de l'allemand
par Jean-Charles Lombard . . . Paris, Flammarion, 1967.
DS557. A6K554   959. 7'04   68-72667

901.   .   Victor Charlie: Viet Cong, Der Unheimlische
Feind. Ein Erlebnis-Bericht mit Dokumentarischem Anhang.
Muenchen, Heyde Bücher, 1968.
DS557. A6K554   959. 7'04   68-72667

902.   Knoll, Erwin & McFadden, Judy, eds.   War Crimes &
American Conscience.   Holt, Rinehart and Winston, 1970.
DS557. A67W3   959. 7'04   76-122254

903.   Kolko, Gabriel, ed.   Three Documents of the National
Liberation Front.   Incl. Principles & Main Content of an
Overall Solution to the Viet Nam Problem: The Ten Points;
Fundamental Resolutions of the South Viet Nam Congress of
People's Representatives; Declaration of the Program of Ac-
tion of the Provisional Revolutionary Government of the Re-
public of South Vietnam.   Beacon Press, Inc. , 1971.

904.   Kolpacoff, Victor, 1938-   The prisoners of Quai Dong.
[New York] New American Library, 1967.
PZ4. K816Pr   67-25937

905.   Koninklijk Institut Voor de Tropen.   Indonesian economics;
the concept of dualism in theory and policy.   The Hague, Van
Hoeve, 1961.
HC447. K65   63-1505

906.   .   Afdeling Agrarisch Onderzoek.   Vietnam (Noord
en Zuid) [Amsterdam, Mauritskade 63] 1968.
DS557. A5K6   74-358547

907.   Korea (Republic) Kongbobu.   Korea and Vietnam.   [Seoul]
Ministry of Public Information, Republic of Korea [1967]
DS557. A64K4   759. 7'04   68-208

908.   Koshyk, Oleksandr Kuz'mych.   Demokratichna Respublika
V'etnam, (Democratic Republic of Vietnam).   (In Ukrainian).
Kiev, 1957.
AS262. T554

909.   Kozhin, Aleksei Ivanovich.   V gorakh i dolinakh V'etnama,
(In the mountains and valleys of Vietnam).   (In Russian).

Moscow, 1956.
DS557. A7K6

910.   Kraslow, David.   The diplomacy of chaos [by] David Kras-
        low and Stuart H. Loory.   London, Macdonald & Company,
        1968.
        DS557. A69K7 1968b   959. 7ʳ04   78-368175

911.   .   The secret search for peace in Vietnam, by
        David Kraslow and Stuart H. Loory.   New York, Random
        House [1968]
        DS557. A692K7 1968   959. 7ʳ04   68-28543

912.   Kroeber, Alfred Louis.   Peoples of the Philippines.   New
        York, Anthropological Handbook Fund, 1928.
        DS665. K7   29-7229

913.   Krueger, Carl, 1908-   Wings of the Tiger; a novel.   New
        York, F. Fell [1966]
        PZ4. K938Wi   66-27604

914.   Kunzli, Arnold.   Vietnam--wie es dazu kam.   Zurich, EVZ-
        Verlag (1965)
        DS557. A6K77   959. 7   66-67943

915.   Kuo, Shou-hau, 1902-   Yueh-nan t'ung chien, (Vietnam
        Handbook), (In Chinese).   Taipei, 1961.
        DS557. A6K8

916.   Kuo, Yuan.   Yueh-nan hsing, (Travelling in Vietnam), (In
        Chinese).   Taipei, 1959.
        DS557. V5K8

917.   De Kwestie Vietnam.   Veiten en achtergronden.   Redactie
        S. J. Bosgra, R. R. Eijbersen.   Eindredactie A. P. E.
        Korver, M. B. H. Visser, H. Amptmeyer e. a. Voor-
        woord van J. Verkuyl.   Amsterdam, Polak & Van Gennep,
        1966.
        DS557. A6K85   67-85462

918.   Kyriak, Theodore E.   North Vietnam, 1957-1961; a bibli-
        ography and guide to contents of a collection of United States
        Joint Publications Research Service translations on microfilm,
        compiled and edited by Theodore E. Kyriak.   Annapolis,
        Research & Microfilm Publications [196-]
        Z3228. V52K9   016. 91597   66-1212

L

919.   Labin, Suzanne.   Sellout in Vietnam?   Introduction by Bry-
        ton Barron.   Updated enl. ed.   Arlington, Virginia, Crest-
        wood Books, 1966.
        DS557. A6L2 1966   959. 7   66-8651

920.   _____. Vietnam: an eye-witness account. Introduction
        by Bryton Barron. Springfield, Virginia, Crestwood [c.]
        1964.
        DS557. A6L2   959.7   64-6886

921.   _____. Vietnam; revelations d'un temoin. Paris, Nou-
        velles Editions latines [1964]
        DS557. A6L22   67-54073

922.   Labor Party (Australia). Western Australian State Executive.
        Facts about Vietnam. [Perth, 1965]
        DS557. A6L23   66-69777

923.   Lacouture, Jean. La Din d'une Guerre, Indochine 1954.
        Paris, Editions du Seuil, 1961.
        DS550. L33   61-48938

924.   _____. Ho Chi Minh: a political biography. Translated
        from the French by Peter Wiles. Translation edited by
        Jane Clark Seitz. [1st American ed.] New York, Random
        House [1968]
        DS557. A76H643   959.7'04'0924 (B)   68-44527

925.   _____. Vietnam: between two truces. With an intro-
        duction by Joseph Kraft. Translated from the French by
        Konrad Kellen and Joel Carmichael. New York, Random
        House [1966]
        DS557. A5L233   320.9597   66-11982

926.   _____. Le Vietnam Entre Deux Paix. Paris, Editions
        du Seuil, 1965.
        DS557. A5L23   65-79869

927.   Lagrilliere-Beauclere, E. . . . A Travers l'Indo Chine.
        Paris, Librairie chez Tallandier, 1900.
        DS534. L17   1-F-3563

928.   Lamb, Alastair. Mandarin Road to Old Hue: Narrative of
        Anglo-Vietnamese Diplomacy from the 17th Century to the
        Eve of the French Conquest. Shoe String Press, Inc., 1970.

929.   Lamb, Helen Boyden. The tragedy of Vietnam; where do we
        go from here? By Helen B. Lamb. [New York, Basic
        Pamphlets, 1964]
        DS557. A6L26   65-4903

930.   Lancaster, Donald. The emancipation of French Indochina.
        London, New York, Oxford University Press, 1961.
        DS541. L28   959.7   61-1998

931.   Lande, Carl Herman. Leaders, factions, and parties; the
        structure of Philippine politics [by] Carl H. Lande. [New
        Haven] Southeast Asia Studies. Yale University [distributor:
        Cellar Book Shop, Detroit, 1965]
        JQ1398. A1L3 1965   329. 9914   65-18996

932.   Landon, Kenneth Perry. Southeast Asia, crossroad of re-
        ligions. Chicago, University of Chicago, 1949.
        BL2050. L3   290. 959   49-840

933.   Landry, Lionel. The land and people of Burma. [1st ed.]
        Philadelphia, Lippincott [1968]
        DS485. B81L3   915. 91   68-10765

934.   Lane, Mark. Conversations with Americans. S & S. 1970.
        DS557. A67L28   959. 7'04   79-129190

935.   Lane, Thomas A. , 1906-   America on trial: the war for
        Vietnam, by Thomas A. Lane. Arlington House, 1971.
        DS557. A63L35   959. 7'04'3373   73-139889

936.   Lang, Daniel. Casualties of war. [1st ed.] New York,
        McGraw-Hill [1969]
        DS557. A67L3   959. 7'04   75-105960

937.   Langer, Paul F. & Zasloff, Joseph J.   North Vietnam & the
        Pathet Lao: Partners in the Struggle for Laos. Harvard
        University Press, 1970.

938.   Langlois, Walter G. Andre Malraux: the Indochina ad-
        venture [by] Walter G. Langlois. New York, Praeger
        [1966]
        PQ2625. A716Z687   959. 7030924   65-24947

939.   Laniel, Joseph. Le drame indochinois; de Dien-Bien-Phu au
        pari de Geneve. Paris, Librairie Plon, 1957.

940.   Larson, Donald Raymond. Vietnam and Beyond. Durham,
        (N. C.) Rule of Law Research Center, Duke University, 1965.
        E183. 8. V5L3   65-6169

941.   Larteguy, Jean, 1920-   Un million de dollars le Viet.
        [Paris] R. Solar [1965]
        DS557. A6L27   66-46625

942.   Lattimore, Owen, 1900-   comp. Silks, spices and empire;
        Asia seen through the eyes of its discoverers. Ed. , anno-
        tated, introduction by Owen & Eleanor Lattimore. [New
        York] Delacorte [1968]
        DS10. L3   915'. 04   67-24633

943.   Laurent, Jacques, 1919-   Les Choses que j'ai vues au
        Vietnam m'ont fait douter de l'intelligence occidentale.

Paris, la Table ronde, 1968.
DS557. A5L37   68-124134

944.   Lawrence, R. John, 1931-   Professional social work in
       Australia [by] R. J. Lawrence.   Canberra, Australian Na-
       tional University [1965]
       HV473. L3   361. 994   66-54736

945.   Lawyers Committee on American Policy Towards Vietnam.
       Consultative Council.   Vietnam and international law; an
       analysis of the legality of the U. S. military involvement.
       [Flanders, N. J.]   O'Hare, 1967.
       JX1573. L38   341. 3'1   67-19573

946.   Leasor, James.   Singapore: the battle that changed the
       world.   [1st ed.]   Garden City, N. Y., Doubleday, 1968.
       DS598. S7L38   959. 5/2/03   67-15355

947.   Le-ba-Khanh.   Standard pronouncing Vietnamese-English and
       English-Vietnamese dictionary.   [New York, F. Ungar Pub-
       lishing Company, 1955]
       PL4376. L48   495. 9232   55-12581

948.   Le-ba-Kong & Le-ba-Khanh, eds.   Standard Vietnamese-
       English, English-Vietnamese Dictionary.   New York, F.
       Ungar, 1971.

949.   Le-Chau.   La Revolution paysanne du sud Viet Nam.   Paris,
       Maspero, 1966.
       HD2080. V5L42   338. 1'09597   68-132983

950.   _____.   Le Viet Nam socialiste: une economie de transi-
       tion.   Paris, F. Maspero, 1966.
       HC443. V5L4   330. 9597   66-72412

951.   Lederer, William J.   1912-   Our own worst enemy [by] Wil-
       liam J. Lederer [1st ed.]   New York, W. W. Norton [1968]
       DS557. A63L4   959. 7'04   68-13487

952.   Le-Duan.   On the Socialist revolution in Vietnam.   Hanoi,
       Foreign Languages Publishing House, 1965.
       DS557. A7L43

953.   _____.   Sur quelques problemes internationaux actuels
       [par] Le Duan.   Hanoi, Editions en langues etrangeres, 1964.
       DS557. A7L4   66-40184

954.   _____.   Vietnamese Revolution.   International Publishers
       Company, Inc., 1971.

955.   Lee Duan.   On the Socialist Revolution.   China Books and
       Periodicals, 1971.

956.   Lee, Kuan Yew, 1923-   The battle for a Malaysian
       Malaysia. [Singapore, Ministry of Culture, 1965]
       DS597. 2. L4   67-113066

957.   Leenhardt, Maurice.   Folk art of Oceania.   New York,
       Tudor, 1950.
       N7410. L   709. 9   A51-2224

958.   Leeson, Ida.   A bibliography of bibliographies of the South
       Pacific.   New York, Oxford University Press, 1954.
       Z4008. 02L4   55-3192

959.   Legge, John David.   Australian colonial policy; a survey of
       native administration and European development in Papua.
       Sydney, Angus and Robertson [1956]
       JQ6311. A2L4   325. 39940995   A 57-1387 rev.

960.   _____ . Indonesia [by] J. D. Legge.   Englewood Cliffs,
       N. J., Prentice-Hall [1965, c. 1964]
       DS634. L44 1965   991   64-23558

961.   Legler, A.   Der Krieg in Vietnam; Bericht und Bibliographie
       bis 30. 9. 1968, von A. Legler und K. Hubinek.   Frankfurt
       am Main, Bernard & Graefe, 1969.
       DS557. A6L32   74-471087

962.   Leichhardt, Ludwig, 1813-1848.   The letters of F. W. Lud-
       wig Leichhardt collected and newly translated from the Ger-
       man, French, and Italian by M. Auronsseau.   London,
       published for the Hakluyt Society by Cambridge University
       Press, 1968.
       G161. H2 2d ser.,   508. 94   68-13538
       no. 135-137

963.   Leifer, Michael.   Cambodia: the search for security.   New
       York, Praeger [1967]
       DS557. C28L4   327. 596   67-18970

964.   Lekomtsev, IUrii Konstantinovich.   Struktura v'etnamskogo
       prostogo predlozheniia, (The Structure of Simple Vietnamese
       sentences).   (In Russian).   Moscow, 1964.
       PL4373. L35

965.   Le May, Reginald Stuart.   The culture of South-east Asia,
       the heritage of India.   London, Allen & Unwin, 1954.
       DS511. L4   915. 9   54-1347

966.   Leont'ev, Aleksei Pavlovich.   V'etnam boretsia, (Vietnam is
       Fighting).   (In Russian).   Moscow, 1965.
       DS557. A6L34

967.   Leont'ev, Lev Abramovich, 1901-   Boriushchiisia V'etnam,
       (Fighting Vietnam).   (In Russian).   Moscow, 1954.
       DS557. V5L4

968.   Le Roy, James Alfred. The Americans in the Philippines;
        a history of the conquest and first years of occupation, with
        an introductory account of the Spanish rule. Boston,
        Houghton Mifflin, 1914.
        DS685. L586   14-6172

969.   Le-thanh-Khoi. Le Viet-nam, histoire et civilisation.
        [Paris] Editions de Minuit [1955]-
        DS557. A5L47   57-15843

970.   Letters from South Vietnam. Hanoi, Foreign Languages
        Publishing House, 1963-
        DS557. A6L37   66-42473

971.   Leur, Jacob Cornelis Van. Indonesian trade and society;
        essays in Asian social and economic history. The Hague,
        W. Van Hoeve, 1955.
        HF3804   A55-8697

972.   Le-van-Chat. Guerre non declaree au Sud Viet Nam.
        Hanoi, Editions en langues etrangeres, 1962.
        DS557. A6L39   S A 65-4977

973.   _____. The undeclared war in South Viet Nam. Hanoi,
        Foreign Languages Publishing House, 1962.
        DS557. A6L4   S A 65-417

974.   Le-van-Hung, Mrs. Vietnamese-English dictionary, with
        the international phonetic system and more than 30, 000
        words and idiomatic expressions. Prepared by Mrs. Le van
        Hung and Dr. Le van Hung. Paris, Editions Europe-Asie
        [1955]
        PL4376. L55   495. 9232   56-4867

975.   Le-van-Ly. Le parler vietnamien; sa structure phonologique
        [sic] et morphologique fonctionnelle. 2. ed. rev. et corr.
        Saigon, Ro Quoc-gia Giao-duc, Vien Khao-co, 1960.
        PL4373. L4 1960   S A 62-73

976.   Levi, Werner, 1912-   American-Australian relations, by
        Werner Levi. . . Minneapolis, University of Minnesota
        press: London, G. Cumberlege, Oxford University Press,
        1947.
        E183. 8. A8L4   327. 730994   47-1789

977.   Levien, Harold. Vietnam, myth and reality. [Rose Bay,
        Sydney, The author, 766 New South Head Road, 1967]
        DS557. A6L44 1967   959. 7'04   68-140044

978.   Levy, Roger. French Interests and Policies in the Far
        East. New York, Institute of Pacific Relations, 1941.
        DS518. 2. L4   327. 44095   41-23698

979. Lidman, Sara 1923-   Samtal i Hanoi. Stockholm, Bonnier,
      1966.
      DS557. A7L5   67-76938

980. Lieban, Richard Warren. Cebuano sorcery; malign magic in
      the Philippines [by] Richard W. Lieban. Berkeley, Uni-
      versity of California Press, 1967.
      GN475. 9. L5   133. 4'09'9145   67-10461

981. Liem, Nguyen Dang. Vietnamese Pronunciation. University
      of Hawaii Press, 1970.

982. Lifton, Robert Jay, 1926-   comp. America and the Asian
      revolutions. [Chicago] Aldine Publishing Company [1970]
      DS557. A63L5   959. 7'04   76-96799

983. Lim, Chong-Yah. Economic development of modern Malaya.
      Kuala Lumpur, London, New York [etc.] Oxford University
      Press, 1967 [i. e. 1968]
      HC445. 5. L45   330. 9595   68-124330

984. Limbourg, Michel. L'economie actuelle du Viet-Nam demo-
      cratique. Hanoi, Editions en langues etrangeres, 1956.
      HC443. V5L45   61-37302

985. _____ . Ekonomike Demokraticheskoi Respubliki V'etnam,
      (The Economy of Vietnamese Democratic Republic). (In
      Russian, translated from French). Moscow, 1957.
      HC443. V5L5

986. Lindholm, Richard Wadsworth, 1914-   Economic develop-
      ment policy with emphasis on Viet-Nam [by] R. W. Lind-
      holm [Eugene] School of Business Administration [University
      of Oregon, 1964]
      HD82. L48   338. 9   64-64520

987. _____ . , ed. Viet-Nam: the first five years; an interna-
      tional symposium. Edited and introduced by Richard W.
      Lindholm. [East Lansing] Michigan State University Press,
      1959.
      DS557. A6L5   959. 7   59-6631

988. Linton, Ralph and Wingert, Paul Stover. Arts of the South
      seas. New York, Simon and Schuster, 1946.
      N7410. L5   709. 9   46-25247

989. Liska, George. War and order; reflections on Vietnam and
      history. Baltimore, Johns Hopkins Press [c. 1968]
      E744. L58   327. 73   68-9697

990. Liss, Howard. The mighty Mekong. Illus. with photos.
      [1st ed.] New York, Hawthorn [1967]
      DS508. 2. L49   915. 9/03   67-24001

991.   Little, David. American foreign policy & moral rhetoric;
        the example of Vietnam. [New York] Council on Religion
        and International Affairs [1969]
        E744. L59   327. 73   74-77373

992.   Lommel, Andreas. Kunst der Sudsee. München, Prestel-
        Verlag, 1952.
        N7410. L6   61-38361

993.   London University. Linguistic Comparisons in South East
        Asia and the Pacific. London, University of London Publi-
        cation, 1963.
        PL492. L53   67-263

994.   _____. School of Oriental and African Studies. Hand-
        book of oriental history. Ed. by C. H. Philips. London,
        Offices of the Royal Historical Society, 1951.
        DS33. 1. L6   950. 02   51-4902

995.   _____. School of Oriental and African Studies. His-
        torical writing on the peoples of Asia. New York, Oxford
        University Press, 1961-62.
        DS32. 5. L6   950. 072   61-4093 rev.

996.   Loridan, Marceline. 17 [i. e. Dix septieme] parallele, la
        guerre du peuple (deux mois sous la terre) [par] Marceline
        Loridan et Joris Ivens. Paris, les Editeurs francais reunis,
        1968.
        DS557. A69L6   959. 7'04   68-112549

997.   Lovy, Andrew. Vietnam Diary: October Nineteen Sixty-
        Seven to July Nineteen Sixty-Eight. Exposition Press, Inc.,
        1970.

998.   Lowenfels, Walter, ed. Where Is Vietnam: American Poets
        Respond. Doubleday, 1967.
        DS557. A61L6   811'. 0080'3   67-11802

999.   _____. Where Is Vietnam: American Poets Re-
        spond. Peter Smith,   1971.

1000.   Lowenstein, James G. Vietnam: December 1969 by James
        G. Lowenstein and Richard M. Moose. A staff report pre-
        pared for the use of the Committee on Foreign Relations,
        United States Senate. Washington, U. S. Government Print-
        ing Office, 1970.
        DS557. A6L67   959. 7'04   73-606022

1001.   Lucas, Jim Griffing, 1914-   Dateline: Viet Nam. New
        York, Award House [dist. Crown, c.] 1966.
        DS557. A6L8   959. 704   66-25709

1002.   _____. Dateline: Vietnam. Rev. ed. Universal
        Pub. and Dist. Corp., 1968.

1003.   Luce, Don. Viet Nam; the unheard voices, by Don Luce and
         John Sommer. Foreword by Edward M. Kennedy. Ithaca,
         [N. Y.] Cornell University Press [1969]
         DS557. A69L8   959. 7'04   69-18361

1004.   Lumb, R. D. The law of the sea and Australian off-shore
         areas [by] R. D. Lumb. [St. Lucia, Brisbane, University
         of Queensland Press, 1966]
         FL957L   347. 75   66-67757

1005.   Luther, Hans Ulrich. Der Vietnamkonflikt. Darstellung
         und Dokumentation. [Graphiken: Ilse Eckart] Berlin,
         Colloquium Verlag [1969]
         DS557. A6L83   70-465222

1006.   Luu-quy-Ky. Escalation war and songs about peace.
         Hanoi, Foreign Languages Publishing House, 1965.
         DS557. A6L85   S A 65-10480

1007.   _____. Vietnamese Problem. China Books and Peri-
         odicals. 1967.

1008.   _____. The Vietnamese problem. Hanoi, Foreign Lan-
         guages Publishing House, 1967.
         DS557. A6L86   959. 7'04   68-6380

1009.   Lynd, Alice. We won't go; personal accounts of war ob-
         jectors. Boston, Beacon Press [1968]
         DS557. A68L9   959. 7'04   68-24371

1010.   Lynd, Staughton. The other side, by Staughton Lynd,
         Thomas Hayden. [New York] New American Library
         [1967, c. 1966]
         DS557. A692L9   959. 704   67-15194

1011.   Lyons, Daniel S. Vietnam Crisis. Twin Circle Publish-
         ing Company, 1967.

                                    M

1012.   Mackay, Ian. Australians in Vietnam. [Adelaide] Rigby
         [1968]
         DS557. A64A84   959. 7'04   67-22944

1013.   Macmillan, David S. Scotland and Australia, 1788-1850:
         emigrations, commerce and investment [by] David S.
         Macmillan. Oxford, Clarendon Press, 1967.
         JV9124. M33   325. 241'0994   67-102004

1014.   Madame Nhu and dictatorship in South Vietnam. (In Viet-
         namese). Saigon, 1964.

1015.   Mahajani, Usha. The role of Indian minorities in Burma

and Malaya. New York, Institute of Pacific Relations,
1960.
DS595. M25   325. 25409591   60-4421

1016.   Mai, Lang, pseud. Chan tou chung ti hsin Yuch-nan, (New
Vietnam in Struggle), (In Chinese). 1948.
DS557. A7M3

1017.   Mailer, Norman. The armies of the night; history as a
novel, the novel as history. [New York] New American
Library [1968]
PS3525. A4152A8   818'. 5'403   68-23406

1018.   Mai-the-Chau. Freedom movement in Viet-Nam. New
Delhi, Indian Council of World Affairs [1947?]
DS557. A5M22   S A 67-487

1019.   Maiwald, Helga. Vietnam. Informationen uber ein ak-
tuelles Weltproblem. (Mit 3 Karten) Berlin, Dietz 1966.
DS557. A6M24   959. 704   66-69157

1020.   Malaysia. Official yearbook. v. 1- 1960?- Kuala
Lumpur.
DS591. M35

1021.   Malcolm, George Arthur. The commonwealth of the
Philippines. New York, Appleton-Century, 1936.
DS655. M34   919. 14   36-8737

1022.   Mali, Tidiane, 1929- Viet-Nam muertri . . . [par le]
Prince Tidiane de Mali . . . Rodez, Subervie, 1967.
DS557. A6M255   959. 7'04   68-72299

1023.   Malinowski, Bronislaw. Argonauts of the western Pacific;
an account of native enterprise and adventure in the
archipelagoes of Melanesian New Guinea. New York,
Dutton, 1922.
GN671. N5M3   22-16057

1024.   Maneli, Mieczyslaw. War of the Vanquished: A Polish
Diplomat in Vietnam. Harper & Row Publishers, Inc.,
1971.

1025.   Mangiolardo, Michael. My days in Vietnam. Illus. with
photos by the author. New York, Vantage [1969]
959. 7'04

1026.   Manning, Robert & Janeway, Michael. Who We Are:
An Atlantic Chronicle of the United States & Vietnam
1966-1969. Little, 1969.
DS557. A68M4   301. 15'4   70-81891

1027.   Mansfield, Michael Joseph, 1903- Vietnam and the Paris

negotiations. The situation in Czechoslovakia and U. S.
forces in Europe. Czechoslovakia: confrontation and
crisis. Reports of Mike Mansfield to the Committee on
Foreign Relations, United States Senate. Washington,
U. S. Government Printing Office, 1968.
DB215. 6. M35   943. 7'04   68-67099

1028.   Marais, Johannes Stephanus. The colonisation of New Zea-
          land. London, Oxford University, 1927.
          DU420. M3   28-9682

1029.   Maretzki, Hans. Was suchen die USA in Vietnam? Berlin,
          Staatsverlag der Deutschen Demokratischen Republik, 1967.
          DS557. A63M3   70-384722

1030.   Markiewicz, Stanislaw. Miedzy Waszyngtonem, Rzymem i
          Sajgonem. [Wyd. 1. Warszawa] Ludowa Spoldzielnia
          Wydawnicza [1965]
          DS557. A6M3   65-79868

1031.   Marks, Richard E., 1946-1966. The letters of Pfc.
          Richard E. Marks, USMC. [1st ed.] Philadelphia,
          Lippincott [1967]
          DS557. A69M3   959. 7'04   66-25410

1032.   Marr, David G. Vietnamese anticolonialism, 1885-1925 by
          David G. Marr. Berkeley, University of California Press,
          1971.
          DS557. A5M228 1971 959. 7'03   75-129611

1033.   _____. Vietnamese anti-colonialism, 1885-1925. Uni-
          versity of California Press, 1972.

1034.   Marshall, Samuel Lyman Atwood, 1900- Ambush; the
          Battle of Dau Tieng, also called the battle of Dong Minh
          Chau, War Zone C, Operation Attleboro, and other deadfalls
          in South Vietnam, by S. L. A. Marshall. Including sket-
          ches by the author. [1st ed.] New York, Cowles Book
          Company [1969]
          DS557. A6M34   959. 7'04   69-19505

1035.   _____. Battles in the monsoon; campaigning in the
          Central Highlands, Vietnam, summer 1966, by S. L. A.
          Marshall. With maps and sketches by Jac Purdon. New
          York, W. Morrow, 1967.
          DS557. A6M35   959. 7'04   67-15157

1036.   _____. Bird; the Christmastide battle, by S. L. A.
          Marshall, assisted by David H. Hackworth. Including
          sketches by the author. [1st ed. New York] Cowles [c. 1968]
          DS557. A62B55   959. 7'04   68-31131

1037.   _____. Fields of Bamboo: Dongtre, Trung Luong &

Hoa Hoi, Three Battles Just Beyond the South China Sea. Dial, 1971.
DS557. A6M355   959. 7'04'34   77-131183

1038. _____. West to Cambodia, by S. L. A. Marshall. Including sketches by the author. [1st ed. New York] Cowles [c. 1968]
DS557. A6M36   959. 704   68-31132

1039. Masson, Andre. Histoire du Vietnam. Paris, Presses Universitaires de France, 1960.

1040. Masson, Andre, 1900-   Histoire du Vietnam . . . 3 edition mise a jour. Paris, Presses universitaires de France, 1967.
DS557. A5M243 1967 959. 7   67-114430

1041. Mate, Gyorgy. Fenyek a dzsungelben. Budapest [Tancsics Konyvkiado] 1964.
DS557. A72M3   68-49763

1042. Mathews, Russell L. Public Investment in Australia: a study of Australian public authority investment and development [by] Russell Mathews. Melbourne, Canberra [etc.] Cheshire [1967]
HC605. M36   338. 994   66-25778

1043. Matthews, John Pengwerne. Tradition in exile; a comparative study of social influences on the development of Australian and Canadian poetry in the nineteenth century. Toronto, University of Toronto, 1962.
PR9469. M3   62-6611

1044. Maxwell-Lefroy, Cecil. The land and people of Burma. London, A. & C. Black; New York, Macmillan [1965, c. 1963]
DS485. B81M36   915. 91   65-10668

1045. Mayer, Henry, 1919-   The press in Australia. [Melbourne] Lansdowne Press [1964]
PN5510. M3   079. 94   64-6686

1046. Mazaev, Al'bert Georgievich. Gosudarstvennyi stroi Demokraticheskoi Respubliki V'etnam, (State Organization of the Democratic Republic of Vietnam). (In Russian). Moscow, 1963.
JQ815. M3 1963

1047. McAleavy, Henry. Black flags in Vietnam; the story of a Chinese intervention, by John [i. e. Henry] McAleavy. [1st American ed.] New York, Macmillan [1968]
DS557. A5M15 1968   327. 51'0597   68-17518

1048.   _____. Black flags in Vietnam: the story of a Chinese
intervention. London, Allen & Unwin, 1968.
DS557. A5M15 1968b   959'. 703   68-111111

1049.   McAlister, John T.   1936-   Viet Nam; the origins of
revolution [by] John T. McAlister, Jr. [1st ed. Princeton, N. J.] Published for the Center of International
Studies, Princeton University [by] Knopf, New York, 1969.
DS557. A5M17 1969   959. 7   69-10690

1050.   _____. Vietnam: The Origins of Revolution.   Doubleday & Company, Inc. , 1971.
A761   959. 7

1051.   _____. The Vietnamese and their revolution, by John
T. McAlister, Jr. , and Paul Mus. [1st ed.] New York,
Harper & Row, 1970.
DS557. A5M18 1970b   320. 9'597   77-10653

1052.   McCarthy, Joseph E.   Illusion of power; American policy
toward Viet-Nam, 1954-1966, by Joseph E. McCarthy.
New York, Carlton Press [1967]
E183. 8. V5M3   327. 597'073   68-461

1053.   McCarthy, Mary Therese, 1912-   Hanoi, by Mary Mc-
Carthy. Harmondsworth, Penguin, 1969.
DS557. A72M29 1969   915. 97   76-490916

1054.   _____. Hanoi [by] Mary McCarthy. London, Weiden-
feld & Nicolson, 1968.
DS557. A72M29 1968b   915. 97   79-368178

1055.   _____. Hanoi [by] Mary McCarthy. [1st ed.] New
York, Harcourt, Brace & World [1968]
DS557. A72M29   915. 97   68-54313

1056.   _____. Vietnam [by] Mary McCarthy. [1st ed.] New
York, Harcourt, Brace & World [1967]
DS557. A68M3   959. 7'04   67-28041

1057.   _____. Vietnam--Report. [Von] Mary McCarthy.
Deutsche Ubersetzung von Klaus Harpprecht. (München,
Zurich Drömer Knaur (1967))
DS557. A68M35   959. 7'04   68-109692

1058.   McClymont, W. G.   The exploration of New Zealand.
2d ed. London, Oxford University Press, 1959.
DU420. M15   993. 1   59-3248

1059.   McCormick, Eric Hall.   New Zealand literature, a survey.
London, Oxford University, 1959.
PR9606. M3   820. 9   59-2038

1060.   McGarvey, Patrick J., comp. Visions of victory: selected
         Vietnamese Communist military writings, 1964-1968.
         Analytical introduction by Patrick J. McGarvey. Stanford,
         California, Hoover Instn. on War, Revolution & Peace,
         Stanford University [1969]
         DS557. A6M22   959. 7'04   69-18374

1061.   McGee, Gale W. The responsibilities of world power, by
         Gale W. McGee. Washington, National Press [1968]
         E183. 8. V5M33   327. 73'0597   68-19118

1062.   McGrady, Mike. A dove in Vietnam. New York, Funk &
         Wagnalls [1968]
         DS557. A6M23   959'. 704   68-23422

1063.   McGregor, Craig. Profile of Australia. Chicago, H.
         Regnery Company [1967, c. 1966]
         DU107. M14 1967   919. 4'03'5   67-14661

1064.   McIntyre, Peter. Peter McIntyre's New Zealand. Welling-
         ton, A. H. & A. W. Reed [1965, c. 1964]
         ND1108. M25A46   65-83473

1065.   McKie, Ronald Cecil Hamlyn. The emergence of Malaysia.
         New York, Harcourt, Brace & World, 1963.
         DS597. M3   991   63-13504

1066.   McLeod, Alan Lindsey, 1928-   The pattern of New Zea-
         land culture. Edited by A. L. McLeod. Ithaca, N. Y.
         Cornell University Press [1968]
         DU418. M3   919. 31'03'3   68-9751

1067.   McLeod, John. The voyage of the Alceste to the Ryukyus
         and Southeast Asia. Rutland, Vermont, Tuttle, 1963.
         DS507. M17   910. 45   63-22228

1068.   McLintock, Alexander H. A descriptive atlas of New Zea-
         land. Wellington, R. E. Owen, Government printer, 1959.
         G2795. M3 1959   Map 60--250

1069.   McNamara, Robert S. 1916-   United States policy in
         Viet-Nam [by Robert S. McNamara. Washington] Bureau
         of Public Affairs, Department of State [1964]
         HF1455. A315 no. 6 1964   64-61852 rev.

1070.   McNelly, Theodore. Sources in Modern East Asian History
         and Politics. New York, Appleton-Century-Crofts, 1967.
         DS511. M27   950. 4   67-18502

1071.   McVey, Ruth Thomas, ed. Indonesia [by] Herbert Feith
         [and others] New Haven, Southeast Asia studies, Yale
         University, by arrangement with HRAF Press [1963]
         DS615. M3   919. 1   62-21842

1072.   Mead, Margaret.   From the South seas; studies of adolescence
        and sex in primitive societies.   New York, Morrow, 1939.
        GN482. M4   572. 995   39-27925

1073.   Mead, Sidney M.   The art of taaniko weaving: a study of its
        cultural context, technique, style, and development, by Sid-
        ney M. Mead.   Wellington, Auckland [etc.] Reed [1968]
        TT848. M39   746. 1   70-363245

1074.   Mecklin, John.   Mission in torment; an intimate account of
        the U. S. role in Vietnam. [1st ed.] Garden City, N. Y.,
        Doubleday, 1965.
        DS557. A6M4   327. 730597   65-10632

1075.   Meeker, Leonard C.   The legality of U. S. participation in
        the defense of Viet Nam.   [Prepared by Leonard C. Meeker.
        Washington] Department of State [Office of Media Services,
        Bureau of Public Affairs; for sale by the Superintendent of
        Documents, Government Printing Office, 1966]
        JX4071. M4   66-61076

1076.   Meeker, Oden.   The little world of Laos.   With a picture
        essay by Homer Page.   New York, Scribner [1959]
        DS557. L2M4   915. 94   59-6175

1077.   Meerssche, Paul van de.   Vrede in Vietnam?   Leuven,
        Davidsfonds [1967]
        DS557. A6M42   320. 9'597   68-71557

1078.   Mekong Documentation Centre.   Viet-Nam: a reading list.
        Bangkok, United Nations Economic Commission for Asia and
        the Far East, 1966.
        Z3228. V5M4   016. 91597   70-8994

1079.   Melin, Karin, 1927-   Vietnamkonflikten i svensk opinion,
        1954-1968. Bibliografi.   Stockholm, Raben & Sjogren, 1969.
        Z3228. V5M43   79-460831

1080.   Mende, Tibor.   South-east Asia between two worlds. London,
        Turnstile, 1955.
        DS518. 1. M45   991   55-27955

1081.   Mensel, Paul.   Moral Argument & the War in Vietnam. Aurora
        Publications, 1971.
        DS557. A6M435   172'. 4   79-143721

1082.   Menzies, Sir Robert Gordon, 1894-   Vietnam; exchange of
        letters between the Prime Minister, the Rt. Hon. Sir Robert
        Menzies, and the Rt. Rev. J. S. Moyes, and certain arch-
        bishops and bishops. [Canberra, Prime Minister's Depart-
        ment, 1965]
        DS557. A692M4   67-1063

1083.   Mertel, Kenneth D. 1924- Year of the horse--Vietnam; 1st
        Air Cavalry in the highlands, by Kenneth D. Mertel. [1st ed.]
        New York, Exposition Press [1968]
        DS557.A6M44   959.7'04   68-24880

1084.   Merton Council for Peace in Vietnam. The truth about Vietnam.
        London, Merton Council for Peace in Vietnam [1967]
        DS557.A6M45   959.7   67-99164

1085.   Merzliakov, Nikolai Semenovich. Demokraticheskaia Respub-
        lika V'etnam, (Democratic Republic of Vietnam). (In Russian).
        Moscow, 1961.
        JQ815.M4 1961

1086.   Meyerson, Harvey. Vinh Long. With an introduction by
        Congressman John V. Tunney. Illustrated with maps by Adam
        Nakamura. Boston, Houghton Mifflin, 1970.
        DS557.A62V5 1970   959.7'04   70-91063

1087.   Mi Ki Khaing, Daw. Burmese Family. Illustrated by E. G. N.
        Kinch. [1st American ed.] Bloomington, Indiana University
        Press [1962]
        DS485.B84M5 1962   915.91   62-8981

1088.   Michigan. State University, East Lansing. Vietnam Advisory
        Group, Saigon. Bibliography of periodicals published in Viet-
        nam. Saigon, 1962.
        Z6958.V5M5   S A 62-1214 rev.

1089.   _____. Final report, covering activities of the Michigan
        State University, Vietnam Advisory Group, for the period May
        20, 1955-June 30, 1962. Saigon, 1962.
        HC443.V5M53   69-63989

1090.   _____. Report. 1st- August 1955- Saigon.
        HC443.V5M5   S A 62-612 rev.

1091.   _____. Report on the organization of the Department of
        Agriculture [Department of Education, Department of Land
        Registration and Agrarian Reform, Department of Information
        and Youth and Sports, Department of National Economy and
        the Special Commissariat for Civic Action. Saigon?] 1956-57.
        JQ831.M5   354.597   59-63338 rev.

1092.   _____. Reports and documents. Saigon, 1960.
        Z7165.V5M5   016.354597   60-63663 rev.

1093.   _____. Review of recommendations of the reorganization
        of the Department of Land Registration and Agrarian Reform.
        [Saigon?] 1957.
        HD2080.V5M5   333.3409597   59-63329 rev.

1094.   _____. Field Administration Division. Research report,

field study of Refugee Commission. Ralph Smuckler, research coordinator; Walter W. Mode, chief of Field Administration Project; Frederic R. Wickert, in-service training coordinator. [East Lansing?] 1955.
HV640.5.V5M5   361.53   59-63330 rev.

1095.   Michigan. State University, East Lansing. Vietnam Project.
         Bibliography of periodicals published in Viet Nam, prepared
         by Nguyen Xuan Dao, special project assistant, Research
         Section, and Richard K. Gardner, library advisor. East
         Lansing, 1958.
         Z6958.V5M54   016.05   59-63325 rev.

1096.   _____. Recent articles on Vietnam: an annotated bibli-
         ography. Compiled by Oral E. Parks and Milan Jan Reban,
         under the general supervision of Frank B. Cliffe, Jr. [East
         Lansing?] 1958.
         Z3226.M5   016.9597   59-63324 rev.

1097.   _____. What to read on Vietnam; a selected annotated bib-
         liography. New York, Institute of Pacific Relations, 1959.
         Z3228.V5M5 1959   016.9597   59-1234 rev.

1098.   Michigan. State University of Agriculture and Applied Sci-
         ence, East Lansing. Vietnam Advisory Group, Saigon. Re-
         view of recommendations on the reorganization of the De-
         partment of Agriculture. Saigon, 1957.
         S471.V47M5   354.5970681   59-63327

1099.   Michigan. University. Survey Research Center. The
         American public's view of U. S. policy toward China; a
         report prepared for the Council on Foreign Relations. New
         York, Council on Foreign Relations [1964]
         E183.8.C5M48   65-3193

1100.   Milc, Stanislaw. Dlaczego wojna? [Wyd. 1.] Warszawa,
         Iskry, 1968.
         DS557.A63M48   77-377571

1101.   Miller, Edmund Morris. Australian literature, a bibliogra-
         phy to 1938, extended to 1950. Rev. ed. Sydney, Angus &
         Robertson, 1956.
         Z4021.M5   A57-6327

1102.   Miller, Harold Gladstone. New Zealand. New York, Hutchin-
         son's University Library, 1960.
         DU420.M55   993.1   51-3103

1103.   _____. Race conflict in New Zealand, 1814-1865 [by]
         Harold Miller. Auckland, Blackwood & J. Paul, 1966.
         DU423.M5   993.101   66-9283

1104.   Miller, Harry, journalist. Prince and Premier; a biography

of Tunku Abdul Rahman Putra Al-Haj, first Prime Minister
of the Federation of Malaya. London, Harrap, 1959.
DS595.6.A2M5   923.2595   59-4954

1105.   _____. A short history of Malaysia. New York,
Praeger [1966, c.1965]
DS596.M52   959.5   66-10946

1106.   Miller, John Donald Bruce. Australian government and
politics: an introductory survey. 2d ed. London, Duck-
worth, 1961.
JQ4018.M5   342.94   59-3147

1107.   Miller, John Owen. Early Victorian New Zealand; a study
of racial tension and social attitudes, 1839-1852. New York,
Oxford University Press, 1958.
DU420.M56   993.1   58-3820

1108.   Mills, Lennox Algernon. British Malaya, 1824-67, by L. A.
Mills. Introductory chapter by D. K. Bassett. Bibliography
by C. M. Turnbull. Kuala Lumpur, London, New York,
Oxford University Press, 1966 [i.e. 1968]
DS592.M5 1966   959.5'1   68-141045

1109.   _____. British Malaya, 1824-1867. Singapore,
Methodist Publishing House, 1925.
DS592.M5   28-14083

1110.   _____. British rule in eastern Asia; a study of con-
temporary government and economic development in British
Malaya and Hong Kong. London, Oxford University, 1942.
HC497.M3M5   A42-5310

1111.   _____. Malaya: a political and economic appraisal.
Minneapolis, University of Minnesota, 1958.
DS596.M53   959.5   58-8132

1112.   Milne, Robert Stephen. Political parties in New Zealand,
by R. S. Milne. Oxford, Clarendon Press, 1966.
JQ5898.A1M5   329.9931   66-70798

1113.   Mintz, Jeanne S. Indonesia; a profile. Drawings by Hans
Guggenheim. Map by Dorothy De Fontaine. Princeton,
N. J., Van Nostrand [1961]
DS615.M5   919.1   61-16174

1114.   Miroshnychenko, Vitalii Heorhiiovych. Dva Roki u V'etnami;
notatki inzhenera, (Two Years in Vietnam; observations of
an Engineer). (In Ukrainian). Kiev, 1959.
DS557.A7M5

1115.   Mirskii, Zinovii IAkovlevich. Burliat vody Mekonga Moskva,
(Waters of Mekong are Stormy). (In Russian). Moscow, 1964.
DS557.A6M5

116   Vietnam

1116.   Mkhitarian, Suren Artemovich. Bor'ba narodov V'etnama,
         Laosa i Kambodzhi za natsional'nuiu nezavisimost', (The
         Struggle of Vietnamese people, Laos and Cambodia for
         National Independence). (In Russian). Moscow, 1954.
         DS557.V5M5

1117.   _____. Bor'ba v'etnamskogo naroda za natsional'nuiu
         nezavisimost', demokratiiu i mir (1945-1955). (Struggle of
         the Vietnamese People for the National Independence,
         Democracy and Peace 1945-1955). (In Russian). Moscow,
         1957.
         DS557.A7M55

1118.   Mkhitarian, Tat'iana Tikhonovna. Fonetika V'etnamskogo
         iazyka, (The phonetics of Vietnamese Language). (In Russian).
         Moscow, 1959.
         PL4379.M55

1119.   Mladenovic, Bora. Vijetnamska rapsodija. Beograd,
         Knjizevni klub RU "Duro Salaj, " 1967.
         PG1419.23.L3V5   68-99983

1120.   Mode, Walter W. Recommendations concerning the Depart-
         ment of Interior, the regions and provinces [by] Walter W.
         Mode, chief, Field Administration Project. Saigon, Michigan
         State University, Vietnam Advisory Team, 1956.
         JQ850.I5M6   352.0597   59-63309

1121.   _____. Review of recommendations concerning proposed
         field organization of the Commissariat for Refugees of
         September 20, 1955 [by] Walter W. Mode [and] Roland Haney.
         Saigon, Michigan State University, Vietnam Advisory Team,
         1956.
         HN700.V5M6   361.53   59-63318

1122.   Moeser, Robert D. U. S. Navy: Vietnam, photography by
         Robert D. Moeser. Annapolis, Maryland, United States
         Naval Institute, 1969.
         DS557.A61M58   959.7'04   71-104004

1123.   Mohn, Albert Henrik. Vietnam. Oslo, Gyldendal, 1965.
         DS557.A6M55   66-7275

1124.   Mohring, Hans. Vietnamesische Malerei. [1. Aufl. Leipzig,
         E. A. Seemann, 1963]
         ND1014.M6   65-78215

1125.   Moinet, Bernard. Opium rouge. Paris, Editions France-
         Empire [1965?]
         PQ2673.03606   66-74737

1126.   Molina, Enrique. Monzon Napalm; ocho poemas. Dibujo de
         Bute. Buenos Aires, Ediciones-Sunda, 1968.
         PQ7797.M534M6   68-132542

1127.   Moller, Per. Indokina efter 1954. Stockholm [Raben &
         Sjogren] 1961.
         DS557.A7M57   65-52030

1128.   Monigold, Glenn W., comp. Folk tales from Vietnam. With
         illustrations by Jeanyee Wong. Mount Vernon, N. Y., Peter
         Pauper Press [1964]
         PZ8.1.M76Fo   64-3909

1129.   Monroe, Malcolm, 1919- The means is the end in Vietnam.
         White Plains, N. Y., Murlagan Press [1968]
         DS557.A63M6   959.7'04   68-2817

1130.   Montagu, Ashley. Coming into being among the Australian
         aborigines; a study of the procreative beliefs of the native
         tribes of Australia. London, Routledge, 1937.
         GN479.M65   572.994   38-17469

1131.   Montagu, Hon. Ivor Goldsmid Samuel, 1904- Vietnam:
         stop America's criminal war, by Ivor Montagu. London,
         Communist Party of Great Britain [1967]
         DS557.A692M6   959.7'04   67-77661

1132.   Montgomery, John Dickey, 1920- Cases in Vietnamese ad-
         ministration [by] John D. Montgomery and the NIA Case
         Development Seminar. [Vietnam, 196-?]
         JQ831.M58   354.597   S A 65-4244

1133.   _____. The politics of foreign aid; American experience
         in Southeast Asia. New York, Published for the Council on
         Foreign Relations by Praeger, 1962.
         HC60.M63   338.9173059   62-16827

1134.   _____. Truong hop hanh chanh Viet Nam [cua] John D.
         Montgomery va Ban Nghien Cuu Phat trien Truong hop cua
         HVQGHC. Saigon, Dai Hoc Duong Tieu Bang Michigan, Phai
         Doan Co Van Tai Viet Nam, 1959.
         JQ831.M6   60-4927

1135.   Moore, Gene D. The killing at Ngo Tho; a novel by Gene
         D. Moore. New York, Norton, 1967.
         PZ4.M8222Ki   67-12445

1136.   Moore, Robert Lowell. The green berets, by Robin Moore.
         New York, Crown Publishers [1965]
         DS557.A6M6   65-15849

1137.   Moore, Robert Lowell. Os boinas verdes: episodios da
         guerra no Vietna, por Robin Moore. Trad. de Jose B.
         Mari. [S. Paulo], Flamboyant [1967]
         PS3563.064G717   68-109982

1138.   Moore, Withers McAlister. Navy chaplains in Vietnam,

1954-1964, by Withers M. Moore. [Washington, Chief of
Chaplains, Bureau of Naval Personnel, 1968]
DS557.A68M6   959.7'04   68-62114

1139.   Moormann, Frank R. Rapport bi-annuel sur l'etude de sol
        au Viet-Nam, par Frank Moormann. Saigon [Bibliotheque
        agronomique] 1959.
        S599.V46M6   S A 65-9316

1140.   Morgenthau, Hans Joachim. Vietnam and the United States,
        Washington, (D.C.) Public Affairs Press, 1965.
        E183.8.V5M6   327.597073   65-28164

1141.   Morrell, William Parket and Hall, David Oswald William.
        A history of New Zealand life. Christchurch, N. Z.,
        Whitcombe & Tombs, 1958.
        DU420.M59   993.1   57-39334

1142.   Morris, Marjorie. And/or; antonyms for our age [by]
        Marjorie Morris, Don Sauers. [1st ed.] New York, Harper
        [1967]
        DS557.A61M6   959.7'04'0222   67-24908

1143.   Morrison, Charles R. Flame in the Icebox. Exposition
        Press Inc., 1968.

1144.   Morrison, Hedda Hammer. Sarawak. London, Macgibbon &
        Kee, 1957.
                                                       A59-1737

1145.   Moscow. Institut mezhdunarodnykh otnoshenii. Piatnadstat'
        let demokraticheskoi Respublika V'etnam, (Fifteen Years of
        the Democratic Republic of Vietnam). (In Russian). Mos-
        cow, 1960.
        DS557.A7M6

1146.   Mouhot, Henry, 1826-1861. Diary: travels in the central
        parts of Siam, Cambodia, and Laos during the years 1858-61.
        Abridged, ed. by Christopher Pym. Kuala Lumpur, New York,
        Oxford, 1966.
        DS524.M7213 1966   915.9   SA66-7431

1147.   Muller, Helmut P. Grune Holle Vietnam. Ein Augenzeugen-
        bericht. [Von] Helmut P. Muller. (Bad Honnef) Osang
        Verlag (1967)
        DS557.A6M76   68-93734

1148.   Mulligan, Hugh A., 1925- No place to die; the agony of
        Viet Nam, by Hugh A. Mulligan. Photos by Horst Faas
        [and others] New York, Morrow, 1967.
        DS557.A6M78 1967   959.7'04   67-20749

1149.   Mulling, Jay. Terror in Viet Nam. Princeton, (N. J.), Van

Nostrand, 1966.
DS557.A6M26   320.9597   66-7632

1150.   Munson, Glenn, ed. Letters from Viet Nam, edited by
        Glenn Munson. Designed by Jacques Chazaud. [New York]
        Parallax Publishing Company [c.1966]
        DS557.A69M8   959.704   67-893

1151.   Muramatsu, Katsu, 1906- Viet-Nam co'ban ngu (Elementary
        Vietnamese) (In Japanese), Tokyo, 1957.

1152.   Murdoch, Walter, comp. A book of Australian and New
        Zealand verse. London, Oxford University, 1949.
        PR9551.M   821.082   A51-8930

1153.   Murti, Bhaskarla Surya Narayana. Vietnam divided; the un-
        finished struggle. New York, Asia Publisher [dist. Tap-
        linger, c.1964]
        DS557.A6M8   959.7   65-526

1154.   _____. Vietnam: the cycle of peace; illusions and reali-
        ties, by B. S. N. Murti. New Delhi, Indian Society of
        International Law [c.1968]
        JX1573.M87   959.7'04   74-903187

1155.   Mus, Paul. Viet-Nam. Paris, Editions du
        Seuil, 1952.
        DS557.A5M77   54-31152

1156.   Myrdal, Gunnar, 1898- USA och Vietnamkriget. Stock-
        holm, Vietnam-press (box 681) 1967.
        DS557.A6M9   959.7'04   68-71439

                              N

1157.   Nach, James. Malaysia and Singapore in pictures. [Rev.
        ed.] New York, Sterling [1966]
        DS592.N3 1966   915.95045   66-6086

1158.   Napalkov, Sergei Nikolaevich. Molodist' vil'noho Vietnamu,
        (Youth of the Free Vietnam). (In Ukrainian). Kiev, 1962.
        DS557.A7N28

1159.   _____. Svobodnyi V'etnam vstrechaet druzei, (The Free
        Vietnam is meeting friends). (In Russian). Moscow, 1960.
        DS557.A7N3

1160.   Narod-geroi, (Heroic People). (In Russian). Hanoi, 1962.
        DS557.A5N27

1161.   National Catholic Welfare Conference. Terror in Vietnam;
        a record of another broken pledge. Washington [1954?]
        DS550.N3   959.7   57-32691

1162.   National Congress of Denunciation of Communist Subversive
         Activities. 2d, Saigon, May, 1956. Achievements of the
         campaign of denunciation of communist subversive activities,
         first phase; published on the occasion of the Second National
         Congress of Anti-Communist Denunciation, May, 1956.
         [Saigon? 1956?]
         DS557.A5N295 1956   64-42050

1163.   National Council of Churches in New Zealand. To church
         people re Vietnam. [Christchurch, 1967]
         DS557.A68N38   301.15'4   68-117314

1164.   National Geographic Society, Washington, D. C. Carto-
         graphic Division. Viet Nam, Cambodia, Laos, and Thailand.
         Wellman Chamberlin, chief cartographer, Athos D. Grazzini,
         associate chief cartographer. Washington, 1967.
         G8010.N3 1967   Map 67-399

1165.   National Symposium on Water Resources, Use and Manage-
         ment, Australian Academy of Science, 1963. Water re-
         sources, use and management; proceedings of a symposium
         held at Canberra by the Australian Academy of Science, 9-
         13 September 1963. [Victoria] Melbourne University Press;
         New York, Cambridge University Press [1964]
         TD321.A1N3 1963   628.10994   64-57187

1166.   Navarre, Henri. Agonie de l'Indochine, 1953-54.   Paris,
         Plon, 1958.
         DS550.N34   57-48723

1167.   Naville, Pierre. La guerre du Viet-Nam. Paris, Revue
         internationale, 1949.
                                                              A 50-941

1168.   Ness, Gayl D. Bureaucracy and rural development in
         Malaysia; a study of complex organizations in stimulating
         economic development in new states [by] Gayl D. Ness.
         Berkeley, University of California Press, 1967.
         HC445.5.N4   338.9595   67-14115

1169.   Netherlands (Kingdom, 1815-) Regeeringsvoorlichtings-
         dienst, New York. The political events in the Republic of
         Indonesia; a review of the developments in the Indonesian
         Republic (Java and Sumatra) since the Japanese surrender.
         Together with statements by the Netherlands and Netherlands
         Indies Governments and complete text of the Linggadjati
         Agreement. New York, Netherlands Information Bureau
         [1947]
         DS644.A5 1947   991   50-55326

1170.   Neumann, Erich Peter. Eindrucke einer Reise nach Viet-
         nam. Bonn, Deutsche Atlantische Gesellschaft, 1967.
         DS557.A6N43   68-101711

1171.   New York.   Museum of Primitive Art.   Three regions of
         Melanesian art, New Guinea and the New Hebrides.   New
         York, University Publishers, 1960.
                                                           60-51988

1172.   New York University.   Burma Research Project.   Annotated
         bibliography of Burma.   Ed. by Frank N. Trager.   New
         Haven, Human Relations Area Files, 1956.
         Z3216.N38   016.91592   56-14758

1173.   _____.   Burma Research Project.   Japanese and Chinese
         language sources on Burma, an annotated bibliography.   Ed.
         by Frank N. Trager.   New Haven, HRAF, 1957.
         Z3216.N44   016.9591   57-13287

1174.   New Zealand.   Department of External Affairs.   Publication,
         no. 1-   Wellington.
         DU400.A33

1175.   _____.   Treaty series.   1945-   Wellington.
         DU400.A33   65-69470

1176.   New Zealand.   General assembly.   . . . Parliamentary
         debates.   1st-   parliament, Legislative council and House
         of representatives. . . 1854/55-19-   Wellington, 1885-19-
         J941.H2   328.93102   46-34611

1177.   New Zealand law journal . . . v.1- March 3, 1925-   Well-
         ington, N. Z., Butterworth & Company (Australia) Ltd.
         [1925]-
         PN53.45   42-23745

1178.   New Zealand official year-book.   [1st]- issue: 1892-
         Wellington.
         DU400.A3   7--21753

1179.   Newman, Bernard, 1897-1968. Background to Viet Nam.   New
         American Library, 1971.

1180.   _____.   Background to Viet-Nam.   New York, Roy [1966,
         c. 1965]
         DS557.A6N45   959.7   66-11016

1181.   _____.   Let's visit Vietnam.   London,   Burke,
         1967.
         DS557.A5N42   915.97'03'4   68-91647

1182.   _____.   Report on Indo-China.   New York, Praeger, 1954.
         DS525   959.7   54-7713

1183.   Newman, Kevin Eugene.   The Anzac Battalion; a record of tour
         of 2nd Battalion, the Royal Australian Regiment, 1st Battalion
         the Royal New Zealand Infantry Regiment (the Anzac

Battalion) in South Vietnam, 1967-68, edited by K. E. Newman. [Brookvale, N. S. W.] Printcraft Press [1968]
DS557. A64A845   959.7'04   70-452345

1184.   News from Viet-Nam. Washington, Press and Information
         Office, Embassy of the Republic of Viet-Nam.
         DS557. A6N47   62-33635

1185.   Newton, Douglas, 1920-   Bibliography of Sepik District
         art annotated for illustrations. [New York, Library, Muse-
         um of Primitive Art] 1965-
         Z5961. N54N4   65-4723 rev.

1186.   _____ .   Malu; openwork boards of the Tshuosh tribe.
         [New York] Museum of Primitive Art, 1963.
         NK9796. N4N4   63-22416

1187.   NFL of South Vietnam; the only genuine and legal repre-
         sentative of the South Vietnam people. [Saigon?] Liberation
         Editions, 1965.
         DS557. A6N23   S A 66-7498

1188.   Nghiem-Dang. Viet-Nam; politics and public administration.
         Honolulu, East-West Center Press [c. 1966]
         JQ831. N46   354.597   65-27935

1189.   Ngo-tat-To, 1892-1954.   When the light is out; novel.
         [Translated by Pham-nhu-Oanh] Hanoi, Foreign Languages
         Publishing House, 1960.
         PZ4. N5686Wh   S A 64-5153

1190.   Nguyen Kien. L'Escalade de la guerre au Vietnam, vers
         un conflit nucleaire mondial? [Suivi d'une declaration du
         Front national de liberation du Sud-Vietnam, 22 mars 1965]
         Paris, Editions Cujas, 1965.
         DS557. A6N478   67-74613

1191.   _____ .   Le Sud-Vietnam depuis Dien-Bien-Phu. Paris,
         F. Maspero, 1963.
         DS557. A6N48   64-42222

1192.   Nguyen-anh-Tuan, Mme. Les forces politiques au Sud
         Viet-Nam depuis les accords de Geneve 1954. (Louvain,
         Offset Frankie), 1967.
         DS557. A6N474   71-350524

1193.   Nguyen-cao-Dam. Vietnam, our beloved land, by Nguyen
         cao Dam and Tran cao Linh.   Adapted and translated by
         Tran The-uy with the assistance of Nguyen quy Bong. Rut-
         land, Vermont, C. E. Tuttle Company [1968]
         DS557. A5N433   915.97'0022'2   68-21116

1194.   Nguyen-cong-Hoan, 1903- Li ming chih ch'ien, (Before

Dawn), (In Chinese).   Shanghai, 1960.
PL4378. 9. N45T72

1195.   Nguyen-cong-Vien, 1914-   Seeking the truth; the inside
         story of Viet Nam after the French defeat, by a man who
         served in Dai's Cabinet.   [1st ed.]   New York, Vantage
         [1967, c. 1966]
         DS557. A5N44   959. 7'04   67-1431

1196.   Nguyen-dac-Kh--   L'independence du Viet-Nam et l'Union
         francaise.   The independence of Viet-Nam and the French
         Union.   (Conferences prononcees au Centre d'etudes
         asiatiques et africaines) Les donnees essentielles du prob-
         leme vietnamien.   The essentials of the Vietnamian problem.
         (Lectures delivered at the Centre for Asian an [i. e. and]
         African Studies, in Paris) Saigon, France-Asie [1954]
         DS557. A5N45   55-22532

1197.   Nguyen-dang-Liem.   A contrastive analysis of English and
         Vietnamese.   Canberra, Australian National University,
         1967-
         PL4374. N45   415   70-365774

1198.   Nguyen-Dinh-Hoa, 1924- Easy Vietnamese. Rev. ed.   C. E.
         Tuttle (Tuttle, Charles E. , Company, Inc.) 1966.

1199.   _____. Quoc-ngu: The modern writing system in
         Vietnam. [Washington?] 1955.
         PL4379. N45   495. 921   55-34796

1200.   _____. Read Vietnamese: A Graded Course in Written
         Vietnamese.   C. E. Tuttle (Tuttle, Charles E. , Company,
         Inc.) 1966

1201.   _____. Say it in Vietnamese.   Rutland, Vermont,
         C. E. Tuttle Company, 1966.
         PL4375. N42   495. 9228342   66-17558

1202.   _____. Verbal and non-verbal patterns of respect-be-
         havior in Vietnamese society: some metalinguistic data.
         Ann Arbor, University Microfilms [1957]
         Microfilm AC-1 no. 19, 991   Mic 57-2482

1203.   _____. Vietnamese-English dictionary.   C. E. Tuttle
         (Tuttle, Charles E. , Company, Inc.) 1966

1204.   _____. Vietnamese-English dictionary.   Saigon, Binh-
         Minh, 1959.
         PL4376. N355   495. 9232   61-4908

1205.   _____. Vietnamese-English Student Dictionary.   rev.
         ed.   S. Ill. U. Press (Southern Illinois University Press)
         1971

1206.   _____ . Vietnamese-English vocabulary. Washington,
          Office of Training, National Security Agency, 1955.
          PL4376. N35   495. 9232   55-4808

1207.   Nguyen-dinh-Thi.   Ch'ung chi. (Attacking), (In Chinese).
          Peking, 1956.
          PL4378. 9. N47X82

1208.   _____ . Front du ciel (Mat tran tren cao), roman.
          Adaptation francaise et presentation de Madeleine Riffaud.
          Paris, Julliard, 1968.
          PL4378. 9. N47M314   68-116401

1209.   Nguyen-dinh-Toan.   Con Duong; truyen dai. [Saigon] Giao-
          Diem, 1965.
          PL4378. 9. N48C6   S A 68-1041

1210.   Nguyen-Du, 1765-1820.   Kim Van Kieu. Traduit du viet-
          namien par Xuan-Phuc et Xuan-Viet. [Paris] Gallimard
          [1961]
          PL4378. 9. N514   65-52944

1211.   Nguyen-duy-Trinh.   Government report on the three year
          plan of North Vietnam, 1958-1960. New York, U. S.
          Joint Publications Research Service, 1959.
          AS36. U56 no. 632   338. 9597   59-60978

1212.   Nguyen-Hong.   Jours d'enfance, et autres recits. Traduit
          du vietnamien par Le Van Chat. [Illustrations de Nguyen
          Tien Chung] Hanoi, Editions en langues etrangeres, 1963.
          PL4378. 9. N516J6   S A 68-4582

1213.   Nguyen-huu-Tho.   Speech. . . [delivered] on the occasion
          of the 5th founding anniversary of the N. F. L. [Saigon?]
          Liberation Editions, 1965.
          DS557. A6N475   66-96485

1214.   Nguyen-huy-Thong.   The frontier campaign: memoirs
          Hanoi, Foreign Languages Publishing House, 1962.
          DS557. A7N43   S A 66-1011

1215.   Nguyen-khac-Hoach.   The social sciences and the problem
          of rural improvement in Viet-Nam. [Saigon? n. d.]
          HN700. V5N45   S A 63-2395

1216.   Nguyen-Ngoc.   Noup, les heros des montagnes. Traduction
          de Dao Trong Sot et D. Boudarel.   Hanoi, Editions en
          langues etrangeres, 1959.
          PL4378. 9. N544   S A 65-4589

1217.   Nguyen-qui-Hung.   Neuf ans de dictature au Sud-Vietnam;
          temoignages vivants sur Mme Nhu et les Ngo [par] Nguyen-
          qui-Hung. Saigon, 1964.
          DS557. A6N483   S A 66-5335

1218.   Nguyen-Thai, 1930-   Is South Vietnam viable? [by]
        Nguyen Thai.   Manila, 1962.
        DS557. A6N487   65-2586

1219.   Nguyen-thai-Binh.   Viet-Nam, the problem and a solution.
        [Paris?]   Viet-Nam Democratic Party, Viet-Nam-Dan-Chu-
        Dang, 1962.
        DS557. A6N49   62-42346

1220.   Nguyen-trung-Viet.   Mon pays, le Vietnam.   Suivi de La
        revolte gronde chez les etudiants americains, par Louis
        Wiznitzer.   [Montreal] Editions Parti pris [1967]
        DS557. A5N465   76-396440

1221.   Nguyen-van-Dam.   Le Viet-nam en marche.   Hanoi, Edi-
        tions en langues etrangeres, 1955.
        DS557. A7N45   62-25821

1222.   Nguyen-van-Luyen.   Le Viet-Nam, une cause de la paix.
        Hanoi, Le van Phuc [1945]
        DS557. A5N47   56-38286

1223.   Nguyen-van Tam, 1895-   Le Vietnam en marche.
        [Montargis? 1952]
        DS557. A5N475   61-20846

1224.   Nguyen-van-Thai.   A short history of Viet-nam, by Nguyen-
        van-Thai and Nguyen-van-Mu'ng.   Saigon, Published for
        the Vietnamese-American Association by the Times Pub-
        lishing Company [1958]
        DS557. A5N48   959. 7   A 59-5075

1225.   Nguyen-van-Thuan.   An approach to better understanding
        of Vietnamese society; a primer for Americans.   Saigon,
        Michigan State University, Vietnam Advisory Group, 1962.
        DS557. A5N49   S A 62-1213

1226.   _____.   A survey of Vietnamese occupational prestige
        and aspiration.   Saigon, Michigan State University, Viet-
        nam Advisory Group, 1962.
        HB2734. V5N45   S A 62-1220

1227.   Nguyen-van-Vinh, Lt. Gen.   The Vietnamese people on the
        road to victory.   Hanoi, Foreign Languages Publishing
        House, 1966.
        DS557. A6N494   959. 7'04   68-1678

1228.   Nguyen-Vien.   Viet-nam is one.   Hanoi, Foreign Languages
        Publishing House, 1956.
        DS557. A5N494   S A 66-4833

1229.   Nguyen-xuan-Dao.   Bibliography of periodicals published
        in Viet Nam, prepared by Nguyen Xuan Dao and Richard K.

Gardner. [East Lansing?] 1958.
Z3227. N5   016. 05   59-63325

1230.   Nhan dan, Hanoi. Selected Nhan dan articles on basic
        construction in North Vietnam. New York, U. S. Joint
        Publications Research Service, 1959.
        AS36. U57 no. 1688   338. 9599   59-61875 rev.

1231.   Nhat-Hanh, Thich. Lotos im Feuermeer Vietnam in
        Geschichte und Krise. [Von] Thich Nhat Hanh. Mit
        einem buddhistischen Friedensvorschlag. [Übersetzung
        aus dem Amerikanischen: Heinz Kloppenburg.) München,
        Kaiser, 1967.
        DS557. A6N4955   72-383514

1232.   _____. Vietnam: lotus in a sea of fire. Foreword by
        Thomas Merton, afterword by Alfred Hassler. [1st ed.]
        New York, Hill & Wang [1967]
        DS557. A6N495   959. 7'04   67-15652

1233.   _____. The Viet Nam; [poems. Santa Barbara, Cali-
        fornia, Unicorn Press, 1967]
        PR6064. H3V5   821   68-1870

1234.   Nichi-Etsu Boekikai. Nichi-Etsu Keizui Koryu Kenkyukai,
        (Research Report of Japanese-Vietnamese Economic Ex-
        change), (In Japanese). Tokyo, 1959.
        HF3828. J3N5

1235.   Nielsen, Jon, 1912-   Artist in South Vietnam, by Jon
        Nielsen, with Kay Nielsen. New York, J. Messner [1969]
        NC1075. N5N5   915. 97   79-81394

1236.   Nighswonger, William A. Rural pacification in Vietnam
        [by] William A. Nighswonger. New York, Praeger [1966].
        HN700. V5N5   309. 1597   66-28775

1237.   Nihon Betonamu Yuko Kyokai. Minami Betonamu baisho to
        ampo kaitei. Reparations and safety treaty for South Viet-
        nam), Tokyo, 1959.

1238.   Nikolaev, T. Velikie peremeny vo V'etname, (Great
        Changes in Vietnam). (In Russian). Moscow, 1953.
        DS557. A5N5

1239.   Nixon, Richard Milhous, 1913-   Cambodia concluded; now
        it's time to negotiate. A report to the Nation by Richard
        Nixon, President of the United States, June 30, 1970.
        [Washington, For sale by the Superintendent of Documents,
        U. S. Government Printing Office, 1970.]
        DS557. A63N56   959. 7'04   75-608136

1240.   _____. Cambodia in perspective, Vietnamization

assured; an interim report, by Richard Nixon. June 3,
1970. [Washington; For sale by the Superintendent of Documents, U. S. Government Printing Office, 1970]
DS557. A63N58   959. 7'04   71-607600

1241. _____. Peace in Vietnam [by] Richard Nixon. [Washing-
ton] Department of State; [for sale by the Superintendent of
Documents, U. S. Government Printing Office, 1969]
DS557. A692N5   959. 7'04   75-602116

1242. _____. The pursuit of peace; an address by Richard
Nixon, November 3, 1969. [Washington; For sale by the
Superintendent of Documents, U. S. Government Printing
Office, 1969]
DS557. A692N53   959. 7'04   73-604671

1243. No more Vietnams? The war and the future of American
foreign policy. Contributors: Eqbal Ahmad [and others]
Edited by Richard M. Pfeffer. [1st ed.] New York, Published for the Adlai Stevenson Institute of International Affairs by Harper & Row [1968]
E840. N6   327. 73   68-58302

1244. No more Vietnams? The war and the future of American
foreign policy. Edited by Richard M. Pfeffer. New York,
Published for the Adlai Stevenson Institute of International
Affairs by Harper & Row [1968]
[E840]   327. 73   76-1933

1245. Nonnemann, H. C. Wir fragten nicht woher sie kamen.
Arzt in Vietnam. [Von] H. C. Nonnemann. (Hamburg)
Hoffmann u. Campe (1968).
DS557. A69N6   959. 7²04   68-69941

1246. Norden, Eric. America's barbarities in Vietnam. [New
Delhi, Mainstream Weekly, 1966]
DS557. A67N6   959. 7'04   S A 67-925

1247. Norden, Hermann. A Wanderer in Indo-China. London,
H. F. & G. Witherby, 1931.
DS534. N6   915. 9   32-340

1248. Nørlund, Ib. Møde med Vietnam. [København] Tiden, 1966.
DS557. A6N6   67-74523

1249. Norodom Sihanouk Varman, King of Cambodia, 1922-
Le Cambodge et ses relations avec ses voisins, par
Norodom Sihanouk. [Phnom Penh?] Ministere de l'in-
formation [1961?]
DS557. C28N57   S A 65-4750

1250. Nu'o'c Viet-Nam Dan chu Cong hoa 15 tuoi, 1945-1960.
Hanoi?, 196-
DS557. A7N8   S A 68-1046

O

1251.   O'Ballance, Edgar.   The Indo-China war, 1945-1954; a
        study in guerrilla warfare.   London, Faber & Faber [Mystic,
        Connecticut, Verry, 1966, c. 1964]
        DS550. 02   959. 703   65-3280

1252.   _____.   Malaya: the communist insurgent war, 1948-60.
        [1st ed.]   Hamden, Connecticut, Archon Books [1966]
        DS597. 02 1966a   323. 2095951   66-31617

1253.   Oberdorfer, Don.   Tet! New York, Doubleday, 1971.
        DS557. A62T46   959. 7'04'342   73-160887

1254.   O'Connell, Daniel Patrick.   International law in Australia:
        edited by D. P. O'Connell, assisted by J. Varsanyi, with
        a foreword by the Rt. Hon. Sir Garfield Barwick.   London,
        published for the Australian Institute of International Af-
        fairs [by] Stevens [Sydney, Law Book Company] 1965 [i. e.
        1966]
        JN3225. 03   341. 0994   66-78506

1255.   O'Connor, John Joseph, 1920-   A chaplain looks at Viet-
        nam, by John J. O'Connor.   Foreword by Everett M.
        Dirksen.   Cleveland, World Publishing Company [1968]
        DS557. A68O57   959. 7'04   68-26834

1256.   O'Daniel, John W.   The nation that refused to starve: the
        challenge of the new Vietnam.   [New, rev. ed.] New York,
        Coward [1963, c. 1962]
        DS557. A6O3   959. 7   62-15303

1257.   O'Daniel, John W.   The nation that refused to starve; the
        challenge of the new Vietnam.   New York, Coward-McCann
        [c. 1960]
        DS557. A6O3   JUV 959. 7   60-6898

1258.   _____.   Vietnam Today: The Challenge of a Divided
        Nation.   rev. ed.   Original Title: Nation That Refused to
        Starve.   Coward-McCann, Inc. , 1962.

1259.   Oglesby, Carl.   Amerikanische Ideologie; zwei Studien uber
        Politik und Gesellschaft in den USA [von] Carl Oglesby
        [und] Richard Shaull.   [Aus dem Amerikanischen ubers.
        von Inge Teichmann.   Frankfurt am Main] Suhrkamp
        [1969]
        E840.O3515   74-464348

1260.   _____.   Containment and Change.   New York, Macmil-
        lan, 1967.
        E744. O35   327. 73   67-13593

1261.   Ognetov, Igor' Aleksandrovich.   Vosstannie Tei-shonov vo

V'etname 1771-1802, (The Insurrection of Tei-shons in Vietnam). (In Russian). Moscow, 1960.
DS557. A5O45

1262. Okamoto, Ryuzo, 1916- Betonamu kaiho e no michi (The road to the Vietnamese liberation; war history of father-land's independence (In Japanese). Tokyo, 1965.

1263. Okamura, Akihiko, 1929- This is war in Vietnam. (In Japanese.) Mainichi Newspapers, [1960]
DS557. A6O37   J 66-129

1264. Oliver, Henry Madison. Economic opinion and policy in Ceylon. Durham, N. C. , Duke University, 1957.
HC437. C4O55   338. 9548   57-13023

1265. Ommaney, Francis Downes, 1903- Eastern windows. Garden City, New York, Doubleday, 1961 [c. 1960]
DS598. S7O48   TR 915. 952   61-11227

1266. Omori, Minoru, 1922- Doro to honoo no Indichina (War sufferings in Indochina) (In Japanese) Tokyo, 1965.
DS557. A6O4

1267. O'Neill, Robert John. The strategy of General Giap since 1964 [by] Robert J. O'Neill. Canberra, Australian Na-tional University Press, 1969.
DS557. A6O47   959. 7'04   71-96464

1268. _____. Strategy of General Giap Since 1964. Inter-national Scholarly Book Service, Inc. , 1964.

1269. _____. Vietnam task; the 5th Battalion, the Royal Australian Regiment, 1966/67 [by] Robert J. O'Neill. [Melbourne] Cassell Australia [1968]
DS557. A64A85   959. 7'04   79-385664

1270. Onorato, Michael Paul, 1934- A brief review of Ameri-can interest in Philippine development, and other essays, by Michael Onorato. Berkeley, California, McCutchan Publishing Corporation [1968]
E183. 8. P5O5   327. 73'0914   68-5791

1271. Opinion Research Corporation, Princeton, New Jersey. The people of South Vietnam: how they feel about the war; a CBS News public opinion survey. Princeton, New Jersey, 1967.
DS557. A68O6   301. 15'4'09597   67-5410

1272. Ord om Vietnam. En international antologi. Traesnit av Palle Nielsen. [Oslo] Gyldendal, 1967.
DS557. A61O73   68-85341

1273.   Ormeling, Ferdinand Jan.   The Timor problem; a geo-
         graphical interpretation of an underdeveloped island.
         Djakarta, Wolters, 1955.
         DS646. 5. O7   919. 24   56-43948

1274.   Osborne, Charles, ed.   Australian stories of today.
         London, Faber & Faber, 1961.
         PZ1. 074AU   62-51925

1275.   Osborne, Leone Neal.   Than Hoa of Viet-Nam.   Illustrated
         by Ruth Boynton, New York.   McGraw [1966]
         HN700. V5O8   j915. 97   66-9155

1276.   Osborne, Milton E.   French Presence in Cochinchina &
         Cambodia: Rule & Response 1859-1905.   Cornell Univer-
         sity Press, 1969.
         DS557. C7O76   959. 7   78-87021

1277.   _____. Singapore and Malaysia.   Ithaca, New York,
         Southeast Asia Program, Department of Asian Studies,
         Cornell University, 1964.
         DS598. S7O8   959. 52   64-55818

1278.   _____. Strategic Hamlets in South Viet-Nam.   Ithaca,
         (New York) Cornell University, 1965.
         DS557. A6O8   355. 42509597   65-64732

1279.   _____. Viet-Nam: the origins of crisis, by Milton E.
         Osborne.   [Toronto] Published for the Canadian Institute
         of International Affairs by the Baxter Publishing Company,
         1965.
         F1034. B4 vol. 25, no. 1   65-9626

1280.   Osipov, V.   Kogda opusteli dzhungli; v'etnamskie ocherki,
         (When we left the jungles; Vietnamese sketches).   (In
         Russian).   Moscow, 1956.
         DS557. A7O8

1281.   Oste, Sven, 1925-   Vietnam--hokens ar.   Stockholm,·
         Aldus /Bonnier, 1966.
         DS557. A6O3   67-97810

1282.   _____. Vietnam--krig utan hopp?   [Samtliga bilder av
         forfattaren] Stockholm, Bonnier, 1965.
         DS557. A6O32   66-77904

1283.   Outvrey, Ernest, 1863-   Nouveau recueil de legislation
         cantonale et communale annamite de Cochinchine, par
         Ernest Outrey . . . Saigon, Imprimerie commerciale
         Menard et Rey, 1905.

1284.   Ozdek, Refik.   Vietnam cikmazi. Istanbul, Yagmur Yayinevi
         [1968]
         DS557. A6O328   N E 68-4455

P

1285.   Paauw, Douglas S.   ed.   Prospects for East Sumatran
         plantation industries, a symposium.   Contributors: Douglas
         S. Paauw, Lim Kim Liat, Sayuti Hasibuan [and] Dahlan
         Thalib.   New Haven, Yale University, Southeast Asia
         Studies; distributed by the Cellar Bookshop, Detroit, 1962.
         HD2085. S7P22 1962   62-3402

1286.   Pagniez, Yvonne, 1896-   Choses vues au Vietnam; nais-
         sance d'une nation.   Paris, La Palatine [1954]
         DS557. A5P2   56-16578

1287.   Paine, Lauran.   Viet-nam.   New York, Roy Publishers
         [1967, c. 1965]
         DS557. A5P23 1967   959. 7   67-11429

1288.   Palfreeman, A. C.   The administration of the White
         Australia policy [by] A. C. Palfreeman.   [Melbourne]
         Melbourne University Press; London, New York, Cambridge
         University Press [1967]
         JV9153. P3 1967   325. 1'0994   67-13258

1289.   Palladin, A. I.   Stikhi poetov V'etnama, (Poems of Viet-
         namese Poets).   (In Russian).   Moscow, 1955.
         PL4378. 9. P3

1290.   Palmer, Vance.   The legend of the nineties.   Carlton,
         Melbourne University, 1954.
         PR9450. P3   54-32906

1291.   Palmier, Leslie H.   Indonesia and the Dutch.   Issued
         under the auspices of the Institute of Race Relations,
         London.   London, New York, Oxford University Press,
         1962.
         DS640. N4P3   327. 492091   62-1482

1292.   P'an Chao-ying, 1908-   Vietnam crisis [by] Stephen Pan
         [and] Daniel Lyons.   New York, East Asian Research In-
         stitute [1966]
         DS557. A6P3   959. 7   66-23533

1293.   Panikkar, Kavalam Madhava.   The Afro-Asian states and
         their problems.   New York, John Day, 1960.
         DS3. P3   309. 15   59-14286

1294.   _____.   Asia and Western dominance; a survey of the
         Vasco da Gama epoch of Asian history, 1498-1945.   New
         ed. London, Allen & Unwin, 1959.
         DS33. P3   950   60-22700

1295.   Pao wei Yin-tu Chih-na ho p'ing, (Maintaining Peace in
         Indochina), (In Chinese).   Hong Kong, 1964.
         DS557. A7P28

1296.   Paret, Peter.   French Revolutionary Warfare from Indo-
        china to Algeria.   (Analysis of a Political and Military
        Doctrine.   Center of International Studies, Princeton) New
        York, Praeger, 1964.
        UA700. P36   355   64-13381

1297.   Parise, Goffredo.   Due, tre cose sul Vietnam.   Milano,
        Feltrinelli, 1967.
        DS557. A6P35   70-364584

1298.   Parkinson, Cyril Northcote, 1909-   British intervention
        in Malaya, 1867-1877.   Singapore, University of Malaya
        Press, 1960.
        DS596. P29   959. 5   60-50031

1299.   Parks, David, 1944-   GI diary.   With photos by the
        author.   [1st ed.]   New York, Harper & Row [1968]
        DS557. A69P35   959. 7'04   68-17037

1300.   Parks, Oral E.   Recent articles on Vietnam: an anno-
        tated bibliography.   Compiled by Oral E. Parks and Milan
        Jan Reban, under the general supervision of Frank B.
        Cliffe, Jr.   [East Lansing?] 1958.
        Z3226. P3   016. 9597   59-63324

1301.   Partridge, Percy Herbert, 1910-   Society, schools, and
        progress in Australia, by P. H. Partridge.   Oxford, New
        York, Pergamon Press [1968]
        LA2101. P3 1968   370'. 994   68-24067

1302.   Passent, Daniel.   Co dzien wojna.   [Wyd. 1. Warszawa]
        Czytelnik, 1968.
        DS557. A5P28   71-230789

1303.   Paton, George Whitecross, 1902-   ed.   The Common-
        wealth of Australia; the development of its laws and consti-
        tution.   Under the general editorship of G. W. Paton.
        With specialist contributors.   London, Stevens, 1952.
        JN248. B7   342. 9409   52-3346

1304.   Patko, Imre.   Vietnam.   Budapest, Kepzomuveszeti Alap
        Kiadovallalata, 1960.
        DS557. A7P3   61-33845 rev.

1305.   Paulsen, Gary.   The special war, compiled and written by
        Gary Paulsen and Raymond Friday Locke.   Los Angeles,
        Sirkay Publishing Company [1966]
        DS557. A6P37   959. 704   66-8542

1306.   Peace, Power and Politics in Asia Conference Committee.
        Peace, power, politics in Asia; the background.   [Welling-
        ton, 1968]
        DS35. P42   959   78-434006

1307.   Peacock, James L. Rites of modernization: symbolic and
        social aspects of Indonesian proletarian drama [by] James
        L. Peacock. Chicago, University of Chicago Press [1968]
        PN2905. J3P4   792'. 0992'2   68-15931

1308.   Pei-ching ta hsuch. Tung fang yu yen hsueh hsi. Yueh-
        nan yu chuan yeh. Yueh-nan hsieu tai tuan p'len hsiao shuo
        chi, (Vietnamese Modern Short Stories), (In Chinese).
        Peking, 1960.
        PL4378. P4

1309.   Pelzer, Karl Josef, 1909- Pioneer settlement in the
        Asiatic tropics; studies in land utilization and agricultural
        colonization in southeastern Asia. New York, American
        Geographical Society, 1945.
        HD855. P4   333. 7   45-9146

1310.   _____. Selected bibliography on the geography of
        Southeast Asia. [New Haven, Yale University, Southeast
        Asia Studies, 1949-]
        Z3221. P4   016. 915   51-3242 rev.

1311.   Penniman, Howard Rae, 1916- Decision in South Vietnam;
        transcript of an interview with Howard R. Penniman.
        [Washington] Free Society Association, 1967.
        JQ892. P4   324'. 2'09597   68-425

1312.   Pentagon Papers (The) as published by the New York Times.
        Written by Neil Sheehan & others. Quadrangle, 1971.
        E183. 8. V5P4   959. 7'0432   75-173846

1313.   People's Viet-Nam pictorial. Hanoi.
        DS557. A7P4   S A 63-1243

1314.   Perlo, Victor. The Vietnam profiteers. [New York, New
        Outlook Publishers, 1966]
        DS557. A68P4   330. 9'597   67-1271

1315.   Permanent Organization for Afro-Asian Peoples' Solidarity.
        Committee of Aid and Assistance to the People of South
        Vietnam. Bulletin. no. 1- November 1963- Cairo.
        DS557. A6P4   N E 64-1801

1316.   Perry, Stuart. The Indecent Publications Tribunal, a social
        experiment. With text of the legislation since 1910 and
        classifications of the tribunal. Foreword by Sir Kenneth
        Gresson. [Christchurch] Whitcombe and Tombs, 1965.
        HV6727. P37   354. 9310076   66-853

1317.   Pfeffer, Richard M. , ed. No More Vietnams: The War &
        the Future of American Foreign Policy. Harper & Row
        Publishers, Inc. , 1968.

1318.   Phan-gia-Ben.   Yueh-nan shou kung yeh fa chan shih ch'u
        kao, (A History of the development of Vietnamese Hand-
        craft industries), (In Chinese).   Peking, 1969.

1319.   Phan-thi-Dac.   Situation de la personne au Viet-Nam . . .
        Paris, Editions du Centre national de la recherche scien-
        tifique, 1966.
        DS557. A5P48   915. 97'03   67-102813

1320.   Phan Tran; roman en vers.   Texte, traduction et notes par
        Maurice Durand.   Paris, Depositaire: Adrien-Maisonneuve,
        1962.
        PL3528. 5. E3 no. 1   64-25965

1321.   Phayre, Sir Arthur Purves, 1812-1885.   History of Burma,
        including Burma proper, Pegu, Tanngu, Tenasserim, and
        Arakan, from the earliest time to the first war with
        British India, by Sir Arthur P. Phayre.   2d ed.   London,
        Santiago de Compostela, Spain, Susil Gupta, 1967.
        DS485. B86P5 1967   959. 1'02   70-370389

1322.   Phelan, John Leddy.   The Hispanization of the Philippines:
        Spanish aims and Filipino responses, 1565-1700.   Madison,
        University of Wisconsin, 1959.
        DS674. P5   991. 402   A59-8602

1323.   Philippines (Republic).   Bureau of the Census and Statistics.
        Facts and figures about the economic and social conditions
        of the Philippines, 1946-   Manila, Bureau of Print.
        HC451. A45   319. 14   48-22034

1324.   Phillips, Arthur Angell.   The Australian tradition; studies
        in a colonial culture.   Melbourne, Cheshire, 1958.
        PR9418. P5   58-39458

1325.   Phillips, Cecil Ernest Lucas, 1898-   Springboard to
        victory [by] C. E. Lucas Phillips.   London, Heinemann,
        1966.
        D767. 6. P48   940. 5425   66-70079

1326.   Pho-can-Tham.   Viet-Han tan-tu-dien, (New Vietnamese-
        Chinese Dictionary).   1958.
        PL4377. P5

1327.   Pic, Roger.   Au coeur du Vietnam.   La Republique demo-
        cratique du Vietnam et le Front national de liberation du
        Sud-Vietnam face a l'agression.   Quatre-vingt seize photos
        de Pic.   Preface de Jean-Paul Sartre.   Paris, F. Mas-
        pero, 1968.
        DS557. A7P5   959. 7'04   68-108767

1328.   Pickerell, James H.   Vietnam in the mud, by James H.
        Pickerell.   With an introduction by Malcolm W. Browne.

Indianapolis, Bobbs-Merrill [1966]
DS557. A6P53   959. 704   66-27883

1329.   Pierce, Robert Willard, 1914- Big day at Da Me, by Bob
         Pierce. With Nguyen Van Duc and Larry Ward. Still
         photography by Joe Gooden. Waco, Texas, Word Books
         [1968]
         DS557. A68P53   959. 7'04   67-30734

1330.   Pike, Douglas. Paradise of dissent; South Australia 1829-
         1857. [2nd ed.] Melbourne, Melbourne University Press;
         London, New York, Cambridge University Press [1967]
         DU320. P5 1967   994'. 2'02   67-29759

1331.   _____. Politics of the Viet Cong. Saigon, 1968.
         DS557. A6P538   320. 9'597   71-924

1332.   _____. Viet Cong; the organization and techniques of
         the National Liberation Front of South Vietnam. Cambridge,
         Massachusetts, M. I. T. Press [1966]
         DS557. A6P54   959. 704   66-28896

1333.   _____. War, peace, and the Viet Cong. Cambridge,
         Massachusetts, M. I. T. Press [1969]
         DS557. A6P548   959. 7'04   70-83403

1334.   _____. War, Peace, & the Viet Cong. M. I. T. Press,
         1970.

1335.   Pilling, Arnold R. Aborigine culture history, a survey of
         publications, 1954-1957. Detroit, Wayne State University
         Press, 1962.
         Z5116. P5   016. 572994   61-12268

1336.   Pis'ma iz IUzhnogo V'etnama, (Letters from South Vietnam).
         (In Russian). Hanoi, 1964.
         DS557. A6P557

1337.   Pizzinelli, Corrado, 1922- Siamo tutti in guerra. Milano,
         Longanesi [1966]
         PQ4876. I88S5   68-42291

1338.   Ploog, Arno. Napalm macht frei; 60 politische Karikaturen
         zum Krieg in Vietnam, mit Texten und Materialien von Jur-
         gen Horlemann. [1. Aufl. Frankfurt am Main, Edition Vol-
         taire, 1968]
         DS557. A61P53   73-442498

1339.   Podkopaev, I. IA. Bor'ba v'etnamskogo naroda za svobodu
         i natsional'nuiu nezavisimost', (Struggle of Vietnamese
         People for Freedom and National Independence). (In Russian).
         Moscow, 1953.
         DS557. V5P59

1340. _____ Demokraticheskaia Respublika V'etnam, (Democratic Republic of Vietnam). (In Russian). Moscow, 1955.
DS557. A5P6

1341. _____ . Demokraticheskaia respublika v'etnam v bor'be
protiv frantsuzskikh imperialistov, (Democratic Republic
of Vietnam fighting against French imperialists). (In Russian). Moscow, 1948.
DS557. V5P6

1342. _____ . Ocherki bor'by v'etnamskogo naroda za neza-
visimost' i edinstvo svoei rodiny, (A Schematic Synopsis
of the War of the Vietnamese People for Independence and
Unity of their Fatherland). (In Russian). Moscow, 1957.
DS557. A5P62

1343. _____ . V'etnam; geograficheskii ocherk, (Vietnam;
Geographical outline). (In Russian). Moscow, 1955.
DS557. A5P63

1344. _____ . V'etnam. Pod red. A. A. Gubera, (Vietnam).
(In Russian). Moscow, 1950.
DS557. V5P63

1345. Poetry in Australia. Berkeley, University of California
Press, 1965.
PR9551. M6 1965   821. 082   65-1832

1346. Polaschek, R. J. Government administration in New Zealand. Wellington, New Zealand Institute of Public Administration, 1958.
JQ5831. P6   354. 931   59-849

1347. The Politics of escalation; a study of United States re-
sponses to pressures for a political settlement of the Viet-
nam War: November 1963-January 1966. Prepared by a
working group organized by scholars at the University of
California, at Berkeley, and Washington University, in St.
Louis. Authors: Franz Schurmann, Peter Dale Scott [and]
Reginald Zelnik. [Berkeley? 1966]
E183. 8. V5P6   327. 730597   66-8081

1348. Poole, Peter A. The Vietnamese in Thailand; a historical
perspective [by] Peter A. Poole. Ithaca [New York]
Cornell University Press [1970]
DS570. V5P6 1970   325. 2'597'09593   73-109337

1349. Portisch, Hugo, 1927- Eyewitness in Vietnam; translated
from the German by Michael Glenny. London, Sydney
[etc.] Bodley Head, 1967.
DS557. A6P613   959. 7'04   67-87884

1350. Poslusajte nas. Slusajtle nas. C. Vsebinsko uredila

Mira Mihelic. Opremil Joze Centa s sodelvanjem ucencev osemletke "Joze Moskric" v Ljubljani. Ljubljana, Republiski center klubov OZN Slovenije, 1967.
DS557. A68P6   68-92214

1351.   Possony, Stefan Thomas, 1913-   Aggression and self-defense: the legality of U. S. action in South Vietnam, by Stefan T. Possony. Philadelphia, University of Pennsylvania, Foreign Policy Research Institute, 1966.
JX1573. P6   959. 7'04   66-25850

1352.   _____ & Pournelle, J. E.   Congress Debates Vietnam. Dunellen Publishing Company, 1971.

1353.   Pour une solution politique du probleme vietnamien. [Le Caire, Secretariat permanent de l'Organisation de la solidarite des peuples afro-asiatiques, 1969]
DS557. A6F574   959. 7'04   71-961019

1354.   Prague. Universita Karlova. Knihovna. Lidove demokraticke zeme Asie: Korea, Vietnam, Mongolsko; [vyberovy seznam literatury. Sest. Miroslav Kaftan. Praha, 1956]
Z3316. P7   57-20258

1355.   Pratt, Don. Salmagundi Vietnam [by] Don Pratt & Lee Blair. With illustrations by Jim Ryan. Rutland, Vermont, C. E. Tuttle Company [1970]
DS557. A61P7   959. 7'04   79-104207

1356.   Pratt, Lawrence. North Vietnam and Sino-Soviet tension. [Toronto, Published for the Canadian Institute of International Affairs by the Baxter Publishing Company] 1967.
F1034. B4 vol. 26.   327. 51'0597   68-86516
no. 6

1357.   Presbyterian Church in the U. S. A.   General Assembly. Vietnam; the Christian, the gospel, the church. Philadelphia [1967]
DS557. A68P7   959. 7'04   68-892

1358.   The present situation of government administration in Vietnam. (Report of Michigan State University Team),   (In Vietnamese). Saigon, 1959.

1359.   Price, Archibald Grenfell. The Western invasions of the Pacific and its continents; a study of moving frontiers and changing landscapes, 1513-1958. Oxford, Clarendon, 1963.
JV61. P68   325. 309   63-2946

1360.   Pridybailo, Andrei Ivanovich.   Narodnaia armiia V'etnama, (Vietnamese People's Army). (In Russian). Moscow, 1959.
DS557. A7P74

138   Vietnam

1361.   Principales victoires des F. A. L. du Sud Vietnam pendant
         la saison seche (de novembre 1965 a mars 1966). [Saigon?
         Editions Liberation, 1966]
         DS557. A6P74   959. 7'04   68-37514

1362.   Pringgodigdo, A. K.   The office of President in Indonesia as
         defined in the three constitutions, in theory and practice.
         Ithaca, New York, Cornell University, 1957.
         JQ771. P7   58-19645

1363.   Printemps sur la montagne [par] Nguyen Ngoc [et al.]
         Hanoi, Editions en langues etrangeres.   1963.
         DS557. A7P76   68-39254

1364.   Profile of an Administration--Thieu & Ky. China Books and
         Periodicals, 1971.

1365.   Pruden, Wesley, Jr.   Vietnam; the war.   National Observer
         [dist. Princeton, New Jersey, Dow Jones, Box 300 c. 1965]
         DS557. A6P78   959. 7   65-26746

1366.   Pugwash Conference on Science and World Affairs.   14th,
         Venice, 1965.   Proceedings; international co-operation for
         science and disarmament.   [London, 1965]
         JX1974. P8 1965   65-6511

1367.   Purcell, Victor William Saunders, 1896-1964.   The Chi-
         nese in Malaya. New York, Oxford University Press, 1948.
         DS595. P8   325. 25109595   48-4242

1368.   _____ . Malaya: communist or free?   Stanford,
         California, Stanford University, 1954.
         DS596. P79   959. 5   54-12854

1369.   _____ . Malaysia. New York, Walker
         [c. 1965]
         DS596. P82   959. 5   65-19260

1370.   Puthucheary, James J.   Ownership and control in the
         Malayan economy.   Singapore, Eastern Universities Press,
         1960.
         HC497. M3P8   61-41660

1371.   Pye, Lucian W. , 1921- Guerrilla communism in
         Malaya, its social and political meaning. Princeton,
         Princeton University, 1956.
         DS596. P9   959. 5   56-10827

1372.   _____ . Politics, personality, and nation build-
         ing: Burma's search for identity. [Study from the Center
         for International Studies, Massachusetts Institute of Tech-
         nology] New Haven, Connecticut, Yale [c.] 1962
         JQ442. P9   959. 1   62-8260

1373.   Pym, Christopher.   The road to Angkor.   [New York,
        Collings] [1959]
        DS525. 2. P9   TR 915. 96   59-4928

Q

1374.   Quan, Lau-King.   Introduction to Asia; a selective guide to
        background reading.   Washington, Library of Congress,
        1955.
        Z3001. Q3   016. 915   54-60018

1375.   Quang-Loi.   IUzhnee 17-i paralleli, (The Southerners of
        the 17th Parallel).   (In Russian).   Moscow, 1960.   Trans-
        lated from French.
        DS557. A6Q37

1376.   _____.   South of the 17th parallel.   Hanoi, Foreign
        Languages Publishing House, 1959.
        DS557. A6Q33   67-111686

1377.   Quigley, Thomas E. , ed.   American Catholics & the Viet-
        nam War.   Eerdmans, William B. , Publishing Company,
        1968.

1378.   Quirno, Carlos.   Magsaysay of the Philippines.   Manila,
        Alemars, 1958.
        DS686. 6. M3Q5   923. 1914   58-40278

R

1379.   Race, Jeffrey.   War Comes to Long An.   University of
        California Press, 1971.

1380.   [Radford, Jim] Indecency in church: hypocrisy, dishonesty,
        injustice at Brighton.   London, Committee of 100 [1967]
                              343'. 4'3094225   68-122892

1381.   Radio Free Europe.   Audience and Public Opinion Research
        Department.   East European attitudes to the Vietnam conflict:
        a study in radio effectiveness.   [Munich?] 1967.
        DS557. A68R3   301. 15'4   68-91948

1382.   _____.   Audience and Public Opinion Research Depart-
        ment.   Identification with North or South Vietnam in eastern
        Europe.   Munich, 1968.
        DS557. A5R3   301. 15'4   77-353715

1383.   Raffaelli, Jean.   Hanoi, capital de la survie.   Paris, B.
        Grasset, 1967.
        DS558. H3R3   959. 7'04   67-111512

1384.   _____.   Hanoi.   Eine Stadt, die uberlebt.   (Aus dem
        Franzosischen ubertragen von Wolfgang Teuschl) [Mit

Abbildungen und Karten] Wien, W. Frick (1968)
DS558.H3R315   959.7'04   74-357180

1385.   Ramparts Editors et al., ed.   Two, Three--Many Vietnams:
        The Wars in Southeast Asia & the Conflicts at Home.   Can-
        field Press, 1971.

1386.   Ramson, William Stanley.   Australian English; an historical
        study of the vocabulary, 1788-1898.   Canberra, Australian
        National University Press [1966]
        PE3601.R3   427.994   66-75820

1387.   Ransom, Robert C., 1944-1968.   Letters from Vietnam, by
        Robert C. Ransom, Jr. [Bronxville? New York, c.1968]
        DS557.A69R28   959.7'04   77-2436

1388.   Raskin, Marcus G., ed.   The Viet-Nam reader; articles
        and documents on American foreign policy and the Viet-Nam
        crisis.   Edited by Marcus G. Raskin and Bernard B. Fall.
        New York, Random House [1965]
        DS557.A6R3   959.704   65-26331

1389.   _____.   The Viet-Nam reader; articles and docu-
        ments on American foreign policy and the Viet-Nam crisis,
        edited by Marcus G. Raskin and Bernard B. Fall.   Rev. ed.
        New York, Vintage Books [1967]
        DS557.A6R3 1967   959.7'04'08   68-1188

1390.   Ratnam, K. J.   The Malayan parliamentary election of 1964,
        by K. J. Ratnam and R. S. Milne.   Singapore, University
        of Malaya Press; [sole distributors, Oxford University Press,
        London] 1967 .
        JQ717.R3   324.911'5   68-2623

1391.   Rawson, Philip S.   The art of Southeast Asia; Cambodia, Viet-
        nam, Thailand, Laos, Burma, Java, Bali [by] Philip Rawson.
        New York, F. A. Praeger, 1967.
        N5877.A8R3 1967   709'.54   67-29399

1392.   Ray, Michele.   Des deux rives de l'Enfer.   Paris, R. Laf-
        font, 1967.
        DS557.A69R3   959.7'04   67-108368

1393.   _____.   The two shores of hell.   Translated by Elizabeth
        Abbott.   New York, D. McKay Company [1968]
        DS557.A69R313   959.7'04   68-22686

1394.   _____.   The two shores of hell; translated [from the French]
        by Elizabeth Abbott and Shirley Deane.   London, Murray,
        1968.
        DS557.A69R313 1968b   959.7'04   68-138756

1395.   Ray, Sibnarayan, 1921- ed.   Vietnam, seen from East and

West; an international symposium.   New York, F. A. Praeger
[1966]
DS557.A6R35   959.704   66-28015

1396.   Razob'em okovy; dokumenty Avgustovskoi revoliutsii 1945
        goda vo V'etname, (We will break the chains; the documents
        of the October revolution in 1945 in Vietnam). (In Russian).
        Moscow, 1960.
        DS557.A7B717

1397.   Razvitie ekonomiki stran narodnoi demokratii Azii; obzor,
        (Economic Development of Asia's Countries of People's
        Democracy). (In Russian). Moscow, 1956.
        HC412.R38

1398.   The Realities of Vietnam; a Ripon Society appraisal.   Edited
        by Christopher W. Beal with Anthony A. D'Amato.   Washing-
        ton, Public Affairs Press [1968]
        DS557.A63R4   959.7'04   68-26541

1399.   Reay, Marie, ed.   Aborigines now; new perspective in the
        study of aboriginal communities.   [Sydney] Angus and
        Robertson [1964]
        DU120.R34

1400.   Recits de la resistance vietnamienne (1925-1945), par Vo
        Nguyen Giap, Bui Lam, Le Van Luong, Hoang Quoc Viet
        . . . [etc.] Textes reunis par L. Puiseux.   Paris, F.
        Maspero, 1966.
        DS557.A5R4   959.7'03   67-79632

1401.   Recto, Claro M.   1890- My crusade.   Manila, P. C. Cali-
        ca & N. Carag [1955]
        DS686.5.R4   327.914   56-47271

1402.   Reed, David E.   Up front in Vietnam [by] David Reed. New
        York, Funk & Wagnalls [1967]
        DS557.A69R35   959.7'04   67-29883

1403.   Reeves, William Pember. The long white cloud, Ao tea roa.
        4th ed. with additional chapters by A. J. Harrop. London,
        Allen & Unwin, 1956.
                                                         25-5983

1404.   Reich, Ebbe, comp.   Til Vietnam. [Digte og grafik]. Redak-
        tion: Ebbe Reich og Vagn Søndergaard. København, Det
        Internationale Krigsforbrydelses Tribunals Københavnskontor
        og Vietnamindsamlingen, Eksp.: Korsgade 49, 1967.
        PT7992.R4   68-94509

1405.   Reicher, Reuben.   Une Paix immediate au Viet-Nam; est-elle
        possible? [par] R. Reicher-Sgradi. [Paris] S. G. R. A. D. I.,
        1966.
        HC443.V5R38   338.9597   67-106038

1406.   _____. Vietnam, nous sommes tous concernes [par]
R. Reicher-Sgradi . . . Paris, Editions de la
S. G. R. A. D. I. , 1967-
D843. R39   909. 82   68-80879

1407.   Reisinan, Michael. Art of the Possible: Diplomatic Alternatives in the Middle East. Princeton University Press, 1971.

1408.   Rennhack, Horst. Das barbarische Engagement. Berlin,
Deutsches Militarverlag, 1968.
DS557. A6R39 1968   70-379262

1409.   Report on Vietnamese refugees and displaced persons, by a
delegation from the American Council of Voluntary Agencies
for Foreign Service, Inc., October, 1965. New York,
[1965?]
DS557. A68R46   959. 7'04   67-4142

1410.   The Reporter (New York, 1949-) Vietnam; why? A col-
lection of reports and comments from the Reporter. [New
York] Reporter Magazine Company [1966]
DS557. A6R4   973. 92   66-9091

1411.   La Republique democratique du Viet-Nam, 1945-1960; impressions de visiteurs etrangers. Hanoi, Editions en
langues etrangeres, 1960.
DS557. A7R4   S A 63-531

1412.   La Republique democratique du Viet Nam sur la voie de
l'industrialisation socialiste. Hanoi, Editions en langues
etrangeres, 1963.
HC443. V5R4   S A 64-7249

1413.   Rhodes, Alexandre de, 1591-1660. Rhodes of Viet Nam; the
travels and missions of Father Alexander de Rhodes in China
and other kingdoms of the Orient. Translated [from French]
by Solange Hertz. Westminster, Maryland, Newman [c.] 1966.
DS506. R413   915. 97043   66-16567

1414.   Riboud, Marc & Devillers, Philippe. Face of North Vietnam.
New York, Holt, Rinehart and Winston, 1970.

1415.   Richard, Pierre. Cinq ans Prisonnier des Viets. Paris,
Editions de la Serpe,   1964.
DS557. A5R48   66-90498

1416.   Riesen, Rene. Jungle Mission. London, Hutchinson, 1957.
DS550. R513   959   57-37872

1417.   Riffaud, Madeleine. Au Nord Viet-nam. (Ecrit sous les
bombes) Paris, Julliard, 1967.
DS557. A635R5   959. 7'04   67-97039

1418.   _____. Bij de Vietcong in het oerwoud. [Vertaling:

R. Fiddelaar] Baarn, De Boekerij [1966]
DS557.A7R512 1966.   67-96975

1419.   . Dans les maquis "vietcong. " Paris, R. Julliard
[1965]
DS557.A7R5   65-67425

1420.   . Unsichtbare Brucken. Ein Vietnam-Bericht. (Uber-
tragen von Tilly Bergner) [Illustriert.] [Wien] Die Buch-
gemeinde [1968]
DS557.A635R55   959.7'04   70-369599

1421.   Rigg, Robert B. How to stay alive in Vietnam; combat survival in the war of many fronts, by Robert B. Rigg. Harrisburg, Pennsylvania, Stackpole Books [1966]
U113.R5   355.4209597   66-20845

1422.   Riklin, Alois, comp. Der Vietnamkrieg. Tatsachen und
Meinungen. (Zurich, Schweizerischer Aufklarungs-Dienst,
1967)
DS557.A6R54   68-89754

1423.   Ritchie, James E. The making of a Maori; a case study of a
changing community, by James E. Ritchie. With a foreword
by Ernest Beaglehole. Wellington, A. H. & A. W. Reed
[1963]
DU423.R5   64-56654

1424.   Rizel y Alonso, Jose. One hundred letters of Jose Rizal to
his parents, brothers, sisters, relatives. Manila, Philippine Historical Society, 1959.
DS675.8.R5A4   923.2914   60-24139

1425.   Robb, Walter Johnson, 1880- Filipinos; pre-war Philippines
essays. Introduction by the author. [Rev.] Rizal. Printed in
the Philippines by Araneta University Press [1963]
[DS659]   919.14   64-9743/CD

1426.   Robequain, Charles. The economic development of French
Indo-China. New York, Oxford University Press, 1944.
HC442.R613   330.959   45-885

1427.   . L'Indo Chine. Paris, A. Colin, 1952.
DS534.R6   63-32280

1428.   . Malaya, Indonesia, Borneo, and the Philippines;
a geographical, economic, and political description. . .
2d ed. New York, Longmans, Green, 1958.
DS601.R752   991   58-4431

1429.   Roberts, John Charles de Villamar, 1925- Vietnam [by
John Roberts] London, Association for World Government
[1968]
DS557.A6R58   68-131120

1430.   Rockefeller, Michael Clark. The Asmat of New Guinea; the
        journal of Michael Clark Rockefeller, edited with an intro-
        duction by Adrian A. Gerbrands. New York, Museum of
        Primitive Art; distributed by the New York Graphic Society,
        Greenwich, Connecticut, 1967 [i.e. 1968]
        DU744.R52   919.5'1   67-28143

1431.   Rodl, Helmut. Vietnam; Hintergrunde, Zusammenhange,
        Losungen. [Jugenheim an der Bergstrasse] Weltkreis Verlag.
        [1966]
        DS557.A6R6   959.7'04   68-102239

1432.   Roff, William R.   The origins of Malay nationalism, by
        William R. Roff. New Haven, Yale University Press, 1967.
        DS596.5.R6   320.1'58'095951   67-13447

1433.   Rogers, William Pierce, 1913- Viet-Nam in perspective;
        an address by William P. Rogers. [Washington] Department
        of State; [for sale by the Superintendent of Documents, U.S.
        Government Printing Office, 1969]
        DS557.A63R6   327.5'073   73-605356

1434.   Rohrer, Daniel M. By weight of arms; America's overseas
        military policy [by] Daniel M. Rohrer, Mark G. Arnold
        and Roger L. Conner. Skokie, Illinois, National Text-
        book Company [1969]
        E840.R57   327.73   73-95359

1435.   Romulo, Carlos Pena. Crusade in Asia; Philippine victory.
        New York, Day, 1955.
        DS686.5.R6   991.4   55-7318

1436.   Roosevelt, Nicholas. The Philippines; a treasure and a
        problem. New York, Sears, 1926.
        DS685.R7   991   26-20745

1437.   Rose, Dale L.   The Vietnamese civil service system [by]
        Dale L. Rose assisted by Vu Van Hoc. [Saigon?] Michigan
        State University Vietnam Advisory Group, 1961.
        JQ847.R6   62-62536

1438.   Rose, Frederick G. G.   The wind of change in Central
        Australia. The aborigine at Angas Downs, 1962 [von]
        Frederick G. G. Rose. Berlin, Akademie-Verlag,
        1965.
        DU120.R58   572.994   66-68921

1439.   Rose, Saul. Socialism in southern Asia. New York, Oxford
        University Press, 1959.
        HX382.R6   335.0959   59-3232

1440.   Rose, William Erle, 1902-   Smouldering fire; international
        affairs 1945-65, and the crisis of Indo-China, summarised

by Erle Rose. Auckland, Graphic Educational Publications [1967]
DS557. A5R58   959. 7   74-374965

1441.   Rosecrance, R. N. Australian diplomacy and Japan, 1945-
        1951. [Parkville] Melbourne University Press; New York,
        Cambridge University Press [1962]
        DU113.5.J3R6 1962   327. 52094   62-5347

1442.   Rosenberg, Milton J., 1925- Vietnam and the silent ma-
        jority: the dove's guide by Milton J. Rosenberg, Sidney
        Verba & Philip E. Converse. Peter Smith, 1971.
        DS557.A68R68   959. 7'04

1443.   _____, et al. Vietnam & The Silent Majority: The Dove's
        Guide. Harper & Row, 1970.
        DS557. A68R68   959. 7'04   72-135749

1444.   Rovere, Richard Halworth, 1915- Reflections on United
        States policy [by] Richard H. Rovere. London, Sydney [etc.]
        Bodley Head, 1968.
        E183. 8. V5R6 1968b   327. 73'0597   68-118545

1445.   _____. Waist deep in the Big Muddy; personal reflec-
        tions on 1968, by Richard H. Rovere. [1st ed.] Boston,
        Little, Brown [1968]
        E183. 8. V5R6   327'. 73'0597   68-22900

1446.   Rowe, James N., 1938- Five years to freedom, by James
        N. Rowe. Boston, Little, Brown, 1971.
        DS557.A675R68   959. 7'04'37   70-128357

1447.   Rowe, John. Count your dead; a novel of Vietnam. [Sydney]
        Angus and Robertson [1968]
        PZ4.R879Co   823   76-366376

1448.   Rowland, Benjamin. The Harvard outline and reading lists
        for Oriental art. Cambridge, Harvard University, 1952.
        N7260.R6   709. 5   52-5040

1449.   Roy, Juoes, 1907- The battle of Dienbienphu. Translated
        from the French by Robert Baldick. Introduction by Neil
        Sheehan. New York, Harper & Row [1965]
        DS550.R6213   959. 7   64-25121

1450.   Rozehnal, Miro. Nad rudou rekou. [1. vyd.] Praha, Orbis,
        1962.
        DS557.A7R6   63-46497

1451.   Rudolf, Walter. Volkerrechtliche Aspekte des Vietnam-
        Konflikts. (Vortrag.) Bad Homburg v. d. H., Berlin,
        Gehlen, 1967.
                                                        68-117903

1452.   Ruehl, Lothar, 1927-   Vietnam. Brandherd eines Weltkon-
         flikts? (Frankfort/-M., Berlin, Ullstein, 1966)
         DS557.A5R8   959.7'04   68-71180

1453.   Runciman, Sir Steven. The white rajahs; a history of Sara-
         wak from 1841 to 1946. Cambridge, University Press,
         1960.
         DS646.36.R9   991.15   60-50589

1454.   Rural reconstruction and development: a manual for field
         workers [by] Y. C. James Yen, Gregorio M. Feliciano and
         the joint staffs of the International Institute of Rural Recon-
         struction and the Philippine Rural Reconstruction Movement.
         Edited by Harry Bayard Price. New York, Praeger [1967]
         HN713.5.R8   309.2'3'09914   67-138 53

1455.   Rusk, Dean, 1909-   The heart of the problem: Secretary
         Rusk [and] General Taylor review Viet-Nam policy in Senate
         hearings. [Washington, Department of State, Office of
         Media Services, Bureau of Public Affairs; for sale by the
         Superintendent of Documents, U.S. Government Printing
         Office, 1966]
         DS557.A6R75   66-61074

1456.   _____. Viet-Nam: four steps to peace. [Washington]
         Department of State [for sale by the Superintendent of Docu-
         ments, U.S. Government Printing Office, 1965]
         DS557.A6R8   65-62055

1457.   Russ, Martin. Happy hunting ground. [1st ed.] New York,
         Atheneum, 1968.
         DS557.A69R8   959.7'04   68-16863

1458.   Russell, Bertrand, 3d Earl Russell, 1872-1970. Appeal to the
         American conscience [by] Bertrand Russell. London,
         Bertrand Russell Peace Foundation [1966]
         DS557.A67R8   67-74275

1459.   _____. War crimes in Vietnam [by] Bertrand Russell.
         [New York, Monthly Review Press, 1967]
         DS557.A6R85 1967   959.7'04   67-23969

1460.   Russell, Richard Joel, 1895-   Australian tidal flats, by
         Richard J. Russell [and] William G. McIntire. Baton Rouge,
         Louisiana State University Press, 1966.
         GB458.5.R8   551.360994   66-21759

1461.   Rutherford, James. Hone Heke's Rebellion, 1844-1846; an
         episode in the establishment of British rule in New Zealand.
         Auckland, 1947.
                                                               48-27753

1462.   Ryan, N. J. The making of modern Malaya; a history from

earliest times to the present. Kuala Lumpur, Oxford University Press, 1963.
DS596.R9   959.5   64-1413

S

1463.   Sack, John. M. [New York] New American Library [1967]
        DS557.A6S14   959.704   67-14220

1464.   Sager, Peter. Report from Vietnam. [Translated from the German by Ian Tickle] [Bern] Swiss Eastern Institute [1968]
        DS557.A6S1483   959.7'04   71-443213

1465.   Sahu, Bhagban, 1944-   Vietnam (Bhietanama), (In Oriya), 1965.
        DS557.A6S15

1466.   Saigon. Hoc-vien Quoc-gia Hanh-chanh. Viet Nam government organization manual, 1957-58. Saigon, National Institute of Administration, Research and Documentation Division, 1958.
        JQ831.S23   S A 62-691 rev.

1467.   Saimong Mangrai, Sao. The Shan States and the British annexation. Ithaca, New York, Department of Asian Studies, Cornell [c.] 1965.
        DS560.S18   959.1   65-8564

1468.   Sainteny, Jean   Histoire d'une paix manquee, Indochine, 1945-1947 . . . Paris, A. Fayard [1967]
        DS550.S35 1967   959.7'03   67-114693

1469.   Sakka, Michel. Vietnam, la guerre chimique et biologique, un peuple sert de champ d'experience. Paris, Editions sociales, 1967.
        DS557.A68S3   959.7'04   67-101341

1470.   Salisbury, Charlotte Y. Asian diary, by Charlotte Y. Salisbury. New York, Scribners [1968 c.1967]
        DS10.S3   915'.04'02   68-11360

1471.   Salisbury, Harrison Evans, 1908- Behind the lines: Hanoi, December 23, 1966-January 7, 1967 [by] Harrison E. Salisbury, New York, Harper & Row [1967]
        DS557.A7S2   959.7'04   67-21219

1472.   Salmon, Malcolm. North Vietnam; a first-hand account of the blitz. [Sydney, Tribune, 1969?]
        DS557.A69S3   959.7'04   77-492329

1473.   Samonte, Quirico S. A situational analysis of public school enrollment in the Philippines, by Quirico S. Samonte. Ann

148   Vietnam

Arbor, Michigan, Printed by Malloy Lithoprinting
[1965]
LC145. P5S3   370. 1934   66-63180

1474.   Sanders, Jacquin. The draft and the Vietnam War. New
York, Walker [1966]
UB343. S27   355. 225   66-25159

1475.   Sandvig, Anders, 1929-   Fred i Vietnam? [Oslo]Normanna-
forlaget; (Bokcentralen) 1968.
DS557. A6S156   70-372497

1476.   Saniel, Josefa M. Japan and the Philippines, 1868-
1898. Quezon City, University of the Philippines,
1962.
DS673. J3S3   327. 520914   64-1292

1477.   Sansom, Robert L. The economics of insurgency in the
Mekong Delta of Vietnam [by] Robert L. Sansom. Cam-
bridge, Massachusetts, M. I. T. Press [1970]
HD2080. V5S35   330. 9597   70-90753

1478.   Sarkar, Chanchal. Window on Asia. New Delhi, Popular
Book Service [1968, c. 1967]
DS10. S35   915'. 03'42   SA 68-948

1479.   Sartre, Jean Paul, 1905-   On genocide. And a summary
of the evidence and the judgments of the International War
Crimes Tribunal, by Arlette El Kaim-Sartre. Boston,
Beacon Press [1968]
DS557. A67S313   959. 7'04   68-54850

1480.   Sarzi Amade, Emilio, 1925-   Rapporto dal Vietnam.
[Torino] Einaudi [1966]
DS557. A6S16   67-3431

1481.   Sawer, Geoffrey. Australian Government today. Rev. &
enl. Parkville, Melbourne University, 1961.
JQ4015. S3 1961   354. 94   62-4734

1482.   Scaff, Alvin H. The Philippine answer to communism.
Stanford, Stanford University Press [1955]
DS686. 5. S35 1955   991. 4   55-9584

1483.   No entry.

1484.   Scharnberg, Carl. Vietnam--blot en begyndelse? Du skal
ikke adlyde ordrer! To radioforedrag. Arhus, Aros;
(D. B. K.) 1967.
DS557. A6S18   79-350384

1485.   Scheer, Robert. How the United States got involved in

Vietnam; a report to the Center for the Study of Democratic Institutions. [Santa Barbara, California, Center for
the Study of Democratic Institutions, 1965]
DS557. A6S2   327. 597073   65-6975

1486.   Schell, Jonathan, 1943-   The military half; an account of
         destruction in Quang Ngai and Quang Tin. [1st ed.] New
         York, Knopf, 1968.
         DS557. A68S3   959. 7'04   68-24317

1487.   _____. The village of Ben Suc. New York, Knopf,
         1967.
         DS557. A68S33   959. 7'04   67-29479

1488.   _____. Village of Ben Suc. Random House, Inc., 1971.

1489.   Schiller, A. Arthur. The formation of Federal Indonesia,
         1945-1949. The Hague, Van Hoeve, 1955.
         JQ762. S35   *320. 991 342. 91   55-2878

1490.   Schlesinger, Arthur Meier, 1917-   The bitter heritage;
         Vietnam and American democracy, 1941-1966 [by] Arthur
         M. Schlesinger, Jr. Boston, Houghton Mifflin, 1967
         [c. 1966]
         E183. 8. V5S3   327. 730597   67-669

1491.   _____. The bitter heritage: Vietnam and American
         democracy, 1941-1966 [by] Arthur M. Schlesinger, Jr.
         London, Deutsch, 1967.
         E183. 8. V5S3 1967b   327. 73'0597   68-86636

1492.   _____. The bitter heritage: Vietnam and American
         democracy, 1941-1968 [by] Arthur M. Schlesinger, Jr.
         Rev. ed. Greenwich, Connecticut, Fawcett Publications
         [1968]
         E183. 8. V5S3 1968   327. 73'0597   67-15978

1493.   _____. Das bittere Erbe. Vietnam, Prufstein der
         Demokratie. [Von] Arthur M. Schlesinger. [Einzig
         berechtigte Ubertragung aus dem Amerikanischen von
         Wolfgang J. und Christa Helbich.) Bern, München, Wien,
         Scherz (1967).
         E193. 8. V5S315   327. 73'0597   68-114022

1494.   _____. Vietna: herenca tragica [por] Arthur M.
         Schlesinger, Jr. Trad. de Aydano Arruda. S. Paulo,
         Ibrasa [1966]
         E183. 8. V5S316   327. 73'0597   68-110618

1495.   Schmitz, Carl August. Oceanic sculpture: sculpture of
         Melanesia. Greenwich, Connecticut, New York Graphic
         Society, 1962.
         NB1111. M4S3   730. 993   62-7574

150   Vietnam

1496.   Schnell, Jonathan, 1943-   The military half; an account of
        destruction in Quang Ngai and Quang Tin.   New York,
        Vintage Books [1968]
        DS557.A68S32 1968b 959.7'04   68-6754

1497.   Schoenbrun, David.   Vietnam; how we got in, how to get
        out. [1st ed.] New York, Atheneum, 1968.
        DS557.A63S28 1968 959.7'04   68-25589

1498.   Schoenman, Ralph.   A glimpse of American crimes in
        Vietnam. [London, Bertrand Russell Peace Foundation]
        1967.
        DS557.A67S4   959.7'04   68-143106

1499.   Schoofs, Rudolf.   Israel, Vietnam: The Horrors of War:
        Hommage to Goya.   Wittenborn, George, Inc., 1968.

1500.   Schrieke, Bertram Johannes Otto, 1890-1945.   Indonesian
        sociological studies.   Selected writings of B. Schrieke. The
        Hague, W. van Hoeve, 1955-
        HN703.5S37   A 55-7350

1501.   Schultz, George F.   Vietnamese legends, adapted from the
        Vietnamese by George F. Schultz.   Rutland, Vermont, C. E.
        Tuttle Company [1965]
        GR313.S38   398.209597   65-25634

1502.   Schultz, Per.   De andres børn.   Redaktion: Per Schultz.
        Tastrup, Unge Paedagoger, Søndertoften 70, 1968.
        DS557.A68S38   68-115127

1503.   Schultz, Gene.   Third Face of War.   Jenkins Publishing
        Company, 1969.

1504.   Schurmann, Herbert Franz.   The politics of escalation; a
        study of United States responses to pressures for a political
        settlement of the Vietnam War: November 1963-January
        1966.   Prepared by a working group organized by scholars
        at the University of California, at Berkeley, and Washington
        University, in St. Louis.   Authors: Franz Schurmann,
        Peter Dale Scott [and] Reginald Zelnik. [Berkeley? 1966]
        DS557.A63S29   327.730597   66-8081 rev.

1505.   _____. The politics of escalation in Vietnam, by Franz
        Schurmann, Peter Dale Scott [and] Reginald Zelnik.   Fore-
        word by Arthur Schlesinger, Jr.   Summary and conclusions
        by Carl E. Schorske.   Boston, Beacon Press [1966]
        DS557.A63S3 1966 973.922   67-1958

1506.   _____. The politics of escalation in Vietnam, by Franz
        Schurmann, Peter Dale Scott [and] Reginald Zelnik.   With
        a foreword by Arthur Schlesinger, Jr.   Summary and con-
        clusions by Carl E. Schorske.   Greenwich, Connecticut,

Fawcett Publications [1966]
DS557. A63S3 1966a   959. 7'04   66-28916

1507. Schweitzer, Carl Christoph. Die U. S. A. und der Vietnam-
Konflikt, 1964-1967. Köln, Westdeutscher Verlag, 1969.
DS557. A63S34   76-397586

1508. Schwimmer, Eric, 1923-   The world of the Maori.
Wellington, A. H. & A. W. Reed [1966]
DU423. S3   919. 31031   67-497

1509. Scigliano, Robert G.   South Vietnam: nation under stress.
Boston, Houghton Mifflin [c. 1963]
DS557. A6S22   959. 7   63-25470

1510. _____ . Technical assistance in Vietnam: the Michigan
State University experience [by] Robert Scigliano [and]
Guy H. Fox.   New York, F. A. Praeger [1965]
HC443. V5S3   309. 223   65-13323 rev.

1511. Scott, Sir James George, 1851-1935.   The Burman; his life
and notions, by Shway Yoe [pseud.] New York, Norton
[1963]
DS485. B81S4 1963   915. 91   63-5970

1512. Segev, Samuel, 1926-   (Vietnam between war and peace),
(In Hebrew). Tel Aviv, Israel, 1966.)
DS557. A6S25

1513. Sein, Kenneth, 1918-   The great Po Sein; a chronicle of
the Burmese theater, by Kenneth (Maung Khe) Sein and
J. A. Withey.   Drawings by Ba Lose Lay.   Bloomington,
Indiana University Press [1966, c. 1965]
PN2960. B8S4   792. 0924 (B)   65-19705

1514. Semmler, Clement, ed.   Twentieth century Australian
literary criticism.   Melbourne, London, Oxford University
Press, 1967.
PR9441. S44

1515. Sergeeva, Natal'ia Sergeevna.   Na v'etnamskoi zemle;
zametki zhurnalista, (On the Vietnamese Soil; observations
of a journalist).   (In Russian).   Moscow, 1955.
DS557. A5S4

1516. Serventy, Vincent.   Landforms of Australia.   [1st American
ed.] New York, American Elsevier, 1968.
GB441. S4   551. 4'0994   67-16091

1517. Shafer, Robert.   Bibliography of the Sino-Tibetan Language.
Wiesbaden, Harrassowitz, 1957.

1518. Shah, Ikbal Ali, sirdar. Viet Nam. London, Octagon Press

[1960]
DS557. A5S46   959. 7   61-24022

1519.   Shang, I. Yueh-nan shu chien, (Letters from Vietnam),
         (In Chinese). Shanghai, 1957.
         DS557. A7S45

1520.   Shaplen, Robert, 1917-   The lost revolution; the story of
         twenty years of neglected opportunities in Vietnam and of
         America's failure to foster democracy there. New York,
         Harper [c. 1955-1965]
         DS557. A5S47   959. 704   65-20438

1521.   _____. Lost Revolution: U. S. in Vietnam,
         1946-1966. Harper & Row, 1966.
         DS557. A5S47 1966   959. 704
                                                              66-4892

1522.   _____. Road from War: Vietnam 1965-1970. Harper &
         Row, 1970.
         DS557. A6S28 1970   959. 7'04   70-123961

1523.   _____. Road from War: Vietnam 1965-1971. Harper &
         Row Publishers, Inc. , 1971.

1524.   Shaw, Alan George Lewers, 1916-   A short history of
         Australia [by] A. G. L. Shaw. [2d ed.] New York,
         Praeger [1967]
         DU112. S5 1967   994   67-24529

1525.   Shchedrov, I. Fighting Vietnam. Moscow, Novosti Press
         Agency Publishing House, 1965.
         DS557. A61S513   67-4782

1526.   _____. Boriushchiisia V'etnam, (Fighting Vietnam).
         (In Russian). Moscow, 1965.
         DS557. A6S17

1527.   _____. IUzhnyi V'etnam segodnia, (South Vietnam To-
         day). (In Russian). Moscow, 1962.
         DS557. A6S3

1528.   Shea, Dick. Vietnam simply. [Coronado, California, Pro
         Tem Publishers, 1967]
         PS3569. H39V5   67-5467

1529.   Sheehan, Susan. Die nicht gefragt werden. Menschen in
         Vietnam. (Aus dem Amerikanischen ubers.: Gunter Eichel.)
         München, Claudius-Verlag (1968)
         DS557. A69S465   73-391994

1530.   _____. Ten Vietnamese. [1st ed.] New York, Knopf,
         1967.
         DS557. A69S46   959. 7'04   67-11129

1531.   Sheldon, Walter J.   Tigers in the Rice: A Short History
        of Vietnam.   Macmillan Company (Subs of Crowell Collier
        & Macmillan, Inc.) 1969.

1532.   Shepard, Elaine.   The doom pussy.   New York, Trident,
        1967.
        DS557. A69S5   959. 704   67-13002

1533.   _____. Doom Pussy. Pocket Books, Inc. , 1968.

1534.   Shields, Archibald John.   Australian weather [by] A. J.
        Shields.   [Brisbane] Jacaranda Press [1965]
        QC992.   551. 50994   66-8362

1535.   Shih chieh chih shih ch'u pan she, Peking.   Chen tou ti
        Yuen-nan (War in Vietnam).   (In Chinese).   Peking, 1965.
        DS550. S52

1536.   _____. Mei-kuo tut Yueh-nan nan fang ti kan she,
        (U. S. A. Policies for interferring & interventing in South
        Vietnam), (In Chinese).   Peking, 1963.
        DS557. A5S475

1537.   _____. Yin-tu-chih-na wen t'i wen chien hui pien,
        (Selected Reports of Indochina Problems).   Peking, 1959.
        DS550. S53

1538.   Shiltova, Alla Petrovna. Natsional'no-osvboditel'noe dvizhenie
        vo V'etname, 1858-1945, (National liberation rising in
        Vietnam, 1858-1945).   (In Russian).   Moscow, 1958.
        DS557. A5S48

1539.   Shitarev, German Ivanovich.   Solntse sotsializma mad
        Krasnoi rekoi, (The sun of socialism over the Red River).
        (In Russian).   Moscow, 1964.
        DS557. A7S47

1540.   Shore, Moyers S.   1941-   The battle for Khe Sanh, by
        Moyers S. Shore, II.   Washington, Historical Branch,
        G-3 Division, Headquarters, U. S. Marine Corps. [for
        sale by the Superintendent of Documents, U. S. Government
        Printing Office] 1969.
        DS557. A62K58   959. 7'04   72-603604

1541.   Silcock, T. H. and Fisk, Ernest Kelvin.   The political
        economy of independent Malaya; a case-study in development.
        Berkeley, University of California, 1963.
        HC497. M3552   64-3049

1542.   Silcock, Thomas Henry, ed.   Readings in Malayan eco-
        nomics.   Singapore, Published by D. Moore for Eastern
        Universities Press, 1961.
        HC497. M3S53

1543.   _____ . Towards a Malayan nation. Singapore, Published by D. Moore for Eastern Universities Press, 1961.
DS597. S5   323. 1595   62-2970

1544.   Simpson, Colin.   Adam in ochre; inside aboriginal
Australia.   New York, Taplinger Publishing Company
[1968, c. 1967]
DU120. S5 1968   572. 9'94   67-26504

1545.   Sinclair, Keith.   A history of New Zealand.   New York,
Oxford University Press, 1961.
DU420. S53   993. 1   61-66687

1546.   _____ . The origins of the Maori wars.   Wellington,
New Zealand University, 1961.
DU420. S55   993. 102   61-35767

1547.   Singapore.   Annual report.   1946-   Singapore, Government Printing Office.
J618. T3S5   352. 0595   49-14197

1548.   Singapore year book.   Singapore, Government Printing
Office.
DS598. S7S6   915. 95'2'005   68-32488

1549.   Sitwell, Osbert.   Escape With Me.   New York: Harrison-
Hilton Books, Inc. , 1940.
DS508. S55   915   40-14026

1550.   Sivaram, M.   The Vietnam war: why?   by M. Sivaram.
Delhi, Atma Ram, 1966.
DS557. A6S5 1966b   S A 68-1101

1551.   _____ . The Vietnam War: Why?   Rutland, Vermont,
Tuttle [1965, c. 1966]
DS557. A6S5   959. 704   66-11009

1552.   Sivko, Vaclav.   Vietnam; Reiseeindrucke eines Malers.
[Deutsch von Norbert Chotas. Prag] Artia [1958]
ND538. S5C47

1553.   Sjahrir, Soetan.   Out of exile.   New York, Day, 1949.
DS644. S513   991   49-7495

1554.   Skinner, George William, 1925-   Local, ethnic, and
national loyalties in village Indonesia; a symposium.   Contributors: Edward M. Bruner [and others.   New Haven?]
Yale University, Southeast Asia Studies, distributed in
cooperation with the Institute of Pacific Relations, New
York, 1959.
HN703. S5 1958   919. 1   59-16784

1555.   Slingsby, H. G. 1921-   Rape of Vietnam [by] H. G.

Slingsby. [Wellington, New Zealand] Modern Books Press, 1966.
DS557. A5S56   959. 7'04   68-4136

1556.   Slizinski, Jerzy, ed.   Legendy i basnie wietnamskie.
[Ksiazke adobu Stanislaw Andrzej Cyrano.   Ilustracje poza tekstem wedlug rysunkow wietnamskich Nguyen Tien Chunga.
Wyd. 1.] Wroclaw, Zaklad im. Ossolinskich, 1956.
GR313. S58   65-34118

1557.   Smith, Bernard William.   Australian painting, 1788-1960.
New York, Oxford University Press, 1962.
ND1100. S55   709. 94   63-2263

1558.   Smith, Donald Eugene, 1927-   Religion and politics in
Burma.   Princeton, New Jersey, Princeton University
Press, 1965.
BL1443. 1. S6   322. 109591   65-14311

1559.   Smith, George E.   P. O. W.   Two Years with the Viet
Cong.   Ramparts, 1971.

1560.   Smith, Mary Benton.   Southeast Asia.   Res., text by
Mary Benton Smith under the direction of Frederic M. Rea.
[1st ed.] Menlo Park, California, Lane [1958]
DS504. S55   915. 9'04   68-26325

1561.   Smith, Nelle Van D., comp.   We care; inspirational mes-
sages, compiled by Nelle Van D. Smith.   New York,
William-Frederick Press, 1968.
DS557. A6S53   959. 7'04   68-19718

1562.   Smith, Peter E.   Letters from a Vietnam Hospital.   International Publications Service, 1969.

1563.   Smith, Ralph.   Vietnam & the West.   International Publications Service, 1968.

1564.   Smith, Ralph Bernard.   Viet-Nam and the West by Ralph
Smith.   Cornell University Press, 1971.
DS557. A5S58 1971   915. 97'03   78-148717

1565.   _____.   Viet-Nam and the West, by Ralph Smith.
London, Heinemann Educational, 1968.
DS557. A5S58   915. 97'03   76-392677

1566.   Smith, Robert Aura, 1899-   Philippine freedom, 1946-1958.
New York, Columbia University Press, 1958.
DS686. 5. S5   991. 4   58-9513

156   Vietnam

1567.   Smith, Roger M.   Cambodia's foreign policy, by Roger M.
         Smith.   Ithaca, New York, Cornell University Press [1965]
         DS557. C28S6   327. 596   65-15375

1568.   Smith, T. E.   Malaysia, by T. E. Smith and John Bastin.
         London, Oxford University Press, 1967.
         DS592. S65   915. 95'03   68-80399

1569.   _____. Population growth in Malaya; an analysis of
         recent trends.   Foreword by Frank W. Notestein.   London,
         New York, Royal Institute of International Affairs [1952]
         HB3640. M3S6   312   52-7567

1570.   Smithsonian Institution.   National Collection of Fine Arts.
         Art and archeology of Viet Nam; Asian crossroad of cul-
         tures.   A traveling exhibition circulated by the National
         Collection of Fine Arts.   Washington, Smithsonian Institu-
         tion, 1961.
         N7314. S6   709. 597   61-60775

1571.   Smits, Alfo.   Ik, een Vietnamees meisje.   Amsterdam,
         Nederlandsche Keurboekerij [1968]
         PT5881. 29. M52I4   68-92333

1572.   Smolik, Milan.   Americane v Saigonu.   [Vyd. 1.] Praha,
         Nakl. politicke literatury, 1962.
         DS557. A6S55   64-26998

1573.   Snyder, Wayne W.   An analysis of government payments in
         Viet Nam during 1955, including details of expenditures by
         the national, regional, provincial, municipal, and prefec-
         torial governments, by Wayne W. Snyder and Nguyen Van
         Hoang.   Saigon, Michigan State University, Viet-Nam Ad-
         visory Team, 1956.
         HJ2158. Z9V6   336. 597   59-63308

1574.   _____. Autonomous state organizations, government
         enterprises and public corporations of Viet Nam; a study
         of the annual reports and the administrative accounts per-
         taining to calendar year 1955 for use in estimating the na-
         tional income of Viet-Nam, a project of the National Bank.
         [Saigon?] Michigan State University, Vietnam Advisory
         Group, National Institute of Administration Division, 1957.
         JQ831. S6   354. 59704   59-63312

1575.   Sobel, Lester A. , ed.   South Vietnam: Communist-U. S.
         Confrontation in Southeast Asia, 1961-1965.   Facts on
         File, 1966.
         DS557. A6S557   959. 704   66-23943

1576.   _____. ed.   South Vietnam: Communist-U. S. Confronta-
         tion in Southeast Asia, Vol. 2. , 1966-1967.   Facts on File,
         Inc., 1969.

1577.   Sochevko, G. G.   V'etnam, (Vietnam).   (In Russian).
        Moscow, 1959.

1578.   Soetrisno Hs.   Teluk Tonkin menggetarkan, disusun oleh
        Soetrisno Hs.   Tjet.   1.   Surabaja, Nirbita, 1965.
        DS557. A6S56   S A 66-3837

1579.   Soljak, Philip Leonard.   New Zealand, Pacific pioneer.
        New York, Macmillan, 1946.
        DU420. S6   993. 1   46-5930

1580.   Solntsev, Vadim Mikhailovich.   V'etnamskii iazyk, (Viet-
        namese Language).   (In Russian).   Moscow, 1960.
        PL4373. S6

1581.   Soloukhin, Vladimir Alekseevich.   Otkrytki iz V'etnama,
        (Views from Vietnam).   (In Russian).   Moscow, 1961.
        DS557. A7S6

1582.   Son, Chu-hwan.   Pult'amun Wo'lam (War is going on in
        Vietnam; diary of a Vietnam war correspondent),   (In
        Korean), 1965.
        DS557. A6S6

1583.   Song, Ong Siang, 1871-   One hundred years' history of
        the Chinese in Singapore.   Singapore, University of Malaya
        Press, 1967.
        DS598. S7S65 1967   301. 453'51'05952   68-4848

1584.   Sontag, Susan, 1933- Trip to Hanoi,   New York, Farrar,
        Straus and Giroux [1969, c. 1968]
        DS557. H3S6 1969   915. 97   69-15403

1585.   South Asian affairs; no. 1- Carbondale, Illinois,
        Southern Illinois University Press, 1960.
        DS335. S6   959. 0082   60-11589

1586.   South Asian affairs; no. 2 [New York] Oxford [c.] 1966.
        DS335. S6   959. 0082   60-11589

1587.   South Vietnam from NFL to PRG.   China Books and Peri-
        odicals, 1970.

1588.   South Vietnam '64.   Hanoi, Foreign Languages Publishing
        House [1964]
        DS557. A7V5 no. 1   65-56473

1589.   South Vietnam: Initial Failure of the U. S. Limited War.
        China Books and Periodicals, 1967.

1590.   South Vietnam.   Initial failure of the U. S. "limited war."
        Hanoi, Foreign Languages Publishing House, 1967.
        DS557. A6S65   959. 7'04   68-1139

1591.   South Vietnam National Front for Liberation.   China Books
        and Periodicals, 1968.

1592.   South Viet Nam National Front for Liberation.   FNLs polit-
        iska program.   Antaget vid FNLs extra kongress i augusti
        1967. [Stockholm] 1967.
        DS557. A6S66   73-396982

1593.   _____. South Vietnam on the road to victory. [n. p.]
        Liberation Publishing House, 1965.
        DS557. A61S6   68-40562

1594.   _____. Central Committee.   Declaration du Comite
        Central du Front national de liberation du Sud Viet-Nam
        sur l'intensification et de l'extension de la guerre d'agres-
        sion americaine au Sud Viet-Nam.   Statement . . . con-
        cening [sic] the intensification and expansion by the U.S.
        imperialists of their aggressive war in South Viet-Nam.
        [n. p. , 1965]
        DS557. A6S68   959. 7'04   67-4992

1595.   South Vietnam Nineteen Sixty-Eight: The DRV at War.
        China Books and Periodicals,   1971.

1596.   South Vietnam: Realities & Prospects.   China Books and
        Periodicals,   1969.

1597.   Southard, Betty Jane.   Provisional government of Viet Nam
        since 1945.   Columbus, Ohio, Capital Properties [1951?]
        JQ811. S6   56-34820

1598.   Spencer, Sir Baldwin and Gillen, Francis James.   The
        native tribes of central Australia.   London, Macmillan,
        1938.
        GN665. S7   572. 9942   1-19198

1599.   Spencer, Joseph Earle.   Land and people in the Philippines;
        geographic problems in rural economy.   Berkeley, Univer-
        sity of California, 1952.
        HD2087. S6   919. 14   52-14536

1600.   Spiro, Melford E.   Burmese supernaturalism; a study in
        the explanation and reduction of suffering.   Englewood
        Cliffs, New Jersey, Prentice-Hall [1967]
        BL2030. B8S67   291'. 1'09591   67-27956

1601.   Spock, Benjamin McLane, 1903-   Dr. Spock on Vietnam
        [by] Benjamin Spock and Mitchell Zimmerman. [New
        York, Dell Publishing Company, 1968]
        DS557. A63S6   959. 7'04   68-3565

1602.   Stamp, Laurence Dudley.   Asia; a regional and economic
        geography. 11th ed. New York, Dutton, 1962.
        HC412. S7   915   62-5766

1603.   Standard, William L.   Aggression: Our Asian disaster by
        William L. Standard.   Random¦ 1971.
        JX1573. Z7U56   959. 7'043373   76-143829

1604.   Starobin, Joseph R.   Eyewitness in Indo-China.   New York,
        Cameron & Kahn, 1954.
        DS550. S8   959   54-3155

1605.   Starobin, Joseph Robert, 1913-   Svoboda se blizi k deltam.
        [Z anglickeho rukopisu "Journey to Free Vietnam" prel.
        Miroslav Jodl.   Vyd. 1.]   Praha, Nase vojsko, 1954.
        DS557. A7S83   57-43630

1606.   _____ . Viet-Nam fights for freedom; the record of a
        visit to the liberated areas of Viet-Nam in March, 1953.
        London, Lawrence & Wishart, 1953.
        DS557. A5S8   959. 7   54-29434 rev.

1607.   Statistical handbook on Vietnam, Saigon, 1949-50.   (In
        Vietnamese).

1608.   Stavens, Ralph, ed.   Warmakers: the Men Who Made the
        Vietnam War & How They Did It.   Outerbridge & Dienstr-
        frey, 1971.

1609.   Steele, Archibald Trojan, 1903-   The American people
        and China [by] A. T. Steele.   [1st ed.]   New York, Pub-
        lished for the Council on Foreign Relations by McGraw-Hill
        [c. 1966]
        E183. 8. C5S8   327. 51073   65-28736

1610.   Steinbeck, John, 1946-   In touch [by] John Steinbeck, IV.
        [1st ed.]   New York, Knopf, 1969.
        CT275. S6763A3   917. 3'03'9230924   69-10685

1611.   Steinberg, David J.   Cambodia: its people, its society, its
        culture.   In collaboration with Chester A. Bain [and others].
        Rev. for 1959 by Herbert H. Vreeland.   New Haven, HRAF
        Press [1959]
        DS557. C2S8 1959   915. 96   59-13226

1612.   Steinberg, David Joel.   Philippine collaboration in World
        War II.   Ann Arbor, University of Michigan Press [1967]
        D802. P5S7   991. 4'035   66-17017

1613.   Steinhaus, Kurt.   Vietnam. Zum Problem der kolonialen
        Revolution und Konterrevolution.   (2. Aufl.)   Frankfurt
        a. M., Verlag Neue Kritik (1967)
        HN700. V5S7   1967   309. 1597   67-103410

1614.   Stern, Kurt, 1907-   Bevor der Morgen graut.   Vietnam
        zwischen Krieg und Sieg.   [Von] Kurt und Jeanne Stern.
        Berlin, Verlag Neues Leben (1969).
        DS557. A72S68   70-448502

1615.   . Reisfelder, Schlachtfelder; Augenzeugenbericht
uber Vietnam in Krieg [von] Kurt und Jeanne Stern. Halle
(Saale) Mitteldeutscher Verlag, 1967.
DS557. A72S7   68-101704

1616.   Stern, Mary.   Come along to Burma.   Minneapolis, Denison
[1966]
DS485. B81S764   j915. 91   66-14846

1617.   Stevens, Joan.   The New Zealand novel, 1860-1960.   New
York, Heinman, 1962.
PR9635. S 7   823. 809   62-52822

1618.   Stevenson, Anne.   High living: a study of family life in
flats [by] Anne Stevenson, Elaine Martin [and] Judith O'Neill.
[Melbourne] Melbourne University Press; London, New York,
Cambridge University Press [1967]
HN920. M4S7 1967   309. 1'94'5   71-353037

1619.   Stewart, Douglas Alexander, ed.   Old bush songs and rhymes
of colonial times.   Enl. & rev.   Sydney, Angus & Robertson, 1957.
PR9560. S82   63-54926

1620.   Stewart, Douglas Alexander and Keesing, Nancy, eds.
Australian bush ballads.   Sydney, Angus & Robertson, 1955.
PR9560. S8   56-406

1621.   Stewart, George, 1922-   What's so funny about Vietnam?
[Tampa, Florida, Tampa Art & Publishing Company, 1968]
DS557. A61S7   959. 7'04   70-9139

1622.   Stockhausen, Hans Wilfried von.   Vietnam, Dynamik eines
Konflikts.   [Diessen/Ammersee] W. Frhr. v. Tucher
[1965]
DS557. A6S7   67-57457

1623.   Stone, Desmond, ed.   Verdict on New Zealand.   Wellington,
Reed, 1959.
DU427. S76   919. 31   59-1424

1624.   Stone, Gerald L.   War without honour [by] Gerald L. Stone.
[Brisbane] Jacaranda Press [1966]
DS557. A6S76   959. 704   66-72162

1625.   Stone, Horace.   From Malacca to Malaysia, 1400-1965.
London, Toronto [etc.] Harrap, 1966.
DS596. S8 1966   959. 5   66-71951

1626.   Strehlow, Theodor Georg Heinrich.   Aranda traditions.
New York, Johnson Reprint [1968]
GN666. S8   572. 994   49-4899

1627. Strel'nikov, Boris Georgievich. Sto dnei vo V'etname; iz putevogo dnevnika, (Hundred Days in Vietnam; from a traveler's Diary). (In Russian). Moscow, 1955.
DS557. V5S78

1628. Strong, Anna Louise, 1885- Cash and violence in Laos and Viet Nam. New York, Mainstream Publishers, 1962.
DS550. S85 327. 730597 62-3766

1629. Studies in the anthropology of Oceania and Asia, presented in memory of Roland Burrage Dixon. Ed. by Carleton S. Coon and James M. Andrews, IV. Cambridge, The Museum, 1943.
44-2765

1630. Studies on Asia. v. 1- 1960- Lincoln, University of Nebraska.
DS2. S8 950. 04 60-15432

1631. Sturt, Charles, 1795-1869. Narrative of an expedition into Central Australia, performed under the authority of Her Majesty's Government, during the years 1844, 5, and 6, together with a notice of the Province of South Australia in 1847. London, T. and W. Boone, 1849. [Adelaide, Libraries Board of South Australia, 1965]
DU80. A88 no. 5

1632. Su, Tzu. Chin jih Yueh-nan, (Vietnam Today), (In Chinese). Mecca, 1952.

1633. Suarez, Luis, 1918- Guerra en la paz: Vietnam, Camboya y Laos. [1. ed. Mexico] Editorial Nuestro Tiempo [1969]
DS550. S9 71-442129

1634. Sudjatmoko, 1922- An approach to Indonesian history: towards an open future; an address before the Seminar on Indonesian History, Gadjah Mada University, Jogjakarta, December 14, 1957 [by] Soedjatmoko. Ithaca, New York, Modern Indonesia Project, Southeast Asia Program, Department of Far Eastern Studies, Cornell University, 1960.
DS635. S3

1635. _____., ed. An introduction to Indonesian historiography. Edited by Soedjatmoko [and others] Ithaca, New York, Cornell University Press [1965]
DS633. 8. S8 991. 0072 64-25273

1636. Sukarno, Pres. Indonesia, 1901- Marhaen and proletarian; speech before the Indonesian Nationalist Party at the party's thirtieth anniversary at Bandung, July 3rd, 1957. [Translated by Claire Holt] Ithaca, New York, Modern Indonesia Project, Southwest Asia Program, Department of Far Eastern Studies, Cornell University, 1960.
JQ763. S8 1960

162   Vietnam

1637.   _____. Sukarno; an autobiography, as told to Cindy
          Adams. Indianapolis, Bobbs-Merrill [1965]
          DS644. 1. S8A3   354. 91030924 (B)   65-26511

1638.   Sully, Francois, ed. We the Vietnamese: Voices from
          Vietnam. Praeger, 1971.
          DS557. A5S85   915. 97'03'08   75-95693

1639.   Sun, Ruth Q. Land of Seagull and Fox. Rutland, Vermont,
          C. E. Tuttle Company, 1967.
          GR313. S9   398. 2'09597   67-23010

1640.   Supeno. Viet Nam berdjoang. [Surabaja] Ksatrya [1949]
          JQ815. S8   55-59548

1641.   Sverige och Vietnamfragan. Anforanden och uttalanden.
          Stockholm [Fritzes hovbokhandel (distr.)] 1968.
          DS557. A6S94   79-370856

1642.   Swearingen, Arthur Rodger, 1923- Communism in Viet-
          nam; a documentary study of theory, strategy, and opera-
          tional practices, by Rodger Swearingen and Hammond Rolph.
          Chicago, American Bar Association [1967]
          HX400. V5S9   335. 43'09597   67-18823

1643.   Sweezy, Paul Marlor, 1910- comp. Vietnam: the end-
          less war; from Monthly Review, 1954-1970. Monthly Re-
          view Press, 1971.
                                959. 7'04   77-127927

1644.   Swettenham, Sir Frank Athelstane, 1850-1946. British Malaya,
          an account of the origin and progress of British influence in
          Malaya. Rev. ed. London, G. Allen & Unwin, 1955,
          c. 1906.
          DS592. S9   49-19163

1645.   _____. Stories and sketches. Selected and
          introduced by William R. Roff. Kuala Lumpur, Oxford Uni-
          versity Press, 1967.
          DS595. 6. S9A25 1967 915. 95'03'3   S A 67-5918

1646.   Sylvester, John F. The eagle and the dragon. Phila-
          delphia, Dorrance [c. 1965]
          DS557. A5S88   959. 704   65-26150

1647.   Syme, Anthony. Vietnam; the cruel war. Sydney,
          London, [etc.] Horwitz [1966]
          DS557. A67S95   959. 7'04   68-105622

1648.   Symposium on America's Stake in Vietnam, Washington,
          D. C. , 1956. A Symposium on America's Stake in Viet-
          nam. [Report] New York, American Friends of Vietnam
          [1956]
          DS557. A5S9 1956   959. 7   56-58707 rev.

1649.   Symposium on the Viet-Nam War, East Carolina University,
        1968. Essays on the Vietnam War. Contributors: Philip
        J. Adler [and others] Editor: Jung-Gun Kim. Greenville,
        N. C., East Carolina University Publications, 1970.
        DS557. A6S97 1968   959. 7'04   70-120959

T

1650.   Taboulet, George. La Geste Francaise en Indo-Chine.
        Paris, Adrian Maisonneuve, 1955.
        DS521. T3   56-24627

1651.   Takman, John, 1912- Krigsforbrytelser i Vietnam. Stock-
        holm, Vietnampress, 1967.
        DS557. A67T3   77-374360

1652.   _____. Var vid Sydkinesiska sjon; en resa i Vietnam
        och Kina, 1958. Stockholm, Tidskriften Clarte [1959]
        DS711. T34   61-28958

1653.   _____. Vietnam; ockupanterna och folket. [1. uppl.
        Malmo] B. Cavefors [1965]
        DS557. A6T34   68-114182

1654.   Tanham, George K. Communist revolutionary warfare;
        the Vietminh in Indochina. New York, Praeger [c. 1961]
        DS557. A5T3   959. 7   61-16698

1655.   _____. War Without Guns. New York, Praeger, 1966.
        HC443. V5T3   309. 22309597   66-13671

1656.   Tanham, George Kilpatrick. Communist revolutionary war-
        fare; from the Vietminh to the Viet Cong [by] George K.
        Tanham. Rev. ed. New York, Praeger [1967]
        DS557. A5T3 1967   959. 7'04   67-21379

1657.   Taruc, Luis. Born of the people. New York, Interna-
        tional Publishers, 1953.
        DS686. 2. T3A3   991. 4   53-10412

1658.   Taylor, Carl. Getting to know Burma. Illustrated by
        Meg Wohlberg. New York, Coward [c. 1962]
        DS485. B81T3   j915. 91   62-14911

1659.   Taylor, George Edward, 1905- The Philippines and the
        United States: problems of partnership. [1st ed.] New
        York, Published for the Council on Foreign Relations by
        Praeger [1964]
        DS672. 8. T3 1964   327. 730914   64-12080

1660.   Taylor, Milton C. The System of excise taxes in Viet-nam.
        [Saigon?] Michigan State University, Viet-Nam Advisory
        Group, 1960.
        HJ5165. Z8V57   336. 2711   60-63879

1661.   Taylor, Nancy M., ed.   Early Travellers in New Zealand.
         Oxford, Clarendon, 1959.
         DU400. T3   919. 31   60-502

1662.   Teller, Charles.   Vietnam 17de [i. e. zeventiende] breed-
         tegraad; roman   (Vertaald door Peter Dietrich)   Brussels,
         D. A. P. (1966)
         PT2682. E4V512   67-99585

1663.   Telles, Carlos de Queiroz.   Vieᴜ em mim.   [n. p.]   Liv.
         Sal. [1968]
         PQ9698. 3. E69V5   68-115636

1664.   Ten years of fighting and building of the Vietnamese Peo-
         ple's Army.   Hanoi, Foreign Languages Publishing House,
         1955.
         UA853. V5T4   S A 66-3741

1665.   Terrorist raids and fascist laws in South Viet Nam; docu-
         ments.   Hanoi, Foreign Languages Publishing House, 1959.
                                                                     S A 66-3743

1666.   Terry, Susan.   House of love: life in a Vietnamese hos-
         pital.   London, Newnes, 1967.
         RA990. V7L65 1967   915. 97'03'4   67-79378

1667.   _____.   House of love; life in a Vietnamese hospital.
         [Melbourne] Lansdowne [1966]
         RA990. V5T47   915. 97034   66-67809

1668.   Thai-van-Kiem.   Viet-Nam d'hier et d'aujourd'hui. Ouvrage
         publie sous le patronage du Departement de l'education
         nationale du Viet-Nam et de la Commission nationale du
         Viet-Nam pour l'UNESCO.   Paris, Commercial Transworld
         Editions [1956]
         DS557. A5T5   57-2178

1669.   _____.   Viet-Nam, past and present.   [Tangier?   Com-
         mercial Transworld Editions, 1957]
         DS557. V5T513   959. 7   60-37048

1670.   They Have Been in North Vietnam.   China Books and Peri-
         odicals, 1968.

1671.   Thompson, Lawrence C.   A Vietnamese Grammar.
         Seattle, University of Washington Press, 1965.
         PL4373. T4   495. 9225   65-25425

1672.   _____.   A Vietnamese reader, by
         Laurence C. Thompson and Nguyen duc Hiep.   Seattle,
         University of Washington Press, 1961.
         PL4378. T48   495. 92   61-14429

1673.   Thompson, Sir Robert Grainger Ker, 1916-   No Exit
        from Vietnam.   rev. ed. New York, McKay, 1970.
        DS557. A6T56 1970   959. 7'04   71-16275

1674.   _____. Defeating Communist insurgency; the
        lessons of Malaya and Vietnam [by] Sir Robert
        Thompson. New York, F. A. Praeger
        [1966]
        U240. T56 1966a   355. 425   66-14507

1675.   _____. No exit from Vietnam, by Robert Thompson.
        [1st American ed.] New York, McKay [1969]
        DS557. A6T56 1969b   959. 7'04   79-86603

1676.   Thompson, Virginia McLean, 1903-   French Indo-
        China. New York, Macmillan Company, 1937.
        DS541. T5   959   38-2122

1677.   _____. French Indo-China, by Virginia Thompson, Ph. D.
        London, G. Allen & Unwin, Ltd. [1937]
        DS541. T5   959   38-2122

1678.   _____. French Indo-China, by Virginia Thompson. New
        York, Octagon, 1968.
        DS541. T5 1968   959   68-17756

1679.   Thomson, Ian, 1912- Changing patterns in South Asia.
        New York, Roy [c. 1962]
        DS509. 3. T55   915. 9   62-13281

1680.   Thorin, Duane.   The need for civil authority over the
        military.   [Bryn Mawr, Pennsylvania, Intercollegiate
        Studies Institute, 1968]
        DS557. A63T47   959. 7'04   68-2557

1681.   Thurk, Harry. Der Tod und der Regen. Roman.   (2.
        Aufl.) (Berlin) Verlag das Neue Berlin (1968)
        PT2682. H8T6 1968   68-138384

1682.   _____. Der Tod und der Regen. Roman.   (Berlin)
        Das Neue Berlin (1967)
        PT2682. H8T6 1967   68-143392

1683.   Tilman, Robert O. Bureaucratic transition in Malaya. Dur-
        ham, North Carolina, Pub. for Duke University Common-
        wealth Studies Center [by] Duke University Press [c.] 1964.
                            959. 5   64-20418

1684.   Tindale, Norman Barnett, 1900· Aboriginal Australians
        [by] Norman B. Tindale and H. A. Lindsay.   Melbourne,
        Children's Library Guild of Australia [distributed by
        Australian Children's Library Distributors, 1963]
        DU120. T66   572. 994   66-5433

1685.   Tinker, Hugh.   The foundations of local self-government in
India, Pakistan, and Burma.   London, Athlone, 1954.
JS7008. T5   54-14610

1686.   _____.   The Union of Burma: a study of the first years
of independence.   4th ed.   London, New York [etc.] issued
under the auspices of the Royal Institute of International Affairs by Oxford University Press, 1967.
DS485. B81T52 1967   915. 91'03'5   67-95770

1687.   _____.   The Union of Burma, a study of the first years
of independence.   2d ed.   London, New York, Oxford University Press, 1959.
DS485. B81T52 1959   959. 1   59-2694

1688.   _____.   The Union of Burma; a study of the first years
of independence.   3d ed.   New York, Oxford [c. 1959, 1961]
DS485. B81T52   959. 1   61-65533

1689.   To Khuy, 1920-   Stikhi.   Perevody s v'etnamskogo,
(Translation of Vietnamese Poetry).   (In Russian).   Moscow,
1961.
PL4378. 9. T63

1690.   Tobing, Philip Oder Lumban.   The structure of the Toba-
Batak belief in the High God.   Amsterdam, Van Campen,
1956.

1691.   Tomizaki, Man'emon, ed.   Minami Betonamu no keizal
kajhatsu, (Economic Development in South Vietnam), (In
Japanese).   Tokyo, 1962.
HC443. V5T6

1692.   Tomlinson, Henry Major.   Malay waters; the story of little
ships coasting out of Singapore and Danang in peace and
war.   London, Hodder & Houghton, 1950.
HE880. M3T6   387. 5   52-735

1693.   Tong, Andre.   Dix mille annees pour le Vietnam!   le
dossier.   Paris, la Table ronde, 1967.
DS557. A6T6   68-96643

1694.   Tongas, Gerard.   J'ai vecu dans l'enfer communiste au
Nord Viet-Nam.   Paris, Nouvelles Editions Debresse
[1960]
DS557. A7T6   61-42749

1695.   Tooze, Ruth.   Cambodia: land of contrasts.   Illustrated
with photos.   New York, Viking [c. 1962]
DS557. C2T6   915. 96   62-18695

1696.   _____.   Our rice village in Cambodia.   Illustrated by
Ezra Jack Keats.   New York, Viking [c. 1963]
PZ9. T5570U   j915. 96   63. 18364

1697.   Tournaire, Helene.   Livre jaune du Viet-Nam; enquete en
        collaboration avec Robert Bouteaud.   Paris, Librairie
        academique Perrin [1966]
        DS550. T67   66-84789

1698.   Toye, Hugh.   Laos: buffer state or battleground.   London,
        New York [etc.]   Oxford University Press, 1968.
        DS557. L25T6 1968   959. 4'04   68-115746

1699.   Le Tractoriste, recueil de nouvelles.   Hanoi, Editions en
        langues etrangeres, 1965.
        PL4382. F8T7   68-43824

1700.   Traditional Vietnam: Some Historical Struggles.   China
        Books and Periodicals, 1964.

1701.   Trager, Frank N.   Building a welfare state in Burma,
        1948-1956.   New York, Institute of Pacific Relations, 1958.
        HC437. B4T67   338. 9591   58-2225

1702.   _____ .   Burma: from kingdom to republic; a historical
        and political analysis [by] Frank N. Trager.   New York,
        Praeger [1966]
        DS485. B86T7   959. 1   65-24936

1703.   _____ .   Burma: land of golden pagodas, by Frank N.
        Trager.   Talking it over, by Helen G. Trager.   [New
        York, Foreign Policy Association] 1954.
        E744. H43 no. 104   959. 1   54-8407
        -------- Copy 2.   DS485. B892T7

1704.   _____ ., ed. Marxism in Southeast Asia; a study of four
        countries.   Edited, with an introduction and conclusion.
        With contributions by Jeanne S. Mintz [and others]
        Stanford, California, Stanford University Press, 1959.
        DS518. 1. T7   335. 40959   59-12469

1705.   _____ .   Why Viet Nam?   [by] Frank N. Trager.   New
        York, F. A. Praeger [1966]
        DS557. A6T63   959. 704   66-14508

1706.   Tran-cu'u-Chan, 1906-   Etude sur le metre populaire
        thu'o'ng luc ha bat.   Saigon, 1953.
        PL4379. T7   S A 66-3833

1707.   Tran-hu'u-Quang.   Cach ve ban do Viet Nam; hinh-the,
        chung-toc, kinh-te.   [Saigon] Nguyen-Du Xuat-ban [1961]
        G2368. V5T7 1961   S A 65-7836

1708.   Tran-minh-Tiet.   Problemes de defense du Sud-Est
        Asiatique. (Le Viet-Nam et ses voisins). Paris, Nouvelles
        editions latines, 1967.
        DS518. 1. T73   68-85704

1709.   Tran-minh-Tiet. Le Viet-Nam dans le contexte mondial
         . . . Paris, Nouvelles editions latines, 1967.
         DS557. A6T64   68-85687

1710.   Tran-Phong. Socialist industrialization in North Vietnam.
         New York, U.S. Joint Publications Research Service, 1959.
         AS36. U56 no. 737   338. 09597   59-61712

1711.   Translations on North Vietnam's Economy, Nos. 1-27.
         New York, Crowell Collier & Macmillan, 1962.

1712.   Tran-van-Khe. La musique vietnamienne traditionelle.
         Paris, Presses universitaires de France, 1962.
                                                              A 66-180/MN

1713.   Tran-van-Tung. Deux mille ans de poesie vietnamienne.
         Paris, Serg, 1965.
         PL4378. 2. T7   841   66-72814

1714.   _____. Le Vietnam face au communisme et a la
         feodalite. Viry-Chatillon [France] Editions du Parc [1962]
         DS557. A6T66   64-26005

1715.   _____. Viet-nam. With a foreword by K. M. Panikkar,
         and an introduction by Michael Edwardes. [Adapted from
         the French by Michael Edwardes] New York, Praeger
         [1959, c. 1958]
         DS557. A5T73   915. 97   58-12093

1716.   Tregaskis, Richard William, 1916- Vietnam Diary. H R & W,
         1963.
         DS557. A6T7   959. 7   63-21877

1717.   _____. Vietnam diary. New York, Popular Lib. [1966,
         c. 1963]
         DS557. A6T7   959. 7   75-1206

1718.   Tregonning, K. G. The British in Malaya; the first forty
         years, 1786-1826 [by] K. C. [i.e. G.] Tregonning. Tuc-
         son, Published for the Association for Asian Studies by
         the University of Arizona Press [c.] 1965.
         DS596. 5. T7   959. 5   64-32755

1719.   _____. A history of modern Malaya [by] K. G.
         Tregonning. New York, McKay [1967, c. 1964]
         DS596. T69 1967   959. 5'1   67-12911

1720.   _____. Under chartered company rule: North Borneo,
         1881-1946. Singapore, University of Malaya, 1959.
         DS646. 33. T7   991. 1   58-2587

1721.   Tribunal Russell, 1st, Stockholm, 1967. Le Jugement de
         Stockholm. [Extraits des debats de la 1 session, 1966-
         1967]. Directeur de redaction: Vladimir Dedijer . . .

Redactrice: Arlette Elkaim. Documentation: Catherine
Russell. [Paris,] Gallimard, 1967.
DS557. A6T72 1967   68-116320

1722.   Tribunal Russell, 1st, Stockholm, 1967. Il Processo di
        Stoccolma. A cura di Paolo Caruso. Bari, De Donato,
        1968.
        DS557. A6T72 1967a 959. 7'04   74-373172

1723.   Truong-buu-Lam. Patterns of Vietnamese response to
        foreign intervention, 1858-1900. [New Haven] Southeast
        Asia Studies, Yale University [distributor: Cellar Book
        Shop, Detroit, c. 1967]
        DS557. A5T733   959. 7'03'08   67-30990

1724.   Tru'o'ng-Chinh. Avgustovskaia revoliutsiia vo V'etname,
        (August Revolution in Vietnam). (In Russian, Translated
        from Vietnamese). Moscow, 1954.
        DS557. V5T717

1725.   _____ . Primer for revolt; the Communist takeover in
        Viet-Nam. A facsim. ed. of the August Revolution and The
        resistance will win. Introduction, notes by Bernard B.
        Fall. New York, Praeger [c. 1963]
        DS557. A5T75   959. 7   63-9456

1726.   _____ . Vpered, pod znamenem partii! (Forward, Under
        the Banners of the Party). (In Russian). Hanoi, 1963.
        JQ898. W6T7

1727.   Truong-Son. A bitter dry season for the Americans. Hanoi,
        Foreign Languages Publishing House, 1966.
        DS557. A6T75   959. 7'04   SA 67-2312

1728.   _____ . Five Lessons of a Great Victory: Winter 1966-
        Spring 1967. China Books and Periodicals, 1967.

1729.   _____ . The Winter 1966-Spring 1967 victory and five
        lessons concerning the conduct of military strategy. Hanoi,
        Foreign Languages Publishing House, 1967.
        DS557. A6T76   959. 7'04   68-2660

1730.   Tru'o'ng-trung-Thu. Ekonomicheskaia politika amerykans-
        kikh neokolonizatorov v IUzhonom V'etname, (Economic
        Policy of American Neo-Colonizers in South Vietnam). (In
        Russian). Moscow, 1965.
        HF1456. 5. V5T777

1731.   Tu Tuong, (Thought) Monthly, 1969-   (In Vietnamese).
        Van Hanh University, 222 Truong Minh Giang, Saigon, South
        Vietnam.

1732.   Tucker, James Guy. Arkansas men at war. [Little Rock,

Arkansas, Pioneer Press, 1968]
DS557. A69T8   959. 7'04   68-29339

1733.   Tucker, Robert W.   Nation or empire?   The debate over
         American foreign policy, by Robert W. Tucker. Baltimore,
         Johns Hopkins Press [c. 1968]
         E840. T8   327. 73   68-9700

1734.   Tung, Tran Van. Vietnam. London, Thames and Hudson,
         1958.
         DS557. A5T73   915. 97   58-12093

1735.   Tung-Phong.   Chinh-de Viet-nam: vi-tri cua Viet-nam trong
         the'gio'i hien'dai; hoan-canh lich-su cua cong-dong quoc-gia;
         cong-san va su phan-chia lanh-tho; du'o'ng loi phat-trien cua
         dan-toc. Saigon, Dong'Nai [1965]
         DS557. A6T8   S A 68-1040

U

1736.   United Nations Association of Great Britain and Northern
         Ireland. Vietnam: a plea for self-determination. London,
         United Nations Association [1966]
         DS557. A6U435   66-76072

1737.   United Nations. Economic Commission for Asia and the
         Far East. Community development and economic develop-
         ment. Bangkok, 1960.
                                                     62-916

1738.   United Nations Educational, Scientific and Cultural Organiza-
         tion. Ceylon: paintings from temple, shrine and rock.
         Greenwich, Connecticut, New York Graphic Society, 1957.
         ND1005. U5   759. 954   57-59245

1739.   United Nations. Fact-Finding Mission to South Viet-Nam.
         Report. Washington, Subcommittee to Investigate the Ad-
         ministration of the Internal Security Act and Other Internal
         Security Laws of the Committee on the Judiciary, U.S.
         Senate, 1964.
         DS557. A6U432   64-60891

1740.   United Nations. General Assembly. 7th session, 1952-53.
         Delegation from New Zealand. The United Nations; summary
         of report of the New Zealand delegation to the resumed part
         of the seventh regular session of the General Assembly,
         held at New York, 24 February to 23 April 1953. Welling-
         ton, Department of External Affairs, 1954.
         DU400. A33 no. 141

1741.   _____ . _____ . 9th session, 1954. Delegation from
         New Zealand. The United Nations; summary of report to
         the ninth regular session of the General Assembly, held at

New York, 21 September 1954 to 17 December 1954.
Wellington, Department of External Affairs, 1956.
DU400. A33 no. 166

1742.   University of Western Australia law review, v. 1-
        1948/50-   Nedlands, Western Australia, University of
        Western Australia Law School.
        PU59

1743.   University Study Group on Vietnam.   Vietnam and Australia;
        history, documents, interpretations.   Gladesville [Sydney,
        1966]
        DS557. A5U57 1966   959. 7   67-90726

1744.   U. S. Agency for International Development.   Statistics and
        Reports Division.   U. S. foreign assistance and assistance
        from international organizations: obligations and loan au-
        thorizations, July 1, 1945-June 30, 1961.   Rev. [Washing-
        ton, 1962]
        HC60. U6I52   62-64730

1745.   U. S. AID Mission in Vietnam.   Diary of an infiltrator.
        Saigon, United States Mission in Vietnam, 1966.
        DS557. A69U5   959. 7'04'0922   67-8473

1746.   U. S. Army.   500th Military Intelligence Group.   A guide to
        the pronounciation of Vietnamese.   [Tokyo] Translation
        Section, 500th Military Intelligence Group, 1956.
        PL4397. U5   495. 9215   57-60256

1747.   U. S. Army Language School, Monterey, California.   Viet-
        namese; basic course.   Presidio of Monterey, 1955-
        PL4373. U5   55-61257

1748.   _____ .   Vietnamese: homework coordinated with basic
        course lessons.   Presidio of Monterey, 1958.
        PL4373. U52   495. 92   58-62085

1749.   _____ .   Vietnamese military interpreting exercises and
        military subjects and situations.   Presidio of Monterey,
        1956.
        PL4375. U52   *495. 92864   56-60641

1750.   _____ .   Vietnamese: military interpreting exercises,
        coordinated with basic course lessons and with military
        subjects and situations.   Presidio of Monterey, 1960.
        PL4373. U529   61-60147

1751.   _____ .   Vietnamese: military interrogation exercises co-
        ordinated with basic course lessons, and with military sub-
        jects and situations.   Rev. Presidio of Monterey, 1958.
        PL4373. U53   495. 92   58-62086

1752. _____. Vietnamese; military map tracking and exercises with military terrain table coordinated with basic course lessons and military subjects and situations. Presidio of Monterey, 1961.
PL4375. U523   61-60995

1753. _____. Vietnamese: military subjects and situations. Presidio of Monterey, 1957-
PL4375. U53   495. 928242   57-62088

1754. _____. Vietnamese; reading selections. Presidio of Monterey, 1956-
PL4375. U54   *495. 92864   56-60825 rev.

1755. _____. Vietnamese (Saigon dialect); special course (12 weeks) Presidio of Monterey, 1962-
PL4373. U56   62-62290

1756. U. S. Congress. House. Committee on Armed Services. Hearing on problems of prisoners of war and their families. Ninety-first Congress, second session. March 6, 1970. Washington, U. S. Government Printing Office, 1970.
KF27. A7 1970   959. 7'04   75-606576

1757. _____. Report by subcommittee of the House committee on Armed Services following a visit to the Republic of Vietnam, January 15-17, 1970, on the progress of the pacification program. Washington, U. S. Government Printing Office, 1970.
KF32. A7 1970   959. 7'04   78-605944

1758. _____. Report of special subcommittee following visit to Southeast Asia, April 7-19, 1966, Eighty-ninth Congress, second session. Washington, U. S. Government Printing Office, 1966.
UA23. 3. A38 1966c   67-60995

1759. _____. Special Subcommittee on Tactical Air Support. Close air support. Hearing, Eighty-ninth Congress, first session. Washington, U. S. Government Printing Office, 1966.
UG633. A412 1966b   358. 4142   66-60590

1760. _____. Special Subcommittee on Tactical Air Support. Close air support; report, Eighty-ninth Congress, second session. Washington, U. S. Government Printing Office, 1966.
UG633. A412 1966c   66-60591

1761. _____. Special Subcommittee to South Vietnam. Report following an inspection tour, June 10-21, 1965. Washington, U. S. Government Printing Office, 1965.
DS557. A6U438   65-62481

U. S.

1762. U. S. Congress. House. Committee on Foreign Affairs. Staff report on field survey of selected projects in Vietnam and Korea. Subcommittee for Review of the Mutual Security Programs. Washington, U. S. Government Printing Office, 1959.
HC443. V5U45   338. 9173   59-61493

1763. U. S. Congress. House. Committee on Government Operations. Military Operations Subcommittee. Military supply systems, 1969. Hearings, Ninety-first Congress, first session. November 20, 25, and December 8, 1969. Washington, U. S. Government Printing Office, 1970.
KF27. G668 1969   355. 3'41   76-605705

1764. U. S. Congress. House. Committee on Merchant Marine and Fisheries. Subcommittee on Coast Guard, Coast and Geodetic Survey, and Navigation. U. S. Coast Guard activities, Southeast Asia; report on a congressional investigation of Coast Guard operations and installations in Thailand and South Vietnam [by Frank M. Clark, Albert J. Dennis, and John H. Bruce] Washington, U. S. Government Printing Office, 1968.
KF32. M436 1968   959. 7'04   68-67110

1765. _____. Subcommittee on Merchant Marine. Vietnam-shipping policy review. Hearings, Eighty-ninth Congress, second session. Washington, U. S. Government Printing Office, 1966-
DS557. A6U44   387. 5   66-61031

1766. U. S. Congress. House. Committee on the Judiciary. Refugee problems in Vietnam, India, and Hong Kong, British Crown Colony; [report] H. Res. 593, Eighty-ninth Congress. Washington, U. S. Government Printing Office, 1966.
HV640. 5. V5U45   325. 21   66-62062

1767. U. S. Congress. House. Special Subcommittee on National Defense Posture. Review of the Vietnam conflict and its impact on U. S. military commitments abroad; report, Ninetieth Congress, second session, under authority of H. Res. 124. Washington, U. S. Government Printing Office, 1968.
KF32. A7732 1968   355. 03'35'73   68-62515

1768. U. S. Congress. House. Subcommittee on National Security Policy and Scientific Developments. American prisoners of war in Southeast Asia, 1970. Hearings,

Ninety-first Congress, second session, April 29, May 1
[and] 6, 1970. Washington, U. S. Government Printing Office, 1970.
KF27. F6483 1970   959. 7'04   74-607562

1769.   . American prisoners of war in Vietnam. Hearings, Ninety-first Congress, first session. November 13
and 14, 1969. Washington, U. S. Government Printing Office, 1969.
KF27. F6483 1969a   959. 7'04   79-604694

1770. U. S. Congress. Joint Economic Committee. Economic
effect of Vietnam spending. Hearings, Ninetieth Congress,
first session. Washington, U. S. Government Printing Office, 1967.
HC106. 6. A47   330. 973   67-61760

1771.   . Economic effect of Vietnam spending; report,
together with supplementary views. Washington, U. S.
Government Printing Office, 1967.
HC106. 6. A474   330. 973   67-62540

1772. U. S. Congress. Senate. Committee on Armed Services.
Preparedness Investigating Subcommittee. Investigation of
the preparedness program; report . . . on airlift and sea-
lift to South Vietnam. Washington, U. S. Government Printing Office, 1967.
DS557. A68U53   959. 7'04   68-60293

1773.   . Investigation of the preparedness program; re-
port . . . on U. S. Air Force tactical air operations in
Southeast Asia. Washington, U. S. Government Printing
Office, 1967.
DS557. A65U5 1967a   959. 7'04   68-60297

1774.   . Investigation of the preparedness program;
report . . . on the U. S. Army in South Vietnam. Washington, U. S. Government Printing Office, 1967.
DS557. A6U443 1967a 959. 7²04   68-60298

1775.   . Investigation of the preparedness program; report . . . on U. S. Navy and U. S. Marine Corps in Southeast Asia. Washington, U. S. Government Printing Office,
1967.
DS557. A645U53   959. 7'04   68-60296

1776.   . Investigation of the preparedness program; sum-
mary report . . . on air war against North Vietnam.
Washington, U. S. Government Printing Office, 1967.
DS557. A65U57   959. 7'04   68-60400

1777.   . Air war against North Vietnam. Hearings,
Ninetieth Congress, first session. Washington, U. S.

U. S.   175

Government Printing Office, 1967-
DS557. A65U55   959. 7'04   67-62358

1778.   U. S. Congress. Senate. Committee on Foreign Relations.
         American prisoners of war in Southeast Asia; report, to
         accompany H. Con. Res. 454. [Washington, U. S. Govern-
         ment Printing Office, 1970]
         KF31. F6 1970   959. 7'04   70-606284

1779.   _____. Background information relating to Southeast
         Asia and Vietnam. 2d rev. ed. Washington, U. S. Govern-
         ment Printing Office, 1966.
         DS550. U5114 1966   327. 730597   66-61002

1780.   _____. Background information relating to Southeast
         Asia and Vietnam. 3d rev. ed. Washington, U. S. Govern-
         ment Printing Office, 1967.
         DS550. U5114 1967   327. 597'073   67-62094

1781.   _____. Background information relating to Southeast
         Asia and Vietnam. 5th rev. ed. Washington, U. S. Govern-
         ment Printing Office, 1969.
         DS550. U5114 1969   327. 597'073   72-601275

1782.   _____. Background information relating to Southeast
         Asia and Vietnam. 4th rev. ed. Washington, U. S. Govern-
         ment Printing Office; for sale by the Superintendent of
         Documents, 1968.
         DS550. U5114 1968   327. 597'073   68-67048

1783.   _____. Briefing on Vietnam. Hearings, Ninety-first
         Congress, first session . . . November 18 and 19, 1969.
         Washington, U. S. Government Printing Office, 1969.
         KF26. F6 1969j   959. 7'04   71-604692

1784.   _____. Changing American attitudes toward foreign
         policy. Hearing, Ninetieth Congress, first session, with
         Henry Steele Commager, professor, Amherst College.
         February 20, 1967. Washington, U. S. Government Print-
         ing Office, 1967.
         E744. U453 1967   327. 73   67-60790

1785.   _____. Conflicts between United States capabilities and
         foreign commitments. Hearing, Ninetieth Congress, first
         session, with Lt. Gen. James M. Gavin (U. S. Army re-
         tired) on February 21, 1967. Washington, U. S. Govern-
         ment Printing Office, 1967.
         E840. A52   327. 73   67-60792

1786.   _____. Impact of the war in Southeast Asia on the U. S.
         economy. Hearings, Ninety-first Congress, second session
         . . . Washington, U. S. Government Printing Office, 1970-
         KF26. F6 1970f   330. 973   70-607454

1787.   _____. Moral and military aspects of the war in Southeast Asia. Hearings, Ninety-first Congress, second session . . . May 7 and 12, 1970. Washington, U. S. Government Printing Office, 1970.
KF26. F6 1970g   959. 7'04   74-607798

1788.   _____. News policies in Vietnam. Hearings, Eighty-
ninth Congress, second session. August 17 and 31, 1966.
Washington, U. S. Government Printing Office, 1966.
DS557. A68U55   327. 730597   66-65775

1789.   _____. Report on Indochina; report of Mike Mansfield
on a study mission to Vietnam, Cambodia [and] Laos.
Washington, U. S. Government Printing Office, 1954.
DS550. U513   54-63240

1790.   _____. Situation in Vietnam. Hearings before the Subcommittee on State Department Organization and Public Affairs of the Committee on Foreign Relations, United States
Senate, Eighty-sixth Congress, first session . . . Washington, U. S. Government Printing Office, 1959-60.
HC443. V5U47 1969   338. 91730597   59-62357 rev.

1791.   _____. Southeast Asia resolution. Joint hearing before
the Committee on Foreign Relations and the Committee on
Armed Services, United States Senate, Eighty-eighth Con-
gress, second session, on a joint resolution to promote the
maintenance of international peace and security in Southeast
Asia. August 6, 1964. Washington, U. S. Government
Printing Office, 1966.
DS557. A63A53   959. 7'04   67-60153

1792.   _____. Submission of the Vietnam conflict to the United
Nations. Hearings, Ninetieth Congress, first session, on
S. Con. Res. 44 . . . [and] S. Res. 180 . . . October
26, 27, and November 2, 1967. Washington, U. S. Govern-
ment Printing Office, 1967.
KF26. F6 1967h   959. 7'04   68-60154

1793.   _____. The truth about Vietnam; report on the U. S.
Senate hearings. Analysis by Wayne Morse. Foreword by
J. W. Fulbright. Ed. by Frank M. Robinson, Earl Kemp,
San Diego, California, Greenleaf Classics [c. 1966]
DS557. A6U446   959. 704   66-4763

1794.   _____. United States aid program in Vietnam. Report
by the Subcommittee on State Department Organization and
Public Affairs to the Committee on Foreign Relations,
United States Senate. Washington, U. S. Government Print-
ing Office, 1960.
HC443. V5U47 1960   338. 91730597   60-60856

1795.   _____. Viet Nam and Southeast Asia, report of Mike

Mansfield, J. Caleb Boggs, Claiborne Pell [and] Benjamin
A. Smith. Washington, U. S. Government Printing Office,
1963.
DS518. 1. U6 1963   63-60861

1796.   . The Vietnam conflict: the substance and the
shadow. Report of Mike Mansfield [and others on a study
mission to Europe and Asia] Washington, U. S. Government
Printing Office, 1966.
DS557. A6U45   66-60454

1797.   . The Vietnam hearings. Introduction by J. William Fulbright. New York, Random [c. 1966]
DS557. A6U447   959. 704   66-4769

1798.   . The Vietnam hearings. With an introduction by
J. William Fulbright. New York, Random House [1966]
DS557. A6U447 1966a   959. 704   66-22357

1799.   . Vietnam policy proposals. Hearings, Ninety-
first Congress, second session. Washington, U. S. Government Printing Office, 1970.
KF26. F6 1970d   353ᵗ. 008ᵗ95   74-606991

1800.   U. S. Congress. Senate. Committee on the Judiciary.
Subcommittee to Investigate Problems Connected with
Refugees and Escapees. Civilian casualty and refugee
problems in South Vietnam; findings and recommendations.
Washington, U. S. Government Printing Office, 1968.
DS557. A68U553   959. 7ᵗ04   68-62612

1801.   . Civilian casualty, social welfare, and refugee
problems in South Vietnam. Hearings, Ninetieth Congress,
first session. Washington, U. S. Government Printing Office, 1968.
DS557. A68U555   959. 7ᵗ04   68-60483

1802.   . Refugee problems in South Vietnam and Laos.
Hearings, Eighty-ninth Congress, first session. Washington, U. S. Government Printing Office, 1965.

1803.   U. S. Congress. Senate. Committee on the Judiciary.
Subcommittee to Investigate the Administration of the Internal Security Act and Other Internal Security Laws. The
anti-Vietnam agitation and the teach-in-movement: the
problem of Communist infiltration and exploitation; a staff
study. Washington, U. S. Government Printing Office, 1965.
E183. 8. V5U48   327. 597073   65-62995

1804.   . Testimony of Jim G. Lucas. Hearing, Ninetieth Congress, second session. March 14, 1968. Washington, U. S. Government Printing Office, 1968.
DS557. A6U453   959. 7ᵗ04   68-61369

178   Vietnam

1805.   U. S. Congress, Senate Foreign Relations Committee.
        China, Vietnam and the United States: Highlights of the
        Hearings of the Senate Foreign Relations Committee.
        Washington, D. C.,   Public Affairs Press, 1966.
        E183. 8. C5U5   327. 51073   66-25442

1806.   U. S. Congress. Senate. Republican Policy Committee.
        The war in Vietnam, prepared by the staff of the Senate
        Republican Policy Committee. Washington, Public Affairs
        Press [1967]
        DS557. A6U455   959. 7'04   67-26288

1807.   U. S. Defense Language Institute. Vietnamese (Hanoi dialect);
        aural comprehension course: Text volume[s]-   [Washington]
        1966-
        PL4375. U56   495'. 922'8342   67-62519

1808.   U. S. Defense Language Institute. West Coast Branch,
        Monterey, California.
        Vietnamese: introduction to the standard writing system of
        Vietnamese. Presidio of Monterey, 1965.
        PL4379. U53   66-61132

1809.   _____. Vietnamese: military interrogation exercises.
        Coordinated with Basic course lessons and with military
        subjects and situations. Rev. 1958. Presidio of Monterey,
        1963.
        PL4373. U57 1963   64-60739

1810.   U. S. Department of State. Bureau of Intelligence and Re-
        search. Summary of principal events in the history of
        Vietnam. [Washington] 1962.
        DS557. A5U53   62-60672

1811.   U. S. Department of State. Division of Research for Far
        East. Political alignments of Vietnamese nationalists.
        [Washington] 1949.
        DS557. A5U52   959. 7   54-22383

1812.   U. S. Department of State. Office of Media Services. Ag-
        gression from the north; the record of North Viet-Nam's
        campaign to conquer South Viet-Nam. [Washington] Depart-
        ment of State [for sale by the Superintendent of Documents,
        U. S. Government Printing Office, 1965]
        DS557. A6U46   65-61214

1813.   _____. The pledge of Honolulu. [Washington] U. S.
        Department of State [for sale by the Superintendent of
        Documents, Government Printing Office, 1966]
        E183. 8. V5U5   66-60787

1814.   _____. Viet-Nam: fact sheet. [Washington, For sale
        by the Superintendent of Documents, U. S. Government

Printing Office, 1963.
DS557. A6U49   63-61406

1815.   . Viet-Nam: the 38th day. [Washington, For
sale by the Superintendent of Documents, Government
Printing Office, 1966]
DS557. A63U52   959. 7'04'08   66-61077

1816.   U. S. Department of State.   Office of Public Services.   A
threat to the peace; North Viet-Nam's effort to conquer South
Viet-Nam. [Washington] Department of State [1961]
DS557. A6U48   959. 7   62-60178

1817.   U. S. Department of State. Office of the Legal Adviser.
The legality of United States participation in the defense of
Viet Nam. [Washington] 1966.
JX4071. U5   327. 597'073   67-61822

1818.   U. S. Department of the Army.   The United States Army in
South Vietnam. [Washington] 1968.
DS557. A6U515   959. 7'04   73-605171

1819.   U. S. Directorate for Armed Forces Information and Educa-
tion.   Know your enemy: the Viet Cong. [Washington,
U. S. Government Printing Office, 1966]
DS557. A6U52   959. 7   66-61525

1820.   U. S. Embassy (Vietnam). Political program of the South
Vietnam National Liberation Front [by] U. S. Mission in
Vietnam.   Saigon, 1967.
JQ898. N37U54   320. 9'597   68-60995

1821.   U. S. Foreign Service Institute.   Vietnamese; basic course,
by Eleanor H. Jorden, Charles R. Sheehan [and] Nguyen-
hy-Quang & associates.   Washington [for sale by the Superintendent of Documents, U. S. Government Printing Office,
1967-
PL4371. U5   495'. 9'228342   67-60913

1822.   U. S. imperialists "burn all, destroy all, kill all" policy
in South Vietnam. [n. p.] Giai Phong (Liberation) Editions,
1967.
DS557. A6U525   959. 7'04   68-978

1823.   U. S. Information Agency.   At stake--the cause of freedom;
the eleven years since the Geneva accords on Vietnam.
[Washington, U. S. Information Service, 1965]
DS557. A6U53   959. 704   66-60460

1824.   U. S. Information Service, Ottawa.   The United States and
Viet-Nam.   Ottawa [1966-67]
DS557. A63   959. 7'04   67-61800

1825.   U.S. International Cooperation Administration. Vietnam,
         fact sheet; mutual security in action. [Washington, Public
         Services Division, Bureau of Public Affairs, 195-
         DS557. A6U5   60-60179

1826.   U.S. Joint Publications Research Service. Industry, trade,
         finance, and labor in North Vietnam. NY-109/1-February
         28, 1958-   New York.
         AS36. U57   338. 9597   58-60909

1827.   _____. North Vietnam's trade and prices. New York,
         1959.
         AS36. U57 no. 2000   382. 09597   60-60353

1828.   _____. Political and military report on North Vietnam.
         NY-108/1-February 28, 1958-   New York.
         AS36. U57   959. 7   58-60944

1829.   _____. Selected newspaper articles on 1959 state plan
         in North Vietnam. New York, 1959.
         AS36. U57 no. 1646   338. 9597   59-61695

1830.   _____. Trade, finance, labor, and standard of living
         in North Vietnam. NY-57/1- February, 25, 1958- New
         York.
         AS36. U57   59-60727

1831.   _____. Translations on North Vietnam's Economy, Nos.
         28-56. New York, Crowell Collier & Macmillan,
         1963.

1832.   _____. Translations on Political & Sociological Informa-
         tion on North Vietnam, Nos. 1-15. New York,
         Crowell Collier & Macmillan, 1962.

1833.   _____. Translations on Political & Sociological Informa-
         tion on North Vietnam, Nos. 16-39. New York,
         Crowell Collier & Macmillan, 1963.

1834.   U.S. Library of Congress. Orientalia Division. Southeast
         Asia; an annotated bibliography of selected reference
         sources. Comp. by Cecil Hobbs. Washington, 1952.
         Z3221. U49   016. 959   52-60056

1835.   U.S. Library of Congress. Reference Department. Indo-
         china; a bibliography of the land and people, compiled by
         Cecil C. Hobbs [and others] New York, Greenwood Press
         [1969]
         Z3221. U53 1969   016. 9159   68-55139

1836.   U.S. Military Assistance Command, Vietnam. Viet Cong
         terminology glossary. [n. p. , 1968]
         U25. U5495   355'. 0003   72-603848

1837.   U. S. Military Assistance Institute. Republic of Vietnam;
         country study. [Rev. and enl. n. p., 1965]
         DS557. A6U54 1965   915. 97   66-2903

1838.   U. S. Naval Mobile Construction Battalion Forty. Fighting
         40, Chu Lai, RVN, 1967-69 [cruise book. Waltham,
         Massachusetts, Woodland-Pembrooke, 1968?]
         DS557. A655E58   959. 7   74-601569

1839.   U. S. Naval Mobile Construction Battalion 74. NMCB 74,
         Danang, 1967-68 [cruise book. Baton Rouge, Army & Navy
         Publishing Company, 1968]
         DS557. A655E6   359. 9'82   71-601989

1840.   U. S. Naval Support Activity, Da Nang. Naval support in I
         Corps, 1968; U. S. Naval Support Activity Danang: its
         mission and men. [Shinjuku-ku, Tokyo, Printed by Dai
         Nippon Printing Company, 1969?]
         DS557. A645U6   959. 7'04   76-600524

1841.   _____. Naval Support I Corps, Vietnam: Danang, Cua
         Viet-Dong Ha, Tan My-Hue, Phu Bai, Chu Lai, Sa Huynh.
         [Shinjuku-ku, Tokyo, Printed by Dai Nippon Printing Com-
         pany, 1969?]
         DS557. A645U62   959. 7'04   77-606129

1842.   U. S. Office of Armed Forces Information and Education.
         A pocket guide to Viet-Nam. [Washington, For sale by
         the Superintendent of Documents, U. S. Government Printing
         Office, 1962]
         DS557. A5U54   63-60665

1843.   U. S. Office of Geography. Northern Vietnam; official
         standard names approved by the United States Board on
         Geographic Names. Washington [U. S. Government Printing
         Office] 1964.
         DS557. A7U5   64-62408

1844.   _____. Southern Vietnam and the South China Sea;
         official standard names approved by the United States Board
         on Geographic Names. Washington, U. S. Government
         Printing Office, 1962.
         DS557. A5U55   915. 97   62-60762

1845.   U. S. Operations Mission to Vietnam. Annual statistical
         bulletin. [Saigon?]
         HC443. V5U49   60-61903

1846.   _____. Provinces of Viet Nam; alphabetical listing with
         names of subordinate districts and cantons and numbers of
         villages in each. USOM/Public Administration Division,
         Unofficial as of October 1, 1963. [Saigon? 1963?]
         JS7225. V5U5 1963   64-54955

1847.   _____. Studies on land tenure in Viet Nam; terminal
          report of J. P. Gittinger, agricultural economist   [n. p.]
          Division of Agriculture and National Resources, U. S.
          Operations Mission to Viet Nam, 1959.
          HD889. V5U6   333. 7609597   61-60202

1848.   _____. Public Safety Division. Resources control by
          the national police of Vietnam, 1 October 1964-March 1965.
          [n. p. , 1965?]
          DS557. A68U58   67-9307

1849.   U. S. Pacific Command. Report on the war in Vietnam, as
          of 30 June 1968. Section I: Report on air and naval cam-
          paigns against North Vietnam and Pacific Command-wide sup-
          port of the war, June 1964-July 1968, by U. S. G. Sharp,
          USN, Commander in Chief Pacific. Section II: Report on
          operations in South Vietnam, January 1964-June 1968, by
          W. C. Westmoreland, USA, Commander, U. S. Military
          Assistance Command, Vietnam. [Washington, For sale by
          the Superintendent of Documents, U. S. Government Printing
          Office, 1969]
          DS557. A6U55   959. 7'04   70-601356

1850.   U. S. President, 1963-   (Lyndon B. Johnson). Foreign
          affairs. [Washington] Department of State [for sale by
          the Superintendent of Documents, U. S. Government Printing
          Office, 1966]
          E840. U65   S D 66-4

1851.   U. S. Senate. Committee on Foreign Relations. Vietnam
          Hearings. Random House, Inc. , 1966.

1852.   U. S. Treaties, etc. 1961-   (Kennedy). Amity and economic
          relations. Treaty between the United States of America
          and Viet-Nam signed at Saigon April 3, 1961. [Washington,
          U. S. Government Printing Office, 1962]
          JX235. 9. A32 no. 4890   62-60501

1853.   _____. Exchange of official publications. Agreement
          between the United States of America and Viet-Nam, effect-
          ed by exchange of notes signed at Saigon, April 4, 1961.
          [Washington, U. S. Government Printing Office, 1961]
          JX235. 9. A32 no. 4717   61-61532

1854.   U. S. Treaties, etc. , 1963-   (Lyndon B. Johnson). Mutual
          waiver of certain claims. Agreement between the United
          States of America and Viet-Nam, effected by exchange of
          notes signed at Saigon February 9, 1965. [Washington,
          for sale by the Superintendent of Documents, U. S. Govern-
          ment Printing Office, 1965]
          JX235. 9. A32 no. 5773   65-61709

1855.   Uspekhi vosstanovleniia narodnogo khoziiaistva Demokratich-

eskoi Respubliki V'etnam (1955-1956), (Achievements in the
Reconstruction of the National Economy of the Democratic
Republic of Vietnam, 1955-1956). (In Russian). Moscow,
1958.
HC443. V5U7

V

1856.   Vance, Samuel. The courageous and the proud. [1st ed.]
         New York, W. W. Norton [1970]
         DS557. A69V3 1970   959. 7'04   69-14710

1857.   Vandenbosch, Amry, 1894-   Australia faces Southeast
         Asia; the emergence of a foreign policy [by] Amry & Mary
         Belle Vandenbosch. Lexington, University of Kentucky
         Press, 1967.
         DS518. 9. A8V3   327. 59'094   67-29340

1858.   _____. The Dutch East Indies, its government, prob-
         lems, and politics. 3d ed. Berkeley, University of
         California, 1942.
         DS615. V3   991   42-36648

1859.   Van der Kroef, Justus Maria. Communism in Malaysia
         and Singapore: a contemporary survey, by Justus M. van
         der Kroef. The Hague, Martinus Nijhoff, 1967.
         HX400. 6. A6V3   335. 43'09595   68-87768

1860.   Van Dyke, Jon M. North Vietnam's Strategy for Survival.
         Pacific Books, Publishers, 1971.

1861.   Van Hanh Bulletin Vol. I. no. 1-111: July, 1969-   Van
         Hanh Bulletin is a shorter English version of Tu Tuong,
         (Thought), the review in Vietnamese, published monthly
         by Van Hanh University, 222 Truong Minh Giang, Saigon,
         South Vietnam.

1862.   Van Niel, Robert. The emergence of the modern Indonesian
         elite. The Hague, W. van Hoeve, 1960.
         HN703. V3   309. 191   60-4603

1863.   Van-Tien-Dung. After political failure, the U. S. imperi-
         alists are facing military defeat in South Vietnam. Hanoi,
         Foreign Languages Publishing House, 1966.
         DS557. A6V3   959. 7'04   67-4392

1864.   _____. Derrotado en lo politico, el imperialismo
         norteamericano esta fracasando tambien en lo militar en
         Vietnam del Sur. Hanoi, Ediciones en Lenguas Extranjeras,
         1966.
         DS557. A6V318   959. 7'04   68-50550

1865.   _____. South Vietnam; U. S. defeat inevitable. Hanoi,

184   Vietnam

Foreign Languages Publishing House, 1967.
DS557. A6V32   959. 7'04   68-1431

1866. _____ . Sud Vietnam, l'inevitabile sconfitta militare
       USA. [Di] Van Tieng Dung. Firenze, Feltrinelli, 1967.
       DS557. A6V326   79-358437

1867. Vanuxem, Paul Fidele Felicien, 1904- Espoir a Saigon
       [par le] General Vanuxem. [Paris,] la Table ronde, 1967.
       DS557. A6V33   959. 7'04   67-98930

1868. Van Vinh, Nguyen. Disengagement & Disenchantment.
       Carlton Press, 1970.

1869. Vaughan, Josephine Budd. The land and people of the
       Philippines. [1st ed.] Philadelphia, Lippincott [1956]
       DS655. V3   991. 4   56-6214

1870. Velev, Veliu. Vietnam. Sofia, 1951. (In Bulgarian).
       DS557. A5V5

1871. Vermeersch, Jeannette, 1910- Pais immediate au Viet-
       Nam, discours prononce a l'Assemblee nationale le 27
       janvier 1950 par Jeannette Vermeersch, suivi d'une
       declaration de Maurice Thorez. [Paris, Parti communiste
       francais, 1950?]
       DS557. A5V43   61-45358

1872. Vernon, Hilda. Vietnam: the war and its background.
       [London, British Vietnam Committee, 1965]
       DS557. A6V37   67-6972

1873. V'etnam; illiustrirovnyi zhurnal, (Vietnam; Illustrated
       Journal). (In Russian). Hanoi, 1962.
       DS557. A7V4

1874. V'etnamsko-russkii slovar', (Vietnamese Russian Diction-
       ary). (In Russian). Moscow, 1961.
       PL4376. V4

1875. Vietnam. Accord entre le Gouvernement de la Republique
       du Vietnam et Michigan State University. [n. p. , 1958?]
                                              NUC63-78964

1876. Viet Nam. [1.]- annee (no.]-); 1 mai 1951- Paris.
       DS557. A6A4   54-34825

1877. Vietnam. L'assassinat par les Viet Minh communistes du
       Colonel Hoang Thuy Nam, chef de la Mission chargee des
       relations avec la Commission internationale de controle.
       Saigon, Gouvernement de la Republique du Viet-Nam, 1962.
                                              NUC69-21071

1878.   Vietnam.   Bilan des realisations gouvernementales: 1954-
        1962.   [Saigon]   1962.
        HC443. V5A46   S A 68-1422

1879.   Vietnam.   Bilan des realisations gouvernementales.
        [Saigon, Nha in Thong Tin]
        JQ824. A3   S A 64-7345 rev.

1880.   Vietnam.   The bogus war of liberation in South Vietnam.
        [Saigon, 1965]
        DS557. A6A412   959. 704   66-48404

1881.   Vietnam.   Bon nam hoat-dong cua Chanh-phu [1954-1958.
        Saigon, 1958]
                                                          NUC67-23596

1882.   Vietnam.   Chinh-nghia Viet-Nam tren the gioi. . . [Saigon]
        Bo thong-tin xuat-ban, 1957.
                                                          NUC68-26210

1883.   Vietnam.   Clearing the undergrowth: what are the facts
        about defoliation in South Vietnam?   Saigon, Ministry of
        Information, 1964.
                                                          NUC69-14354

1884.   Vietnam.   Communist aggression against the Republic of
        Viet-nam.   Saigon, 1964.
                                                          NUC67-32788

1885.   Vietnam.   Communist aggression against the Republic of
        Viet-nam.   Saigon, 1964.
        DS557. A6A413   64-54470

1886.   Vietnam.   Communist Viet-minh aggressive policy and
        communist subversive warfare in South Vietnam, period
        from May 1961 to June 1962.   Saigon, 1962.
                                                          NUC67-22802

1887.   Vietnam.   [Decrees, reports and other official documents
        relating to agricultural reform in Vietnam.   Saigon, 1955]
        HD2080. V5A52   56-45421

1888.   Vietnam.   Eight years of the Ngo dinh Diem administra-
        tion, 1954-1962.   [Saigon? 1962?]
        DS557. A6A42   64-2438

1889.   Vietnam.   General specifications of services for investiga-
        tion, planning, design, and project evaluation of the Upper
        Sesan basin, Republic of Viet-nam.   [n. p., 1960]
                                                          NUC67-24153

1890.   Vietnam.   The measure of aggression; a documentation of
        the Communist effort to subvert South Vietnam. Saigon, 1966.
                                                          NUC69-19806

1891.   Vietnam.   The murder of Colonel Hoang Thuy Nam, chief
        of the Vietnamese mission in charge of relations with the
        International Commission for Control by the Vietminh com-
        munists.   Saigon, 1962.
                                                    NUC67-83124

1892.   Vietnam.   [New Delhi, Consulate-General of the Democratic
        Republic of Vietnam in India]
        DS557. A7A3   S A 63-3942

1893.   Vietnam.   Ngo Dinh Diem of Viet-Nam.   Saigon, Press
        office, Presidency of the Republic of Viet-Nam, 1957.

1894.   Vietnam.   Oanh tac Bac Viet.   [Saigon, Bo Thong tin Tam
        ly Chien, 1965]
                                                    NUC68-26889

1895.   Vietnam.   Official government report on 1960 census in
        North Vietnam.   Washington, U.S. Joint Publications Re-
        search Service, 1961.
                                                    NUC63-78965

1896.   Vietnam.   Plan d'action sociale pour les pays montagnards
        du sud du Domaine de la couronne.   [Saigon] Editions de
        la Delegation imperiale du Domaine de la couronne [1953]
        HD889. V5A5   56-17741

1897.   Vietnam.   Plan de developpement economique pour les
        pays montagnards du sud du domaine de la couronne.
        [n. p.] Editions de la Delegation imperiale du domaine de
        la couronne [1952?]
        HC443. V5A52   54-32968

1898.   Vietnam.   Plan d'equipement pour les Pays montagnards du
        Sud du Domaine de la Couronne.   [Saigon?] Editions de la
        Delegation imperiale du Domaine de la Couronne [1952]
        HC443. V5A5   55-59543

1899.   Vietnam.   La politique agressive des Viet Minh commu-
        nistes et la guerre subversive communiste au Sud Vietnam:
        periode de mai 1961 a juin 1962.   Saigon, 1962.
        DS557. A6A44   S A 64-723

1900.   Vietnam.   Preliminary report on the achievements of the
        war cabinet from June 19, 1965 to September 29, 1965.
        [Saigon, 1965]
                                                    NUC 68-26252

1901.   Vietnam.   President Ngo Dinh Diem.   Saigon, Presidency
        of the Republic of Viet-Nam, Press Office, 1957.

1902.   Vietnam.   Programme of activities of the Government of
        the Republic of Vietnam.   Saigon, 1964.
                                                    NUC67-23672

1903.   Vietnam.   Record of governmental achievements, July 1955-
        July 1956. [Saigon, 1956?]
                                                        NUC67-7315

1904.   Vietnam.   Seven years of the Ngo Dinh Diem administra-
        tion, 1954-1961.   Published on the 6th anniversary of the
        Republic of Vietnam, October 26, 1961.   [Saigon] 1961.

1905.   Vietnam.   So ket thanh tich hoat dong cua Noi cac Chien
        tranh, tu 19-6-1965 den 29-9-1965.   [Saigon? 1965?]
                                                        NUC69-23387

1906.   Vietnam.   State visit to Vietnam of their Majesties, the
        King and Queen of Thailand, December 18-21, 1959;
        speeches by His Majesty Bhumibol Adulyadej and His Ex-
        cellency President Ngo Dinh Diem.   [Saigon] Press office,
        Presidency, Republic of Vietnam [1960]

1907.   Vietnam.   Un danger pour la paix mondiale; l'agression
        communiste au Sud Viet-Nam, periode de juin 1962 a
        juillet 1963.   Saigon, 1963.
                                                        NUC67-23462

1908.   Vietnam.   Les violations des accords de Geneve par les
        communistes Viet-Minh.   Saigon, 1959.
        DS557. A6A453   61-26411

1909.   Vietnam.   Violations of the Geneva agreements by the
        Viet-Minh Communists, from July 1959 to June 1960.
        Saigon, 1960.
        DS557. A6A454   S A 63-2154

1910.   Vietnam.   Violations of the Geneva agreements by the Viet-
        Minh Communists.   Saigon, 1959.
        DS557. A6A45   959. 7   60-25806

1911.   Vietnam.   Y nghia ngay bau cu Quoc-hoi Lap-hien 11-9-
        1966.   [Saigon, 1966]
                                                        NUC68-76216

1912.   Viet Nam; a nation on the march.   [n. p., 195-]

1913.   Viet Nam; a nation on the march.   [n. p., 1954?]
        DS557. A5V48   62-26006

1914.   Vietnam, a new stage in her history.   A[b]dication state-
        ment, declaration of independence, constitution, national
        anthem, address by President Ho-chi-Minh.   Bangkok,
        Vietnam News, 1947.
        DS557. V5V5   959. 7   51-29449

1915.   Viet Nam; a report on a Wingspread briefing.   [Racine?
        Wisconsin, 1964]
        DS557. A6V48   66-3738

188   Vietnam

1916.   Viet-nam; a sketch.   Hanoi, Foreign Languages Publishing
        House [1956?]

1917.   Vietnam advances.   [Hanoi: Distributed by Xunhasaba, etc.]
        DS557. A7V42   65-9582

1918.   Vietnam and the Sino-Soviet dispute, edited by Robert A.
        Rupen and Robert Farrell.   New York, published for the
        Institute for the study of the USSR [by] Praeger [1967]
        DS557. A6V413   959. 7'04   67-16684

1919.   Vietnam and trade unionists [written and compiled by
        Martin Bernal and others] London, Vietnam Solidarity Cam-
        paign [1967]
        DS557. A6V415   959. 7'04   68-96672

1920.   Vietnam.   Artikler og noter 1945-1967.   Udarbejdet pa
        grundlag af artikler i Frit Danmark under redaktion af
        Marianne Kruse, Per Jacobsen, Ulla Koppel, Peter Bjer-
        rum og Knud Jensen.   København, Frit Danmark og De
        Storkøbenhavnske Vietnamkomiteer, [1967]
        DS557. A6V427   68-91727

1921.   Vietnam.   Aspecten van een tragedie.   Uitg. in samenwer-
        king met het Oost-West Instituut, 's-Gravenhage.   Alpen
        aan den Rijn.   N. Samsom, 1967.
        DS557. A6V43   67-96531

1922.   Vietnam.   Bo Cai-tien Nong thon.   Bao ve mua mang.
        [Saigon, 196-]
                                                         NUC68-76217

1923.   Vietnam.   Bo Canh-Nong.   General soil map [of] Republic
        of Vietnam.   [Saigon] 1961.
                                                        NUC69-107579

1924.   Vietnam.   Bo Canh-Nong.   Pham chat gao va pho san.
        Normes du riz derives.   Rice and by-products standards.
        Saigon, Nha Quoc-gia Canh-nong, 1960.
                                                         NUC67-80629

1925.   Vietnam.   Bo Canh-Nong.   Truong Quoc-gia nong-lam Muc,
        Bao-loc.   The National College of agriculture, Blao.
        [Saigon] 1960.
                                                         NUC67-22051

1926.   Vietnam.   Bo Kinh-te.   Economic survey of free Viet-
        Nam; statistical analysis data through 1959. [Saigon] 1960.

1927.   Vietnam.   Bo Kinh-te.   Investing in Viet-nam.   [Saigon,
        Department of National Economy, Industrial Development
        Center, 1958?]
        HC443. V5A55   332. 673597   60-4931

1928.   Vietnam.   Bo Kinh-te.   Nhung dieu nen biet ve the le nhap
         cang trong chu'o'ng trinh ngoai te so huu.   [Saigon, Bo
         Kinh-te, 1964]
                                                        NUC69-25211

1929.   Vietnam.   Bo Lao-Dong.   Apercu sur les activities du
         secretariat d'etat au travail.   [Saigon]   1959.
                                                        NUC69-20635

1930.   Vietnam.   Bo Lao Dong.   . . . Bo luat Lao-dong ve cac
         nong-nghiep, du so 26 ngay 26 thang sau nam 1953.   Code
         du travail des entreprises agricoles; ordonnance n 26 du
         26 juin 1953.   Che-do phu-cap Gia-dinh, du so 2 ngay thang
         gieng nam 1953.   Regime des allocations familiales;
         ordonnance n 2 du 20 janvier 1953.   The-le lap hoi va
         thanh-lap nghiep-doan, du so 10 va 23 ngay mong 6 thang
         tam nam 1950 va ngay 16 than muoi mot nam 1952.   Re-
         gime des associations & syndicats professionnels; ordon-
         nances nos. 10 et 23 des 6 aout 1950 et 16 novembre 1952.
         [Saigon]   1961.
                                                        NUC67-23162

1931.   Vietnam.   Bo Lao-Dong.   . . . Tap-luc cac ban van ap-
         dung bo luat lao-dong.   Recueil de textes d'application du
         Code du travail.   Sai-gon, Nha in Cac Cong-Bao, 1958.
                                                        NUC67-24215

1932.   Vietnam.   Bo Ngoai-giao.   Infiltration d'elements armes
         communistes et introduction clandestine d'armes du Nord au
         Sud Vietnam.   Saigon, Ministere des affaires etrangeres,
         Republique du Vietnam, 1967.
                                                        NUC69-7624

1933.   Vietnam.   Bo Nogai-giao.   Realites vietnamiennes (les
         realites permanentes) 2. ed., entierement revue et corrigee.
         Saigon, Ministere des affaires etrangeres du Vietnam, 1966.
                                                        NUC67-79765

1934.   Vietnam.   Bo Ngoai-giao.   The so-called war of liberation
         in South Viet-Nam.   Saigon, 1965.
                                                        NUC68-40934

1935.   Vietnam.   Bo Ngoai-Giao.   The Viet-Nam-Cambodia border
         issue before the U.N. Security Council. Saigon, Ministry
         of Foreign Affairs, 1964.
                                                        NUC67-47458

1936.   Vietnam.   Bo Ngoai-giao.   Vietnamese realities.   [3d ed.
         Saigon] Ministry of Foreign Affairs.
                                                        NUC69-8547

1937.   Vietnam.   Bo Quoc-gia Giao-duc.   Activites du Depart-
         ment de l'education nationale de 1954 a 1961.   [Saigon,

190   Vietnam

Impr. Tan-Phat] 1961
                                                 NUC67-23210

1938.   Vietnam.   Bo Quoc-gia Giao-duc.   Activities of the De-
        partment of National Education from July 7, 1954 to July 7,
        1961. [Saigon] Department of National Education, 1961.
                                                  NUC67-6933

1939.   Vietnam.   Bo Quoc-gia Giao-duc.   Activities of the Depart-
        ment of National Education from 1954 to 1959. [Saigon?]
        1959.
        L586.V5A5   S A 66-3739

1940.   Vietnam.   Bo Quoc-gia Giao-duc.   Elementary education
        curriculum. [Saigon?] Department of National Education,
        1960.
        LB1564.V5A52   61-65459

1941.   Vietnam.   Bo Quoc-gia Giao-duc.   Progress of education
        in Vietnam during the school year, 1965-1966; progres de
        l'enseignement au Vietnam du cours de l'annee scolaire,
        1965-1966. [Seoul?] Republic of Vietnam, Ministry of
        Education, 1966.
                                                 NUC69-25905

1942.   Vietnam.   Bo Quoc-gia Giao-duc.   Secondary education
        curriculum. [Saigon] Republic of Vietnam, Department
        of National Education [1960]
        LB1617.V5A5   65-9505

1943.   Vietnam.   Bo Quoc-gia Giao-duc.   Statistiques de l'En-
        seignement. [Hanoi?] Service d'Etude et du Plan, Bureau
        Statistique, 1956-57.

1944.   Vietnam.   Bo Thong-tin va Thanh-nien.   Ba Cahn; a story
        of revolutionary development. [Saigon, Ministry of In-
        formation, 1966?]
                                                 NUC67-77755

1945.   Vietnam.   Bo Thong-tin va Thanh-nien.   Mot nam thanh tich
        hoat dong cua chanh phu cach mang, tu 1-11-1963 den 1-11-
        1964. [Saigon] 1964.
                                                 NUC68-81758

1946.   Vietnam.   Bo Thong-tin va Thanh-nien.   Policy of the
        Military Revolutionary Council and the provisional govern-
        ment of the Republic of Vietnam. Saigon, Ministry of
        Information, 1963.
        DS557.A6A48 1963   65-89114

1947.   Vietnam.   Bo Thong-tin va Thanh-nien.   The problem of
        reunification of Viet-nam. [Saigon?] 1958.
        DS557.A6A48   60-4933

1948.   Vietnam.   Bo Thong-tin va Thanh-nien.   The truth of the
        National Liberation Front in South Vietnam.   [Saigon?]
        Published by the Ministry of Information and Chieu Hoi
        [1967]

                                                    NUC69-35542

1949.   Vietnam.   Bo Thong-tin va Thanh-nien.   Viet Cong atroci-
        ties and sabotage in South Vietnam.   Rev. ed.   [Saigon?
        Published by the Ministry of Information and Chieu Hoi,
        Directorate of Psy-War Planning, 1967]

                                                    NUC69-58802

1950.   Vietnam.   Bo tu'-phap.   To-chu'c tu'-phap Viet-nam Cong-
        boa.   [Saigon] Bo tu'phap xuat ban, 1962.

                                                    NUC68-88189

1951.   Vietnam bulletin.   [Washington, Office of Cultural Affairs
        and Information, Embassy of Vietnam]
        DS557. A6A19   959. 7'04   79-3037

1952.   Vietnam.   Central Committee for Community Development.
        Community development; definition, organization, planning,
        operations.   Prepared by the General Direction of Plan-
        ning.   [n. p. , 1957?]

1953.   Vietnam.   Centre national de recherches scientifiques et
        techniques.   Archives geologiques du Vietnam.   no. 1-
        Saigon, Impr. Le Van Tan, 1954-

                                                    G S 56-298

1954.   Vietnam (Compiled by the Government of the Republic of
        Vietnam).   Violations of the Geneva Agreements by the
        Viet-Minh Communists.   Saigon, 1959.
        DS557. A6A45   959. 7   60-25806

1955.   Vietnam.   Constitution.   The Constitution of the Republic
        of Viet Nam, October 26, 1956.   Washington, Press and
        Information Office, Embassy of the Republic of Viet-Nam,
        1956.

                                                    NUC67-23310

1956.   Vietnam.   Constitution.   Constitution of the Republic of
        Vietnam . . .   Prepared by the Office of the SJA, USMACV.
        [n. p.] 1967.

                                                    NUC68-76227

1957.   Vietnam.   Constitution. . . . Constitution [Saigon, Kim
        Lai An-Quan]   1956.

1958.   Vietnam.   Constitution.   The Constitution of the Republic
        of Vietnam.   Saigon, Secretariat of State for Information,
        1956.
                        342. 59701   59-39021

1959.   Vietnam. Constitution. The constitution of Vietnam; an
        analysis and comparison. [n. p. 1967?]
                                                    NUC69-86347

1960.   Vietnam. Constitution. Constitution; translated by the
        Bureau of the Constituent Assembly. [Saigon?] 1956.
                                                    59-36799

1961.   Vietnam. Constitution. Hien-phap. [Saigon?] So' Nghien-
        cuu va Tai-lieu Quoc-Hoi, 1967.
                                                    NUC68-75741

1962.   Vietnam. Consulate. Delhi. Vietnam through Indian eyes.
        New Delhi [1959]

1963.   Vietnam Courier--Information Weekly, 1946-64 Tran Hung
        Dao Street, Hanoi.

1964.   Vietnam, crimen del imperialismo [por] Luis Quintanilla
        [et al. 1. ed. Mexico] Editorial Nuestro Tiempo [1968]
        DS557. A6V446   959. 7'04   68-122259

1965.   Viet-Nam Dan-chu Dang. American blood for freedom or
        tyranny? [Edited by Nguyen-thai-Binh. Paris, Printed
        by Serg] 1963.
                                                    NUC63-7744

1966.   Le Vietnam d'aujourd'hui. Hanoi, Editions en langues
        etrangeres, 1965.
        DS557. A7V425   66-86123

1967.   Vietnam (Democratic Republic, 1946-). Breaking our
        chains; documents on the Vietnamese revolution of August
        1945. Hanoi, Foreign Languages Publishing House, 1960.
                                                    NUC67-24906

1968.   Vietnam (Democratic Republic, 1946-). Couleurs, hymne
        et armoiries de la Republique democratique du Vietnam.
        Flag, anthem and emblem of the Democratic Republic of
        Viet-nam. [Hanoi, Editions en langues etrangeres, 1956]

1969.   Vietnam (Democratic Republic, 1946-). The Democratic
        Republic of Viet Nam. Hanoi, Foreign Languages Pub-
        lishing House, 1960.
                                                    NUC67-24233

1970.   Vietnam (Democratic Republic, 1946-). Documents on
        the National Assembly of the Republic of Vietnam: Or-
        ganization & functioning of the administrative services;
        the civil service status; the law codification committee.
        [Saigon, 1961?]
                                                    NUC67-80841

1971.   Vietnam (Democratic Republic, 1946-).   XVth anniversary
        of the Democratic Republic of Viet Nam, 1945-1960.
        Hanoi, Foreign Languages Publishing House [1960?]
                                                        NUC63-78975

1972.   Vietnam (Democratic Republic, 1946-).   Le XVe [i. e.
        quinzieme] anniversaire de la Republique Democratique du
        Viet Nam, 1945-1960.   Hanoi, Editions en langues
        etrangeres, 1961.

1973.   Vietnam (Democratic Republic, 1946-).   Memorandum.
        [Hanoi] 1965.
        DS557. A602A5   67-4783

1974.   Vietnam (Democratic Republic, 1946-).   Plan triennal de
        developpement et de transformation de l'economie et de
        developpement de la culture; documents officiels.   Hanoi,
        Editions en langues etrangeres, 1959.

1975.   Vietnam (Democratic Republic, 1946-).   Les Problemes
        vietnamiens de 1961: economie, culture, reunification
        nationale [et] relations etrangeres.   Hanoi, Editions en
        langues etrangeres [1961]
                                                        NUC63-78976

1976.   Vietnam (Democratic Republic, 1946-).   The Problems
        facing the Democratic Republic of Viet Nam in 1961:
        Economy, culture, national reunification [and] foreign re-
        lations.   Hanoi, Foreign Languages Publishing House
        [1961]
                                                        NUC63-78977

1977.   Vietnam (Democratic Republic, 1946-). Relevement
        economique et developpement culturel dans la Republique
        Democratique du Vietnam.   Hanoi, Editions en langues
        etrangeres, 1958.

1978.   Vietnam (Democratic Republic, 1946-).   The Three-year
        plan to develop and transform economy and to develop
        culture (1958-1960) Hanoi, Foreign languages publishing
        house, 1959.

1979.   Vietnam (Democratic Republic, 1946-).   Central Joint
        Supply and Marketing Cooperative.   Supply and marketing
        co-operatives in the Democratic Republic of Viet Nam.
        Hanoi [Foreign Languages Publishing House] 1959.
                                                        NUC63-78978

1980.   Vietnam (Democratic Republic, 1946-).   Commission for
        Investigation on the American Imperialists' War Crimes in
        Vietnam.   American crimes in Vietnam.   [Hanoi?] 1966.
                                                        NUC69-71969

1981.   Vietnam (Democratic Republic, 1946-). Commission for In-
         vestigation on the American Imperialists' War Crimes in
         Vietnam. Chronology of the Vietnam war, 1941-1966.
         [By] Democratic Republic of Vietnam Commission for In-
         vestigation of the U.S. Imperiali[s]ts' War Crimes in Viet-
         nam. [Paris, Distributed by: Association d'amitie franco-
         vietnamienne, 1969-   ]
                                                        NUC69-139689

1982.   Vietnam (Democratic Republic, 1946-). Conseil des
         ministres. La cooperation agricole au Nord Viet Nam;
         rapport du Vice-President du Conseil Truong Chinh a la
         10e Session de l'Assemblee nationale, mai 1959. Hanoi,
         Editions en langues etrangeres, 1959.

1983.   Vietnam (Democratic Republic, 1946-). Constitution. Con-
         stitution de la Republique democratique du Viet-Nam.
         Hanoi, Editions en langues etrangeres, 1960.

1984.   Vietnam (Democratic Republic, 1946-). Constitution.
         Constitution of the Democratic Republic of Viet-Nam.
         Hanoi, Foreign Languages Publishing House, 1960.
                                                        S A 64-327

1985.   Vietnam (Democratic Republic, 1946-). Constitution.
         Konstitutsiia Demokraticheskoi Respubliki V'etnam, (Con-
         stitution of the Democratic Republic of Vietnam).   (In
         Russian). Hanoi, 1960.

1986.   Vietnam (Democratic Republic, 1946-). Constitution.
         Yueh-nan min chu kung ho kuo hsien fa, (Constitution of
         the Democratic Republic of Vietnam), (In Chinese).
         Hanoi, 1962.

1987.   Vietnam (Democratic Republic, 1946-). Embassy. Bul-
         garia. Deset godini agresiia na amerikanskite imperialisti
         v IUzhen Vietnam, (Ten Years of Aggression of American
         imperialists in South Vietnam).   (In Bulgarian).   Sofia,
         1964.
         DS557. A6A53

1988.   Vietnam (Democratic Republic, 1946-).   Viet Nam U.S.
         Biggest Operation Foiled (February-April 1967), Hanoi,
         Foreign Languages Publishing House, 1967.
         DS557. A6I54   959. 7'04   68-980

1989.   Vietnam (Democratic Republic, 1946-). Laws, statutes,
         etc.   Criminal legislation in the Democratic Republic of
         Vietnam.   New York, U.S. Joint Publications Research
         Service, 1958.
         AS36. U56 no. 408   343. 0959701   59-60137

1990.   Vietnam (Democratic Republic, 1946-). Laws, statutes,

etc. Demokraticheskaia Respublika V'etnam; konstitutsiia,
zakonodatel'nye akty, dokumenty, (Democratic Republic of
Vietnam; Constitution, legislative acts, documents). (In
Russian). Moscow, 1955.

1991. Vietnam (Democratic Republic, 1946-). Laws, statutes,
etc. Loi sur la reforme agraire votee par l'Assemblee
nationale de la Republique democratique du Viet-Nam en sa
3 session pleniere le 4-12-1953. [Hanoi, Editions en
langues etrangeres, 1955]

60-46203

1992. Vietnam (Democratic Republic, 1946-). Ministry of
Foreign Affairs. The criminal activities of the United
States and its agents in North Viet Nam. Hanoi, Press and
Information Department, 1964.

NUC69-19817

1993. Vietnam (Democratic Republic, 1946-). Ministry of
Foreign Affairs. Memorandum of the Government of the
Democratic Republic of Viet Nam on the expansion of the
aggressive war in Laos by the U. S. imperialists in the
S. E. A. T. O. military bloc. [Hanoi] Ministry of Foreign
Affairs, Democratic Republic of Vietnam, 1961.

NUC68-97973

1994. Vietnam (Democratic Republic, 1946-). Ministry of
Foreign Affairs. Memorandum of the Ministry for foreign
affairs of the Democratic Republic of Viet Nam concerning
the military aggression of the U. S. government in South
Viet Nam. Hanoi, 1962.

NUC67-22152

1995. Vietnam (Democratic Republic, 1946-). Ministry of
Foreign Affairs. Statement by the spokesman of the
D. R. V. Foreign Ministry on so-called "peace efforts"
made recently by the U. S. [Hanoi, 1966]

NUC67-50860

1996. Vietnam (Democratic Republic, 1946-). Ministry of
Foreign Affairs. U. S. intervention and aggression in Viet
Nam during the last twenty years. Hanoi, 1965.
DS557. A7A55   959. 704   66-2885

1997. Vietnam (Democratic Republic, 1946-). Ministry of Foreign Affairs. Press and Information Department. Les
activites criminelles des Etats-Unis et de leurs agents
au Nord Viet Nam. Hanoi, Ministere des affaires
etrangeres, Departement de la presse et information, 1964.

NUC67-23744

1998. Vietnam (Democratic Republic, 1946-). Ministry of
Foreign Affairs. Press and Information Department.

Documents related to the implementation of the Geneva
agreements concerning Viet-nam.   Ha-noi, 1956.
JX1573. V5   327. 597   59-39391

1999.   Vietnam (Democratic Republic, 1946-). Ministry of Foreign
         Affairs.   Press and Information Department.   Imperialist
         schemes in Vietnam against peace and reunification.
         Hanoi, 1958.

2000.   Vietnam (Democratic Republic, 1946-). Ministry of Foreign
         Affairs.   Press and Information Department.   Memorandum
         of the Ministry of foreign affairs of the Democratic Repub-
         lic of Viet Nam concerning U. S. "special warfare" in South
         Viet Nam nine years after the signing of the Geneva agree-
         ments on Viet Nam.   Hanoi, Press and Information depart-
         ment, Ministry of Foreign affairs, 1963.
                                                         NUC67-23323

2001.   Vietnam (Democratic Republic, 1946-). Ministry of Foreign
         Affairs.   Press and Information Department.   Les menees
         imperialistes au Viet-nam contre la paix et la reunification.
         Hanoi, Departement de la presse et de l'information, Min-
         istere des affaires etrangeres, 1958.
                                                         NUC67-23540

2002.   Vietnam (Democratic Republic, 1946-). Ministry of Foreign
         Affairs.   Press and Information Department.   La politique
         d'intervention et d'agression des Etats-Unis au Sud Viet
         Nam.   Hanoi, 1962.
         DS557. A6A55   S A 63-1677

2003.   Vietnam (Democratic Republic, 1946-). Ministry of Foreign
         Affairs.   Press and Information Department.   Principaux
         documents officiels de la Republique democratique du Viet-
         nam concernant le probleme du Laos.   Hanoi, Departement
         de presse et d'information, Ministere des affaires
         etrangeres, 1961.
                                                         NUC67-22353

2004.   Vietnam (Democratic Republic, 1946-). Ministry of Foreign
         Affairs.   Press and Information Department.   The U. S.
         policy of intervention and aggression in South Viet Nam.
         Hanoi, 1962.
                                                         NUC67-81043

2005.   Vietnam (Democratic Republic, 1946-). Ministry of Foreign
         Affairs.   Press and Information Department.   U. S. "Spe-
         cial war" in South Viet Nam.   Hanoi, Press and Informa-
         tion Department, Ministry of Foreign Affairs, 1964.
                                                         NUC67-81321

2006.   Vietnam (Democratic Republic, 1946-). Ministry of Foreign
         Affairs.   Press and Information Department.   U. S. war

crimes in North Viet Nam.   Hanoi, 1966.
DS557. A7A555   959. 704   66-31816

2007.   Vietnam (Democratic Republic, 1946-). National Assembly.
Against U. S. aggression; main documents of the National
Assembly of the Democratic Republic of Vietnam, 3d
legislature- 2d session, April 1965.   [Second ed.] Hanoi,
Foreign Languages Publishing House, 1966.
NUC67-78971

2008.   Vietnam (Democratic Republic, 1946-). National Assembly.
Against U. S. aggression; main documents of the National
Assembly of the Democratic Republic of Vietnam, 3rd
Legislature, 2nd session [held . . . April 8, 9, and 10,
1965] Hanoi, Foreign Languages Publishing House, 1965.
NUC67-29394

2009.   Vietnam (Democratic Republic, 1946-). National Assembly.
L'aventure militaire des imperialistes americains au Sud
Viet Nam.   Hanoi, Editions en langues etrangeres, 1962.
NUC67-80446

2010.   Vietnam (Democratic Republic, 1946-). National Assembly.
L'aventure militaire des imperialistes americains au Sud
Viet Nam.   Hanoi, Editions en langues etrangeres, 1962.
NUC63-78980

2011.   Vietnam (Democratic Republic, 1946-). National Assembly.
Contre l'agression americaine; principaux documents de
l'Assemblee nationale de la R. D. V. 3e legislature.   2e
session.   Hanoi, Editions en Langues etrangeres, 1965.
NUC67-84510

2012.   Vietnam (Democratic Republic, 1946-). National Assembly.
Some documents of the National Assembly of the Demo-
cratic Republic of Vietnam; 3rd Legislature, 1st session,
June-July 1964.   Hanoi, Foreign Languages Publishing
House, 1964.
DS557. A7A56   65-89129

2013.   Vietnam (Democratic Republic, 1946-). Prime Minister.
Forward!   Final victory will be ours! [By] Pham van
Dong.   Hanoi, Foreign Languages Publishing House, 1968.
DS557. A635V5   959. 7'04   79-9633

2014.   Vietnam (Democratic Republic, 1946-). Prime Minister.
Report of Premier Pham Van Dong at the eighth session of
National Assembly, Democratic Republic of Vietnam. New
York, U. S. Joint Publications Research Service [1958?]
AS36. U56 no. 294   959. 7   58-62069

2015.   Vietnam (Democratic Republic, 1946-). Prime Minister.
Text of report by North Vietnamese Premier Van Dong to

National Assembly on 15 April 1966. [Washington] 1966.
                                                    NUC67-823

2016.   Vietnam (Democratic Republic, 1946-). State Committee of
        Science and Technology. Statement by the Democratic Re-
        public of Vietnam State Committee of Science and Technology
        on the use of toxic chemicals and poison gas by the aggress-
        ive U.S. imperialists in South Vietnam. [n. p., 1965 or 6]
        UG447.V5   358.34   66-5223

2017.   Vietnam (Democratic Republic of) sponsored report. Viet-
        namese Intellectuals Against U.S. Aggression. Hanoi,
        Foreign Language Publishing House, 1966.
        DS557.A68V53   959.7'04   68-1192

2018.   Vietnam. Department of Labour. Insight into the activities
        of the Department of Labour. [Saigon] 1959.

2019.   Vietnam. Department of Land Registration and Agrarian
        Reform. . . . Agrarian reform in Viet-nam. [Saigon?] 1958.

2020.   Vietnam. Det Norske studentersamfunds teach-in i Oslo den
        16, april 1966. Redigert av Per Frydenberg, Liv Mellum
        [og] Eilert Struksnes. [Oslo] Norsk utenrikspolitisk in-
        stitutt, 1966.
        DS557.A6V44   68-77134

2021.   Vietnam. Direction generale de l'information. Bilan des
        realisations gouvernementales (1945-1958). Ed. par le Ser-
        vice des publications du Secretariat d'etat a l'information.
        Saigon, 1959.

2022.   Vietnam. Direction generale de l'information. Cai-San;
        the dramatic story of resettlement and land reform in the
        "Rice Bowl" of the Republic of Viet-Nam. Saigon [1956?]

2023.   Vietnam. Direction generale de l'information. The problem
        of reunification of Viet-nam. [Saigon?] Ministry of In-
        formation, 1958.

2024.   Vietnam. Directorate General of Civil Service. Central
        executive agencies in Vietnam. Saigon, 1958.
                                                    NUC67-7113

2025.   Vietnam. Directorate General of Civil Service. Personnel
        recruitment in Vietnam. Saigon, 1958.

2026.   Vietnam. Directorate General of Civil Service. The presi-
        dential system of government and the executive power in
        Vietnam. Saigon, 1958.
                                                    NUC67-7277

2027.   Vietnam. Directorate General of Civil Service. The

problem of training in Vietnam.   Saigon, 1958.

2028.   Vietnam.   Directorate General of Civil Service.   The pro-
        vincial administrator in Vietnam.   Saigon, 1958.

2029.   Vietnam.   [Door] John Bultinck, Bruno de Roeck, Jet Turf
        [en] Piet Reckman.   Uitg. verzorgd door Diepgang & Sjal-
        oom.   [Apeldoorn, Demper Agendo, 1967]
        DS557.A68V45   959.7'04   68-96272

2030.   Vietnam.   Embassy.   U.S.   Documents on the Buddhist
        issue in Viet-Nam.   Washington, D.C., 1963.
                                                    NUC67-22956

2031.   Vietnam.   Embassy.   U.S.   Flight to freedom; a story of
        courage, sacrifice, and a faith in the free world.   [Washing-
        ton, Office of Information and Cultural Affairs, Embassy of
        Viet Nam, 1955]
        DS550.V5   56-34531

2032.   Vietnam.   Embassy.   U.S.   A guide to Viet-Nam.   [Washing-
        ton, Press and Information Office, Embassy of Viet Nam,
        1959?]
        DS557.A5A48   915.97   61-20674

2033.   Vietnam.   Embassy.   U.S.   In violation of the Tet truce.
        Washington, [1968]
                                                    NUC69-13698

2034.   Vietnam.   Embassy.   U.S.   The presidential election, Sep-
        tember 3, 1967.   Washington, Embassy of the Republic of
        Vietnam [1967]
                                                    NUC68-75739

2035.   Vietnam.   Embassy.   U.S.   Viet Minh violations of the
        Geneva armistice agreement.   Washington [1954]
        DS557.A5A5   56-17786

2036.   Vietnam.   Embassy.   U.S.   Viet-Nam at the crossroads of
        Asia.   [Washington, 1959?]
        DS557.A6A5 1959   60-26424

2037.   Vietnam.   Embassy.   U.S.   Viet-Nam at the crossroads of
        Asia.   [Washington, 1959]
                                                    NUC68-79158

2038.   Vietnam.   Embassy.   U.S.   Vietnam.   [Washington, 1955]
        DS557.A6A5   60-21494

2039.   Vietnam; en dokumentasjon i tekst og bilder.   [Oslo, For-
        laget Ny dag, 1965]
        DS557.A61V5   67-49152

2040.   Vietnam en het recht.   Bijzonder nummer van het juridisch
         studentenblad Ars Aequi.   Amsterdam, Polak & Van Gen-
         nep, 1968.
         JX4521. V54   75-355268

2041.   Vietnam--en tva høring.   Redaktion: Henrik Antonsen.
         Odense, Danmarks Radio [1967]
         DS557. A6V 52   959. 7'04   67-108104

2042.   Viet-Nam et ses relations internationales.   Viet-Nam 1962;
         etudes nationales et internationales.   Studies on national and
         international affairs.   Saigon [1962]
                                                     NUC67-80615

2043.   Le Vietnam et ses relations internationales. Vietnam in
         world affairs.   [Saigon] Secretariat d'etat aux affaires
         etrangeres.
         DS557. A5A43   S A 63-2279

2044.   Viet-Nam Fatherland Front and the struggle for national
         unity.   Hanoi, Foreign Language Publishing House, 1956.
         DS557. A7V43   S A 66-4578

2045.   Viet-nam Fatherland Front and the struggle for national
         unity.   Hanoi, Foreign Language Publishing House, 1956.

2046.   Vietnam Foreign Language Press.   Nan fang lai hsin,
         (Letters from the South), (In Chinese).   Peking, 1964.
         PL4378. N312

2047.   Viet Nam government organization manual, 1957-58.   Saigon,
         National Institute of Administration, Research and Documen-
         tation Division, 1958.

2048.   Vietnam hearings: voices from the grass roots; a transcript
         of testimony given at the hearing on the war in Vietnam con-
         ducted by Robert W. Kastenmeier.   Garden City, New York,
         Doubleday [1966]
         DS557. A6V49   355. 0335597   66-31905

2049.   Vietnam.   Hoa xa. Bulletin officiel.   annee 1- juin/dec.
         1952- Saigon.
         HE3319. V5A3   S A 63-197

2050.   Vietnam; la huella del imperialismo.   [Departamento de
         Publicacion de Accion Sinideal Uruguaya para D. I. P. U. L.,
         1967]
         DS557. A5V49   79-415283

2051.   Vietnam i dokument.   Sammanstallda av Teddy Arnberg,
         Erik Eriksson, Bengt Liljenroth [m. fl.] Stockholm, Prisma;
         [Solna, Seelig], 1968.
         DS557. A6A552   68-133093

Vietnam

2052. Vietnam in dieser Stunde. Kunstlerische Dokumentation. Hrsg. von Werner Braunig, Fritz Cremer [u. a.] Halle/Saale, Mitteldeutscher Verlag, 1968.
DS557.A6V447 1968b   70-383847

2053. Vietnam in dieser Stunde. Kunstlerische Dokumentation. Hrsg. von Werner Braunig. [u. a.]. Zürich, Limmat-Verlag, (1968).
DS557.A6V447 1968   71-382940

2054. Vietnam in Frage und Antwort. (Pfaffenhofen/Ilm, Ilmgau-Verlag, 1967.)
DD1.0712 1967,   959.7'04   68-113407
no. 1

2055. Viet-Nam in world affairs. Viet-Nam 1960 [i.e. dix neuf cent soixante]; etudes nationales et internationales. Studies on national and international affairs. Saigon [1960]

2056. Viet-Nam information notes. no. 1- [Washington, For sale by the Superintendent of Documents, U.S. Government Printing Office, 1967-
DS557.A6A193   915.97   68-60068

2057. The Vietnam Inquirer. [Saigon]
DS557.A47   959.7'04   77-2507

2058. Vietnam. Institut de la statistique et des etudes economiques. Thong ko nien giam Viet-nam. Annuaire statistique du Vietnam. v. 1- [Saigon]
HA1780.5.A32   55-39210

2059. Viet-Nam kinh-te tap-san. Bulletin economique du Viet-Nam. nam thu 1 Gieng 1950- [Saigon]
HC443.V5V552   56-30692

2060. Vietnam-konferansen pa-Hawaii: Komunikeet og Honolulu-erklaeringen.   Oslo, 1966.
E183.8.V5V5   67-71211

2061. Viet Nam Lao Dong Party. Central Committee of Propaganda. Thirty years of struggle of the party. Hanoi, Foreign Languages Publishing House, 1960-

2062. Vietnam. Laws, statutes, etc. Bo luat lao-dong (Du so 15 ngay mong 8 thang bay nam 1952, bo-tuc sua doi boi so 9 va so 10 ngay mong 8 thanh hai nam 1955) [Code du travail (Ordonnance no. 15 du 8 juillet 1952, complete at modifiee par les ordonnances nos. 9 et 10 du 8 fevrier 1955)] Saigon, Quoc-Gia Viet-Nam, Bo La-Dong, 1958.

2063. Vietnam. Laws, statutes, etc. . . . Code civil du Nord Vietnam mis a jour au 30. 6. 1956. Saigon, 1956.

2064. Vietnam. Laws, statutes, etc. Code de la famille. [Saigon, 1959]

NUC67-80959

2065. Vietnam. Laws, statutes, etc. Code de procedure penale. [Saigon] So Tai-lieu Quoc-hoi, 1960.

NUC66-91073

2066. Vietnam. Laws, statutes, etc. . . . Code of the family. [n. p., 1959]

2067. Vietnam. Laws, statutes, etc. Codes annamites: Code d'organisation des juridictions annamites du Tonkin, Code de procedures civile et commerciale [et] Code penal (appli- cables au Tonkin) Nouvelle ed. [Saigon?] 1960.

NUC67-22485

2068. Vietnam. Laws, statutes, etc. English translations of basic Vietnamese land tenure legislation. [Saigon] U.S. Operations Mission to Viet Nam, 1957.

2069. Vietnam. Laws, statutes, etc. The investment laws and procedures in Vietnam: an analysis, with comparisons and recommendations, by Andrew Jackson Bennett. . . [Saigon] 1964.

NUC68-16222

2070. Vietnam. Laws, statutes, etc. Law on the organization of People's Councils and Administrative Committees of all echelons. Washington, U.S. Department of Commerce, Of- fice of Technical Services, Joint Publications Research Ser- vice, 1962.

NUC67-22606

2071. Vietnam. Laws, statutes, etc. . . . Luat-le noi-thuong . . . [Saigon] 1960.

NUC67-24872

2072. Vietnam. Laws, statutes, etc. Official documents on in- vestments in Vietnam . . . June ---- Saigon, 1964.

NUC68-15576

2073. Vietnam. Laws, statutes, etc. The thuc bua cu Tong thong, Pho tong thong va Nhgi si thuong nghi vien (Ngay 3-9-1967) [Saigon, Nha sa hoach Tam ly chien, Tong bo Thong tin Chien hon 1967]

NUC68-75740

2074. Vietnam, l'heure decisive, l'offensive du Tet (fevrier 1968) . . . Paris, R. Laffont, 1968.
DS557.A6V448   68-116314

2075. Vietnam [magasinet] Utg. av Arbeidernes ungdomsfylking,

det Norske studentersamfund [o. a.] [Redaktør: Bjørn Bjørn-
sen.] [Oslo] Pax [1966]
DS557.A6V45   67-95412

2076.   Vietnam.   Military Revolutionary Council.   Le remaniement
du Conseil militaire revolutionnaire: motifs et objectifs.
Saigon, 1964.
NUC69-46963

2077.   Vietnam. Ministere des finances, du plan et de la reconstruction.   Budget; textes et documents annexes. Saigon.
HJ70.I8A32   54-20428

2078.   Vietnam. Ministry of Agriculture and Forestry.   Agricultural
production in North Vietnam during last 15 years. Washington, U.S. Joint Publications Research Service, 1961.

2079.   Vietnam News Service. see Vietnam, a new stage in her
history. Bangkok, 1947.
DS557.V5V5   959.7   51-29449

2080.   Vietnam News Service. Ho Chi Minh, the "Father" of his
people. [Bangkok? 1947?]
DS557.A5V5   923.2597   51-32982

2081.   Vietnam. Nha Giam-Doc Khi-Tu'o'ng. Resumes climatologiques; modeles A, B, C, D, K.   Climatological summaries;
models A, B, C, D, K. Station: Saigon-Tansonnhut, 48900.
[Saigon] 1966.
QC990.V5A56   75-216689

2082.   Vietnam. Nha Khao-Cu'u Va Su'u-Tam Nong-Lam-Suc.
Notes et rapports sur les conditions pedologiques et
hydrologiques au PMS. [Saigon] Bibliotheque agronomique
[1960]
NUC67-23205

2083.   Vietnam. Nha Khao-Cu'u va Su'u-Tam Nong-Lam-Suc. Re-
searches on acid sulphate soils and their amelioration by
liming. [Saigon] Agronomic Library, 1961.
NUC67-22643

2084.   Vietnam. Nha Tong Giam-doc Ngan-sach va Ngoai- vien.
National budget, c[alendar] y[ear] 1963. Translated by Eco-
nomic and Financial Planning Division, USOM, Vietnam.
[Saigon? 196-]
HJ2158.Z9V63   67-55735

2085.   Vietnam. Nha Tong Giam-doc Quan-thue. Tarif des
douanes; tableau des droits d'entree et de sortie applicables
au Viet-Nam. Saigon, 1959.
HJ6316.V5A54   60-4932

2086.   Viet-Nam nhan-vat-chi vu'ng-bien [cua]. Thai-van-Kiem va Ho-
        dac-Ham bien-soan. [Saigon] Bo Quoc-gia Giao-duc, 1962.
                                                    NUC67-80340

2087.   Vietnam.   Office national du tourisme.   Vietnam as a tourist
        centre.   Saigon, 1953.
        DS557.A5A54   915.97   56-34528

2088.   Vietnam, old nation--young state.   [Paris, 1952]
        DS557.A5V53   915.97   53-26406

2089.   Viet Nam Peace Committee.   Five years of the implementa-
        tion of the Geneva agreements in Viet Nam. [Hanoi, Foreign
        Languages Publishing House, 1959]
        DS557.A6V5   S A 64-7958

2090.   Viet Nam Peace Committee.   The peace movement in Vietnam.
        Hanoi, Foreign Languages Publishing House, 1958.
                                                    NUC67-81724

2091.   Viet Nam Peace Committee.   Six years of the implementation
        of the Geneva Agreements in Viet Nam.   [Hanoi, Foreign
        Languages Publishing House, 1960]
                                                    NUC67-22127

2092.   Viet Nam Peace Committee.   Six years of the implementation
        of the Geneva Agreements in Viet Nam.   [Hanoi, Foreign
        Languages Publishing House, 1961]
                                                    NUC67-22127

2093.   Vietnam peace proposals. [Editor: Robert S. Woito.
        Berkeley, California, World Without War Council, 1967]
        DS557.A692V5   959.7'04   67-9049

2094.   Vietnam.   People's Directive Committee for the campaign of
        Denunciation of Communist Subversive Activities.   Viet Nam
        and the fight against communism.   [Saigon] 1956

2095.   Vietnam.   Phu Tong-dy Dinh-Dien.   L'oeuvre de developpe-
        ment agricole au Viet Nam au 30 juin 1959. [Saigon? 1959]
                                                    NUC67-24232

2096.   Vietnam.   Phu Tong-uy Dinh-Dien.   The work of land de-
        velopment in Viet Nam up to June 30, 1959.   [Saigon? 1959]
        HD1516.V5A5   S A 63-1619

2097.   Vietnam. Phu Tong-uy Ho'p-tac-xa va   Nong-tin.   Agricul-
        tural credit in Vietnam.   [Saigon] 1960.
        HG3729.V5A55   S A 64-6748

2098.   Vietnam. Phu Tong-uy Ho'p-tac-xa va Nong-tin.   Agricul-
        tural credit in Vietnam. Translation of the lecture delivered
        by Tran-ngoc-Lien before the League of the Civil Servants of

the National Revolution at the City Hall in Saigon on June
26, 1959. [Saigon, 1959]

NUC67-22879

2099.   Vietnam.   Phu Tong-uy Ho'p-tac-xa va Nong-tin.   The co-
operative movement in Viet-nam and the establishment of
the Commissariat General for Cooperatives and Agricultural Credit.   [Saigon, 1959?]

NUC67-16384

2100.   Vietnam.   Phu Tong-uy Ho'p-tac-xa va Nong-tin.   The co-
operative movement in Vietnam.   Saigon, 1960.
HD3542. V5A49   S A 64-6747

2101.   Vietnam.   Phu Tong-uy Ho'p-tac-xa va Nong-tin.   Cooperative operations of corn-hog program in strategic hamlets of
the Republic of Viet-nam, March 1, to September 30, 1963.
[Saigon] 1963.

NUC67-18600

2102.   Vietnam.   Phu Tong-uy Hop-tac-xa va Nong-tin.   The co-
operative research and training center.   [Saigon] 1960.

NUC63-78970

2103.   Vietnam.   Phu Tong-uy Ho'p-tac-xa va Nong-tin.   The
establishment of cooperatives in Vietnam, June 30, 1959.
[Saigon?] 1959.
HD3542. V5A52   61-4910

2104.   Vietnam.   Phu Tong-uy Ho'p-tac-xa va Nong-tin.   The
growth of agricultural credit in Vietnam, June 30, 1959.
[Saigon?] 1959.
HG2051. V47A5   61-4911

2105.   Viet Nam.   Pref. de Paul Levy; photos de Michel Huet
[et al. Choix de textes vietnamiens et mise en pages de
Simone Jeanson] Lausanne, Guilde du livre [1951]
DS557. A5V54   915. 97   53-34306

2106.   Viet Nam.   Pref. de Paul Levy; photos de Michel Huet
[et al. Choix de textes vietnamiens et mise en pages de
Simone Jeanson] Paris, Editions Hoa-Qui [1951]
A 52-10079

2107.   Vietnam.   President, 1955- (Ngo-dinh-Diem). The emer-
gence of free Viet-Nam; major addresses delivered by
President Ngo-Dinh-Diem during his official visit to the
United States of America, May 8-18, 1957.   Saigon,
Presidency of the Republic of Viet-Nam, Press Office,
1957.

2108.   Vietnam. President, 1955- (Ngo-dinh-Diem). Major policy
speeches. 3d ed. Saigon, Presidency of the Republic of
Viet-Nam, Press Office, 1957.

2109.   Vietnam.   President, 1955-   (Ngo-dinh-Diem). Major policy
          speeches.   Saigon, Press Office, Presidency of the Repub-
          lic of Viet Nam, 1956.

                                                        NUC63-78971

2110.   Vietnam.   President, 1955-   (Ngo-dinh-Diem). Major
          policy speeches. 2d expanded ed.   Saigon, Press Office,
          Presidency of the Republic of Viet Nam, 1956.

2111.   Vietnam.   President, 1955-   (Ngo-dinh- Diem). Message of
          President Ngo dinh Diem to the National Assembly (Opening
          session, 6 October 1958) [Saigon] Department of Informa-
          tion [1958]

2112.   Vietnam.   President, 1955-   (Ngo-dinh-Diem). Message of
          the President of the Republic to the National Assembly,
          5 Oct. 1959.   [Saigon] Department of Information [1959]

2113.   Vietnam, President, 1955-   (Ngo-dinh-Diem). Pour une
          meilleur comprehension mutuelle.   Saigon, Presidence de
          la Republique du Vietnam, Service de Presse, 1957.

                                                        NUC67-22655

2114.   Vietnam, President, 1955-   (Ngo-dinh-Diem). President
          Ngo Dinh Diem on Asia; extracts from speeches by Presi-
          dent Ngo Dinh Diem. 2d expanded ed.   Saigon, Presidency
          of the Republic of Viet-Nam, Press Office, 1958.

                                                        NUC63-78972

2115.   Vietnam.   President, 1955-   (Ngo-dinh-Diem). President
          Ngo dinh Diem on Asia (extracts from speeches. . .)
          Saigon, Press Office, Presidency of the Republic of Viet-
          nam, 1957.

2116.   Vietnam, President, 1955-   (Ngo-dinh-Diem). President
          Ngo dinh Diem on democracy (addresses relative to the
          constitution) Saigon, Press Office, Presidency of the Re-
          public of Viet-nam, 1957.

2117.   Vietnam.   President, 1955-   (Ngo-dinh-Diem). Press inter-
          views with President Ngo Dinh Diem [and] Political Coun-
          selor Ngo Dinh Nhu.   [Saigon] 1963.

                                                        NUC69-25972

2118.   Vietnam.   President, 1955-   (Ngo-dinh-Diem). Toward
          better mutual understanding; speeches delivered by Presi-
          dent Ngo dinh Diem during his state visits to Thailand,
          Australia and Korea.   Saigon, Press Office, Presidency
          of the Republic of Vietnam, 1957.

2119.   Vietnam.   President, 1955-   (Ngo-dinh-Diem).   Toward
          better mutual understanding; speeches delivered by Presi-
          dent Ngo Dinh Diem during his state visits to Thailand,

Australia, Korea. Saigon, Presidency of the Republic of
Vietnam, Press Office, 1958.

2120.   Vietnam. President, 1955-1963. (Ngo-dinh-Diem). Mes-
         sage of the President of the Republic to the National As-
         sembly [Oct. 1st, 1962] Message du President de la Re-
         publique a l'Assemblee Nationale [ler oct. 1962, Saigon,
         Directorat General of Information, 1962?]
                                                          NUC67-81529

2121.   Vietnam. President, 1955-1963. (Ngo-dinh-Diem). Mes-
         sage of the President of the Republic to the National As-
         sembly, opening session, October 2, 1961. [Saigon? 1961?]
                                                          NUC67-77455

2122.   Vietnam Press. The Buddhist question; basic documents.
         Saigon, 1963-
                                                          NUC67-22471

2123.   Vietnam Press. Phuc va bao chi Viet Nam. Tahnh tich
         hoat dong trong nam 1965 cua Viet Nam Thong tan xa.
         [Saigon, 1965]
                                                          NUC69-20705

2124.   Vietnam Press. Vietnam Press. Viet-nam Thong tan xa.
         [Saigon, 1958?]
                                                          NUC63-78981

2125.   Vietnam Press. The World Assembly of Youth. W. A. Y.
         Asian seminar-Saigon 1961. Special issue. [Saigon]
         1961.
                                                          NUC69-67453

2126.   Vietnam. Regie des chemins de fer non conceaes du
         Viet-Nam. Reconstruction du chemin de fer Trans-Viet-
         nam. Railway reconstruction. [Saigon] 1959.

2127.   Viet-Nam; review of a test case on the border of the free
         world. [n. p. , 1958]
                                                          NUC63-78982

2128.   Viet Nam, Secretariat of State for Information. The Con-
         stitution of the Republic of Viet Nam. Saigon, 1956.
                          342. 59701   59-39021

2129.   Vietnam. Service du protocole. Liste des personnalites
         residant sur le territoire de Saigon-Giadinh. Saigon.
         JQ821. A36   60-26206

2130.   Vietnam. Service geologiques du Viet-Nam. no. 1-
         Saigon, 1954-
                                                          G S 56-298 rev.

2131.   Vietnam. So Thong-va Kinh-te Nong-nghiep. Phuc-trinh
         va kiem-tra canh-nong tai Vietnam. Report on the
         agriculture census of Vietnam, 1960-1961. [Saigon? 196-]
         S471. V47A57   S A 67-6870

2132.   Vietnam. So Thong ke ca Tai-lieu. Viet-Nam canh-nong
         thong-ke. Vietnamese agricultural statistics. [Saigon]
         HD2080. V5A34   S A 63-420

2133.   Vietnam Solidarity Campaign. National Council. Why
         Vietnam solidarity? Policy statement by the National
         Council of the Vietnam Solidarity Campaign. London,
         Vietnam Solidarity Campaign, 1967.
         DS557. A6V527   959. 7'04   68-91223

2134.   Vietnam. Toa Dac-su . Laos. De giup kieu bao hien
         dang sinh song tren dat nuoc ban Af-lao. Vientiane, 1958.
                                                       NUC63-78973

2135.   Vietnam today. Hanoi, Foreign Languages Publishing
         House, 1965.
         DS557. A5A55   309. 1597   66-95941

2136.   Vietnam today. Hanoi, Foreign Languages Publishing
         House, 1965.
         DS557. A5V535   68-1538

2137.   Vietnam. Treaties, etc., 1949- (Bao Dai).
         Conventions inter-etats, conclues en application
         de l'Accord franco-vietnamien du 8 mars 1949 . . .
         [Saigon, Impr. d'Extreme-Orient, 1951]

                                                       55-42155

2138.   Vietnam. Treaties, etc., 1949- (Bao Dai). [see France.
         Treaties, etc., 1947-1954 (Auriol).] Accords franco-viet-
         namiens du 8 mars 1949. Conventions d'application . . .
         [Saigon, Ideo, 1950?]
         JX945. V5A513   54-23208

2139.   Vietnam. Treaties, etc., 1949- (Bao Dai). Mutual
         defense assistance in Indochina. Agreement . . .
         signed at Saigon December 23, 1950. [Washington,
         Government Printing Office, 1953]
         JX235. 9. A32 no.   355   54-61026
         2447

2140.   Vietnam. Treaties, etc., 1949- (Bao Dai). Mutual
         security assurances under Mutual security act of 1951.
         Agreement . . . effected by exchange of notes dated at
         Saigon December 18, 1951, and January 3, 16, and
         19, 1952.

Vietnam   209

[Washington, Government Printing Office, 1954]
JX235.9.A32 no.   355   54-61434
2623

2141.   Vietnam. Treaties, etc., 1951. Economic cooperation.
        Agreement and notes . . . signed at Saigon September
        7, 1951 [Washington, Government Printing Office,
        1952]
        JX235.9.A32   338.9597   52-61449
        no. 2346

2142.   Vietnam. Treaties, etc., 1949-1955 (Bao Dai).
        Mutual defense assistance in Indochina. Agreement
        between the United States of America and Cambodia,
        France, Laos, and Viet-Nam, amending annex to
        Agreement of December 23, 1950 . . . [Washington,
        Government Printing Office, 1955.
        JX235.9.A32   355   56-60213
        no. 3131

2143.   Vietnam. Treaties, etc., 1949-1955 (Bao Dai). Economic
        cooperation; informational media guaranty program. Agree-
        ment . . . effected by exchange of notes signed at Saigon
        October 11 and November 3, 1955. [Washington, Govern-
        ment Printing Office 1955]
        JX235.9.A32   56-60153
        no. 3402

2144.   Vietnam. Treaties, etc., 1949-1955 (Bao Dai).
        Economic cooperation, support of Vietnamese Armed
        Forces. Agreement . . . amending paragraph 3 of
        Agreement of April 22 and 23, 1955, effected by ex-
        change of notes signed at Saigon June 24 and 25, 1955.
        [Washington, Government Printing Office, 1956]

2145.   Vietnam. Treaties, etc., 1949-1955 (Bao Dai).
        Economic cooperation, support of Vietnamese Armed
        Forces. Agreement . . . effected by exchange of
        notes signed at Saigon April 22 and 23, 1955. [Wash-
        ington, Government Printing Office, 1956]

2146.   Vietnam. Treaties, etc., 1949-1955 (Bao Dai).
        Mutual defense assistance in Indochina. Agreement
        . . . amending annex A to Agreement of December
        23, 1950, as amended . . . [Washington, Government
        Printing Office, 1956]

2147.   Vietnam. Treaties, etc., 1949-1955 (Bao Dai).
        Relief supplies and equipment; duty-free entry
        and exemption from internal taxation. Agreement
        . . . effected by exchange of notes dated at

Saigon August 20 and 26, 1954. [Washington,
Government Printing Office, 1955]
JX235. 9. A32   55-63763
no. 3115

2148.   Vietnam.   Treaties, etc., 1949-1955 (Bao Dai).
        Trade-marks.   Declaration . . . effected by exchange
        of notes signed at Washington November 3, 1953, and
        October 15, 1954.
        [Washington, Government Printing Office, 1955]
        JX235. 9. A32   55-63718
        no. 3100

2149.   Vietnam.   Treaties, etc., 1955- (Ngo Dinh Diem).
        Exchange of notes between . . . Gt. Britain and
        . . . Vietnam, for the protection of trade marks. Saigon,
        October 3/14, 1955 . . . London, HMSO,
        1956.

2150.   Vietnam, Treaties, etc., 1955- (Ngo Dinh Diem).
        Economic cooperation; informational media guaranty
        program.   Agreement . . . effected by exchange of
        notes signed at Saigon October 11 and November 3,
        1955. [Washington, Government Printing Office,
        1955]
        JX235. 9. A32   56-60153
        no. 3402

2151.   Vietnam.   Treaties, etc., 1955- (Ngo-dinh-Diem). Accords
        et conventions entre la Republique du Viet-Nam et le Roy-
        aume du Laos.   Signes a Vientiane le 11 juin 1959. [Saigon,
        Kimiaian quan, 1959]

2152.   Vietnam.   Treaties, etc., 1955-1963 (Ngo-dinh-Diem). Hiep-
        uoc than-huu va lien-lac kinh-te giua Viet-Nam, Cong-Hoa
        va Hiep Chung Quoc Hoa-Ky. [Treaty of amity and eco-
        nomic relations between the United States of America and
        the Republic of Viet-Nam.   Saigon, 1961]
                                                       NUC67-23770

2153.   Vietnam.   Trung-tam Khuech-tru'o'ng Ky-nghe.   Investing
        in Viet-Nam.   Saigon [1956?]
        HG5750. V5A5   S A 63-897

2154.   Vietnam.   Vien Quoc-gia Thong-ke.   Economic expansion
        of Viet-Nam in 1964.   [Saigon] National Institute of Statis-
        tics, 1965.
                                                       NUC67-78184

2155.   Vietnam.   Vien Quoc-gia Thong-ke.   Enquete demographique
        a Saigon en 1962.   Saigon, Institut national de la statistique
        [1963]
        HB3644. V5A57 1962   65-46911

2156.   Vietnam.   Vien Quoc-gia Thong-ke.   Enquete sur la con-
        sommation du riz et des conditions sanitaires.   [Saigon]
        1963.
                                                        NUC67-6836

2157.   Vietnam.   Vien Quoc-gia Thong-ke.   Enquetes demographiques
        au Vietnam en 1958.   [Saigon, 1960]
        HB3644. V5A57   60-4934

2158.   Vietnam.   Vien Quoc-gia Thong-ke.   Recensement des
        establissements au Viet-Nam, 1960.   [Saigon] Institut na-
        tional de la statistique, 1962-63.
        HA1780. 5. A48   73-203644

2159.   Vietnam.   Vien Quoc-gia Thong-ke.   Recensement pilote de
        la province de Phu'o'c-tuy, effectue le 6 novembre 1959.
        [Saigon? 1959?]
        HA37. V6A5   60-4925

2160.   Vietnam.   Vien Quoc-gia Thong-ke.   Su tien-trien cua nen
        kinh-te Vietnam trong nam 1960.   [Saigon] 1961.
                                                        NUC63-69078

2161.   Vietnam.   Vien Thong-ke va Khao Cu-u Kinh-te.   Su tien-
        trien kinh-te Viet-Nam trong nam 1955.   Evolution eco-
        nomique du Vietnam en 1955.   [Saigon?] 1956.
                                                        NUC67-81628

2162.   Vietnam.   Vien Thong-ke va Khao Cieu Kinh-te.   Tinh-
        hinh tien-trien kinh-te Viet-Nam trong nam 1952.   Evolu-
        tion economique du Vietnam en 1952.   [Saigon?] 1953.
        HC443. V5A56   60-4926

2163.   Vietnam: the view beyond the battle.   [n. p., 1967]
        DS557. A6V528   309. 1'597   67-62658

2164.   The Vietnam War: Christian perspectives.   Edited by
        Michael P. Hamilton.   Grand Rapids, Eerdmans [1967]
        DS557. A68V5   959. 7'04   67-28380

2165.   Vietnam: which way to peace?   A discussion by Roger
        Hilsman & others.   University of Chicago, Center for
        Policy Study, 1970.
        DS557. A63V53   959. 7'0431   70-22148

2166.   Viet Nam Workers' Party.   Cac dan toc thieu so tru'ong
        thanh duoi ngon co vinh quang cua Dang.   Ha-noi, Su That,
        1960.
                                                        NUC69-18604

2167.   Viet Nam Workers' Party.   Communique du 9e plenum du
        Comite central du Parti des travailleurs du Viet Nam.
        Hanoi, Editions en langues etrangeres, 1964.
                                                        NUC65-24447

2168.   Viet Nam Worker's Party.   Offensive against poverty and
         backwardness.   Hanoi, Foreign Languages Publishing
         House, 1963.

                                                        NUC65-43301

2169.   [Viet Nam Workers' Party]   Offensive against poverty and
         backwardness.   Hanoi, Foreign Languages Publishing
         House, 1963.
         HD2080.V5V5   68-7436

2170.   Viet Nam Workers' Party.   Offensive contre la pauvrete
         et le retard economique.   Hanoi,   Editions en langues
         etrangeres, 1963.
         HD2080.V5V5   66-88142

2171.   Viet Nam Workers' Party.   Resolution of the 9th confer-
         ence of the Viet Nam Workers' Party Central Committee,
         December 1963.   [Translated by the U.S. Mission in
         Vietnam.   Saigon, 1967?]

                                                        NUC68-89257

2172.   Viet Nam Workers' Party.   Thirty years of struggle of
         the party.   Hanoi, Foreign Languages Publishing House,
         1960-
         JQ898.W6A613   67-116300

2173.   Viet Nam Workers' Party.   III [i. e. Tretii] s'ezd Partii
         trudiashchikhsia V'etnama, Khanoi, 5-12 septiabria, 1960
         goda, (The Third Congress of Vietnamese Workers, Hanoi,
         5-12 September, 1960).   (In Russian).   Moscow, 1961.

2174.   Viet Nam Workers' Party.   Congress.   3d, Hanoi, 1960.
         Documentary record of the Third National Congress of the
         Vietnam Lao Dong Party.   Washington, U.S. Joint Publi-
         cations Research Service, 1961.

                                                        NUC63-69517

2175.   Viet Nam Workers' Party.   Congress.   3d, Hanoi, 1960.
         III [i. e. Tretii] s'ezd Partii trudiashchikhsia V'etnama,
         Khanoi, 5-12 septiabria 1960 goda.   Moskva, Gospolitiz-
         dat, 1961.

                                                        NUC68-6546

2176.   Viet Nam Worker's Party.   Youth group.   By-laws of the
         Vietnam Lao Dong Youth Group.   Washington, U.S. Joint
         Publications Research Service, 1961.

                                                        NUC63-69518

2177.   Vietnam Youth Action Committee.   Conscription?   [Upper
         Moutere, 1967]
         DS557.A64N45   355.2'23'09931   76-35862

2178.   [Vietnamese documents translated and released to the

press by the United States Mission in Saigon, including
some which were captured from the Viet Cong and North
Vietnamese forces, with the addition of reports of inter-
rogations of Communist defectors and captured Communist
troops, airgrams to the U. S. Department of State from the
American Embassy in Saigon, etc. n. p. , Distributed by
the Office of Media Services, Department of State, Washington, 1949?-
DS557. A5V58   959. 7   68-101750

2179.   Vietnamese gramophone records. Hanoi, National Printing
        Office of Vietnam, Office for the Export of Books and Peri-
        odicals.
        ML156. 4. N3V5   66-34582/MN

2180.   Vietnamese handicrafts. Hanoi, Foreign Languages Pub-
        lishing House, 1959.

2181.   Vietnamese intellectuals against U. S. aggression.   Hanoi,
        Foreign Languages Publishing House, 1966.
        DS557. A68V53   959. 7'04   68-1192

2182.   Vietnamese intellectuals against U. S. aggression.   Hanoi,
        Foreign Languages Publishing House, 1966.
                                                NUC67-80194

2183.   The Vietnamese music. Special ed. Saigon, Review Hori-
        zons [195-?]
        ML345. V5V5   68-128458/MN

2184.   The Vietnamese Nationalist Revolutionary Congress. [Paris,
        1956]

2185.   Vietnamese studies. Agricultural problems. Hanoi,
        Foreign Language Publishing House, 1964.
                                                NUC67-82047

2186.   Vietnamese studies. no. 1-   Hanoi, Foreign Languages
        Publishing House [1964-]
        DS557. A7V5   S A 65-4487

2187.   Vietnamese-American Association. Chuong trinh trinh dien
        cua Hoi Tieu Nhac Hoa tau Nu'u Uoc. Little Orchestra
        Society of New York. Saigon, 1959.
                                                NUC68-47484

2188.   Vietnamese-English Dictionary, Vols. 1-2. New York,
        Crowell Collier & Macmillan, 1960.

2189.   Vietnamese-English Dictionary Romanized. Shalom P. ,
        Publications, Inc., 1971.

2190.   Vinde, Victor. Vietnam--den beskidte krig. Overs. fra

svensk of Conrad Raun. [København] Det Udenrigspolitiske
Selskab og Det Danske Forlag, 1966.
DS557. A6V532   67-75213

2191.   . Vietnam--det smutsiga kriget.   2. bearb. uppl.
Stockholm, Raben & Sjøgren, 1967.
DS557. A6V53 1967   67-90949

2192.   . Vietnam--det smutsiga kriget.   3. bearb. uppl.
Stockholm, Raben & Sjøgren, 1968.
DS557. A6V53 1968   68-133841

2193.   . Vietnam--det smutsiga kriget.   Stockholm,
Raben & Sjøgren, 1966.
DS557. A6V53   66-77234

2194.   Viravong, Maha Sila. History of Laos [Translated from
Laotian by the U. S. Joint Publications Research Service]
New York, Paragon [c.] 1964.
AS36. U57   959. 4

2195.   Vitorovic, Nikola, 1927-   Oslobodilaeki front Juznog Vijet-
nama. Beograd, "Sedma sila, " 1966.
D839. 3. S4 br. 142   68-101790

2196.   Vittachi, Tarzie. The fall of Sukarno. New York,
Praeger [1967]
DS644. 4V5

2197.   Vlekke, Bernard Hubertus Maria. Nusantara; a history of
Indonesia. Wholly rev. ed. The Hague, W. van Hoeve,
1959.
DS634. V55   991   59-4657

2198.   Vo-duc-Hanh, Etienne. La place du catholicisme dans les
relations entre la France et le Viet-Nam de 1851 a 1870,
par E. Vo Duc Hanh. Leiden, Brill, 1969.
DC277. 4. V64   72-482643

2199.   Die Volksarmee Vietnams; Beitrage und Dokumente zum
Befreiungskampf des vietnamesischen Volkes. [Ubersetzung
aus dem Englischen und Franzosischen: Heinz Eder und
Reinhard Sommer] Berlin, Verlag des Ministeriums fur
Nationale Verteidigung, 1957.
UA853. V5V615   65-48834

2200.   Vo-Nguyen-Giap. "Big victory, great task"; North Viet-
Nam's Minister of Defense assesses the course of the war.
Introduction by David Schoenbrun. New York, Praeger
[1968]
DS557. A6V58   959. 7'04   67-31381

2201.   . Dien Bien Phu. Hanoi, Foreign Language Publishing House, 1959.

2202.   _____. Guerre du peuple, armee du peuple. Paris, F.
Maspero, 1966.
DS557. A6V614   959. 7'04   67-82924

2203.   _____. Narod IUzhnogo V'etnama pobedit, (People of
South Vietnam Will Win the War) (In Russian). Hanoi,
1966.
DS577. A6V6

2204.   _____. People's war; People's Army [by] Vo Nguyen
Giap. Hanoi, Foreign Languages Publishing House, 1961.
DS557. A7V593   S A 68-2027

2205.   _____. People's war, People's Army; the Viet Cong
insurrection manual for underdeveloped countries. Foreword by Roger Hilsman, Profile of Giap by Bernard B.
Fall. New York, Praeger [c. 1962]
DS557. A7V6   959. 7   62-19110

2206.   _____. The South Vietnam people will win. Hanoi,
Foreign Languages Publishing House, 1965.
DS557. A6V64   67-3328

2207.   _____. Una vez mas venceremos. Hanoi, Ediciones
en Lenguas Extranjeras, 1966.
DS557. A63V6   973. 923   68-49813

2208.   _____. Victoire totale, tache grandiose. Introduction
de David Schoenbrun. Paris, J. Didier, 1968.
DS557. A6V5814   77-382691

2209.   _____. La vittoria del Vietcong. Roma, Editori riuniti,
1968.
DS557. A6V66   79-414791

2210.   Vu-do-Thin. Evolution economique du Viet-Nam. Paris,
Librairie generale de droit et de jurisprudence, 1954-
HC443. V5V8   54-36101

2211.   Vu-hoang-Chu'o'ng. Communion; poems. Drawings by
Ysabel Baes. Saigon, Edition Ng. Khang [1960]
PL4378. 9. V8   S A 65-6036

2212.   Vu-quoc-Thuc, 1920-   L'economie communaliste du Viet-
Nam. Pref. de Gaston Leduc. Hanoi, Presses universi-
taires du Viet-Nam, 1951.
HC443. V5V85   64-36292

W

2213.   Wagenaar, Dan. Letters from Nam. Carlton Press, 1971.

2214.   Walinsky, Louis Joseph. Economic development in Burma,
         1951-1960. New York, Twentieth Century Fund, 1962.
         HC437. B8W2   338. 9591   62-13330

2215.   Wallace, Alfred Russel. The Malay Archipelago, the land
         of the orangutan and the bird of paradise; a narrative of
         travel, with studies of man and nature. New York, Dover,
         1962.
         DS601. W18   574. 991   62-2568

2216.   Wallace-Crabbe, Chris, ed. Six voices: contemporary
         Australian poets. Sydney, Angus & Robertson, 1963.
         PR9558. W3   821. 914082   64-6488

2217.   Walt, Lewis W. Strange War, Strange Strategy: A
         General's Report on Vietnam. Funk and Wagnalls, 1970.
         DS557. A6W27   959. 7'04   74-127054

2218.   _____. Strange War, Strange Strategy. Universal
         Publishing & Distributing Corp. , 1971.

2219.   Wang, Gungwu, ed. Malaysia, a survey. New York, F. A.
         Praeger [1964]
         DS597. 2. W3 1964   959. 5   64-24586

2220.   Wang, Hua-hsing. Yueh-nan chan wang, (Foreseeing Viet-
         na.). (In Chinese). Taipei, 1962
         DS557. A6W3

2221.   Wannan, Bill, ed. A treasury of Australian humour. Mel-
         bourne, Lansdowne, 1962.
         PR9535. W37   61-36095

2222.   War--Vietnam; memorabilia for the U.S. Armed Forces.
         [Pyrmont, Sydney, Hay & Son, 1968]
         DS557. A61W28   959. 7'04   71-440140

2223.   Warbey, William. Vietnam: The Truth. London, Merlin
         Press, 1965.
         DS557. A6W33   959. 704   66-2648

2224.   Warnenska, Monika. Alarm auf den Reisfeldern. Von der
         Reise eines Kriegsberichterstatters. (Übersetzung aus dem
         Polnischen von Caesar Rymarowicz. Illustrationen von
         Jozef Czerwinski.) Berlin, Kinderbuchverlag (1968)
         DS557. A7W2815   71-350429

2225.   _____. Front w dzungli; Woetnam 1965. [Wyd. 1.]
         Warszawa, Ludowa Spoldzielnia Wydawnicza [1967]
         DS557. A69W3   67-109257

2226.   _____. Most na rzece Ben Hai. [Wyd. 1. Warszawa]
         Ludowa Spoldzielnia Wydawnicza [1964]
         DS557. A7W3   65-34842

2227.   Warner, Denis Ashton, 1917-   The last Confucian.   New
         York, Macmillan [c. 1963]
         DS550. W3   959. 7   63-14185

2228.   Waterhouse, Charles H.   Vietnam sketchbook; drawings
         from delta to DMZ, by Charles Waterhouse.   Rutland,
         Vermont, C. E. Tuttle Company [1968]
         DS557. A61W3   741. 9'73   68-21114

2229.   _____. Vietnam war sketches, from the air, land, and
         sea, by Charles Waterhouse.   Rutland, Vermont, C. E.
         Tuttle Company [1970]
         DS557. A61W32 1970 959. 7'04   71-109410

2230.   Waters, Mary A.   G. I. s & the Fight Against War.   New
         York, Pathfinder Press, 1971.

2231.   Watt, Sir Alan Stewart, 1901- The evolution of Australian
         foreign policy, 1938-1965, by Alan Watt.   London, Cam-
         bridge University Press, 1967.
         DU117. W3   327. 94   67-10782

2232.   _____. Vietnam, an Australian analysis, by Alan
         Watt.   Melbourne, Canberra [etc.] Cheshire for the
         Australian Institute of International Affairs [1968]
         DS557. A6W35   959. 7'04   79-385053

2233.   _____. Vietnam: An Australian Analysis.   Interna-
         tional Publications Service, 1968.

2234.   _____. Vietnam--an Australian Analysis.   Verry,
         Lawrence, Inc. , 1968.

2235.   Wavell, Stewart.   The Naga King's daughter.   New York,
         Atheneum, 1965 [c. 1964]
         DS509. 3. W3   915. 95   65-10915

2236.   Weatherly, Marjorie.   Pig follows dog [by] Lorraine Sal-
         mon [pseud.]   Hanoi, Foreign Languages Publishing House,
         1960.
         DS557. A7W4   S A 64-2287

2237.   Wehl, David.   The birth of Indonesia.   London, G. Allen
         & Unwin, 1948.
         DS644. W44   992   49-16619

2238.   Weil, Charles A.   Curtains Over Vietnam: A Strategic
         Appraisal of Suppressed Aspects of U. S. Security Stake
         in Vietnam.   Exposition, 1969.
         UA23. W3696   959. 7'04   72-5982

2239.   Weiler, Heinrich, 1924- Vietnam: eine volkerrechtliche
         Analyse des amerikanischen Krieges und seiner Vorges-

chichte.   Vorwort von Wolfgang Abendroth.   Frankenthal,
H. Wolf, 1969.
JX1573.W39   73-464826

2240.   Weinstein, Franklin B.   Vietnam's Unheld Elections; the
Failure to Carry out the 1956 Reunification Elections and
the Effect on Hanoi's Present Outlook.   Ithaca, New York.
Southeast Asia Program.   Department of Asian Studies,
Cornell University, 1966.
JX1573.W4   320. 9597   66-65159

2241.   Weiss, Peter, 1916- Diskurs uber die Vorgeschichte und
den Verlauf des lang andauernden Befreiungskrieges in Viet
Nam als Beispiel fur die Notwendigkeit des bewaffneten
Kampfes der Unterdruckten gegen ihre Unterdrucker, sowie
uber die Versuche der Vereinigten Staaten von Amerika die
Grundlagen der Revolution zu vernichten. [Frankfurt am
Main] Suhrkamp [1968, 1967]
PT2685. E5D5   832'. 9'14   68-121709

2242.   _____.   "Limited bombing" in Vietnam: report on the
attacks against the Democratic Republic of Vietnam by the
U. S. Air Force and the Seventh Fleet, after the declaration of 'limited bombing' by President Lyndon B. Johnson
on March 31, 1968 by Peter Weiss [and] Gunilla Palmstierna Weiss; translated [from the German] by Anna
Bjorkwall & Davis Jones.   London, Bertrand Russell
Peace Foundation [1969]
DS557. A7W45   959. 7'04   77-8421

2243.   _____.   Notes on the cultural life of the Democratic
Republic of Vietnam.   Translated from the German.   [New
York, Dell Publishing Company, 1970]
DS557. A74W43   915. 97'03'4   70-13444

2244.   _____.   Notes sur la vie culturelle en Republique
democratique du Viet Nam.   Traduit de l'allemand par
Michel Bataillon.   Paris, Editions du Seuil, 1969.
DS557. A74W44   75-494265

2245.   _____.   Notizen zum kulturellen Leben in der Demo-
kratischen Republik Viet Nam.   [Frankfurt am Main]
Suhrkamp [1968]
DS557. A74W4   70-384828

2246.   _____.   Rapport om Forenta staternas forstarkta angrepp
mot Nordvietnam efter den 31 mars 1968.   [Av] Peter
Weiss [och] Gunilla Palmstierna.   Den svenska red. i
samarbete med Erik Eriksson.   Malmo, Cavefors; [Solna,
Seelig] 1968.
DS557. A65W4   76-405867

2247.   _____.   Reponse a Johnson sur les bombardements

limites ou l'Escalade U. S. au Vietnam d'avril a juin 1968.
[Paris] Editions du Seuil, 1968.
DS557. A65W42   71-406103

2248.   Weltmacht USA; internationale Politik und Selbstverstandis
        der Vereinigten Staaten, mit Beitragen von Abraham Ash-
        kenasi [et al] Stuttgart, E. Klett [1969]
        E744. W532   73-495669

2249.   Wepf, Reinhold. Vietnam. Vom Mekongdelta zum Song
        Ben Hai. (Farbaufnahmen: Reinhold Wepf. [Texte:]
        Reinhold Wepf, [u. a.]) Bern, Kummerly & Frey, (1968)
        DS557. A5W45   76-362255

2250.   Werfel, Roman. Wietnam bez ostatniego rozdzialu. [Wyd.
        1.] Warszawa, Iskry, 1967.
        DS557. A63W4   68-89812

2251.   Wernstedt, Frederick L.   The Philippine Island world: a
        physical, cultural, and regional geography, by Frederick
        L. Wernstedt and J. E. Spencer, Berkeley, University of
        California Press, 1967.
        DS660. W47   919. 14   67-14001 rev.

2252.   Wertheim, Willem Frederik, 1907-   Indonesian society
        in transition, a study of social change.   2d rev. ed. The
        Hague, W. van Hoeve [1959]
        HN703. W45   309. 191   56-59029

2253.   West, Francis J. , Jr.   Small Unit Action in Vietnam:
        Summer 1966.   Arno Press, 1968.

2254.   _____.   Small unit action in Vietnam, summer, 1966,
        by Francis J. West, Jr.   Washington, Historical Branch,
        G-3 Division, Headquarters U. S. Marine Corps, 1967.
        DS557. A6W4   959. 7'04   67-60937

2255.   West, Fred. Getting to know the two Vietnams. Illus-
        trated by Polly Bolian. New York, Coward [c. 1963]
                             j915. 97   63-15548

2256.   West, Katharine. Power in the Liberal Party: a study in
        Australian politics.   Melbourne, Canberra [etc.]
        Cheshire [1965]
        JQ4098. L5W47   329. 994   66-74268

2257.   West, Richard.   Sketches from Vietnam; illustrated by
        Gerald Scarfe.   London, Cape, 1968.
        DS557. A5W47   915. 9'7'034   68-118056

2258.   _____. Sketches from Vietnam.   International Publi-
        cations Service, 1968.

2259.   . Sketches from Vietnam.   Verry, Lawrence,
Inc. , 1968.

2260.   Wheatley, Paul.   The Golden Khersonese; studies in the
historical geography of the Malay Peninsula before A. D.
1500. [dist. New York, Oxford, c.] 1961.
DS596. W45   HIS 959. 5   61-65521

2261.   . Impressions of the Malay Peninsula in ancient
times. Singapore, Published by D. Moore for Eastern
University Press. [Detroit, Cellar Book, 1965, c. 1964]
DS596. 5. W5   959. 503   66-26

2262.   White, Ralph K.   Nobody wanted war; misperception in
Vietnam and other wars [by] Ralph K. White. [1st ed.]
Garden City, New York, Doubleday, 1968.
DS557. A6W45   959. 7'04   68-10553

2263.   . Nobody Wanted War: Misperception in Vietnam
& Other Wars. rev. ed. Doubleday & Company, Inc. , 1970.

2264.   Whiteside, Thomas, 1918- Defoliation.   Foreword by George
Wald.   New York, Ballantine Books [1970]
QH545. P4W48   632'. 954   72-13059

2265.   Whitmore, Terry.   Memphis, Nam, Sweden: the autobiography of a Black American exile, by Terry Whitmore
as told to Richard Weber.   New York, Doubleday, 1971.
DS557. A69W48   959. 7'0438   79-157638

2266.   Whittemore, Lewis Bliss, Bp.   Struggle for freedom;
history of the Philippine Independent Church.   Greenwich,
Connecticut [Seabury Press, 1961]
BX4795. I5W5 1961   279. 14   61-10457

2267.   Why Vietnam.   [Washington, For sale by the Superintendent
of Documents, U. S. Government Printing Office, 1965]
DS557. A6W47   65-62680

2268.   Why Vietnam.   Washington, The White House (distributed
by the U. S. Information Service, 1965]
DS557. A6W47 1965   959. 7   66-61020

2269.   Why Vietnam.   Washington, U. S. Government Printing
Office, 1965.
DS557. A6W47 1965a 959. 7   66-60301

2270.   Wickberg, Edgar.   The Chinese in Philippine life, 1850-
1898.   New Haven, Yale University Press, 1965.
DS666. C5W5   301. 451510914   65-22475

2271.   Wiernik, Bronislaw.   Cien kapitana Daileya; korespondent
sajgonski zmienia zdanie. [Wyd. 1. Warszawa] Ksiazka i

Wiedza, 1967.
DS557. A63W5   68-129915

2272.   _____. Rok tygrysa; o Wietnamie . . . i nie tylko o
Wietnamie. [Wyd. 1.] Warszawa] Ksiazka i Wiedza, 1964.
DS557. A7W5   65-39300

2273.   _____. Wschod jest czerwony, slonce wschodzi . . .
[Wyd. 1.] Warszawa, Wydawn. Ministerstwa Obrony
Narodowej, 1953.
DS902. W5   54-43916

2274.   Williams, Iain McLean.   Vietnam; a pictorial history of
the Sixth Battalion, the Royal Australian Regiment, re-
searched and written by Iain McLean Williams.   Assisted
by Bryan Wickens [and] David Sabben.   Drawings by
James Kenna.   Brookvale, Sydney, R. W. Newton and
W. Crooks (Printcraft Press), 1967.
DS557. A64A87   959. 7'04   68-82572

2275.   Williams, Lea E.   Overseas Chinese nationalism; the
genesis of the Pan-Chinese movement in Indonesia, 1900-
1916.   Glencoe, Illinois, Free Press, 1960.
DS632. C5W5   325. 2510991   60-9582

2276.   Williams, Marion.   My Tour in Vietnam: A Burlesque
Shocker.   Vantage Press, Inc. , 1970.

2277.   Williams, Maslyn.   Five journeys from Jakarta; inside
Sukarno's Indonesia. New York, W. Morrow, [1965,
1966]
DS620. W5   919. 1043   66-11592

2278.   Williams, Roger Neville.   The new exiles: American war
resisters in Canada.   Liveright, 1971.
F1035. A5W5   959. 7'04'31   78-148662

2279.   Williamson, Robert Wood.   Religion and social organization in central Polynesia.   Cambridge, University Press,
1937.
BL2600. W52   299. 9   38-10069

2280.   _____. Religious and cosmic beliefs of central Polynesia.   Cambridge, University Press, 1933.
BL2600. W5   299. 9   34-22783

2281.   Willmott, Donald Earl.   The Chinese of Semarang: a
changing minority community in Indonesia.   Ithaca, New
York, Cornell University, 1968.
DS632. C5W52   301. 451   60-51392

2282.   Wilson, Patrick.   South Asia, a selected bibliography on
India, Pakistan, Ceylon.   New York, American Institute

of Pacific Relations,   1957.
Z3185.W5   016.954   57-810

2283.   Wilson, Peter J.   A Malay village and Malaysia: social
         values and rural development [by] Peter J. Wilson.   New
         Haven, HRAF Press [1967]
         HN700.6.A8W5   309.1595'1   66-27877

2284.   Wilson, Trevor Gordon.   The Grey government, 1877-79;
         an episode in the rise of liberalism in New Zealand.
         Auckland, Auckland University College, 1954.

2285.   Winstedt, Sir Richard Olof.   Malaya and its history.   6th
         ed.   London, Hutchinson University Library, 1962.
         DS596.W515 1962   959.5   63-1005

2286.   _____, Malaya and its history.   [7th ed.]
         London, Hutchinson University Library [1966]
         DS596.W515 1966   959.5   63-1005

2887.   Woito, Robert S., ed.   Vietnam Peace Proposals.   World
         Without War Council Publications, 1967.

2288.   Wolf, Charles.   The Indonesian story; the birth, growth
         and structure of the Indonesian Republic.   New York, Day,
         1948.
         DS644.W6   992   48-7301

2289.   Wolff, Leon.   Little brown brother; how the United States
         purchased and pacified the Philippine Islands at the cen-
         tury's turn.   Garden City, New York, Doubleday, 1961.
         DS682.A1W6   991.403   61-6528

2290.   Wolfkill, Grant F.   Reported to be alive, by Grant Wolf-
         kill with Jerry A. Rose.   Foreword by Robert F. Kennedy.
         New York, S. & S.   [c.1965]
         DS557.L28W6   959.404   65-18650

2291.   Wolin, Marian.   Agresja amerykanska w Wietnamie;
         problemy wojskowe i polityczne.   [Wyd. 1. Warszawa]
         Wydawn.   Ministerstwa Obrony Narodowej [1967]
         DS557.A6W58   68-121889

2292.   Wood, Hugh Bernard.   Nepal bibliography.   Eugene, Ore.,
         American-Nepal Education Foundation, 1959.
         Z3207.N4W6   016.915426   59-16488

2293.   Woodman, Dorothy.   The making of Burma.   London,
         Cresset Press, 1962.
         DS485.B86W6   959.1   62-2969

2294.   Woodruff, Lloyd Wilbur.   Local administration in Viet Nam;
         its future development.   Saigon, Michigan State University

Advisory Group, National Institute of Administration, Republic of Vietnam, 1961.

NUC65-9528

2295. _____. Local finance in South Viet-Nam; a study of 25 villages in the two southern regions. Saigon, Michigan State University Advisory Group, National Institute of Administration, Republic of Vietnam, 1961.

NUC65-9527

2296. _____. The study of a Vietnamese rural community: administrative activity by Lloyd W. Woodruff assisted by Nguyen ngoc Yen. Annex: Village government in Viet-Nam, a survey of historical development, by Nguyen xuan Dao. [Saigon?] Michigan State University, Viet-Nam Advisory Group, 1960.
JS7225.V5W6   352.0597   60-64305

2297. Woodruff, William. The Suez Canal and the Australian economy [by] W. Woodruff & L. McGregor. [Carlton] Melbourne University Press [1957]
HE513.W6   386.43   58-23976

2298. Woodside, Alexander B. Vietnam & The Chinese Model: A Comparative Study of Nguyen & Ch'ing Civil Government in the First Half of the Nineteenth Century. Harvard University Press, 1971.

2299. Woolf, Cecil. Authors take sides on Vietnam; two questions on the war in Vietnam answered by the authors of several nations, edited by Cecil Woolf and John Bagguley. New York, Simon and Schuster [1967]
DS557.A68W6 1967b 959.7'04   67-28040

2300. World Conference of Lawyers for Vietnam, Grenoble, 1968. Conference mondiale de juristes pour le Vietnam. Grenoble 6-10 juillet 1968. Bruxelles, Editions de l'Association internationale des juristes democrates, av. Jupiter, 49, [1969]
JX1995.W58 1968   70-446374

2301. World Conference on Vietnam, Stockholm, 1967. World conference on Vietnam, Stockholm, July 6-9, 1967. Documents. [Wien, gazzetta Zeitschriften Ges. m. b. H., 1967]
DS557.A6W63 1967   959.7'04   68-94894

2302. World Congress for Peace, National Independence, and General Disarmament, Helsinki, 1965. Vietnam; documents, messages, speeches. [Wien, Gazzetta Zeitschriften, 1965.]
DS557.A6W6 1965aa   66-7260

2303.   . Vietnam; Dokumente, Ansprachen, Botschaften.
        [Wien, Gazzetta 1965]
        DS557. A6W6   959. 7'04   65-70988
        1965aab

2304.   Wright, Harrison M.   New Zealand, 1769-1840; early years
        of western contact.   Cambridge, Massachusetts, Harvard
        University, 1959-
        DU420. W75   993. 101   59-12979

2305.   Wright, Judith, ed.   A book of Australia verse.   London,
        Oxford University, 1956.
        PR9551. W7   821. 082   57-3031

2306.   Wright, Judith, comp.   New land, new language; an antholo-
        gy of Australian verse.   New York, Oxford University
        Press, 1962.
        PR9551. W73   821. 082   58-3069

2307.   Wu, Kuan-ch'i.   Yueh-nan, (Vietnam), (In Chinese).
        Peking, 1965.
        DS557. A7W8

2308.   Wyllie, Robert Gurner.   Brief aus Vietnam.   Ein australis-
        cher Arzt berichtet uber seine Erlebnisse wahrend eines
        sechsmonatigen freiwilligen Einsatzes in Vietnam.   (Von
        R. G. Wyllie)   Wien, Australische Botschaft, [1968]
        DS557. A67W945   77-492388

                                    Y

2309.   Yale Southeast Asia studies.   no. 1-   New Haven, Yale
        University Press, 1965-
        DS503. 4Y17

2310.   Yale University.   Graduate School.   Southeast Asia Studies.
        Monograph series.   no. 1-   New Haven, 1961-
        DS503. 4Y18

2311.   . Translation series.   no. 1-   [New Haven]
        Yale University Southeast Asia Studies.
        DS503. 4Y35

2312.   Yamin, Muhammad.   Presiden Ho-chi-Minh; uraian mend-
        jelas alasan-alasan menganugerahkan gelar doctor honoris
        causa dalam ilmu hukum oleh Universitas Padjadjaran pada
        tanggal 2 Maret 1959 dikota Bandung kepada P. J. M. Ho Chi
        Minh, Presiden Republik Demokratis Vietnam.   Diutjapkan
        oleh H. Muhammad Yamin.   [Bandung] Universitas Padjad-
        jaran [cover 1959]
        DS557. A7Y3   S A 65-3297

2313.   Yi, Kyu-t'ae P'mudun yonkkot (Blood spreaded lotus flower

(Report on Vietnam war) (In Korean) 1965.
DS557. A6Y5

2314.   Yugoslavia and Vietnam. Documents on Yugoslavia's sup-
        port to the liberation struggle of Vietnam. [Translator:
        Andelija Vujovic.   Dimce Belovski: Introduction]. Beo-
        grad, "Medunarodna stampa-Interpress, " 1968.
        JX1977. 2. Y8D6   959. 7'04   68-144356
        no. 15

                                Z

2315.   Zabilka, Gladys, 1917- Customs and culture of the
        Philippines. Illustrated by M. Kuwata. [1st ed.] Tokyo,
        Rutland, Vermont, C. E. Tuttle Company [1963]
        DS663. Z3   919. 14   63-8566

2316.   Zablocki, Clement J. Report on Vietnam, by Clement J.
        Zablocki, Wisconsin, of the Committee on Foreign Affairs,
        House of Representatives. Washington, U. S. Government
        Printing Office, 1966.
        DS557. A6Z25   309. 1597   66-61297

2317.   Zagoria, Donald S. Vietnam triangle; Moscow, Peking,
        Hanoi, by Donald S. Zagoria. New York, Pegasus [1967]
        DS557. A635Z3   959. 7'04   67-25501

2318.   Zaide, Gregorio F. The Philippine revolution. Manila,
        Modern Book, 1954.
        DS675. Z3   54-37073

2319.   Zalamea, Jorge, 1905-   comp. Las aguas vivas del
        Vietnam; antologia de la poesia vietnamita combatiente.
        Versiones, prologo y notas de Jorge Zalamea. [1. ed.]
        Bogota, Editorial Colombia Neuve, 1967.
        PQ3973. 5. Z3   741   67-103529

2320.   Zasloff, Joseph Jermiah. The role of the sanctuary in
        insurgency; Communist China's support to the Vietminh, 1946-
        1954, by J. J. Zasloff. Santa Monica, California, Rand
        Corp. , 1967.
        Q180. A1R36   355. 03'2'597   67-8262
        no. 4618

2321.   _____ . Rural resettlement in Vietnam; an agroville in
        development [by] Joseph J. Zasloff. [Saigon] Michigan
        State University, Vietnam Advisory Group [1961?]
        DS557. A6Z3   64-64288

2322.   _____ . A study of administration in Binh Minh district
        [by] Joseph J. Zasloff and Nguyen-Khac-Nhan. Saigon,
        Michigan State University Viet Nam Advisory Group and
        National Institute of Administration, 1961.
                                                    NUC64-50379

2323.   Zelentsov, Vsevolod Alekseevich.   Narod V'etnama pobedit,
         (The Vietnamese People will Win).   (In Russian). Moscow,
         1966.
         DS557. A6Z44

2324.   Zeri i popullit, Tirana.   Expose to the end the double-
         faced stand of the Khrushchevite revisionists towards the
         struggle of the Vietnamese people. Tirana, Naim Frasheri
         Publishing House, 1965.
         DS557. A7Z4   65-29369

2325.   Zhukov, IUrii Aleksandrovich. V'etnam, 1965; iz zapisnykh
         knizhek zhurnalistov, (Vietnam, 1965; from journalists'
         notebooks).   (In Russian). Moscow, 1965.
         DS557. A6Z48

2326.   Zils, Maria Susanne.   Vietnam, Land ohne Frieden.
         Weilheim/Oberbayern, O. W. Barth-Verlag [1965]
         DS557. A5Z5   66-37604

2237.   Zimmer, Egon Maria, 1910- Der Tag des Zorns.   Roman.
         [Von] C. C. Bergius.   (Gutersloh) Mohn (1967)
         PT2653. I54T3   68-78953

2328.   Zinkin, Maurice. Development for free Asia. New ed.
         New York, Oxford University Press, 1963.
         HN666. Z55   309. 15   63-6290

2329.   Zinn, Howard, 1922-   Vietnam: the logic of withdrawal.
         Boston, Beacon Press [1967]
         DS557. A63Z5   973. 92   67-14112

2340.   _____. Vijetnam: logika povlacenja.   Preveli s engleskog:
         Nikola Catipovic [i] Stevan Majstorovic.   Naslovna strana:
         Pavle Ristic.   Beograd, "Sedma sila, " 1968.
         D839. 3. S4 br. 190-191   68-113585

2331.   Zwartboek Vietnam. [Samengesteld door S. Bosgra, C. le
         Pair en Fr. de Vries. 6. herz. en aangevulde uitg.   Am-
         sterdam, Stichting Uitg. Bevrijding, 1967]
         DS557. A6Z9 1967   68-95894

SUBJECT INDEX

Part I -- Vietnam

Vietnam (General) 5, 31, 38, 39, 62, 69, 75, 93, 99, 117, 133,
143, 155, 162, 173, 182, 183, 190, 199, 205, 212, 226, 239,
249, 252, 257, 280, 296, 310, 313, 315, 341, 350, 356, 363,
374, 397, 400, 405, 426, 428, 431, 456, 461, 473, 485, 513,
522, 523, 558, 564, 567, 568, 569, 570, 595, 600, 637, 653,
657, 663, 667, 682, 687, 688, 707, 733, 756, 762, 763, 764,
773, 775, 785, 793, 815, 846, 851, 871, 872, 880, 882, 885,
888, 903, 906, 928, 937, 948, 954, 955, 969, 981, 987, 997,
999, 1002, 1007, 1011, 1014, 1024, 1033, 1050, 1143, 1149,
1171, 1179, 1198, 1200, 1203, 1205, 1223, 1238, 1258, 1268,
1317, 1334, 1343, 1344, 1352, 1358, 1364, 1377, 1379, 1385,
1407, 1414, 1427, 1461, 1483, 1488, 1499, 1503, 1509, 1523,
1531, 1533, 1535, 1559, 1562, 1563, 1576, 1587, 1588, 1589,
1591, 1595, 1596, 1607, 1608, 1629, 1643, 1668, 1669, 1670,
1700, 1711, 1715, 1728, 1795, 1814, 1825, 1831, 1832, 1833,
1835, 1837, 1851, 1860, 1868, 1870, 1876, 1883, 1889, 1912,
1913, 1933, 1936, 1962, 2036, 2037, 2038, 2088, 2096, 2135,
2136, 2163, 2186, 2188, 2189, 2213, 2218, 2230, 2233, 2234,
2253, 2258, 2259, 2263, 2276, 2287, 2298, 2321, 2326.

Abdul Rahman, Tunku, 1903-
1104
Administrative & Political Di-
visions 1846
Adolescence 1072
Africa 1293
Aggression (International Law)
1603
Agricultural Colleges 1925
Agricultural Colonies--Dutch 1309
Agricultural Colonies--Philippine
Islands 1309
Agricultural Credit 2097, 2098,
2104
Agricultural Education 1922
Agricultural Laborers 1930
Agricultural Societies, Asia 1737
Agriculture 624, 927, 1098,
1139, 2019, 2095
Agriculture--Annam 58
Agriculture--Economic Aspects
1887
Agriculture--Economic Aspects--
Australia 365

Agriculture--Economic Aspects--
New Zealand 365
Agriculture--Economic Aspects--
Philippine Islands 1599
Agriculture--Statistics 2131, 2132
Agriculture--Tropics 1922
Alceste (ship) 1067
Allotment of Land 2096
American Poetry 998, 1152
Americans in Canada 2278
Ancestor--Worship 543
Angkor, Cambodia 331, 643,
1373, 1549
Annam 48, 49
Annam--Industries 58
Annam--Laws, Statutes, etc. 54,
56, 57, 1283
Annam--Politics and Government
58
Annamese Language--Spoken Anna-
mese 844
Anti-Communist--Vietnam 2094
Appropriations and Expenditures
1573, 2084

Japan 1441

Australia--Foreign Relations--U.S.
976

Australia--Foreign Relations and
Economic Conditions 88

Australia--Geology 196

Australia--Harbors 145

Australia--History 94, 150, 322,
1524

Australia--Imprints 91, 269

Australia in Literature--Bib-
liography 1101

Australia--International Law--His-
tory 1254

Australia--Investment, American
36

Australia--Journalism 1045

Australia--Labor Disputes 191

Australia--Land Tenure 234

Australia--Landforms 1516

Australia--Law 1303

Austarlia--Law--Periodicals
1742

Australia--Legal Research 266

Australia--Libraries 105

Australia, Literature--History
and Criticism 479

Australia, Melbourne--Social
Conditions 1618

Australia--Meteorology 1534

Australia--Native Races 1399

Australia--Natural History 112

Australia--Northern Territory--
Economic Conditions 440

Australia--Official Handbook 86

Australia--Physical Geography
827

Australia--Political Parties--
Liberal Party 2256

Australia--Politics and Government 472, 1106, 1481

Australia--Shipping 2297

Australia--Social Conditions 386

Australia--Social Workers 944

Australia, South--History 1330

Australia--Sydney--Opera House
119

Australia--Taxation 702

Australia--Territorial Waters
1004

Australia--Treaty-making Power
411

Australia--Wages and Labor

Productivity 814

Australia--Water Supply--Con-
gresses 1165

Australian Ballads and Songs
1619, 1620

Australian Literature 2221

Australian Literature--Addresses,
Essays, Lectures 1324

Australian Literature--Bibliography
1101

Australian Literature--History and
criticism 632, 666, 1101,
1290, 1514

Australian Literature--Wit and
Humor 2221

Australian Poetry 633, 1345

Australian Poetry (Collections)
2305, 2306

Australian Poetry--History and
Criticism 209

Australian Poetry--19th Century--
History and Criticism 1043

Australian Poetry--20th Century
672, 2216

Australian Poetry--Year-books 92

Authors, Australian 722

Banks and Banking, Central-Asia
387

Barter 1023

Batak 1690

Batakland--Religion 1690

Batakland--Social Life and
Customs 1690

Bay of Islands, New Zealand 875

Bibliography 27, 842, 883, 1088,
1095, 1096, 1097, 1300, 1354

Biography 2086

Birth (in rel., folk-lore) 1130

Bo Quoc-gia giao-duc 1941, 1943

Borneo 781

Borneo--Description 1144

Borneo--History 813

Botany--Economic 232

Botany--Malay Peninsula 232

Boundaries--Cambodia 406

British in Malaya 1298

British North Borneo Company
1720

Budda and Buddhism 466, 2030,
2122

Buddhism and State 2030

Budget 2077, 2084

Mines and Mineral Resources--
Malay Peninsula 232
Ministry of Agriculture and
Forestry 2078
Missions--Indo-China 337
Modjokerto, Indonesia--Economic
Conditions 580
Modjokerto, Java--Religion 581
Mohammedans in Indonesia 131
Moi (Tongking Hill Tribes) 1416
Music--Discography 2179
Music--History & Criticism
1712, 2183
Mythology--Oriental 71
Mythology--Polynesian 206, 638,
2279, 2280

National Characteristics, New
Zealand 1623
National Front for the Liberation
of South Vietnam 24, 1332,
1948
National History--Malay Archi-
pelago 2215
Nationalism 228, 1032
Nationalism--Asia, Southeastern
757
Nationalism--China 2275
Nationalism--Indonesia 855
Native Races--Borneo 1144
Natural History--Indo-China
927, 1146
Natural History--South Island,
New Zealand 321
Negri Sembilan--Politics and
Government 659
Nepal--Bibliography 2292
Netherlands--Colonies--Ad-
ministration 471, 1858, 2197
Netherlands--Colonies--Dutch
East Indies 115
Netherlands--Colonies--East
Indies 471, 571
Netherlands--Foreign Relations
Indonesia 1291
New Caledonia--Politics and
Government 129
New Guinea--Art--Asmat 1430
New Guinea--Art--Bibliography
1185
New Guinea--Biography 886
New Guinea, Dutch--Politics and
Government 164

New Guinea--Ethnology 127
New Guinea--Politics and Govern-
ment 532, 959
New Guinea--Wood-Carving 1186
New Hebrides--Politics and
Government 129
New Zealand 130, 1174, 1403
New Zealand--Biography 231
New Zealand--Censorship 1316
New Zealand Company, London
1028
New Zealand--Description and
Travel 370, 1064
New Zealand--Description and
Travel--Collections 1661
New Zealand--Description and
Travel--Views 175
New Zealand--Discovery and Ex-
ploration 122, 436, 1058
New Zealand--Economic Condi-
tions 1068
New Zealand Fiction--History
and Criticism 1617
New Zealand--Foreign Relations
619
New Zealand--Foreign Relations--
Treaties 1175
New Zealand--History 344, 362,
1028, 1102, 1107, 1141, 1545,
1546, 1579, 2304
New Zealand--Intellectual Life
1066
New Zealand--Law--Periodicals
1177
New Zealand Literature--History
and Criticism 1059
New Zealand--Maoris 1423,
1508
New Zealand--Native Races
1103, 1107
New Zealand Poetry 287, 273,
1152
New Zealand--Political Parties
1112
New Zealand--Politics and
Government 1176, 1346
New Zealand--Social Conditions
1107
New Zealand--Statistics 1178
New Zealand--United Nations
1740, 1741
New Service 2079
Ngo-dinh-Diem, 1901 1888,

Southeastern 890
U.S.--Foreign Relations--China
(People's Republic of China,
1949-) 1805
U.S.--Foreign Relations--Indo-
china, French 1628
U.S.--Foreign Relations--Laos
1993
U.S.--Foreign Relations--
Philippine Islands 648
U.S.--Foreign Relations--Russia
697
U.S. Marine Corps 1st Division
790
U.S. Marine Corps--Military
Life 1031
U.S.--Military Policy 2238
U.S.--Politics and Government
621
U.S.--Relations (General) with
Foreign Countries 1260
University Publications 1731,
1861

Veterans--U.S. 881
Vietnam Workers' Party--
Congress--3d, Hanoi 2174
Vietnam Workers' Party--
Party Work 2173
Vietnam Workers' Party--
Youth Groups 2176
Vietnamese in Thailand 214, 1348
Vietnamese-American Association
2187
Villages 2296
Villages--Community Develop-
ment 1236
Villages--Juvenile Literature
1275
Vinhlong, (Province) 2322
Voyages and Travels 1413

War 275, 1934
War Crimes 434, 902
War--Destruction and Pillage
1486
War (International Law)--
Compends. 2040
Washington, D. C.--Demon-
stration, April 18-23,
1971 881
Water--Conservation 2082
Wheat Trade--Australia 444

Women in Burma 884
World Assembly of Youth 2125
World Politics 1260
World War, 1939-1945--Indo-
nesia 131
World War, 1939-1945--Malay
Peninsula 1692
Wuoc-Gia Nong-Tin Cuoc. 2104

Youth 2125
Youth Movement 2125

SUBJECT INDEX

Part II -- Democratic Republic of Vietnam

SUBJECT INDEX

Part III -- Vietnamese Conflict, 1961-

Vietnamese Conflict, 1961- (General) 23, 25, 41, 44, 136, 140,
142, 152, 160, 161, 166, 179, 185, 189, 198, 202, 203, 204,
215, 222, 223, 227, 228, 229, 256, 268, 290, 299, 319, 324, 357,
378, 380, 422, 425, 435, 448, 464, 474, 475, 476, 482, 506,
510, 521, 539, 540, 545, 563, 572, 598, 599, 609, 610, 650, 655,
656, 662, 677, 696, 744, 755, 759, 774, 779, 811, 816, 862, 890,
898, 899, 900, 901, 917, 949, 961, 977, 1000, 1005, 1008, 1017,
1022, 1035, 1062, 1147, 1148, 1154, 1170, 1190, 1227, 1248,
1259, 1260, 1267, 1281, 1284, 1297, 1302, 1312, 1327, 1333,
1349, 1351, 1398, 1406, 1418, 1431, 1451, 1459, 1464, 1471,
1475, 1480, 1487, 1497, 1522, 1584, 1594, 1614, 1615, 1622,
1633, 1641, 1653, 1673, 1675, 1682, 1727, 1757, 1758, 1760,
1761, 1763, 1783, 1785, 1786, 1787, 1799, 1848, 1863, 1864,
1867, 1872, 1890, 1919, 1921, 1932, 1948, 1964, 1980, 2013,
2040, 2054, 2056, 2075, 2133, 2190, 2191, 2192, 2200, 2206,
2208, 2209, 2217, 2239, 2262, 2291, 2300, 2329, 2331

Addresses, Essays, Lectures
484, 2041
Addresses, Sermons, etc. 63,
267, 381, 530, 535, 1156,
1306, 1353, 1422, 1484, 1561,
1649, 1918, 2020, 2052, 2053,
2301
Aerial Operations, American 28,
195, 429, 588, 589, 700, 830,
1773, 1776, 1777, 2242, 2246,
2247
Aerial Operations, North Vietnamese 1208
Atrocities 30, 43, 258, 271,
434, 591, 636, 684, 716,
720, 795, 808, 809, 902, 934,
936, 1246, 1458, 1479, 1498,
1647, 1651, 1822, 1949, 1981
Australia 1012

Bibliography 961
Biography 34, 65, 615

Campaigns 60, 106, 437, 556,
794, 1029, 1034, 1037, 1038,
1060, 1361, 1590, 1729, 1804,
1818, 1849, 1865, 1866, 1988,
2074
Campaigns--Binh Dinh (Tinh)
1036
Campaigns--Cambodia 433,
1240
Campaigns--Cambodia--Addresses
Essays, Lectures 628
Campaigns--Hue, Vietnam 450
Campaigns--Khe Sanh 1540
Campaigns--Khe Sanh--Pictorial
Works 437
Campaigns--My Lai (4), Viet-
nam 591, 636, 720
Campaigns--Son My 684
Campaigns--Vinh Long (Province)
1086
Causes 859
Censorship--U.S. 1788
Chemistry 40, 1469
Children 379, 477
Children--Pictorial Works
1502
China (People's Republic of
China, 1949-) 323
Civilian Relief 124, 194, 1329,
1800, 1801
Collections 1081

244

TITLE INDEX

Aboriginal Australians. 1684
Aborigine culture history, a survey of publications. 1954-1957. 1335
Aborigines now; new perspective in the study of aboriginal communities. 1399
Abuse of power. (1967) 425
Abuse of power. (1971) 426
Accord entre le Gouvernement de la Republique du Vietnam et Michigan State University. 1875
Accords et conventions entre la Republique du Viet-Nam et le Royaume du Laos. Signes a Vientiane le 11 juin 1959. 2151
Accords franco-vietnamiens du 8 mars 1949. Conventions d'application. La presente publication est faite d'accord parties entre le gouvernement du Vietnam et le Haut Commissariat de France en Indochine. 551
Accords franco-vietnamiens du 8 mars 1949. Conventions d'application. . . 2138
Accords franco-vietnamiens du 8 mars 1949. The Franco-Vietnamese agreement of March 8th, 1959. 4
Achievements of the campaign of denunciation of communist subversive activities, first phase; published on the occasion of the Second National Congress of Anti-Communist Denunciation, May, 1956. 1162
(Les) activities criminelles des Etats-Unis et de leurs agents au Nord Viet Nam. 1997
Activites du Departement de l'education nationale de 1954 à 1961. 1937
Activities of the Department of National Education from July 7, 1954 to July 7, 1961. 1938
Activities of the Department of National Education from 1954 to 1959. 1939
Activities of the U.S. Army Surgical Team WRAIR--Vietnam; a technical report, for the period 17 June, 1967 to 20 January 1968. 712
Adam in ochre; inside aboriginal Australia. 1544
Adelaide (Australiana facsimile editions, no. 1) 94
(The) administration of the White Australia policy 1288
(The) Afro-Asian states and their problems. 1293
After political failure, the U.S. imperialists are facing military defeat in South Vietnam. 1863
Against the Crime of Silence. 434
Against the crime of silence; proceedings of the Russell International War Crimes Tribunal, Stockholm, Copenhagen. 808
Against U.S. Aggression for National Salvation. (China Books) 742
Against U.S. aggression for national salvation. (Hanoi, Foreign

247

American dilemma in Viet-Nam; a report on the vic.
citizens in thirty-three cities. 235
American Failure & Dry Season Offensives. 31
American foreign policy & moral rhetoric; the example of Vietnam.
991
American heroes of Asian wars, by the editors of the Army times.
34
(The) American people and China. 1609
American Policy and Vietnamese Nationalism 1950-1954. 443
American power and the new mandarins. 311
American prisoners of war in Southeast Asia, 1970. Hearings,
Ninety-first Congress, second session. April 29, May 1 and 6,
1970. 1768
American prisoners of war in Southeast Asia; report, to accompany
H. Con. Res. 454. 1778
American prisoners of war in Vietnam. Hearings, Ninety-first
Congress, first session. November 13 and 14, 1969. 1769
(The) American public's view of U.S. policy toward China; a report
prepared for the Council on Foreign Relations. 1099
American uses of war gases and world public opinion. 40
American-Australian relations. 976
Americane v Saigonu. 1572
(The) Americans in the Philippines; a history of the conquest and
first years of occupation, with an introductory account of the
Spanish rule. 968
America's barbarities in Vietnam. 1246
America's Vietnam policy; the strategy of deception. 715
Amerikanerne i junglen. Udg. af Arhus-konferencens Kobenhavns-
udvalg. 41
Amerikanische Ideologie; zwei Studien uber Politik und Gesellschaft
in den USA [von] Carl Oglesby [und] Richard Shaull. 1259
Amity and economic relations. Treaty between the United States of
America and Viet-Nam signed at Saigon April 3, 1961. 1852
Amongst the Shans. 337
Analyse critique de l'intervention americaine au Vietnam [par]
Charles Chaumont. . . 289
(An) analysis of government payments in Viet Nam during 1955, in-
cluding details of expenditures by the national, regional, pro-
vincial governments. 1573
Anatomy of error; the inside story of the Asian war on the Potomac,
1954-1969. 176
Anatomy of error: the secret history of the Vietnam war. 177
And/or: antonyms for our age. 1142
André Malraux: the Indochina adventure. 938
(De) andres born. Redaktion: Per Schultz. 1502
(An) anecdotal history of old times in Singapore, from the foundation
of the settlement under the Honorable the East India Company on
February 6th, 1819, to the transfer to the Colonial Office as part
of the colonial possessions of the Crown on April 1st, 1867. 208
Angels over the altar; Christian folk art in Hawaii and the South
Seas. 552
Angkor: an introduction. 331

Angkor et Cambodge au XVIe siecle d'apres les sources portugaises
   et espagnoles.   643
Annam.   Bulletin administratif. . .   48
L'Annam en 1906.   49
Annam.   Ministere de l'economic rurals.   58
(An) annotated bibliography of climatic maps of North Vietnam.   640
Annuaire general du Vietnam.   Tong nien giam Viet-Nam.   General
   directory of Vietnam.   59
Annual catalogue of Australian publications.   no. 1-25; 1936-60.   269
Annual statistical bulletin.   1845
(An) anthology of New Zealand verse.   287
(An) anthropological bibliography of South Asia, together with a direc-
   tory of recent anthropological field work.   570
Anthropology and religion.   206
(The) anti-Vietnam agitation and the teach-in-movement: the prob-
   lem of Communist infiltration and exploitation; a staff study   1803
Anybody here from Arizona?   A look at the Vietnam war.   393
The Anzac Battalion; a record of tour of 2nd Battalion, the Royal
   Australian Regiment, 1st Battalion, the Royal New Zealand Infantry
   Regiment (the Anzac Battalion) in South Vietnam, 1967-68.   1183
Ap Bac; les grandes batailles, 1963-1964, au Sud Vietnam.   60
Apercu sur les activities du secretariat d'etat au travail.   1929
Appeal to the American conscience.   1458
(An) approach to better understanding of Vietnamese society; a primer
   for Americans.   1225
(An) approach to Indonesian history: towards an open future; an ad-
   dress before the Seminar on Indonesian History, Gadjah Mada Uni-
   versity, Jogjakarta, Dec. 14, 1957.   1634
Aranda traditions.   1626
Archives geologiques du Vietnam. no. 1- (Vietnam. Centre national
   de recherches scientifiques et techniques.)   1953
Archives geologiques du Viet-Nam.   no. 1- (Vietnam. Service
   geologique)   2130
Area handbook for North Vietnam.   37
Area handbook for South Vietnam.   38
Area handbook for Vietnam.   39
(Un) argentino en Vietnam.   816
Argonauts of the western Pacific; an account of native enterprise and
   adventure in the archipelagoes of Melanesian New Guinea.   1023
Arkansas men at war.   1732
(The) Armies of the Night: History as a Novel, the Novel as History.
   1017.
Arriere-plan revolutionnaire de la guerre du Vietnam.   359
Art and archeology of Viet Nam; Asian crossroad of cultures.   A
   traveling exhibition circulated by the National Collection of Fine
   Arts.   1570
Art in Arnhem Land.   467
Art in Indonesia; continuities and change.   758
(The) Art of Indochina.   641
(The) art of Southeast Asia; Cambodia, Vietnam, Thailand, Laos,
   Burma, Java, Bali.   1391
(The) art of taaniko weaving: a study of its cultural context, tech-
   nique, style, and development.   1073

Art of the Possible: Diplomatic Alternatives in the Middle East.
    1407
(The) art of the South Sea Islands, including Australia and New Zea-
    land. 212
Artillery Medic in Vietnam. 173
Artist in South Vietnam. 1235
Arts musulmans. Extreme-Orient: Inde, Indo-chine, Insulinde,
    Chine, Japon, Asie centrale, Tibet. 67
Arts of the South seas. 988
Asia; a regional and economic geography. 11th ed. 1602
Asia and Western dominance; a survey of the Vasco de Gama
    epoch of Asian history, 1498-1945. 1294
Asian culture. 69
Asian diary. 1470
Asian nationalism and the West; a symposium based on documents
    and reports of the eleventh conference, Institute of Pacific Rela-
    tions. 757
(The) Asian-African Conference, Bandung, Indonesia, April 1955. 852
Asia's lands and peoples; a geography of one-third the earth and two-
    thirds its people. 2d ed. 367
Asiatic mythology; a detailed description and explanation of the
    mythologies of all the great nations of Asia. 71
(Die) Asiatischen Lander der Volksdemokratie. Lehreft der Erdkunde
    fur das 8. Schuljahr. 72
(The) Asmat of New Guinea; the journal of Michael Clark Rockefel-
    ler. 1430
L'assassinat par les Viet Minh communistes du Colonel Hoang Thuy
    Nam, chief de la Mission chargee des relations avec la Commis-
    sion internationale de controle. 1877
Assumptions underlying Australian education. 243
At stake--the cause of freedom; the eleven years since the Geneva
    accords on Vietnam. 1823
At War with Asia. (Pantheon. 1970) 312
At War with Asia. (Random House, Inc. 1971) 313
Atrocities in Vietnam: Myths & Realities. 716
Au coeur du Vietnam. La Republique democratique du Vietnam et
    le Front national de liberation du Sud-Vietnam face á l'agression.
    1327
Au Nord Viet-nam. (Ecrit sous les bombes) 1417
Australia and the Pacific. 88
Austtalia, Britain and the EEC, 1961 to 1963. 583
Australia faces Southeast Asia; the emergence of a foreign policy.
    1857
Australia goes to press. 756
Australia; official handbook. (Melbourne) 86
Australian atrocities in Vietnam. 271
Australian bush ballads. 1620
Australian colonial policy; a survey of native administration and Euro-
    pean development in Papua. 959
Australian Council for Educational Research. Research series. no.
    1- (Melbourne) 87
Australian diplomacy and Japan, 1945-1951. 1441
Australian economic background, from the Report of the Committee of
    Economic Enquiry. 78

Australian education, 1788-1900; church, state, and public education
in Colonial Australia.   76
Australian English; an historical study of the vocabulary, 1788-1898.
1386
Australian government and politics: an introductory survey. 2d ed.
1106
Australian Government today. 1481
Australian libraries.   105
Australian literature, a bibliography to 1938, extended to 1950.   1101
Australian literature; a critical account to 1955.   666
Australian national bibliography.   Jan. 1961-   91
Australian painting, 1788-1960. 1557
Australian poetry. 92
Australian policies and attitudes toward China.   12
(The) Australian political party system.   90
Australian short stories. 1st- series. 93
Australian short stories: second series. 822
Australian society; a sociological introduction.   386
Australian stories of today.   1274
Australian tidal flats.   1460
Australian trade policy 1942-1966; a documentary history.   364
(The) Australian tradition; studies in a colonial culture.   1324
Australian weather. 1534
(The) Australian wheat-growing industry, 1788-1948.   444
Australians in Vietnam.   1012
Authors take sides on Vietnam; two questions on the war in Vietnam
answered by the authors of several nations.   2299
Autonomous state organizations, government enterprises and public
corporations of Viet Nam; a study of the annual reports and the
administrative accounts pertaining to calendar year 1955 for use
in estimating the national income of Vietnam, a project of the
National Bank.   1574
L'aventure militarie des imperialistes americains au Sud Viet Nam.
(NUC67-80446) 2009
L'aventure militaire des imperialistes americains au Sud Viet
Nam.   (NUC63-78980) 2010
Avgustovskaia revoluitsiia vo V'etname, (August Revolution in
Vietnam). (In Russian, translated from Vietnamese)   1724
Az arany teknosbeka foldjen; vietnami utirajz. 369

Ba Canh; a story of revolutionary development. 1944
Background information relating to Southeast Asia and Vietnam. 2d
rev. ed. 1779
Background information relating to Southeast Asia and Vietnam.
3d rev. ed. 1780
Background information relating to Southeast Asia and Vietnam.
• 5th rev. ed. 1781
Background information relating to Southeast Asia and Vietnam.
4th rev. ed. 1782
(The) background of nationalism and other essays.   358
Background to betrayal; the tragedy of Vietnam. 139
Background to Viet Nam. (1971) 1179

(A) chaplain looks at Vietnam. 1255
(Le) Chemin du bonheur et de la prosperite. 293
Chen tou ti Yueh-nan (War in Vietnam). (In Chinese) 1535
Chieh fang chung ti Yueh-nan, (Vietnam in Freedom), (In Chinese)
    769
Chien si nhan dan; tap truyen ngan ky su phuc vu le ky niem 15 nam
    ngay thanh lap quan doi nhan dan Viet-Nam 22-12-59 [cua] Nguyen-
    minh-Chau [et. al.] 305
Chin jih Yueh-nan, (Vietnam Today). (In Chinese) 1632
China and the Vietnam war--will history repeat? Report to the Com-
    mittee on Foreign Relations, United States Senate. 323
China, Vietnam and the United States: Highlights of the Hearings of
    the Senate Foreign Relations Committee. 1805
China's Relations with Burma and Vietnam. 730
(La) Chine et le Vietnam, un probleme pour la conscience chretienne
    [par] Lily Abeg, Carl-J. Keller-Senn, Ernst Kux, Alois Riklin
    . . . [etc.] Traduit par [l'abbe] Marcel Grandclaudon. 309
(The) Chinese Communists' role in the war in Vietnam. 299
(The) Chinese in Malaya. 1367
(The) Chinese in Philippine life, 1850-1898. 2270
(The) Chinese of Semarang: a changing minority community in Indo-
    nesia. 2281
Chinh-de Viet-nam: vi-tri cua Viet-nam trong the-gioi hien-dai;
    hoan-canh lich-su cua cong-dong quoc-gia; cong-san va su phan-
    chia lanh-tho; du'o'ng loi phat-trien cua dan-toc. 1735
Chinh-nghia Viet-Nam tren the-gioi. . . 1882
(Les) Choses que j'ai vues au Vietnam m'ont fait douter de l'intelli-
    gence occidentale. 943
Choses vues au Vietnam; naissance d'une nation. 1286
(Die) Christen und der Krieg in Vietnam. Ein Memorandum
    deutscher Katholiken. 135
Chronology of the Vietnam war, 1941-1966. 1981
Ch'ung chi, (Attacking), (In Chinese) 1207
Chung Yueh liang kuo jen min ti yu hao kuan hsi ho wen hua chiao liu,
    (Sino-Vietnamese Friendship & Cultural Exchange), (In Chinese)
    294
Chung Yueh yu i, (Long Life for Chinese-Vietnamese Friendship),
    (In Chinese) 826
Chuong trinh trinh dien cua Hoi Tieu Nhac Hoa tau Nu'u Uoc. 2187
Cien kapitana Daileya; korespondent sajgonski zmienia zdanie. 2271
Cinq Ans Prisonnier des Viets. 1415
Civilian casualty and refugee problems in South Vietnam; findings
    and recommendations. 1800
Civilian casualty, social welfare, and refugee problems in South
    Vietnam. Hearings, Ninetieth Congress, first session. 1801
Clearing the undergrowth: what are the facts about defoliation in
    South Vietnam? 1883
Close air support. Hearing, Eighty-ninth Congress, first session.
    1759
Close air support; report, Eighty-ninth Congress, second session.
    1760
Co dzien wojna. 1302
. . . Code annamite. Lois et reglements du royaume d'Annam;

(A) contrastive analysis of English and Vietnamese. 1197
Contre l'agression americaine; principaux documents de l'Assemblee
    nationale de la R.D.V. 3e legislature. 2e session. 2011
Contribution à l'etude des colonies vietnamiennes en Thailand. 214
Contribution à l'histoire de la nation vietnamienne. 300
Conventions inter-etats, conclues en application de l'Accord franco-
    vietnamien du 8 mars 1949 . . . 2137
Conversations with Americans. 934
(La) cooperation agricole au Nord Viet Nam; rapport du Vice-Presi-
    dent du Conseil Truong Chinh à la 10e session de l'Assemblee
    nationale, mai 1959. 1982
(The) co-operative movement in Indonesia. 705
(The) cooperative movement in Vietnam. 2100
(The) cooperative movement in Viet-nam and the establishment of
    the Commissariat General for Cooperatives and Agricultural
    Credit. 2099
Cooperative operations of corn-hog program in strategic hamlets of
    the Republic of Viet-nam, March 1 to September 30, 1963. 2101
(The) cooperative research and training center. 2102
Couleurs, hymne et armoiries de la Republique democratique du
    Vietnam. Flag, anthem and emblem of the Democratic Republic
    of Vietnam. 1968
Count your dead; a novel of Vietnam. 1447
Counterinsurgency: principles and practices in Viet-Nam. 503
(The) courageous and the proud. 1856
(The) Court Martial of Lieutenant Calley. 683
Creative writing in Australia; a selective survey. 479
(The) crescent and the rising sun; Indonesian Islam under the
    Japanese occupation, 1942-1945. 131
(The) criminal activities of the United States and its agents in North
    Viet Nam. 1992
Criminal legislation in the Democratic Republic of Vietnam. 1989
(A) critical study of American intervention in Vietnam. 290
(The) cross and the Bo-tree; Catholics and Buddhists in Vietnam. 597
Crusade in Asia; Philippine victory. 1435
Cry of Vietnam. 687
(The) cultural ecology of a chinese village; Cameron Highlands,
    Malaysa [sic] 325
(The) culture of South-east Asia, the heritage of India. 965
Curtains Over Vietnam: A Strategic Appraisal of Suppressed
    Aspects of U.S. Security Stake in Vietnam. 2238
Customs and culture of the Philippines. 2315
Customs and culture of Vietnam. 363

Dagbok fran Nordvietnam. 474
(Un) danger pour la paix mondiale; l'agression communiste au Sud
    Viet-Nam, periode de juin 1962 a juillet 1963. 1907
Dans les maquis "vietcong." 1419
Darkness of the sun; the story of Christianity in the Japanese Empire.
    102
Dateline: Viet Nam. (1966) 1001
Dateline: Vietnam. (1968) 1002

Derrotado en lo politico, el imperialismo norteamericano esta
    fracasando tambien en lo militar en Vietnam del Sur. 1864
(A) descriptive atlas of New Zealand. 1068
Deset godini agresiia na amerikanskite imperialisti v IUzhen Vietnam,
    (Ten Years of Aggression of American imperialists in South
    Vietnam). (In Bulgarian) 1987
Destroy or die: the true story of Mylai. 591
(Les) deux guerres du Vietnam; de Valluy à Westmoreland. 277
Deux mille ans de poesie vietnamienne. 1713
(Des) deux rives de l'Enfer. 1392
Development for free Asia. 2328
(The) development of British Malaya, 1896-1909. 279
Development of the Economy of the Chinese, Vietnamese, Korean, &
    Mongolian Peoples Republic in 1961. 400
(The) development of the Javanese economy: a socio-cultural ap-
    proach. 582
Diary of a Shortimer in Vietnam. 190
Diary of an infiltrator. 1745
Diary: travels in the central parts of Siam, Cambodia, and Laos
    during the years 1858-61. 1146
Dick Adair's Saigon: A Vietnam Sketchbook. 5
(A) dictionary of the economic products of the Malay peninsula. 232
Dictionnaire vietnamien, chinois, francais. 622
Dien Bien Phu. 2201
(Le) Differend khmero-vietnamien devant le Conseil de securite des
    Nations-Unies, mai, juin, juillet, 1964; a document. 406
(The) diplomacy of chaos. 910
(The) discovery of New Zealand. 122
Disengagement & Disenchantment. 1868
Diskurs uber die Vorgeschichte und den Verlauf des lang andauernden
    Befreiungskrieges in Viet Nam als Beispiel fur die Notwendig-
    keit des bewaffneten Kampfes der Unterdruckten gegen ihre
    Unterdrucker, sowie uber die Versuche der Vereinigten Staaten
    von Amerika die Grundlagen der Revolution zu vernichten. 2241
Dix mille annees pour le Vietnam! le dossier. 1693
Dlaczego wojna? 1100
Doctor at Dienbienphu. 629
Doctor Spock on Vietnam. 1601
Doctor Tom Dooley's three great books: Deliver us from evil, The
    edge of tomorrow [and] The night they burned the mountain. 417
Documentary record of the Third National Congress of the Vietnam
    Lao Dong Party. 2174
Documents on the Buddhist issue in Viet-Nam. 2030
Documents on the National Assembly of the Republic of Vietnam:
    organization & functioning of the administrative services; the civil
    service status; the law codification committee. 1970
Documents related to the implementation of the Geneva agreements
    concerning Viet-nam. 1998
Doing business in and with Australia. 36
Doing business in the new Indonesia. 236
(Le) domaine maudit; roman. 372
(The) doom pussy. (1967) 1532
Doom Pussy. (1968) 1533

Doro to honoo no Indichina (War sufferings in Indochina) (In Japanese)
    1266
(A) dove in Vietnam. 1062
(The) draft and the Vietnam War. 1474
(Le) drame indochinois; de Dien-Bien-Phu au pari de Geneve. 939
(Le) Drapeau-repere; recits de la resistance vietnamienne [par] Huu
    Mai. 424
Druzhestvennyi V'etnam, (Friendly Vietnam). (In Russian, Translated
    from English)   548
DRV in the Face of U.S. Aggression. 431
Du colonialism au communisme, l'experience du Nord-Vietnam . . .
    736
Due, tre cose sul Vietnam. 1297
(The) Dutch colonial system in the East Indies. 893
(The) Dutch East Indies, its government, problems, and politics.
    1858
Dva Roki u V'etnami; notatki inzhenera, (Two Years in Vietnam;
    observations of an Engineer). (In Ukrainian)   1114
(The) dynamics of the Western New Guinea (Irian Barat) problem.
    164
Dzikie banany; u bujnych Tajow i meznych Meo. 516

(The) eagle and the dragon. 1646
(The) eagle and the lotus; western intervention in Vietnam 1847-1968.
    251
Early American-Philippine trade: the journal of Nathaniel Bowditch
    in Manila, 1796. 172
(The) early Chinese newspapers of Singapore, 1881-1912. 298
Early Travellers in New Zealand. 1661
Early Victorian New Zealand; a study of racial tension and social
    attitudes, 1839-1852. 1107
East European attitudes to the Vietnam conflict: a study in radio
    effectiveness. 1381
Eastern windows. 1265
Easy Vietnamese. 1198
Economic Commission for Asia and the Far East. Community de-
    velopment and economic development. 1737
Economic cooperation. Agreement and notes . . . signed at Saigon
    September 7, 1951. 2141
Economic cooperation; informational media guaranty program. Agree-
    ment . . . effected by exchange of notes signed at Saigon October
    11 and November 3, 1955. 2143
Economic cooperation; informational media guaranty program. Agree-
    ment . . . effected by exchange of notes signed at Saigon October
    11 and November 3, 1955. 2150
Economic cooperation, support of Vietnamese Armed Forces. Agree-
    ment . . . amending paragraph 3 of Agreement of April 22 and
    23, 1955, effected by exchange of notes signed at Saigon June 24
    and 25, 1955. 2144
Economic cooperation, support of Vietnamese Armed Forces. Agree-
    ment . . . effected by exchange of notes signed at Saigon April
    22 and 23, 1955. 2145

Enquetes demographiques au Vietnam en 1958. 2157
Envoye special au Vietnam. 378
Era of challenge. 197
Erlebtes Vietnam. Mit einem Nachwort von Erwin Zucker-Schilling.
    828
L'Escalade de la guerre au Vietnam, vers un conflit nucleaire mon-
    dial? 1190
Escalation war and songs about peace. 1006
Escape with me. 1549
Espoir a Saigon [par le] General Vanuxem. 1867
Essays in poetry, mainly Australian. 209
Essays on economic growth, capital formation, and public policy in
    Viet-Nam. 306
Essays on the Vietnam War. 1649
Essentials of the Philippine educational system. 557
(The) establishment of cooperatives in Vietnam, June 30, 1959. 2103
(The) ethnohistory of norther Luzon. 870
Etude sur le metre populaire thu'o'ng luc ha bat. 1706
Evolution economique du Viet-Nam. 2210
(The) evolution of Australian foreign policy, 1938-1965. 2231
(The) evolution of the Netherlands Indies economy. 159
(The) evolution of Vietnamese literature: from "nom" to romanized
    characters. 478
Exchange of notes between . . . Gt. Britain and . . . Vietnam, for
    the protection of trade marks. 2149
Exchange of official publications. Agreement between the United
    States of America and Viet-Nam, effected by exchange of notes
    signed at Saigon April 4, 1961. 1853
(The) exploration of New Zealand. 1058
Expose to the end the double-faced stand of the Krushchevite revision-
    ists towards the struggle of the Vietnamese people. 2324
Eye of the Storm: A People's Politics for the Seventies. 621
Eyewitness in Indo-China. 1604
Eyewitness in Vietnam; translated from the German by Michael
    Glenny. 1349

Face of North Vietnam. 1414
(The) face of South Vietnam. 185
(The) face of war: Vietnam, the full photographic report! 708
Facts about Vietnam. 922
Facts and dates on the problem of the reunification of Viet-Nam. 481
Facts and figures about the economic and social conditions of the
    Philippines. 1946-47-- 1323
(The) fall of Sukarno. 2196
(The) federal story; the inner history of the federal cause, 1880-1900.
    391
Fenyek a dzsungelben. 1041
Fields of Bamboo: Dongtre, Trung Luong & Hoa Hoi, Three Battles
    Just Beyond the South China Sea. 1037
XVth anniversary of the Democratic Republic of Viet Nam, 1945-
    1960. (DS557.A7F53) 520
XVth anniversary of the Democratic Republic of Viet Nam, 1945-1960.

(NUC63-78975) 1971
(Le) XVe [i. e. quinzieme] anniversaire de la Republique Democratique
    du Viet Nam, 1945-1960. 1972
Fighting 40, Chu Lai, RVN, 1967-69 [cruise book]   1838
Fighting Vietnam. 1525
Filipinos; pre-war Philippines essays. 1425
(La) Fin d'Une Guerre, Indochine, 1954. 923
Final report, covering activities of the Michigan State University,
    Vietnam Advisory Group for the period May 20, 1955-June 30,
    1962. 1089
Financing provincial and local government in the Republic of Vietnam.
    333
Firewinds; poems [on the Vietnam War]   351
(The) First Air Cavalry Division, Vietnam. 789
First Marine Division, Vietnam. 790
First Vietnam Crisis: Chinese Communist Strategy & United States
    Involvement, 1953-1954. (1968) 663
(The) first Vietnam crisis; Chinese Communist strategy and United
    States involvement, 1953-1954. (1967) 664
Five journeys from Jakarta; inside Sukarno's Indonesia. 2277
Five Lessons of a Great Victory: Winter 1966-Spring 1967. 1728
Five women I love; Bob Hope's Vietnam story. 765
Five years of the implementation of the Geneva agreements in Viet
    Nam. 2089
Five years to freedom. 1446
Flame in the Icebox. 1143
Flight to freedom; a story of courage, sacrifice, and a faith in the
    free world. 2031
FNLs politiska program.   Antaget vid FNLs extra kongress i
    augusti 1967. 1592
Folk art of Oceania. 957
Folk tales from Vietnam. 1128
Fonetika V'etnamskogo iazyka, (The phonetics of Vietnamese Lan-
    guage).   (In Russian) 1118
For a political solution of the Vietnam issue. 535
(Les) forces politiques au Sud Viet-Nam depuis les accords de
    Geneve 1954. 1192
Foreign affairs. 1850
Foreward! Final victory will be ours! 2013
(The) formation of Federal Indonesia, 1945-1949. 1489
(The) formation of Malaysia; new factor in world politics; an analytical
    history and assessment of the prospects of the newest state in
    Southeast Asia, based on a series of reports written for the Amer-
    ican Universities Field Staff. 690
Forty days with the enemy. 433
Forty-two faces. 722
(The) foundations of local self-government in India, Pakistan, and
    Burma. 1685
(The) fourth Cosmos Club award: McGeorge Bundy. 215
France. Commissariat de la Republique francaise dans le Nord
    Viet-Nam. (Bulletin officiel. 1.-4. annee; 15 jan. 1948-15 dec.
    1951). 550
(La) France et le Viet-Nam, le Paix qui s'impose [par] Ferdinand
    Lop. 510

Headhunters of Borneo.   818
Hearing on problems of prisoners of war and their families.   Ninety-
    first Congress, second session.   March 6, 1970.   1756
(The) heart of the problem: Secretary Rusk [and] General Taylor
    review Viet-Nam policy in Senate hearings.   1455
Hell in a very small place: the siege of Dien Bien Phu.   486
Here is your enemy; complete report from North Vietnam.   261
(A) Heroic people: memoirs from the revolution.   717
Heros et heroines des forces armees de liberation du Sud Vietnam.
    718
Hien-phap.   1961
Hiep-uoc than-huu va lien-lac king-te giua Viet-Nam Cong-Hoa va Hiep
    Chung Quoc Hoa-Ky.   [Treaty of amity and economic relations
    between the United States of America and the Republic of Viet-
    Nam]   2152
High living: a study of family life in flats.   1618
Hinduism and Buddhism; an historical sketch.   466
(The) Hispanization of the Philippines: Spanish aims and Filippino
    responses, 1565-1700.   1322
Histoire du Vietnam.   (1960)   1039
Histoire du Vietnam. . . 3e edition mise a jour.   (1967)   1040
Histoire d'une paix manquee, Indochine, 1945-1947. . .   1468
Histoire et philosophie du caodaisme; bouddhisme remove spiritisme
    vietnamien, religion nouvelle en Eurasie.   611
Historical interaction of China and Vietnam: institutional and cultural
    themes.   732
Historical studies: selected articles, second series.   733
Historie du Viet-Nam de 1940 A 1952.   402
History and philosophy of Caodaism; reformed Buddhism, Viet-
    namese spiritism, new religion in Eurasia.   612
(A) history of Asia.   646
(A) history of Australia.   322
(A) history of Australian literature, pure and applied; a critical re-
    view. . .   632
(A) history of Burma.   772
History of Burma from the earliest times to 10 March 1824, the be-
    ginning of the English conquest.   701
History of Burma, including Burma proper, Pegu, Tanngu, Tenas-
    serim, and Arakan, from the earliest time to the first war with
    British India.   1321
History of Laos.   2194
(A) history of Malaya.   877
(A) history of modern Burma.   247
(A) history of modern Malaya.   1719
(A) history of New Zealand.   1545
(A) history of New Zealand life.   1141
(A) history of the Pacific area in modern times.   695
(The) history of Viet-Nam from the French penetration to 1939.   100
Ho Chi Minh: a political biography.   924
Ho Chi Minh dan negaranja.   800
Ho Chi Minh, derniere chance, la conference franco-vietnamienne de
    Fontainebleau, juillet 1946. . .   98
Ho Chi Minh, the "Father" of his people.   2080

Hone Heke's Rebellion, 1844-1846; an episode in the establishment of
British rule in New Zealand. 1461
House of love: life in a Vietnamese hospital. (London, Newnes,
1967) 1666
House of love; life in a Vietnamese hospital. (Landsowne, 1966)
1667
How my brother Leon brought home a wife, and other stories. 62
How the United States got involved in Vietnam; a report to the Center
for the Study of Democratic Institutions. 1485
How to get out of Vietnam; a workable solution to the worst problem
of our time. 575
How to stay alive in Vietnam; combat survival in the war of many
fronts. 1421
Hung-ho sh'en ko, (Singing Morning Songs Along the Red River), (In
Chinese) 509

I lived in Burma. 544
I protest! 437
Identification with North or South Vietnam in eastern Europe. 1382
Ik, een Vietnamees meisje. 1571
Illusion of power; American policy toward Viet-Nam, 1954-1966.
1052
Im Lande der wilden Bananen; Begegnungen mit den Tai und Meo. 57
Imagens e paisagens do Vietnam. 162
Images du Viet-Nam. 792
Impact of the war in Southeast Asia on the U.S. economy. Hearings,
Ninety-first Congress, second session . . . 1786
Imperialist schemes in Vietnam against peace and reunification.
1999
Impressions of the Malay Peninsula in ancient times. 2261
In Face of American Aggression: 1965-1967. 793
In opposition; images of American dissent in the sixties. (Da Capo
Press, 1968) 512
In Opposition: Images of American Dissent in the Sixties. (Plenum Pub-
lishing Corporation, 1971) 513
In search of wealth; a study of the emergence of commercial opera-
tions in the Melanesian society of southeastern Papua. 128
In South Viet Nam U.S. Biggest Operation Foiled (February-April
1967) 1988
In South Vietnam. U.S. biggest operation foiled (February-March
[i.e. April] 1967) 794
In the name of America; the conduct of the war in Vietnam by the
armed forces of the United States as shown by published reports,
compared with the laws of war binding on the United States govern-
ment and on its citizens. 795
In the Teeth of War: Photographic Documentary of the March 26th,
1966 Demonstration Against the War in Vietnam. 521
In touch. 1610
In violation of the Tet truce. 2033
Incident at Muc Wa. 537
Indecency in church: hypocrisy, dishonesty, injustice at Brighton.
1380

Jours d'enfance, et autre recits. Traduit du vietnamien par Le Van
   Chat. 1212
(Le) Jugement de Stockholm. [Extraits des debats de la 1re session,
   1966-1967.] Directeur de redaction: Vladimir Dedijer. . . Re-
   dactrice: Arlette Elkaim. Documentation: Catherine Russell.
   1721
(Le) Jugement final. Directeur de publication: Jean Paul Sartre.
   Redactrice: Arlette El Kaim . . .   809
Jungle Mission. 1416
(La) Justice dans l'ancien Annam; code de procedure, traduction et
   commentaire, par Raymond Deloustal. 54

(Der) kampfbereite Drache. Vietnam nach Dien Bien Phu. (Aus
   dem Engl. v. Walter Hacker.) 237
The Kennedys & Vietnam. (Interim History Ser: The Bridge Between
   Today's News & Tomorrow's History)   880
(The) key to peace in Vietnam. 587
Kiki: ten thousand years in a lifetime, a New Guinea autobiography.
   886
(The) killing at Ngo Tho; a novel by Gene D. Moore. 1135
Kim--a gift from Vietnam. 310
Kim Van Kieu. Traduit du vietnamien par Xuan-Phuc et Xuan-Viet.
   1210
King Dick, a biography of Richard John Seddon. 230
Know your enemy: the Viet Cong. 1819
Kogda opusteli dzhungli; v'etnamskie ocherki, (When we left the
   jungles; Vietnamese sketches). (In Russian) 1280
Konstitutsiia Demokraticheskoi Respubliki V'etnam, (Constitution of
   the Democratic Republic of Vietnam). (In Russian) 1985
Korea and Vietnam. 907
(Der) Krieg in Vietnam; Bericht und Bibliographie bis 30. 9. 1968,
   von A. Legler und K. Hubinek. 961
Kriegserklarung. 180
Krigen i Vietnam i økonomisk og folkeretslig belysning. 381
Kriget i Vietnam. 863
Kriget i Vietnam. Av Per-Olof Karlsson. 862
Krigsforbryterser i Vietnam. 1651
Kunst der Sudsee. 992
(De) Kwestie Vietnam. Feiten en achtergronden. Redactie S. J.
   Bosgra, R. R. Eijbersen. Eindredactie A. P. E. Korver,
   M. B. H. Visser, H. Amptmeyer e. a. Voorwoord van J.
   Verkuyl. 917

Land and people in the Philippines; geographic problems in rural
   economy. 1599
(The) Land and people of Burma. (Lippincott) 933
(The) land and people of Burma. (London, A. & C. Black; New York,
   Macmillan) 1044
(The) land and people of the Philippines. 1869
(The) land and the people of Malaysia. 326
Land of Seagull and Fox. 1639

Medics in action.   719
Mei-kuo tut Yueh-nan nan fang ti kan she, (U.S.A. Policies for in-
    terferring & interventing in South Vietnam), (In Chinese)   1536
Memorandum.   1973
Memorandum of the Government of the Democratic Republic of Viet
    Nam on the expansion of the aggressive war in Laos by the U.S.
    imperialists in the S.A.A.T.O. military bloc.   1993
Memorandum of the Ministry for foreign affairs of the Democratic
    Republic of Viet Nam concerning the military aggression of the
    U.S. government in South Viet Nam.   1994
Memorandum of the Ministry of foreign affirss of the Democratic
    Republic of Viet Nam concerning U.S. "special warfare" in South
    Viet Nam nine years after the signing of the Geneva agreements on
    Viet Nam.   2000
Memphis, Nam, Sweden: the autobiography of a Black American
    exile.   2265
Men, stress and Vietnam.   170
(Les) menees imperialistes au Viet-nam contre la paix et la reuni-
    fication.   2001
Message of President Ngo dinh Diem to the National Assembly (Open-
    ing session, 6 October 1958)   2111
Message of the President of the Republic to the National Assemble
    [October 1st, 1962] Message du President de la Republique a
    l'Assemblee Nationale [1er oct. 1962.]   2120
Message of the President of the Republic to the National Assembly,
    5 Oct. 1959.   2112
Message of the President of the Republic to the National Assembly,
    opening session, October 2, 1961.   2121
Michigan. State University, East Lansing. Vietnam Advisory Group,
    Saigon. Report.   1090
Miedzy Waszyngtonem, Rzymem i Sajgonem. [Wyd. 1. Warszawa]
    1030
(The) mighty Mekong.   990
Military Art of People's War. Selected Writings.   600
Military developments in Viet Nam.   488
(The) military half; an account of destruction in Quang Ngai and
    Quang Tin. (Knopf) 1486
(The) military half; an account of destruction in Quang Ngai and
    Quang Tin. (Vintage Books) 1496
Military supply systems, 1969. Hearings, Ninety-first Congress,
    first session.   November 20, 25, and December 8, 1969. 1763
Military surgical practices of the United States army in Viet Nam.
    711
(Un) million de dollars le Viet.   941
Minami Betonamu baisho to ampo kaitei. (Reparations and safety
    treaty for South Vietnam)   1237
Minami Betonamu no keizal kajhatsu, (Economic Development in
    South Vietnam), (In Japanese)   1691
Mission de la France en Asie.   553
Mission in torment; an intimate account of the U.S. role in Vietnam.
    1074
Mission to Hanoi.   61
Mission to Hanoi; a chronicle of double-dealing in high places, a

(The) new exiles: American war resisters in Canada. 2278
(The) new face of war. (1965) 201
(The) new face of war. (1968) 202
New Guinea on the threshold; aspects of social, political, and eco-
    nomic development. 532
New impulses in Australian poetry. 672
(A) new kind of war. 584
New land, new language, an anthology of Australian verse. 2306
(The) new legions. (Gollanez) 438
(The) new legions. (Random House) 439
(The) new soldier. 881
(The) new states of Asia, a political analysis. 184
New Zealand. (Berkeley, University of California) 130
New Zealand. (New York, Hutchinson's University Library) 1102
New Zealand, a regional view. 370
New Zealand becomes a Pacific power. 619
New Zealand, Department of External Affairs. Publication, no. 1- 174
New Zealand. Department of External Affairs. Treaty series.
    1945- 1175
New Zealand, gift of the sea. 175
New Zealand law journal. . . v. 1- March 3, 1925- 1177
New Zealand literature, a survey. 1059
New Zealand notables. 231
(The) New Zealand novel, 1860-1960. 1617
(The New Zealand official year-book. [1st]- 1892- 1178
New Zealand, Pacific pioneer. 1579
New Zealand, 1769-1840; early years of western contact. 2304
New Zealand short stories. 388
(The) New Zealand wars. A history of the Maori campaigns and the
    pioneering period. 362
News from Viet-Nam. 1184
News policies in Vietnam. Hearings, Eighty-ninth Congress, second
    session. August 17 and 31, 1966. 1788
(The) NFL of South Vietnam; the only genuine and legal representa-
    tive of the South Vietnam people. 1187
Ngo Dinh Diem of Viet-Nam. 1893
Nhan, a boy of Viet-Nam. 541
Nhung dieu nen biet ve the le nhap cang trong chuong trinh ngoai te
    so huu. 1928
Nichi-Etsu Keizui Koryu Kenkyukai, (Research Report of Japanese-
    Vietnamese Economic Exchange), (In Japanese) 1234
(Die) nicht gefragt werden. Menschen in Vietnam. (Aus dem
    Amerikanischen ubers.: Gunter Eichel) 1529
Niente e cosi sia. 500
Night flight to Hanoi; war diary with 11 poems. 140
(The) 1954 Geneva Conference; Indo-China and Korea. 585
Nineteenth-century Borneo; a study in diplomatic rivalry 's-Graven-
    hage, Nijhoff, 1955. 813
Nineteenth-century Malaya; the origins of British political control.
    361
NMCB 74, Danang, 1967-68 [cruise book.] 1839
No Exit from Vietnam. (1970) 1673
No Exit from Vietnam. (1969) 1675

Peddlers and princes; social change and economic modernization in
 two Indonesian towns.   580
(The) Penguin book of New Zealand verse.   373
Pentagon Papers (The) as published by the New York Times.   1312
(The) People of French Indochina.   823
(The) people of South Vietnam: how they feel about the war; a CBS
 News public opinion survey.   1271
(The) peoples of Asia.   245
(The) peoples of Malaysia.   334
Peoples of the Philippines.   912
People's Viet-Nam pictorial.   1313
People's War, People's Army.   (Praeger)   601
People's War; People's Army.   (Foreign Languages Publishing House)
 2204
People's War, People's Army; the Viet Cong insurrection manual for
 underdeveloped countries.   2205
Perang Vietnam & netralisasi Asia Tenggara.   791
Permanent Organization for Afro-Asian Peoples' Solidarity. Commit-
 tee of Aid and Assistance to the People of South Vietnam. Bulletin.
 1315
Personnel recruitment in Vietnam.   2025
Pham chat gao va pho san.   Normes du riz et derives. Rice and by-
 products standards.   1924
Phan Tran; roman en vers.   Texte, traduction et notes par Maurice
 Durand.   1320
(Le) phenomene national vietnamien, de l'independence unitaire à l'in-
 dependance fractionnee.   Pref. de Michel-Henry Fabre.   817
(The) Philippine answer to communism.   1482
Philippine collaboration in World War II.   1612
Philippine freedom, 1946-1958.   1566
Philippine independence; motives, problems, and prospects.   891
(The) Philippine Island world: a physical, cultural, and regional
 geography.   2251
(The) Philippine Islands.   536
(The) Philippine plaza complex: a focal point in culture change.   698
(The) Philippine presidential election of 1953.   355
(The) Philippine revolution.   2318
Philippine Studies Program. Selected bibliography of the Philippines,
 topically arranged and annotated.   Fred Eggan, director. Pre-
 liminary ed.   304
Philippine writing; an anthology.   7
(The) Philippines, a study in national development.   710
(The) Philippines; a treasure and a problem.   1436
(The) Philippines and the United States.   648
(The) Philippines and the United States: problems of partnership.
 1659
(Les) Philippines et le Pacifique, des Iberiques (XVIe, XVIIe,
 XVIIIe siecles)   291
(The) Philippines: public policy and national economic development.
 613
(The) Philippines to the end of the Commission government; a study
 in tropical democracy.   468
Phuc vu bao chi Viet Nam.   Thanh tich hoat dong trong nam 1965 cua

conscription. 13
(The) politics of escalation; a study of United States responses to pres-
sures for a political settlement of the Vietnam War: November
1963-January 1966. (E183.8.V5P6) 1347
(The) politics of escalation; a study of United States responses to
pressures for a political settlement of the Vietnam War: November
1963-January 1966. (DS557.A63S29) 1504
(The) politics of escalation in Vietnam. (Beacon Press) 1505
(The) politics of escalation in Vietnam. (Fawcett Publications) 1506
(The) politics of foreign aid; American experience in Southeast Asia.
1133
Politics of the Viet Cong. 1331
Politics, personality, and nation building: Burma's search for identity.
[A study from the Center for International Studies, Massachusetts
Institute of Technology] 1372
(La) politique agressive des Viet Minh communistes et la guerre sub-
versive communiste au Sud Vietnam: periode de mai 1961 á juin
1962. 1899
(La) politique d'intervention et d'agression des Etats-Unis au Sud
Viet Nam. 2002
Polynesian mythology, and ancient traditional history of the Maori as
told by their priests and chiefs. 638
Population growth in Malaya; an analysis of recent trends. 1569
Por voce, por mim [por] Ferreira Gullar. [Rio de Janeiro] 515
Postmark: Mekong Delta. 834
(The) postwar development of the Republic of Vietnam; policies and
programs. (1970) 838
(The) postwar development of the Republic of Vietnam: policies and
programs. (1969) 839
Postwar development of Viet Nam; a summary report. 840
Postwar settlement in Western Australia. 519
Pour une meillure comprehension mutuelle. 2113
Pour une solution politique du probleme vietnamien. [Le Caire,
Secretariat permanent de l'Organisation de la solidarite des
peuples afro-asiatiques, 1969] 1353
Pourquoi le Vietcong gague [par] Wilfred Burchett. Traduit de l'anglais
par J.-P. [Jean-Pierre] Rospars. 222
P.O.W. Two Years with the Viet Cong. 1559
Power in the Liberal Party: a study in Australian politics. 2256
Preliminary checklist of Indonesian imprints during the Japanese
period (March 1942-August 1945) with annotations. 451
Preliminary report on the achievements of the war cabinet from June
19, 1965 to September 29, 1965. 1900
(The) present situation of government administration in Vietnam,
(Report of Michigan State University Team), (In Vietnamese)
1358
Presiden Ho-chi-Minh; uraian mendjelas alasan-alasan menganugerah-
kan gelar doctor honoris causa dalam ilmu hukum oleh Universitas
Padjadjaran pada tanggal 2 Maret 1959 dikota Bandung kepada
P.J.M. Ho Chi Minh, Presiden Republik Demokratis Vietnam.
Diutjapkan oleh H. Muhammad Yamin. 2312
President Ho chi Minh answers President L. B. Johnson. 749
President Ngo Dinh Diem. 1901

Australia. 525
Provinces of Viet Nam; alphabetical listing with names of subordinate
    districts and cantons and numbers of villages in each. USOM/
    Public Administration Division, Unofficial as of Oct. 1, 1963.
    1846
(The) provincial administrator in Vietnam. 2028
Provincial government in Viet Nam; a study of Vinh Long province.
    526
Provisional government of Viet Nam since 1945. 1597
Public administration in Hong Kong. 335
Public administration in Malaya. 845
Public investment in Australia: a study of Australian public au-
    thority investment and development. 1042
Pugwash Conference on Science and World Affairs. 14th, Venice,
    1965. Proceedings; international co-operation for science and
    disarmament. 1366
Pult'anun Wo'lam (War is going on in Vietnam; diary of a Vietnam
    war correspondent), (In Korean) 1582
(The) pursuit of peace; an address. 1242

Quickie lessons in Vietnamese, using the absorbomatic method. 501
(The) quicksand war; prelude to Vietnam. 157
(The) quiet American. 635
Quoc ngu. The modern writing system in Vietnam. 1199
Quotations Vietnam: Nineteen Fifty to Nineteen Seventy. 461
Quotations Vietnam: 1945-1970. 462
(The) Quynh Luu uprisings. 70

Rabbi Feinberg's Hanoi diary. 506
Race conflict in New Zealand, 1844-1865. 1103
Raffles of Singapore. 360
Rape of Vietnam. 1555
Rapport bi-annuel sur l'etude du sol au Viet-Nam, par Frank
    Moormann. 1139
Rapport om Forenta staternas forstarkta angrepp mot Nordvietnam
    efter den 31 mars 1968. [Av] Peter Weiss [och] Gunilla Palm-
    stierns. Den svenska red. i samarbete med Erik Eriksson. 2246
Rapporto dal Vietnam. 1480
Razob'em okovy; dokumenty Avgustovskoi revoliutsii 1945 goda vo
    V'etname, (We will break the chains; the documents of the October
    revolution in 1945 in Vietnam). (In Russian) 1396
Razvitie ekonomiki stran narodnoi demokratii Azii; obzor, (Economic
    Development of Asia's Countries of People's Democracy). (In
    Russian) 1397
Read Vietnamese: A Graded Course in Written Vietnamese. 1200
Readings in Malayan economics. 1542
Realites vietnamiennes (les realites permanentes) 2. ed., entiere-
    ment revue et corrigee. 1933
(The) Realities of Vietnam; a Ripon Society appraisal. 1398
Realization of the production plan for the first six months of 1958
    (North Vietnam) 383

Recensement des etablissements au Viet-Nam, 1960.   2158
Recensement pilote de la province de Phu'o'c-tuy, effectue le 6
     novembre 1959.   2159
Recent articles on Vietnam: an annotated bibliography.   (Z3226. M5)
     1096
Recent articles on Vietnam: an annotated bibliography.   (Z3226. P3)
     1300
Recent exchanges concerning attempts to promote a negotiated settle-
     ment of the conflict in Viet-Nam.   651
Recits de la resistance vietnamienne (1925-1945), par Vo Nguyen Giap,
     Bui Lam, Le Van Luong, Hoang Quoc Viet. . . [etc.] Textes re-
     unis par L. Puiseux.   1400
Recommendations concerning the Department of Interior, the regions
     and provinces.   1120
Reconstruction du chemin de fer Trans-Vietnam.   Railway construc-
     tion.   2126
Record of governmental achievements, July 1955-July 1956.   1903
Recueil de la legislation en vigueur en Annam et au Tonkin, depuis
     l'origine du protectorat jusqu'au i mai, 1895.   2. ed., publiee
     d'apres les textes officiels et classee dans l'ordre alphabetique et
     chronologique par D. Ganter. . . 55
Recueil des principales ordonnances royales edictees depuis la promul-
     gation du Code annamite et en vigueur au Tonkin.   Traduction de
     R. Deloustal.   Revue, annotee et completee d'une table alpha-
     betique et analytique de ce recueil et du Code annamite (traduc-
     tion Philastre) par Gabriel Michel.   56
Reflections on Australian foreign policy.   463
Reflections on United States policy.   1444
Refugee problems in South Vietnam and Laos.   Hearings, Eighty-
     ninth Congress, first session.   1802
Refugee problems in Vietnam, India, and Hong Kong, British Crown
     Colony; [report] H. Res. 593, Eighty-ninth Congress.   1766
Regime de la propriete fonciere dans les concessions francaises en
     Annam et au Tonkin; (decreta des 21 juillet 1925 et 6 septembre
     1927)   57
Reisfelder, Schlachtfelder; Augenzeugenbericht uber Vietnam in
     Krieg [von] Kurt and Jeanne Stern.   1615
Relevement economique et developpement culturel dans la Republique
     Democratique du Vietnam.   1977
Relief supplies and equipment; duty-free entry and exemption from
     internal taxation.   Agreement . . . effected by exchange of notes
     dated at Saigon August 20 and 26, 1954.   2149
Religion and politics in Burma.   1558
Religion and politics in rural central Java.   [New Haven?] Yale
     University, Southeast Asia Studies.   824
Religion and social organization in central Polynesia.   2279
(The) religion of Java.   581
Religion, politics, and economic behavior in Java: the Kudus
     cigarette industry.   273
Religious and cosmic beliefs of central Polynesia.   2280
(Le) remaniement du Conseil militaire revolutionnaire: motifs et
     objectifs.   2076

Resources control by the national police of Vietnam, 1 October
1964-31 March 1965.   1848
(The) responsibilities of world power.   1061
Responsible government in South Australia.   Adelaide?   339
Resumes climatologiques; modeles A, B, C, D, K.   Climatological
summaries; models A, B, C, D, K.   Station: Saigon-Tansonnhut,
48900.   2081
(Je) reviens du Viet-Nam libre (notes de voyage) Pref. de Marcel
Cachin.   522
Review of recommendations concerning proposed field organization
of the Commissariat for Refugees of September 20, 1955.   1121
Review of recommendations of the reorganization of the Department
of Land Registration and Agrarian Reform.   1093
Review of recommendations on the reorganization of the Department
of Agriculture.   1098
Review of the Vietnam conflict and its impact on U.S. military
commitments abroad; report, Ninetieth Congress, second session,
under authority of H. Res. 124.   1767
(La) Revolution paysanne du Sud Viet Nam.   949
Rhodes of Viet Nam; the travels and missions of Father Alexander
de Rhodes in China and other kingdoms of the Orient.   1413
Rites of modernization: symbolic and social aspects of Indonesian
proletarian drama.   1307
(The) Riverina, 1861-1891: an Australian regional study.   244
Rizal.   Philippine nationalist and martyr.   329
Road from War: Vietnam 1965-1970.   1522
Road from War: Vietnam 1965-1971.   1523
(The) road to Angkor.   1373
(The) road to victory in Vietnam.   860
Rok tygrysa; o Wietnamie . . . i nie tylko o Wietnamie, (Year of
the Tiger; about Vietnam . . . and not only about Vietnam).   (In
Polish)   2272
(The) role of Indian minorities in Burma and Malaya.   1015
(The) role of the sanctuary in insurgency; Communist China's sup-
port to the Vietminh, 1946-1954.   2320
Roots of involvement: the U.S. in Asia, 1784-1971.   859
Rot Leuchtet der Song Cai.   480
Rural pacification in Vietnam.   1236
Rural reconstruction and development: a manual for field workers.
1454
Rural resettlement in Vietnam; an agroville in development.   2321
Russelltribunalen.   Fran sessionera i Stockholm och Roskilde.
Urval och redigering: Peter Limqueco och Peter Weiss.   Over-
sattning av Teddy Arnberg m. fl.   810

Saigon à l'heure des coups d'etat [par] Hai Thu [et] Binh Thanh.
668
Saigon Diary.   155
Saigon, U.S.A.   704
Salmagundi Vietnam.   1355
(The) Salmon King of Oregon; R. D. Hume and the Pacific fisher-
ies.   410

discoverers. 942
Singapore and Malaysia. 1277
Singapore. Annual report. 1946- 1547
Singapore: the battle that changed the world. 946
Singapore year book. 1548
(A) sinister twilight; the fall of Singapore, 1942. 108
Situation de la personne au Viet-Nam. . . 1319
Situation in Vietnam. Hearings before the Subcommittee on State
    Department Organization and Public Affairs of the Committee on
    Foreign Relations, United States Senate, Eighty-Sixth Congress,
    first session. . . 1790
(A) situational analysis of public school enrollment in the enroll-
    ment in the Philippines. 1473
(The) six legal dimensions of the Vietnam war. 482
Six voices: contemporary Australian poets. 2216
Six years of the implementation of the Geneva Agreements in Viet
    Nam. (1960) 2091
Six years of the implementation of the Geneva Agreements in Viet
    Nam. (1961) 2092
Sketches from Vietnam. (Cape) 2257
Sketches from Vietnam. (International Publications Service) 2258
Sketches from Vietnam. (Verry, Lawrence, Inc.) 2259
Skhvatka v dzhungliakh, (Pursuit in Jungles) 117
Small Unit Action in Vietnam: Summer 1966. (Arno Press) 2253
Small unit action in Vietnam, summer, 1966. (Francis J. West,
    Jr. , Washington, Historical Branch, G-3 Division, Head-
    quarters U. S. Marine Corps) 2254
Smaller Dragon. 239
(The) smaller dragon; a political history of Vietnam. 238
Smouldering fire; international affairs 1945-65, and the crisis of
    Indo-China, summarised by Erle Rose. 1440
So ket thanh tich hoat dong cua Noi cac Chien tranh, tu 19-6-1965.
    1905
(The) so-called war of liberation in South Viet-Nam. 1934
(The) social sciences and the problem of rural improvement in
    Viet Nam. 1215
Socialism and private enterprise in equatorial Asia, the case of
    Malaysia and Indonesia. 554
Socialism in southern Asia. 1439
Socialist industrialization in North Vietnam. 1710
Society, schools and progress in Australia. 1301
Sociology in the Philippine setting. 782
Solntse sotsializma mad Krasnoi rekoi, (The sun of socialism
    over the Red River). (In Russian) 1539
Some aspects of guerilla warfare in Vietnam. 740
Some documents of the National Assembly of the Democratic
    Republic of Vietnam; 3rd Legislature, 1st session, June-July
    1964. 2012
(A) source book on Vietnam; background to our war. 343
Sources in Modern East Asian History and Politics. 1070
South Asia, a selected bibliography on India, Pakistan, Ceylon.
    2282
South Asian affairs; no. 2. 1585

South of the 17th parallel. 1376
South Vietnam. 1575
South Vietnam: A Political History 1954-1970. (1970)   871
South Vietnam: A Political History 1954-1970. (1971)   872
South Vietnam: Communist-U. S. Confrontation in Southeast Asia.
   1961-1965. 1575
South Vietnam: Communist-U. S. Confrontation in Southeast Asia,
   Vol. 2. 1966-1967. 1576
South Vietnam from NFL to PRG. 1587
South Vietnam: Initial Failure of the U. S. Limited War. (China
   Books) 1589
South Vietnam. Initial failure of the U. S. "limited war." (Foreign
   Languages Publishing House) 1590
South Vietnam: nation under stress. 1509
South Vietnam National Front for Liberation. 1591
South Vietnam '64. 1588
South Vietnam Nineteen Sixty-Eight: The DRV at War. 1595
South Vietnam on the road to victory. 1593
(The) South Vietnam people will win. 2206
South Vietnam: Realities & Prospects. 1596
South Viet-Nam: reality and myth. 216
South Vietnam: U. S. -Communist confrontation in Southeast Asia,
   1961-65. 1575
South Vietnam; U.S. defeat inevitable. 1865
South Vietnam, victim of misunderstanding. 192
Southeast Asia. (Atheneum) 447
Southeast Asia. (Time, 62-20816) 867
Southeast Asia. (Time-Life Books, 68-851) 868
Southeast Asia. (Lane) 1560
Southeast Asia, a selected bibliography. 469
Southeast Asia; an annotated bibliography of selected reference
   sources. 1834
Southeast Asia between two worlds. 1080
Southeast Asia, crossroad of religions. 932
Southeast Asia resolution. Joint hearing before the Committee on
   Foreign Relations and the Committee on Armed Service, United
   States Senate, Eighty-eighth Congress, second session, on a
   joint resolution to promote the maintenance of international
   peace and security in Southeast Asia. August 6, 1964. 1791
Southeast Asia: selected annotated bibliography of Japanese publi-
   cations. 812
Southeast Asian history; a bibliographic guide. 709
(The) Southeast Asian world; an introductory essay. 205
Southern Vietnam and the South China Sea; official standard names
   approved by the United States Board on Geographic Names. 1844
Special Report to the Co-Chairman of the Geneva Conference on
   Indo-China, Saigon, 13 Feb. 1965. 805
Special report to the co-chairmen of the Geneva Conference on
   Indo-China, Saigon, 27, February, 1965. 806
(The) special war. 1305
Speciale opdracht in Vietnam. Naar het Frans bewerkt door M.
   Stevens. Nukerke, Uitg. 380
Speech . . . [delivered] on the occasion of the 5th founding

(The) Three-year plan to develop and transform economy and to
    develop culture (1958-1960) 1978
Through the valley of the Kwai. 620
(The) thuc bua cu Tong thong, Pho tong thong va Nghi si thuong
    nghi vien (ngay 3-9-1967) 2073
Thud Ridge. 195
(Der) Tiger kommt nicht mehr; vietnamesische Reisen. 895
Tigers in the Rice: A Short History on Vietnam. 1531
Til Vietnam. [Didte og grafik]. Redaktion: Ebbe Reich og Vagn
    Sondergaard. København, Det Internationale Krigsforbrydelses
    Tribunals Københavnskontor og Vietnamindsamlingen, Eksp.:
    Korsgade 49, 1967. 1404
(The) Timor problem; a geographical interpretation of an under-
    developed island. 1273
Tinh-hinh tien-trien kinh-te Viet-Nam trong nam 1952.   Evolution
    economique du Vietnam en 1952. 2162
To church people re Vietnam. 1163
To what end; report from Vietnam 850
To-chuc'c'c tu'-phap Viet-nam Cong-hoa. 1950
(Der) Tod und der Regen. Roman. [2. Aufl. (Berlin)(1968)] 1681
(Der) Tod und der Regen. Roman. (Berlin) (1967) 1682
Toward a policy for economic growth in Vietnam. 307
Toward better mutual understanding; speeches delivered by Presi-
    dent Ngo dinh Diem during his state visits to Thailand,
    Australia and Korea. (1957) 2118
Toward better mutual understanding; speeches delivered by Presi-
    dent Ngo Dinh Diem during his state visits to Thailand,
    Australia, Korea. (1958) 2119
Toward Peace in Indochina. 458
Toward the economic development of the Republic of Vietnam;
    report. 455
Towards a Malayan nation. 1543
(Le) Tractoriste, recueil de nouvelles. 1699
Trade, finance, labor, and standard of living in North Vietnam.
    1830
Trade-marks. Declaration . . . effected by exchange of notes
    signed at Washington November 3, 1953, and October 25, 1954.
    2148
Tradition in exile; a comparative study of social influences on the
    development of Australian and Canadian poetry in the nineteenth
    century. 1043
Traditional Vietnam: Some Historical Struggles. 1700
(La) Tragedie vietnamienne vue par des Quakers americains
    (American Friends Service Committee). Propositions nouvelles
    pour la paix. 562
(The) tragedy of Vietnam; where do we go from here? 929
Traitors. 188
Transitional nationalism in Viet-Nam 1903-   288
Translations on North Vietnam's Economy, Nos. 1-27. 1711
Translations on North Vietnam's Economy, Nos. 28-56. 1831
Translations on Political & Sociological Information on North
    Vietnam, Nos. 1-15. 1832
Translations on Political & Sociological Information on North

308   Vietnam

Original Title: Nation That Refused to Starve. 1258
Vietnam triangle; Moscow, Peking, Hanoi. 2317
Vietnam under the shadows; a chronological and factual book that
    records the tragedy of Vietnam. 66
(Le) Viet-Nam, une cause de la paix. 1222
Vietnam--USA: s krig. Diskussionskurs. [Av Erik Eriksson och
    Bengt Liljenroth. Utg. pa uppdrag av och i samarbete med
    ABF. Studiehandledning till Sven Oste: Vietnam--hokens ar
    och John Takman: Napalm] 475
Viet-nam van-hoa su'-cu'o'ng. Esquisse d'histoire de la civilisa-
    tion annamite. 382
Vietnam viewpoints; a handbook for concerned citizens. 755
Il Vietnam vincera. Politica, strategia, organizzazione. Scritti
    di Ho Chi Minh, Vo Nguyen Giap, Pham Van Dong, Nguyen Kach
    Vien, Pham Ngoc Thach, Truong Son, Enrica Collotti Pischel.
    336
Vietnam; vital issues in the great debate. 540
Vietnam. Vom Mekongdelta zum Song Ben Hai. (Farbaufnahmen:
    Reinhold Wepf. [Texte:] Reinhold Wepf, [u. a.]) 2249
(The) Vietnam war and international law. (1968) 484
Vietnam War & International Law. (1967) 485
(The) Vietnam War: Christian perspectives. 2164
Vietnam war sketches, from the air, land, and sea. 2229
(The) Vietnam war: why? (Delhi, Atma Ram) 1550
(The) Vietnam War: Why? (Rutland, Vt., Tuttle) 1551
Viet Nam; where East & West meet. 421
Vietnam: which way to peace? A discussion. 2165
Vietnam: who cares? 124
Vietnam; why? a collection of reports and comment from the Re-
    porter. 1410
Vietnam--why? An American citizen looks at the war. 147
Vietnam--wie es dazu kam. 914
Vietnam will win! Why the people of South Vietnam have already
    defeated U. S. imperialism--and how they have done it--by the
    internationally famous Western correspondent whose first-hand
    dispatches from Vietnam have become a part of the history of
    our times, Wilfred G. Burchett. 229
Viet-Nam witness, 1953-66. 498
Vietnam yesterday and today. 682
Vietnam. Zum Problem der kolonialen Revolution und Konterrevolution.
    1613
(The) Vietnamese and their Revolution. 1051
Vietnamese anticolonialism, 1885-1925. (1971) 1033
Vietnamese Anti-colonialism, 1885-1925. (1972) 1032
Vietnamese; basic course. 1821
Vietnamese; basic course. Presidio of Monterey, 1955- 1747
(The) Vietnamese civil service system. 1437
(A) Vietnamese district chief in action. 18
Vietnamese documents translated and released to the press by the
    United States Mission in Saigon, including some which were cap-
    tured from the Viet Cong and North Vietnamese forces, with
    the addition of reports of interrogations of Communist defectors
    and captured Communist troops, airgrams to the U. S. Department

of State from the American Embassy in Saigon, etc.   2178
Vietnamese gramaphone records.   2179
(A) Vietnamese Grammar.   1671
Vietnamese handicrafts.   2180
Vietnamese (Hanoi dialect); aural comprehension course: text
    volumes.   1807
Vietnamese: homework coordinated with basic course lessons.   1748
(The) Vietnamese in Thailand; a historical perspective.   1348
Vietnamese intellectuals against U. S. aggression.   (68-1192)   2181
Vietnamese intellectuals against U. S. aggression.   (NUC 67-80194)
    2182
Vietnamese: introduction to the standard writing system of Viet-
    namese.   1808
Vietnamese legends, adapted from the Vietnamese.   1501
Vietnamese military interpreting exercises and military subjects
    and situations.   1749
Vietnamese: military interpreting exercises, coordinated with
    basic course lessons and with military subjects and situations.
    1750
Vietnamese: military interrogation exercises co-ordinated with
    basic course lessons, and with military subjects and situations.
    (1958)   1751
Vietnamese: military interrogation exercises.   Coordinated with
    Basic course lessons and with military subjects and situations.
    (1963)   1809
Vietnamese; military map tracking and exercises with military
    terrain table, coordinated with basic course lessons and mili-
    tary subjects and situations.   1752
Vietnamese: military subjects and situations.   1753
(The) Vietnamese music.   Special ed.   2183
(The) Vietnamese Nationalist Revolutionary Congress.   2184
(The) Vietnamese people on the road to victory.   1227
Vietnamese phrase book, and English-Vietnamese dictionary.   137
Vietnamese problem.   1007
Vietnamese Pronunciation.   981
(A) Vietnamese reader.   1672
Vietnamese; reading selections.   1754
Vietnamese realities.   1936
Vietnamese Revolution.   954
Vietnamese (Saigon dialect); special course [12 weeks]   1755
Vietnamese studies.   no. 1-   2186
Vietnamese-English Dicionary.   (C. E. Tuttle [Tuttle, Charles E.,
    Company, Inc.] 1966) 1203
Vietnamese-English dictionary.   (Saigon, Binh-Minh, 1959)   1204
Vietnamese-English Dictionary Romanized.   2189
Vietnamese-English Dictionary, Vols. 1-2.   2188
Vietnamese-English dictionary, with the international phonetic
    system and more than 30, 000 words and idiomatic expressions.
    974
Vietnamese-English Student Dictionary.   1205
Vietnamese-English vocabulary.   1206
Vietnamesische Lehrjahre, sechs Jahre als deutscher Arzt in Viet-
    nam 1961-1967. [Von] Georg W. Alsheimer.   23

Vietnamesische Malerei. 1124
Vjetnamin palavat tuulet [kirj.] Pentti Halme [ja] Mikko Valtasaari.
673
(Der) Vietnamkonflikt. Darstellung und Dokumentation. [Graphiken:
Ilse Eckart] 1005
Vietnamkonflikten i svensk opinion. 1954-1968. Bibliografi. 1079
(Der) Vietnamkrieg. Tatsachen und Meinungen. 1422
(Der) Vietnamkrieg und die Presse [von] Urs Jaeggi, Rudolf
Steiner [und] Willy Wyniger. 821
Vietnam's Unheld Elections; the Failure to Carry Out the 1956 Re-
unification Elections and the Effect on Hanoi's Present Outlook.
2240
Vietnamsko surtse, (Heart of Vietnam). (In Bulgarian) 592
Vijetnam demokratska republika u Istocnoj Aziji, (The Democratic
Republic of Vietnam in East Asia). (In Yugoslav) 841
Vijetnam: logika povlacenja. Preveli s engleskog: Nikola
Capipovic [i] Stevan Majstorovic. Naslovna strana: Pavle
Ristic. 2330
Vijetnam, savest covecanstva. 435
Vijetnamska rapsodija. 1119
Vijetnamski rat. Naslovna strana: Pavle Ristic. 572
Village in Vietnam. 727
Village life in modern Thailand. 405
(The) village of Ben Suc. (New York, Knopf, 1967) 1487
Village of Ben Suc. (Random House, Inc., 1971) 1488
Vinh Long. 1086
(Les) violations des accords de Geneve par les communistes Viet-
Miny. 1908
Violations of the Geneva agreements by the Viet-Minh Communists.
1910
Violations of the Geneva agreements by the Viet-Minh Communists,
from July 1959 to June 1960. 1909
Vision accomplished? The enigma of Ho Chi Minh. 788
Visions of victory: selected Vietnamese Communist military writings,
1964-1968. 1060
Visit beautiful Vietnam; ABC der Aggressionen heute. 44
Vitnam Al-chenobia Towachih Al-asiffah. (Vietnam in the storms of
war). (In Arabic) 505
(La) vittoria del Vietcong. 2209
Volkerrechtliche Aspekte des Vietnam-Konflikts. (Vortrag.) 1451
(Die) volkerrechtliche Stellung Vietnams; ein Beitrag zue Problematik
der volkerrechtlichen Situation geteilter Staaten. Mie einem
Geleitwort von F. J. Berber. 685
(Die) Volksarmee Vietnams; Bietrage und Dokumente zum Befreiungs-
kampf des vietnamesischen Volkes. [Ubersetzung aus dem Englischen
und Franzosischen: Heinz Eder und Reinhard Sommer] 2199
Vosstannie Tei-shonov vo V'etname 1771-1802, (The Insurrection
of Tei-shons in Vietnam). (In Russian) 1261
(The) voyage of the Alceste to the Ryukyus and Southeast Asia.
1067
(The) voyage of the Astrolabe, 1840; an English rendering of the
journals of Dumont d'Urville and his officer. . . 436
Vpered, pod znamenem partii! (Forword, Under the Banners of